OXFORD MONOGRAPHS
IN INTERNATIONAL HUMANITARIAN
AND CRIMINAL LAW

General Editors

SUZANNAH LINTON

Distinguished Professor at the Law School of Zhejiang Gongshang University, China

ROBERT CRYER

Professor of International and Criminal Law at the University of Birmingham Law School, UK

SALVATORE ZAPPALÀ

Professor of International Law at the University of Catania

Internationalized Armed Conflicts in International Law

OXFORD MONOGRAPHS IN INTERNATIONAL HUMANITARIAN AND CRIMINAL LAW

The aim of this series is to publish original and innovative books on fundamental, topical, or cutting-edge issues in international humanitarian law and international criminal justice. The primary purpose of the series is to publish books which, in addition to critically surveying existing law, also suggest new avenues for improving the law.

Special attention will be given to works by young scholars.

Internationalized Armed Conflicts in International Law

KUBO MAČÁK

OXFORD
UNIVERSITY PRESS

OXFORD
UNIVERSITY PRESS

Great Clarendon Street, Oxford, OX2 6DP,
United Kingdom

Oxford University Press is a department of the University of Oxford.
It furthers the University's objective of excellence in research, scholarship, and education by publishing worldwide. Oxford is a registered trade mark of Oxford University Press in the UK and in certain other countries

First Edition published in 2018

Published in the United States of America by Oxford University Press
198 Madison Avenue, New York, NY 10016, United States of America

British Library Cataloguing in Publication Data
Data available

Library of Congress Control Number: 2018934171

ISBN 978–0–19–881986–8

To Tomáš

Foreword

The law is all about making distinctions. One of the longest-standing distinctions in public international law has been between the notions of inter-state war, or what today is called international armed conflict (IAC), and civil war, or non-international armed conflict (NIAC). These types of armed conflict have been governed for a long time by different legal rules. In 1625 Hugo Grotius wrote that, by the Law of Nations, prisoners of war may be made slaves only if 'taken in a solemn [inter-State] War', while in 'civil Wars [. . .] Prisoners are generally put to the Sword, because they cannot be made Slaves'. Only in a solemn War 'both Sides' had the right of killing enemies, and only in a solemn War the property of the enemy could be acquired simply by taking possession, while 'in civil Wars, whether they be great or small, there is no Change in Property but by the Sentence of a Judge'. While the law applicable to the two types of armed conflict has seen change and a certain convergence over the centuries, present-day international humanitarian law (IHL) still draws a clear distinction between IACs and NIACs.

Life, however, is often more complex than the law. Actual armed conflicts these days rarely conform to this strict dichotomy of IACs and NIACs. As recent complex conflict situations in Afghanistan, Libya, Syria, Yemen, and Ukraine have shown, armed conflicts may start as classic NIACs between a rebel group and the state's government but, due to outside intervention or other factors, may later develop into IACs. In some cases, armed conflicts may even be transformed from non-international to international, and then back again to non-international, with important consequences for the applicable law. Armed conflicts that have been transformed from a NIAC to an IAC are referred to as 'internationalized' armed conflicts. Internationalized armed conflicts differ from classic inter-state IACs in their intra-state origin and the continued intra-state setting in which they are conducted. Outside intervention in a NIAC raises the question of whether such conflict should be considered as one single internationalized armed conflict or as two or more separate but parallel international and non-international armed conflicts. Above all, the notion of internationalized armed conflict poses the question of the legal rules applicable to these conflicts and, in particular, whether and, if so, to what extent the rules applicable to classic IACs are equally applicable to internationalized armed conflicts.

There is much here that needs careful, painstaking, and historically informed analysis. Kubo Mačák provides all this. In his well-researched, well-reasoned, and well-written work he develops a comprehensive typology of the ways in which armed conflicts are internationalized and de-internationalized. With the notion of 'operational autonomy' of the conflict parties he offers a workable criterion for the classification of complex conflict situations involving more than two conflict parties as either one single internationalized conflict or two or more international and non-international armed conflicts existing independently side by side. Mačák challenges the perceived wisdom that the application of the rules of IHL relating to combatant status and belligerent occupation are predicated on the existence of an inter-state IAC. He argues that members of non-state groups participating in an internationalized armed conflict are eligible, in principle, to combatant status and that the law of belligerent occupation may be applied to internationalized armed conflicts. Even if one may not fully agree with all aspects of Mačák's findings on the applicable law, one has to admire the seriousness and profoundness of his scholarship. The work makes a significant contribution to our understanding of the notion of internationalized armed conflicts and will establish its author as one of the pre-eminent experts in the field of IHL of the coming generation.

Stefan Talmon
Institute for Public International Law, Bonn University
8 March 2018

Series Editors' Preface

We are very happy to publish Kubo Mačák's book, *Internationalized Armed Conflicts in International Law*, in the Oxford Monographs in International Humanitarian and Criminal Law Series. This preface highlights a few reasons why this book takes its place in this Series and why it represents a major contribution to the study of one of the most delicate aspects in international law and International Humanitarian Law (IHL).

Firstly, the author Dr Mačák exemplifies the aims and profile of this Series (see Series Editor's Preface to *Fairness in International Criminal Trials* by Yvonne McDermott, at x as well as *Detention in Non-International Armed Conflict* by Lawrence Hill-Cawthorne, at v) and we take this opportunity to further encourage young colleagues (and their mentors) to keep the Series in mind for their works. There is little doubt that the area of IHL has been profoundly reshaped by the changes in contemporary armed conflicts as well as by the advent of International Criminal Law. The implication of these changes must continue to be studied and analysed with great depth. Kubo Mačák makes an excellent contribution in deepening our understanding of certain phenomena, including by linking these specific aspects to more general public international law. The Series was created by having in mind the need to address new realities through a new generation of scholars, all of whom would be ready to look at both old and emerging issues with a solid background and an open mind, combining tradition and evolving trends.

Secondly, Mačák's book deals with a traditional topic, and focuses very ably on one of the most delicate current problems in IHL: the conundrum of how to address the tormented relationships between (the law of) international armed conflict and (the regulations of) non-international armed conflicts in a world where conflicts often change nature many times. In particular, this is true when discussing what could now be seen as a nearly twenty-year single conflict: the so-called 'war on terrorism' or 'war on terror', which to a large extent has radically transformed if not the law of armed conflicts at least the political discourse around it and to a large extent its implementation.

Thirdly, the ideas, and the approach to them taken in this book have the merit to address a traditional issue with new lens, offering an interesting perspective from a solid legal standpoint, as well as a constructive and creative interpretation. It is always difficult for law, and for lawyers, to deal with transitions; normally, law is more suited to capturing the static aspects of reality, while the dynamics are often too blurred to be captured and are frequently left aside. The binary construction 'international *v* non-international armed conflicts' is usually seen as the basis for the application of IHL and its study. At the same time, armed conflicts, almost by definition, are full of movements and are inevitably expression of (often unlawful and yet) successful or unsuccessful transitions. The book revolves around one of the most sensitive of these potential transitions; it is a successful attempt to capture the multifaceted nature of the problems raised by these transitions and represents a serious addition to the reflections in this field.

Finally, the book contains a detailed analysis of cases and practice which makes it a useful tool not only for academics, but also for practitioners. Mačák's ability to show the evolving nature of armed conflicts, the insufficiency of the binary distinction between their characterization as international and non-international, the eventuality of shifts (such as their 'internationalization'), and potential consequences, makes this book an incredibly useful prism to understand better the realities of today's armed conflicts. Hence, we are very pleased to publish it in this Series.

The Editors

Acknowledgements

The story of this book begins over a decade ago at the Jean-Pictet Competition in International Humanitarian Law (IHL). I was an undergraduate law student then, studying at KU Leuven on a yearlong Erasmus exchange from Charles University in Prague. *Concours Jean-Pictet* was my first true encounter with IHL and the many legal, military, and political issues raised by this body of law. It was thanks to my participation in this competition that I came to appreciate the central importance of the question of conflict qualification and, gradually, conceived of the research question at the heart of this book. My first words of thanks thus must go to my coach Bruno Demeyere, teammates Griet Seurs and Leen Chanet, and the whole family of *Picteists* for setting me on the journey of which this publication is the latest step.

The book itself has grown out of my doctoral project at the University of Oxford. I therefore owe my greatest intellectual debt to my supervisor, Professor Stefan Talmon, who has given me in equal measure his wise counsel, subtle guidance, and constant encouragement. After each meeting with him, I was brimming with ideas and feeling even more enthusiastic about the project. It has been a true privilege to be able to work with Professor Talmon and to learn from him over the years.

I am grateful to scholars who have examined parts of this work at the MPhil level (Professors Dapo Akande and Lindsay Moir), DPhil confirmation of status (Professors Mark Janis and Catherine Redgwell), and as the entire doctoral thesis (Professors Dapo Akande and Noam Lubell). Their comments and suggestions have been extremely helpful in shaping the following stages of my research and writing. I thank them all.

I am also grateful to the three anonymous reviewers who further improved the manuscript with their insights and advice. Moreover, I especially acknowledge the help of those friends and colleagues who have read parts of this book and provided valuable comments on their contents, including Russell Buchan, Martin Faix, Barbara Havelková, Lawrence Hill-Cawthorne, Professor Mike Schmitt, Noam Zamir, and Ruvi Ziegler.

My thanks also go to the entire editorial team at OUP, particularly Merel Alstein, Kimberly Marsh, and Jack McNichol, for guiding me through the publication process. I am further grateful to Michele Marietta for her careful and precise copyediting, to Ashirvad Moses Thyagarajan and Afrose of Newgen for overseeing the production of the book, and to my old friend Victor Breiner for allowing me to use one of his photographs for the book cover.

Since my time as a doctoral candidate, I have had the privilege of friendship and support of many fellow members of the postgraduate international law community at Oxford, including Farid Ahmadov, Eirik Bjorge, Nic Croquet, Ernesto Feliz, Asif Hameed, Jarrod Hepburn, Gleider Hernández, Lawrence Hill-Cawthorne, Jessica Howley, Miles Jackson, Travers McLeod, Greg Messenger, Nikki Palmer, Martins

Paparinskis, Masha Puchyna, James Upcher†, Lema Uyar, Meg Wong, Noam Zamir, and Ruvi Ziegler. Many ideas that eventually found their way into the text of this book can be traced back to our discussions at the Wednesday morning research seminars led by Professors Guy Goodwin-Gill and Vaughan Lowe or, perhaps more plausibly, to one of the pubs in central Oxford. It is often said that pursuing a PhD can be a lonely experience, but thanks to all the friends I met in Oxford, this was not so for me.

I was also fortunate in being offered a lectureship at the University of Exeter as I was completing my doctorate. My colleagues at the Exeter Centre for International Law, who have over the years included Professor Michael Addo, Ana Beduschi, Christine Bicknell, Jess Duggan-Larkin, Rachel Gimson, Jarrod Hepburn, Agnieszka Jachec-Neale, Annika Jones, Joseph Lee, Professor Hitoshi Nasu, Mike Sanderson, Aurel Sari, Julia Schmidt, and Professor Mike Schmitt, have all contributed to the creation of a fruitful and friendly atmosphere that stimulates research and fosters intellectual exchange. In addition, I acknowledge the excellent research assistance of Exeter Law School students Chloe Abbott, Kier Childs, and Lucia Jamrichová. I am grateful to them all.

This research was enabled by the generosity of many individuals and institutions. I am particularly grateful to the donors of the Weidenfeld Scholarships and Leadership Programme, who had made it possible for me to study at Oxford and complete much of the work on this project. I acknowledge further generous support from the Europaeum, the International Law Fund (Cambridge), Somerville College, and the SPP Foundation (Slovakia), all of whom have funded specific aspects of the research and associated travel. I am especially thankful to Somerville College, which became my second home during the years spent in Oxford and whose law academics, including Professors Julie Dickson and Steve Weatherill, have given me much support and guidance throughout my studies. I am also grateful to those institutions that have hosted me and provided me with access to their libraries or archives while I was working on this book, including the Graduate Institute of International and Development Studies in Geneva, the International Committee of the Red Cross in Geneva, the Max Planck Institute for Comparative Public Law and International Law in Heidelberg, and the Institute for Public International Law at the University of Bonn.

My deepest thanks must go to my family. I am grateful to my parents Slávka and Dodo for giving me a wonderful and happy childhood and for making me understand the importance of education and hard work later in life. I am indebted to my brother Matej for always being close by and ready to share a word of advice or a good laugh. My grandparents Mikuláš and Mária, and Jozef and Helena, have all instilled in me a sense of curiosity about the world around me from a very early age, and each of them has been a role model to me in a different way. Perhaps at least the dog persons among the readers will forgive me for also noting the unique contribution of my senior canine assistant Gaby, who has slept through the drafting of many pages, including this one. Finally, I thank my wife Ana who has not only supported me every step of the way, but has also read and helped me tweak every word of the manuscript. It is no exaggeration to say that without Ana's love and kindness I could never have seen this book's story to its completion.

Note
This book reflects the state of the law as of January 2018. Similarly, unless expressly noted otherwise in the text, all online sources were last accessed in January 2018.

Table of Contents

Detailed Table of Contents

III. BELLIGERENT OCCUPATION

IV. CONCLUSION

Table of Cases

INTERNATIONAL

Permanent Court of International Justice (PCIJ)

International Military Tribunal (IMT), Nuremberg

International Military Tribunal for the Far East (IMTFE)

International Court of Justice (ICJ)

Table of Treaties, Legislation, and Other Instruments

INTERNATIONAL INSTRUMENTS

NATIONAL INSTRUMENTS

Algeria

Bosnia and Herzegovina

Germany

Libya

Peru

Uganda

United Kingdom

United States

List of Abbreviations

AIDI	Annuaire de l'Institut de Droit International
AJICL	African Journal of International and Comparative Law
AJIL	American Journal of International Law
AP I	Protocol Additional to the Geneva Conventions of 12 August 1949, and relating to the Protection of Victims of International Armed Conflicts (Protocol I) (signed 12 December 1977, entered into force 7 December 1978) 1125 UNTS 3
AP II	Protocol Additional to the Geneva Conventions of 12 August 1949, and relating to the Protection of Victims of Non-International Armed Conflicts (Protocol II) (signed 12 December 1977, entered into force 7 December 1978) 1125 UNTS 609
APs	Additional Protocols
APCML	Asia Pacific Centre for Military Law
Art(s)	Article(s)
ASDI	Annuaire Suisse de Droit International
ASIL	American Society of International Law
AUILR	American University International Law Review
AULR	American University Law Review
BGE	Decisions of the Swiss Federal Supreme Court [*Bundesgerichtsentscheide*]
BGer	Swiss Federal Supreme Court [*Bundesgericht*]
BYBIL	British Year Book of International Law
C2	Command and control
CA	Court of Appeal[s]
CCW	Convention on Prohibitions or Restrictions on the Use of Certain Conventional Weapons Which May Be Deemed to be Excessively Injurious or to Have Indiscriminate Effects (signed 10 October 1980, entered into force 2 December 1983) 1342 UNTS 137
CDDH	Diplomatic Conference on the Reaffirmation and Development of International Humanitarian Law Applicable in Armed Conflicts [*Conférence diplomatique sur la réaffirmation et le développement du droit international humanitaire applicable dans les conflits armés*]
Chinese JIL	Chinese Journal of International Law
CJEU	Court of Justice of the European Union
CPN	Communist Party of Nepal
CUP	Cambridge University Press
Doc	Document
DoD	Department of Defense (United States)
DRC	Democratic Republic of the Congo
Duke J Comp & Int'l L	Duke Journal of Comparative and International Law
ECCC	Extraordinary Chambers in the Courts of Cambodia
ECHR	European Convention on Human Rights
ECJ	European Court of Justice

ECOWAS	Economic Community of West African States
ECtHR	European Court of Human Rights
edn	edition
EECC	Eritrea–Ethiopia Claims Commission
EJIL	European Journal of International Law
ELN	National Liberation Army [*Ejército de Liberación Nacional*] (Colombia)
EU	European Union
EUFOR Tchad/RCA	European Union Force Chad/Central African Republic [*Tchad/République centrafricaine*]
FARC	Revolutionary Armed Forces of Colombia [*Fuerzas Armadas Revolucionarias de Colombia*]
FMLN	*Farabundo Martí* National Liberation Front (*Frente Farabundo Martí para la Liberación Nacional*)
FRELIMO	Mozambique Liberation Front [*Frente de Libertação de Moçambique*]
FRY	Federal Republic of Yugoslavia
GC I	Geneva Convention (I) for the Amelioration of the Condition of the Wounded and Sick in Armed Forces in the Field (signed 12 August 1949, entered into force 21 October 1950) 75 UNTS 31
GC II	Geneva Convention (II) for the Amelioration of the Condition of Wounded, Sick and Shipwrecked Members of Armed Forces at Sea (signed 12 August 1949, entered into force 21 October 1950) 75 UNTS 85
GC III	Geneva Convention (III) relative to the Treatment of Prisoners of War (signed 12 August 1949, entered into force 21 October 1950) 75 UNTS 135
GC IV	Geneva Convention (IV) relative to the Protection of Civilian Persons in Time of War (signed 12 August 1949, entered into force 21 October 1950) 75 UNTS 287
GCs	Geneva Conventions
GYIL	German Yearbook of International Law
Hague Regulations	Regulations concerning the Laws and Customs of War on Land, Annex to Hague Convention (IV) respecting the Laws and Customs of War on Land (signed 18 October 1907, entered into force 26 January 1910) 205 CTS 277
HCJ	High Court of Justice (Israel)
HR H-B	Croatian Republic of Herzeg-Bosnia [*Hrvatska Republika Herceg-Bosna*]
HRLR	Human Rights Law Review
HRW	Human Rights Watch
HVO	Croatian Defence Council [*Hrvatsko vijeće obrane*]
HZ H-B	Croatian Community of Herzeg-Bosnia [*Hrvatska zajednica Herceg-Bosna*]
IAC	international armed conflict
IACmHR	Inter-American Commission of Human Rights
IACtHR	Inter-American Court of Human Rights
ICC	International Criminal Court
ICG	International Crisis Group
ICISS	International Commission on Intervention and State Sovereignty
ICJ	International Court of Justice
ICJ Rep	International Court of Justice, Reports of Judgments
ICJ Statute	Statute of the International Court of Justice, of 26 June 1945, annexed to the UN Charter
ICL	international criminal law

ICLQ	International and Comparative Law Quarterly
ICRC	International Committee of the Red Cross
ICTR	International Criminal Tribunal for Rwanda
ICTY	International Criminal Tribunal for the former Yugoslavia
IHL	international humanitarian law
IHRL	international human rights law
IIFFMCG	Independent International Fact-Finding Mission on the Conflict in Georgia
IIHL	International Institute of Humanitarian Law
ILA	International Law Association
ILC	International Law Commission
ILC ASR	International Law Commission, Articles on the Responsibility of States for Internationally Wrongful Acts, UN GA Res 56/83 annex, UN Doc A/RES/56/83 (12 December 2001)
ILC DARIO	International Law Commission, ILC Draft Articles on Responsibility of International Organizations, UN Doc A/66/10 (2011)
ILM	International Legal Materials
ILR	International Law Reports
IMT	International Military Tribunal for the Trial of German Major War Criminals
IMTFE	International Military Tribunal for the Far East
IRRC	International Review of the Red Cross
ISAF	International Security Assistance Force (Afghanistan)
ISIS	Islamic State of Iraq and Syria
Isr L Rev	Israel Law Review
IYHR	Israel Yearbook on Human Rights
JCSL	Journal of Conflict and Security Law
JICJ	Journal of International Criminal Justice
JIHLS	Journal of International Humanitarian Legal Studies
KFOR	Kosovo Force
KLA	Kosovo Liberation Army
KUFNS	Kampuchean United Front for National Salvation
LJIL	Leiden Journal of International Law
LNTS	League of Nations Treaty Series
LOAC	law of armed conflict
LRA	Lord's Resistance Army
LTTE	Liberation Tigers of Tamil Eelam (Sri Lanka)
MACV	Military Assistance Command, Vietnam
MJIL	Melbourne Journal of International Law
MLC	Movement for the Liberation of the Congo
MLR	Military Law Review
n	note
NATO	North Atlantic Treaty Organization
NDFP	National Democratic Front of the Philippines
NIAC	non-international armed conflict
NILR	Netherlands International Law Review
NLM	National Liberation Movement
NTC	National Transitional Council (Libya)
NYBIL	Netherlands Yearbook of International Law
NYU JILP	New York University Journal of International Law and Politics

ONLF	Ogaden National Liberation Front
ONUC	United Nations Operation in the Congo [*Organisation des Nations Unies au Congo*]
OUP	Oxford University Press
para(s) #(–#) or [#](–[#]) or §(§)#(–#)	paragraph(s) #(–#)
PCIJ	Permanent Court of International Justice
PKK	Kurdistan Workers' Party [*Partiya Karkerên Kurdistan*]
PLO	Palestinian Liberation Organization
POW(s)	Prisoner(s) of War
RCD	Rally for Congolese Democracy
Res	Resolution
RIAA	Reports of International Arbitral Awards
Rome Statute	Rome Statute of the International Criminal Court (opened for signature 17 July 1998, entered into force 1 July 2002) 2187 UNTS 90
RPF	Rwandan Patriotic Front
s (ss)	section(s)
SCSL	Special Court for Sierra Leone
SFRY	Socialist Federal Republic of Yugoslavia
SWAPO	South West African People's Organisation
Temp Int'l & Comp LJ	Temple International and Comparative Law Journal
UCLA(s)	Unilaterally Controlled Latino Asset(s)
UDI	Unilateral Declaration of Independence
UK	United Kingdom
UN	United Nations
UN Charter	Charter of the United Nations (signed 26 June 1945, entered into force 24 October 1945) 1 UNTS XVI
UNGA	United Nations General Assembly
UNGAOR	United Nations General Assembly Official Records
UNHCR	United Nations High Commissioner for Refugees
UNITA	National Union for the Total Independence of Angola [*União Nacional para a Independência Total de Angola*]
UNOSOM	United Nations Operation in Somalia
UNSC	United Nations Security Council
UNTS	United Nations Treaty Series
US	United States
US MT	United States Military Tribunal (Nuremberg)
USSR	Union of Soviet Socialist Republics
VCLT	Vienna Convention on the Law of Treaties (concluded 23 May 1969, entered into force 27 January 1980) 1155 UNTS 331
VJIL	Virginia Journal of International Law
vol	volume
VRS	Army of Republika Srpska [*Vojska Republike Srpske*]
WCC	War Crimes Chamber (Serbia)
YIHL	Yearbook of International Humanitarian Law
YJIL	Yale Journal of International Law

1
Introduction

In a distant land, tensions are brewing. After long years of suffering under a military regime described by many as despotic, racist, and corrupt, the opposing factions have finally united and risen up to depose the hated government. Under the banner of national liberation and supported by much of the population, the insurgents quickly consolidate control over a large part of the territory. However, after the initial shock at the opposition's rapid progress, the government armed forces soon mount a powerful counteroffensive. And then, as the fighting stalls, the rebels' morale receives a sudden boost when several neighbouring countries issue public declarations of support. Some even pad their words with wads of cash. However, not all neighbours are equally supportive. One country makes a statement that because the conflict has now reached the level of a 'true civil war', strict neutrality must be observed in dealings with all belligerents. Another sends in its troops, stripped of their official insignia, to assist the embattled government. Refugees are now fleeing the country by the tens of thousands, further destabilizing the region. Meanwhile, the rebel leadership, keen not to lose the momentum and the popular support it now enjoys in parts of the country, declares an independent republic there. As the hostilities continue, gradually, a sizable proportion of the international community recognize the nascent state. However, the actual control over territory continues to shift over time, with the erstwhile rebels establishing authority over several areas outside their new state, and vice versa. Hundreds of enemy fighters are captured and held by both sides. The end of conflict is nowhere in sight.

If this factual pattern sounds more than faintly familiar, it is because parts of it play out around the world at almost all times. It is true that most armed confrontations, like this hypothetical example, begin as internal conflicts.[1] However, in a world defined by the twin forces of globalization and fragmentation,[2] virtually no armed conflict remains confined to the territory of one state, free from foreign involvement. This holds true for nearly all major conflicts that have shaped the post-Cold War era: ex-Yugoslavia, Rwanda, Afghanistan, Iraq, Libya, Syria, Yemen, and so on. As this book goes to press, the armed conflict in eastern Ukraine continues

[1] M Allansson, E Melander, and L Themnér, 'Organized violence, 1989–2016' (2017) 54 Journal of Peace Research 574, 576.
[2] See generally I Clark, *Globalization and Fragmentation: International Relations in the Twentieth Century* (OUP 1997).

to simmer, with conflicting claims made by both sides as to the extent of Russian involvement in the fighting.[3]

This is not a book about any of these conflicts, and yet it is a book about all of them. Each of them illustrates, albeit in differing ways, that an originally internal conflict may change and evolve, acquiring gradually additional elements of international character. Such developments have profound implications for the application of international law to these situations. This is because international humanitarian law (IHL), as the branch of international law that regulates armed conflict, is based on a persisting bifurcation between international armed conflicts (IACs) and non-international armed conflicts (NIACs).[4] Each of these legal categories is governed by a different legal framework, and traditionally the regulation of the former has been much more comprehensive than the regulation of the latter.[5] Although the last few decades have seen a progressive trend of convergence between the two, the distinction between IACs and NIACs is here to stay. It is therefore essential to understand at what point a NIAC transforms into an IAC and what consequences that transformation brings from the legal point of view.

And that is the focus of this book. Rather than examining the nature of specific conflict situations at a given *static* point in time, it adopts a *dynamic* lens for its scrutiny. Accordingly, it searches for the tipping points that may convert NIACs into IACs. On that basis, the book argues for a specific conceptualization of internationalized armed conflict in international law. Such conflicts are understood here as prima facie NIACs, the legal nature of which has transformed, with the effect that the law of IAC becomes applicable to them.[6] However, the intra-state origin of such conflicts provides for an uneasy match with many of the precepts of the law of IAC, which has historically evolved as a regulatory framework for inter-state wars. Of those, the regulation of combatancy and the law of belligerent occupation are where the principal legal questions lie and which will be examined in depth in this book.

[3] Compare, eg, Russia, Remarks by Deputy Permanent Representative of the Russian Federation to the OSCE Dmitry Balakin on the situation in Ukraine (7 November 2017) <www.mid.ru/en/foreign_policy/news/-/asset_publisher/cKNonkJE02Bw/content/id/2939398> (referring to the situation as to 'the internal Ukrainian conflict') and Russia, Comment by Foreign Ministry Spokesperson Maria Zakharova (14 December 2017) <www.mid.ru/en/foreign_policy/news/-/asset_publisher/cKNonkJE02Bw/content/id/2990728> (describing the anti-government forces as 'the Donbass self-defence forces'), with Ukraine, Statement of the Ministry of Foreign Affairs of Ukraine on Escalation in Donbas (21 July 2017) <http://mfa.gov.ua/en/press-center/comments/7576-zajava-mzs-ukrajini-shhodo-zagostrennya-situaciji-na-donbasi> (referring to the situation as to 'Russia-instigated international armed conflict') and Ukraine, Statement on 'Russia's ongoing aggression against Ukraine and illegal occupation of Crimea' (14 December 2017) <http://mfa.gov.ua/en/press-center/news/61906-statement-on-russias-ongoing-aggression-against-ukraine-and-illegal-occupation-of-crimea> (protesting against 'Russia's presence as an invasion force in Donbas').

[4] The distinction between IACs and NIACs is discussed further in Section 1.2.

[5] E Crawford, *The Treatment of Combatants and Insurgents under the Law of Armed Conflict* (OUP 2010) 2; S Sivakumaran, *The Law of Non-International Armed Conflict* (OUP 2012) 1; L Hill-Cawthorne, *Detention in Non-International Armed Conflict* (OUP 2016) 1.

[6] The notion of internationalization is discussed further in Section 1.3.

1.1 Research Overview

1.1.1 Aim, objectives, and scope

The aim of this book is to provide a comprehensive examination of the notion, process, and effects of internationalization of armed conflicts in international law. In achieving that aim, this research project has been guided by three primary objectives: (1) to set forth a clear, reasoned, and practical conceptualization of conflict internationalization; (2) to comprehensively identify the existing forms of conflict internationalization in contemporary international law; and (3) to establish how the law of armed conflict applies to conflicts that have been internationalized in this sense. Together, the fulfilment of these objectives should confirm the continuing relevance of the concept of internationalized armed conflicts for the theory and practice of international law.

A few remarks should be made regarding the scope of enquiry of the present work. First and foremost, this book does not purport to exhaust all legal questions concerning conflict internationalization. Rather, its focus and methodological approach is grounded in the discipline of public international law. In particular, that means that the enquiry is not into standards for conflict qualification under domestic laws, nor into the domestic regulation of military operations that may qualify as internationalized armed conflicts. To the extent that the analysis refers to such materials (for instance, domestic military manuals or amnesty laws issued by various states), it is only with the aim of assessing their relevance for the international legal rules governing the situations within the scope of this study.

Secondly, the book examines conflict internationalization from the viewpoint of IHL (also referred to as the law of armed conflict throughout the text). Accordingly, the enquiry is restricted to the law applicable in armed conflicts (*jus in bello*) and excludes questions of the lawfulness of the use of force (*jus ad bellum*).[7] Moreover, the study touches only incidentally on the related areas of international human rights law (IHRL) and international criminal law (ICL). It is important to note that IHRL

[7] The literature on the distinction between *jus in bello* and *jus ad bellum* is vast: see, eg, H Lauterpacht, 'The Limits of the Operation of the Law of War' (1953) 30 BYBIL 206; C Greenwood, 'The Relationship between *Ius ad Bellum* and *Ius in Bello*' (1983) 9 Review of International Studies 221; R Kolb, 'Origin of the Twin Terms *Jus ad Bellum/Jus in Bello*' (1997) 37 IRRC 553; J Martinez et al, 'The Relationship between *Jus ad Bellum* and *Jus in Bello*: Past, Present, Future' (2006) 100 ASIL Proceedings 109, 109–24 (proceedings from a panel discussion); A Orakhelashvili, 'Overlap and Convergence: The Interaction Between *Jus ad Bellum* and *Jus in Bello*' (2007) 12 JCSL 157; J Moussa, 'Can *Jus ad Bellum* Override *Jus in Bello*? Reaffirming the Separation of the Two Bodies of Law' (2008) 90 IRRC 963; RD Sloane, 'The Cost of Conflation: Preserving the Dualism of *Jus ad Bellum* and *Jus in Bello* in the Contemporary Law of War' (2009) 34 YJIL 47; K Okimoto, *The Distinction and Relationship between Jus ad Bellum and Jus in Bello* (Hart 2011); JHH Weiler and A Deshman, 'Far Be It from Thee to Slay the Righteous with the Wicked: An Historical and Historiographical Sketch of the Bellicose Debate Concerning the Distinction between *Jus ad Bellum* and *Jus in Bello*' (2013) 24 EJIL 25; K Okimoto, 'The Relationship between *Jus Ad Bellum* and *Jus In Bello*' in M Weller (ed), *The Oxford Handbook of the Use of Force in International Law* (OUP 2015) 1209–23.

does not cease to operate in times of armed conflict[8] and it may thus provide additional protection to victims of internationalized armed conflicts, although the exact relationship between IHL and IHRL remains subject to ongoing debate.[9] For its part, ICL primarily contributes to the enforcement of IHL by criminalizing serious violations of IHL.[10] Additionally, international criminal tribunals have refined and developed IHL by applying the rules relevant to cases involving such violations.[11] Although the present study recognizes these important overlaps, it looks to IHRL and ICL only to the extent that these bodies of law bear upon the correct understanding of the rules of IHL applicable to conflict internationalization.

Thirdly, within IHL, the focus of the enquiry is on (1) the rules governing conflict qualification, and (2) the regulation of combatancy and belligerent occupation. The former are, in a way, meta-rules of IHL, determining which legal framework (or part thereof) applies to a particular situation. Accordingly, the book examines those rules to identify the specific modalities of conflict transformation. The enquiry then turns to the latter sets of rules in its analysis of the effects of internationalization. This is because combatancy and belligerent occupation are widely accepted as the two main areas of crucial difference between the law of IAC and NIAC, as attested by the wealth of literature referring to them in this connection.[12] That difference,

[8] *Legality of the Threat or Use of Nuclear Weapons Case* (Advisory Opinion) [1996] ICJ Rep 226 [25] (hereafter *Nuclear Weapons* Advisory Opinion); *Legal Consequences of the Construction of a Wall in the Occupied Palestinian Territory* (Advisory Opinion) [2004] ICJ Rep 136 [106].

[9] Again, the relevant literature is particularly extensive: see, eg, R Provost, *International Human Rights and Humanitarian Law* (CUP 2002); MJ Dennis, 'Application of Human Rights Treaties Extraterritorially in Times of Armed Conflict and Military Occupation' (2005) 99 AJIL 119; R Arnold and N Quénivet (eds), *International Humanitarian Law and Human Rights Law: Towards a New Merger in International Law* (Martinus Nijhoff 2008); C Droege, 'Elective Affinities? Human Rights and Humanitarian Law' (2008) 90 IRRC 501; M Sassòli and LM Olson, 'The Relationship Between International Humanitarian and Human Rights Law Where it Matters: Admissible Killing and Internment of Fighters in Non-International Armed Conflicts' (2008) 90 IRRC 599; I Scobbie, 'Principle or Pragmatics? The Relationship between Human Rights Law and the Laws of Armed Conflict' (2009) 14 JCSL 449; O Ben-Naftali (ed), *International Humanitarian Law and International Human Rights Law* (OUP 2011); M Milanovic, 'A Norm Conflict Perspective on the Relationship Between International Humanitarian Law and Human Rights Law' (2012) 23 EJIL 121; D Bethlehem, 'The Relationship between International Humanitarian Law and International Human Rights Law in Situations of Armed Conflict' (2013) 2 Cambridge J Int'l & Comp L 180; L Hill-Cawthorne, 'Humanitarian Law, Human Rights Law and the Bifurcation of Armed Conflict' (2015) 64 ICLQ 293; A Clapham, 'The Complex Relationship Between the Geneva Conventions and International Human Rights Law' in A Clapham, P Gaeta, and M Sassòli (eds), *The 1949 Geneva Conventions: A Commentary* (OUP 2015) (hereafter Clapham et al, *Geneva Conventions*); C De Koker and T Ruys, 'Foregoing *Lex Specialis*: Exclusivist v. Symbiotic Approaches to the Concurrent Application of International Humanitarian and Human Rights Law' (2016) 49 RBDI 244; M Hakimi, 'The Theory and Practice at the Intersection Between Human Rights and Humanitarian Law' (2017) 111 AJIL 1063.

[10] P Gaeta, 'Geneva Conventions and International Criminal Law' in Clapham et al, *Geneva Conventions* (n 9) 739 [3].

[11] M Sassòli, 'Humanitarian Law and International Criminal Law' in A Cassese (ed), *The Oxford Companion to International Criminal Justice* (OUP 2009) 114.

[12] See, eg, R Baxter, '*Ius in Bello Interno*: The Present and Future Law' in JN Moore (ed), *Law & Civil War in the Modern World* (Johns Hopkins University Press 1974) 530–31; M Bothe, KJ Partsch, and WA Solf, *New Rules for Victims of Armed Conflicts: Commentary on the two 1977 Protocols Additional to the Geneva Conventions of 1949* (Martinus Nijhoff 1982) 671–72; WA Solf, 'The Status of Combatants in Non-International Armed Conflicts under Domestic Law and Transnational Practice' (1983) 33 AUILR 53, 57–59; Y Sandoz, C Swinarski, and B Zimmermann (eds), *Commentary on the Additional*

however, is certainly not exhausted by those two matters and other issues might also be mentioned in this connection.[13] To some extent, the analysis may be applicable *mutatis mutandis* to these other issues. Additionally, it may serve as a bellwether of sorts: in other words, if the two cardinal bastions of the law of IAC are found to be transposable to internationalized armed conflicts, this may be taken as an inductive indicator with respect to other matters subject to different regulation. However, such considerations are excluded from the scope of the present enquiry.

1.1.2 Methodology

The analytical thrust of the study is on what the law is (analysis *de lege lata*), not on what the law should be (*de lege ferenda*). Admittedly, the distinction between *lex ferenda* and *lex lata* is not always strictly pronounced in international law.[14] In fact, arguments as to the existence and interpretation of specific international legal rules (dimension *lex lata*) quite frequently feature elements of policy, desirability and progressiveness (dimension *lex ferenda*).[15] Moreover, it is acknowledged that

Protocols of 8 June 1977 to the Geneva Conventions of 12 August 1949 (ICRC 1987) 1332 [4397] (hereafter Sandoz et al, *APs Commentary*); C Greenwood, 'International Humanitarian Law (Laws of War)' in F Kalshoven (ed), *The Centennial of the 1st International Peace Conference: Reports & Conclusions* (Kluwer Law International 2000) 234; M Sassòli, 'The Legal Qualification of the Conflicts in the Former Yugoslavia: Double Standards or New Horizons for International Humanitarian Law?' in S Yee and Wang Tieya (eds), *International Law in the Post-Cold War World: Essays in Memory of Li Haopei* (Routledge 2001) 312; R Kolb and R Hyde, *An Introduction to the International Law of Armed Conflicts* (Hart Publishing 2008) 69; R Kolb, 'International Humanitarian Law and Its Implementation by the Court' in J Doria, H-P Gasser, and MC Bassiouni (eds), *The Legal Regime of the International Criminal Court: Essays in Honour of Professor Igor Blishchenko* (Brill 2009) 1018–19; N Lubell, *Extraterritorial Use of Force against Non-State Actors* (OUP 2010) 93; GS Corn, 'Thinking the Unthinkable: Has the Time Come to Offer Combatant Immunity to Non-State Actors?' (2011) 22 Stanford Law & Policy Review 253, 277; Crawford (n 5) 47; Sivakumaran (n 5) 513; E Mikos-Skuza, 'International Law's Changing Terms: "War" becomes "Armed Conflict"' in ME O'Connell (ed), *What Is War?: An Investigation in the Wake of 9/11* (Martinus Nijhoff 2012) 28; H Harrison Dinniss, *Cyber Warfare and the Laws of War* (CUP 2012) 142; Fleck (n 13) 604–05; Y Sandoz, 'Land Warfare', 116–17, P Spoerri, 'The Law of Occupation', 185, and N Melzer, 'The Principle of Distinction Between Civilians and Combatants', 318, all in A Clapham and P Gaeta (eds), *The Oxford Handbook of International Law in Armed Conflict* (OUP 2014); M Sassòli, 'The Concept and the Beginning of Occupation' in Clapham et al, *Geneva Conventions* (n 9) 1415 [57].

[13] See, eg, D Akande, 'Classification of Armed Conflicts: Relevant Legal Concepts' in E Wilmshurst (ed), *International Law and the Classification of Conflicts* (OUP 2012) 36 (considering 'the rules relating to detention of combatants and civilians' as one of 'two key parts' of IHL regulated differently in IACs and NIACs); D Fleck, 'The Law of Non-International Armed Conflicts' in D Fleck (ed), *The Handbook of International Humanitarian Law* (3rd edn, OUP 2013) 604–05 (listing, additionally, '[p]ublic property', '[r]elease of persons deprived of their liberty', '[b]elligerent reprisals', and '[m]ilitary objectives'). But see Section 9.4.2.3 in this book (discussing the rules on the seizure of public property in occupied territories in the context of the treatment of the law of belligerent occupation).

[14] cf, eg, R Higgins, *Problems and Process: International Law and How We Use It* (OUP 1995) 10 (arguing that the distinction between *lex lata* and *lex ferenda* in international law is 'in large measure a false dichotomy').

[15] See further K Mačák, 'Military Objectives 2.0: The Case for Interpreting Computer Data as Objects under International Humanitarian Law' (2015) 48 Isr L Rev 55, 60–62 (discussing the distinction between *lex lata* and *lex ferenda* from the perspective of the horizontal legal framework of international law).

the norms of applicability of IHL in particular have been decried as ambiguous,[16] arbitrary,[17] archaic,[18] and artificial,[19] to name just a few of the unflattering epithets. Nevertheless, the focus of the study is not on how the law should be developed or what the preferred policy of conflict parties should be.

In determining what the law is, the sources of analysis in this book mirror closely the two main sources of international law,[20] namely international treaties and customary international law.[21] The study may thus be considered orthodox in its methodological approach; in particular, it does not interpret the law applicable to armed conflicts 'liberally' to include 'soft law'[22] and it does not consider practice of armed groups to contribute in and of itself towards the creation of international custom.[23] Rather, soft law, non-state practice, and other sources are considered relevant to the extent that they lead to reactions by states, because it is those reactions that form the 'building block[s] in the edifice of . . . customary rule[s]'.[24]

The identification and analysis of norms arising from treaties present few methodological difficulties. The relevant international conventions are few in number and easy to access; the canons of interpretation are well-known and generally free from controversy. The present work principally relies on the 1899 and 1907 Hague Conventions governing land warfare,[25] the 1949 Geneva Conventions (GCs),[26]

[16] JG Stewart, 'Towards a Single Definition of Armed Conflict in International Humanitarian Law: A Critique of Internationalized Armed Conflict' (2003) 85 IRRC 313, 349.

[17] RJ Dupuy and A Leonetti, 'La notion de conflict armé à caractère non international' in *The New Humanitarian Law of Armed Conflict*, vol 1 (Editoriale scientifica 1979) 258.

[18] R Ehrenreich Brooks, 'War Everywhere: Rights, National Security Law, and the Law of Armed Conflict in the Age of Terror' (2004) 153 University of Pennsylvania Law Review 675, 755.

[19] R Abi-Saab, 'Humanitarian Law and Internal Conflicts: The Evolution of Legal Concern' in AJM Delissen and GJ Tanja (eds), *Humanitarian Law of Armed Conflict: Challenges Ahead: Essays in Honour of Frits Kalshoven* (Martinus Nijhoff 1991) 209.

[20] cf H Thirlway, *The Sources of International Law* (OUP 2014) 11.

[21] Art 38(1)(a)–(b) ICJ Statute.

[22] cf S Rondeau, 'Participation of Armed Groups in the Development of the Law Applicable to Armed Conflicts' (2011) 93 IRRC 649, 651 ('reference to "the law applicable to armed conflicts" should be interpreted liberally, as to include . . . soft law').

[23] cf J-M Henckaerts and L Doswald-Beck (eds), *Customary International Humanitarian Law* (CUP 2005) (hereafter *ICRC CIHL Study*) vol 1, xxxvi (considering the legal significance of non-state actors' practice as 'unclear'); but see, eg, R McCorquodale, 'An Inclusive International Legal System' (2004) 17 LJIL 477, 498; J-M Henckaerts, 'The ICRC Customary International Humanitarian Law Study: A Rejoinder to Professor Dinstein' (2007) 37 IYHR 259, 261; M Sassòli, 'Taking Armed Groups Seriously: Ways to Improve Compliance with International Humanitarian Law' (2010) 1 JIHLS 5, 22; Sivakumaran (n 5) 3–4 (all suggesting that some weight should be given to non-state practice in determining the content of customary IHL).

[24] M Mendelson, 'The Formation of Customary International Law' (1999) 272 RdC 155, 266 fn 299.

[25] Hague Convention (II) with Respect to the Laws and Customs of War on Land (signed 29 July 1899, entered into force 4 September 1900) 32 Stat 1803, TS 403; Hague Convention (IV) respecting the Laws and Customs of War on Land (signed 18 October 1907, entered into force 26 January 1910) 205 CTS 277.

[26] Geneva Convention (I) for the Amelioration of the Condition of the Wounded and Sick in Armed Forces in the Field (signed 12 August 1949, entered into force 21 October 1950) 75 UNTS 3 (hereafter GC I); Geneva Convention (II) for the Amelioration of the Condition of Wounded, Sick and Shipwrecked Members of Armed Forces at Sea (signed 12 August 1949, entered into force 21 October 1950) 75 UNTS 85 (hereafter GC II); Geneva Convention (III) relative to the Treatment of Prisoners of War (signed 12 August 1949, entered into force 21 October 1950) 75 UNTS 135 (hereafter GC III);

and their 1977 Additional Protocols.[27] The interpretive approach taken throughout the book is based on the relevant rules of the Vienna Convention on the Law of Treaties.[28] In general, that means that any treaty provisions should be interpreted in good faith in accordance with the ordinary meaning of the terms in their context and in the light of their object and purpose.[29] More specifically, the indeterminate duration and the humanitarian nature of the principal IHL treaties justify an evolutive approach to their interpretation,[30] in particular with respect to the generic terms[31] contained therein.[32] Finally, the *travaux préparatoires* and the subsequent practice of states parties to the treaties are also taken into account in the analysis.[33]

By contrast to treaties, working with international custom in this area is generally more challenging. Although the traditional, cumulative test of state practice and *opinio juris* is well-known,[34] its ingredients are not always easy to identify. The central problem in this respect is in the reluctance of states to engage publicly in the legal qualification of armed conflicts.[35] On occasion, states even admit as much themselves: for instance, the UK military manual notes that 'states have been, and always will be, reluctant to admit that a state of armed conflict exists'.[36] Even when states do acknowledge the applicability of IHL to a particular situation in which they are not themselves involved, they often refrain from specifically qualifying the type of conflict at hand.[37] For example, the Australian foreign minister stated in 1991

Geneva Convention (IV) relative to the Protection of Civilian Persons in Time of War (signed 12 August 1949, entered into force 21 October 1950) 75 UNTS 287 (hereafter GC IV).

27 Protocol Additional to the Geneva Conventions of 12 August 1949, and relating to the Protection of Victims of International Armed Conflicts (signed 12 December 1977, entered into force 7 December 1978) 1125 UNTS 3 (hereafter AP I); Protocol Additional to the Geneva Conventions of 12 August 1949, and relating to the Protection of Victims of Non-International Armed Conflicts (signed 12 December 1977, entered into force 7 December 1978) 1125 UNTS 609 (hereafter AP II).

28 Vienna Convention on the Law of Treaties (concluded 23 May 1969, entered into force 27 January 1980) 1155 UNTS 331 (hereafter VCLT).

29 Art 31(1) VCLT.

30 *The Right to Information on Consular Assistance in the Framework of the Guarantees of the Due Process of Law* (Advisory Opinion) (Ser A) No 16 (1 October 1999) (IACtHR) [114]; S Jacquement, 'The Cross-Fertilization of International Humanitarian Law and International Refugee Law' (2001) 83 IRRC 651, 658; V Chetail, 'The Contribution of the International Court of Justice to International Humanitarian Law' (2003) 85 IRRC 235, 259.

31 cf *Dispute regarding Navigational and Related Rights (Costa Rica v Nicaragua)* (Judgment) [2009] ICJ Rep 213 [66] ('[W]here the parties have used generic terms in a treaty, the parties necessarily having been aware that the meaning of the terms was likely to evolve over time, and where the treaty has been entered into for a very long period or is "of continuing duration", the parties must be presumed, as a general rule, to have intended those terms to have an evolving meaning.').

32 See further Mačák (n 15) 68–71 (arguing in favour of the evolutive interpretation of AP I).

33 cf Arts 32 and 31(3)(b) VCLT.

34 *North Sea Continental Shelf cases (Federal Republic of Germany/Denmark; Federal Republic of Germany/Netherlands)* [1969] ICJ Rep 3 [74].

35 See, eg, J Pejić, 'Status of Armed Conflicts' in E Wilmshurst and SC Breau (eds), *Perspectives on the ICRC Study on Customary International Humanitarian Law* (CUP 2007) 78; E Wilmshurst, 'Conclusions' in E Wilmshurst (ed), *International Law and the Classification of Conflicts* (OUP 2012) 479; N Zamir, *Classification of Conflicts in International Humanitarian Law: The Legal Impact of Foreign Intervention in Civil Wars* (Edward Elgar 2017) 3.

36 UK Ministry of Defence, *The Manual of the Law of Armed Conflict* (OUP 2004) 386 [15.3.1].

37 Wilmshurst (n 35) 480.

that the attacks of the Yugoslav National Army against civilian targets throughout Croatia had been 'quite contrary to the precepts of international humanitarian law', without specifying whether it was the 'precepts' of the law of IAC or NIAC that he deemed applicable to the situation. Similarly, when referring to their own conduct, states often hide behind ambiguous terms as 'operations' or terms with questionable legal valence such as 'armed conflict short of war' rather than use the established categories of IAC or NIAC.[38] Overall, this reluctance may perhaps be due to the states' desire to 'avoid contaminating humanitarian questions with the political considerations which are inseparable from their international relations in periods of conflict.'[39] Whatever the motivation, it makes the identification of customary rules in this area rather challenging.

In order to abate this problem to some extent, the present author attempted to gauge the relevant *opinio juris* by way of direct collection of data conducted in the early phases of the research project. A questionnaire concerning states' views on the applicability of IHL to internationalized armed conflicts was prepared and dispatched to all states with diplomatic representation in the UK and to the UK itself. The questionnaire was sent on 20 June 2011 by post to 163 diplomatic and consular missions in London and to the UK's Inter-departmental Committee for International Humanitarian Law. The addressees were requested to either answer the questions set out in the questionnaire or to forward it to the appropriate department of the respective state's government. Out of the 33 responses received in the following seven months, only 11 contained substantial or otherwise relevant answers. Given this limited number, the utility of the returned questionnaires thus remains illustrative at best.[40] The full text of the questionnaire and the replies thereto are available online for interested readers.[41]

1.1.3 Structure

This book is structured into eleven chapters. Following this brief research overview, the remainder of the present introductory chapter lays out the conceptual and normative framework for the entire analysis. It first justifies the need for this study by confirming the continuing distinction between IACs and NIACs in IHL (Section 1.2); and it then puts forward a conception of internationalization that expresses the transformation from a NIAC to an IAC (Section 1.3).

Part I of the book examines the process of conflict transformations. Chapter 2 provides a comprehensive map of the currently available modalities of conflict internationalization. Chapter 3 specifically considers the legal qualification of complex situations that feature more than two conflict parties. Chapter 4 then contrasts the mechanism of internationalization of armed conflicts with the reverse process of de-internationalization. The book then turns from the question of process to the effects that are produced by conflict internationalization in IHL.

[38] See further Zamir (n 35) 3.

[39] 'The International Committee of the Red Cross and Torture' (1976) 16 IRRC 610, 613.

[40] See, eg, note 160 in this chapter.

[41] See <www.kubomacak.org> (tab Data).

Part II focuses on the issue of combatant status. Since internationalized conflicts at their outset necessarily feature at least one non-state party, the traditional understanding would bar persons belonging to such entities from being eligible for combatant status. Accordingly, Chapter 5 examines the access to combatant status by members of non-state armed groups from a historical perspective. Chapter 6 then considers the normative underpinnings of the present-day regulation of combatancy. Finally, Chapter 7 analyses whether fighters engaged in internationalized armed conflicts may actually qualify for combatant status in practice.

Part III is concerned with the law of belligerent occupation. An internationalized armed conflict breaks out in the territory of a single state, which poses a number of difficulties vis-à-vis the applicability of occupation law, premised as it is on the existence of two independent warring states. In that regard, Chapter 8 traces the development of the law of occupation in order to identify trends relevant to its applicability to internationalized conflicts. Chapter 9 then considers the theoretical ramifications of extending the law of occupation to such conflicts. Chapter 10 rounds off the analysis by considering the practical application of the law in its temporal, geographical, and personal dimensions.

The final chapter summarizes the argument of the book. In particular, it argues that the study stands for a specific understanding of the notion of internationalized armed conflicts, which is subject to an extensive application of IHL. Nonetheless, the book also uncovers a number of gaps in the legal regulation that result from the particular features of internationalized conflicts. The conclusion thus sketches potential directions, in which the law and practice may develop to alleviate these deficiencies.

1.2 Distinction Between International and Non-international Armed Conflicts

1.2.1 Historical overview[42]

1.2.1.1 Pre-modern times: religion as the dividing line

Before the modern concept of state sovereignty took hold in international law, the extent of the rules applicable to armed conflict depended on religious affiliations of the belligerents rather than on the type of territories they controlled.[43] On the one hand, inter-religious conflicts were purportedly waged in the name of God and limited by few rules.[44] In this vein, the thirteenth-century canonist Hostiensis

[42] For a more detailed discussion see, eg, L Perna, *The Formation of the Treaty Law of Non-International Armed Conflicts* (Martinus Nijhoff 2006) 1–112; R Bartels, 'Timelines, Borderlines and Conflicts: The Historical Evolution of the Legal Divide between International and Non-international Armed Conflicts' (2009) 91 IRRC 35, 42–64; Zamir (n 35) 10–47.

[43] See also L Arimatsu, 'Territory, Boundaries and the Law of Armed Conflict' (2009) 12 YIHL 157, 161–65 (emphasizing that in pre-modern era, before the emergence of cartography, spatial conceptions were markedly different to those prevailing today: boundaries did not exist and rulers controlled people, not territories).

[44] cf Zamir (n 35) 11–12.

considered as legitimate those wars that Christian rulers waged against 'infidels'.[45] Even the otherwise progressive sixteenth-century theologian and jurist Francisco de Vitoria still considered it 'indubitably lawful to carry off both the children and the women of the Saracens into captivity and slavery' although he duly warned that such 'enslaving is not lawful in a war between Christians'.[46] Similarly, at least until the twelfth century, the prevailing view among Muslims was that holy war (*jihad*) was 'the only kind of relationship that could exist between those who believed in Islam and those who did not'.[47] These inter-religious wars were placed under very few restraints as their goal was to secure the domination of one religion over another using all available means.

On the other hand, intra-religious conflicts—that is, conflicts waged between princes of the same religious affiliation—were much more strictly regulated both in the Christian and the Muslim worlds. Hostiensis condemned such conflicts as illegitimate unless one of the strict exceptions was met.[48] By contrast, Vitoria was willing to grant that 'Christians may serve in war and make war' against one another,[49] but he still subjected their conduct to stringent rules.[50] Certain means and methods of warfare had been outlawed long before: for instance, already in 1139, the Second Lateran Council banned the use of crossbow in armed disputes between Christian princes, determining it to be 'suitable for use only against heathens'.[51] Similarly, a tenth-century Baghdadi scholar Al-Mawardi divided intra-religious wars between Muslim princes into three classes, each of which was supposed to be waged with different methods and based on a different set of obligations towards the enemy.[52]

In addition to religiously motivated conflicts, popular uprisings against rulers were frequent even in the pre-Westphalian times. In the Christian world, virtually no limitations were imposed on the means used to quell domestic rebellions.[53] Given that the authority of rulers was seen as deriving directly from God, rebels were to be treated in the same way as heathens.[54] By contrast, the Muslim scholar Al-Mawardi did consider the *ahl al baghi* ('war against rebels') to be one of the types of intra-religious war that were subject to constraints on permissible conduct.[55] However, as the role of religion in international relations continued to decline following the Thirty Years' War (1618–48), wars against rebels gradually evolved into a separate category even in the Christian-dominated part of the world.

[45] GM Reichberg, H Syse, and E Begby, *The Ethics of War: Classic and Contemporary Readings* (Blackwell 2006) 160–61.

[46] F de Vitoria, *De Indis and De Jure Belli* (JP Bate tr, 1557) vol I, book VI, §42.

[47] Bartels (n 42) 43.

[48] Reichberg et al (n 45) 161.

[49] de Vitoria (n 46) vol I, book VI, §1.

[50] ibid §§3–60.

[51] M Van Creveld, *The Transformation of War* (Free Press 1991) 138.

[52] ibid 140 (listing wars against apostasy (*ahl al ridda*), against rebels (*ahl al baghi*), and against those who had renounced the authority of the *imam* (*ahl al muharabin*)).

[53] See, eg, de Vitoria (n 46) vol I, book VI, §18 ('it is lawful to employ all appropriate measures . . . against internal foes, that is, against bad citizens').

[54] Perna (n 42) 2; Zamir (n 35) 12.

[55] Van Creveld (n 51) 140.

1.2.1.2 Westphalian era: remit of the law defined by state borders

The Peace of Westphalia (1648) is often seen as the starting point for the development of modern international law.[56] In contradistinction to the war it concluded, it established an international community based on the principle of religious equality—albeit initially only with respect to denominations of the Christian faith—and thus contributed to the decline of the influence of religious ideas on the international plane.[57] With respect to the typology of conflicts, the emergence of a sovereign order contributed to a different treatment of inter-state and civil wars. This was also reflected in the seventeenth-century writings on the law of nations.

Already in 1625, Hugo Grotius divided wars into public and private based on the parties involved: wars between sovereign powers were public, while wars between persons without authority from the state were private.[58] He further introduced a subdivision of public wars into 'formal' and 'less formal' categories, the former being a war waged under the authority of state sovereigns on both sides and observing certain formalities (such as a declaration of war).[59] The latter subtype included conflicts that did not meet those conditions, for example if the war was 'waged against private persons'.[60] For Grotius, civil wars were thus seen as either private wars (if no sovereign power was involved) or as less formal public wars (if such a war was waged by the sovereign against his subjects).[61]

Later in the seventeenth century, the German jurist Samuel von Pufendorf made the distinction clearer and more express. Building on the categories introduced previously by Grotius, he expressly stated that 'civil wars', together with undeclared wars and those waged against private citizens, belonged to the class of 'informal' wars.[62] However, similarly to his predecessor, von Pufendorf left open the question whether the limits to permissible conduct in war should also extend to conflicts we would today describe as non-international.[63] Accordingly, the idea that some forms of internal wars should be subject to international law constraints only started to develop in the next period.[64]

[56] See, eg, D Anzilotti, *Cours de droit international* (G Gidel tr, Sirey 1929) vol 1, 5; L Gross, 'The Peace of Westphalia, 1648–1948' (1948) 42 AJIL 20, 26; P Malanczuk, *Akehurst's Modern Introduction to International Law* (7th edn, Routledge 2002) 9–11; but see, eg, V Lowe, *International Law* (OUP 2007) 9–10 (criticizing 'the fixation with Westphalia as the birth of international law'); Arimatsu (n 43) 165–66 (highlighting the emergence of cartography as an independent discipline in the period of Enlightenment and its importance for the development of the notion of territorial jurisdiction).

[57] Bartels (n 42) 44; see also Gross (n 56) 26 (arguing that the Peace of Westphalia 'promoted the laicization of international law by divorcing it from any particular religious background').

[58] H Grotius, *The Law of War and Peace in Three Books* (FW Kelsey tr, 1625), book I, ch III, s I, §1.

[59] ibid, book I, ch III, s IV, §1.

[60] ibid, book I, ch III, s IV, §2.

[61] At the outset of the chapter entitled 'Distinction Between Public and Private War; Explanation of Sovereignty', Grotius also referred to 'mixed wars' as those that are 'on one side public, on the other side private'. He did not elaborate on the relationship of this category to less formal public wars waged against private persons. It appears that such conflicts could fall simultaneously into both of these categories. See ibid, book I, ch III, s I, §1; see further SC Neff, *War and the Law of Nations* (CUP 2005) 253–54.

[62] S von Pufendorf, *On The Duty of Man And Citizen According to the Natural Law* (F Gardner Moore tr, John Hayes 1682), ch XVI, §7.

[63] See further Bartels (n 42) 45.

[64] Zamir (n 35) 15.

In the eighteenth century, the Swiss scholar Emmerich de Vattel argued that the laws of war should apply in full in those civil wars, which in their intensity resembled an international war. To Vattel, as soon as the rebels acquired 'sufficient strength to give [the sovereign] effectual opposition', the bands of society and government were broken, there was no common superior recognized by the enemy parties, and the war between them was equivalent in every respect to a public war between two states.[65] Because a true civil war was fully tantamount to an inter-state war, it activated the law of neutrality, thus affecting not only the conflict parties, but also all foreign countries.[66] Conversely, the sovereign was not bound by the laws of war when suppressing rebellions of lower intensity.[67] The only duty incumbent upon him by operation of international law in those cases was one of clemency, requiring him to grant amnesty where the offenders were numerous.[68]

The doctrine of belligerency, developed in the nineteenth century, resolved the difficulty of distinguishing between rebellions that triggered the application of the laws of war and those that did not.[69] It stipulated that an internal conflict could only come within the scope of international law if the insurgents were recognized as belligerents. According to Lassa Oppenheim, a civil war was not a 'real war in the strict sense of the term in International Law'[70] because 'war is an armed contention between *States*.'[71] However, such a conflict could be elevated to the international plane by way of recognition.[72] The process of recognition structured the status acquired by the anti-government forces into three stages: rebellion, insurgency, and belligerency.[73]

A *rebellion* was an internal conflict characterized by non-recognition both by the territorial government and the outside states. As such, it was to be dealt with exclusively by domestic law.[74] If a rebellion was sustained and presented a credible threat to the ruling government, it could evolve into an *insurgency*.[75] The territorial state could recognize the existence of an insurgency, indicating that it regarded the insurgents as legal contestants and not as mere lawbreakers.[76] Finally, a formal recognition of the non-state party to the conflict as *belligerents* by the incumbent

[65] E de Vattel, *The Law of Nations or the Principles of Natural Law* (J Chitty tr, 1758), book III, ch XVIII, §§292–93, 295.

[66] Neff (n 61) 258.

[67] It is controversial whether Vattel's view was motivated by humanitarian concerns or simply by the fact that the conflicts in question were similar in magnitude: compareL Moir, *The Law of Internal Armed Conflict* (CUP 2004) 3 and Perna (n 42) 20–22.

[68] de Vattel (n 65), book III, ch XVIII, §§290–91.

[69] See further Neff (n 61) 258–68.

[70] L Oppenheim, *International Law: A Treatise* (1st edn, Longmans, Green & Co. 1905 & 1906) vol II, 67.

[71] ibid 65 (emphasis original).

[72] ibid 65–66.

[73] cf YM Lootsteen, 'The Concept of Belligerency in International Law' (2000) 166 MLR 109, 113; Bartels (n 42) 48; Zamir (n 35) 16.

[74] BR Roth, *Governmental Illegitimacy in International Law* (Clarendon Press 1999) 173.

[75] Moir (n 67) 4; Lootsteen (n 73) 113–14.

[76] R Higgins, 'International Law and Civil Conflict' in E Luard (ed), *The International Regulation of Civil Wars* (NYU Press 1972) 170; see also RA Falk, 'Janus Tormented: The International Law of Internal War' in JN Rosenau (ed), *International Aspects of Civil Strife* (Princeton University Press 1964) 200 (stating that rebels, whose insurgency was recognized, acquired an intermediate legal status, causing 'a partial internationalization of the conflict, without bringing the state of belligerency into being').

government made the laws of war applicable to the conflict in full;[77] recognition by a third state also invoked the law of neutrality between this third state and the parties to the conflict.[78] It was on this basis that, for instance, Great Britain was held liable for the violation of her neutrality obligations by allowing the construction and sale of warships to the Confederacy during the American Civil War (1861–65).[79] Over time, recognition of belligerency became less and less frequent, with the last known express recognition by the territorial state having been granted during the Boer War (1899–1902).[80] Critically, no recognition was issued during the Spanish Civil War in the 1930s, leading some scholars to argue that the doctrine had fallen into *desuetude*.[81] It will be shown later in this work that the present author does not share that view.[82]

As for inter-state conflicts, traditional international law developed von Pufendorf's distinction between formal and informal wars to require a formal declaration of war in order to trigger the application of the laws of war.[83] The 1907 Hague Convention (III) relative to the Opening of Hostilities codified this customary law requirement, stipulating that hostilities must only commence by either an explicit declaration of war or an ultimatum with a conditional declaration of war.[84] More than twenty years later, the 1928 Kellogg-Briand Pact prohibited the use of war in international relations.[85] Although in theory, these steps were taken to liberate humanity from the scourge of war altogether, or at least to subject its outbreak to rigid rules, their actual outcome was markedly different.[86] As a result, by denying the existence of war

[77] cf also Zamir (n 35) 15 fn 37 (noting that in this regard, the doctrine of belligerency echoed Vattel's approach).

[78] D Schindler, 'The Different Types of Armed Conflicts According to the Geneva Conventions and Protocols' (1979) 163 RdC 117, 145 (hereafter Schindler, 'Different Types of Armed Conflicts'); Moir (n 67) 7–10.

[79] *Alabama Claims (United States v Great Britain)* (Award) (1872) 29 RIAA 125, 129–31.

[80] H-P Gasser, 'International Humanitarian Law' in H Haug (ed), *Humanity for All: The International Red Cross and Red Crescent Movement* (P. Haupt 1993) 559; E La Haye, *War Crimes in Internal Armed Conflicts* (CUP 2008) 14 fn 87.

[81] See, eg, RR Oglesby, *Internal War and the Search for Normative Order* (Martinus Nijhoff 1971) 100; R Higgins, 'International Law and Civil Conflict' in E Luard (ed), *The International Regulation of Civil Wars* (New York University Press 1972) 171; L Doswald-Beck, 'The Legal Validity of Military Intervention by Invitation of the Government' (1985) 56 BYBIL 189, 252; J Crawford, 'First Report on State Responsibility', UN Doc A/CN.4/490 and Adds 1-6 (1998) [270]; Provost (n 9) 279; R Kolb, *Ius contra bellum: Le droit international relatif au maintien de la paix* (2nd edn, Helbing Lichtenhahn 2009) 326; E David, *Principes de droit des conflits armés* (5th edn, Bruylant 2012) 138; A Sanger, 'The Contemporary Law of Blockade and the Gaza Freedom Flotilla' (2010) 13 YIHL 397, 424–25; Hill-Cawthorne (n 5) 13; see also Baxter (n 12) 520 ('[the] institution [of recognition of belligerency has] fallen into disuse'); A Cullen, *The Concept of Non-International Armed Conflict in International Humanitarian Law* (CUP 2010) 8 fn 2 ('the doctrine of belligerency . . . has fallen into disuse and is now considered obsolete'); Moir (n 67) 41 (arguing that the doctrine 'has fallen into disuse as a legal concept'); D Guilfoyle, 'The Mavi Marmara Incident and Blockade in Armed Conflict' (2011) 81 BYBIL 1, 192 (considering it doubtful that the doctrine had survived the nineteenth century).

[82] See Section 2.5.1.1.

[83] See Pufendorf (n 62) ch XVI, §7; see also, eg, de Vattel (n 65), book III, ch IV, §51; JC Bluntschli, *Le droit international codifié* (C Lardy tr, 5th edn, Guillaumin 1895) 296 §521.

[84] Hague Convention (III) relative to the Opening of Hostilities (signed 18 October 1907, entered into force 26 January 1910) 205 CTS 263, Art 1.

[85] Kellogg-Briand Pact (signed 27 August 1928, entered into force 24 July 1929) 94 LNTS 57, Art 1.

[86] cf Neff (n 61) 293–96.

in a *formal* sense, states could escape allegations of violations of both *jus ad bellum* and *jus in bello*.[87] The interbellum American jurist John Bassett Moore had simple advice for states involved in drafting the Pact: 'When once you have outlawed war, do not use the word war any more.'[88] And indeed, instead of refraining from the use of force in the settlement of their disputes, states resorted to practising what has been described as the 'art of avoiding war'.[89] For instance, after the Sino-Japanese conflict broke out in 1937, the Chinese and Japanese governments both denied that a state of war existed between them, despite the intense fighting and the subsequent Chinese occupation of Manchuria.[90]

In summary, traditional international law stipulated rules that applied almost exclusively to inter-state wars understood in the formal sense. Conflicts taking place within one state's borders were beyond the reach of international law—unless they reached intensity similar to that observed in inter-state conflicts and were formally recognized as such by one of the relevant international actors. In 1949, the adoption of the four GCs dramatically changed this state of affairs.

1.2.2 Current dichotomy

1.2.2.1 International armed conflicts

The 1949 GCs developed the pre-existing 'Geneva law' which had dated back to the second half of the nineteenth century.[91] Crucially, the decision to revise and expand the prior treaties[92] was prompted by the unprecedented violence and human suffering during the Second World War.[93] The events of that war had exposed a number of deficiencies in the legal framework valid at the time that were to be addressed by the new treaties.[94] Among other developments, the Conventions radically modified the approach to the applicability of IHL in inter-state conflicts.[95] The bedrock

[87] See also Provost (n 9) 249 ('With the prohibition of war in international law by way of the Briand-Kellogg Pact … there was an even greater incentive not to admit to being in a state of war with another country.').

[88] Q Wright, 'The Meaning of the Pact of Paris' (1933) 27 AJIL 39, 51.

[89] Neff (n 61) 296.

[90] CC Hyde, *International Law, Chiefly as Interpreted and Applied by the United States* (2nd rev edn, Little, Brown & Co 1947) vol III, 1687 fn 5.

[91] See, eg, F Kalshoven and L Zegveld, *Constraints on the Waging of War: An Introduction to International Humanitarian Law* (4th edn, CUP 2011) 16–19.

[92] On the relationship of the 1949 Conventions with the older Geneva Conventions, see generally P Benvenuti, 'Relationship with Prior and Subsequent Treaties', in Clapham et al, *Geneva Conventions* (n 9) 694–97 [16]–[25].

[93] J-M Henckaerts and H Niebergall-Lackner, 'Introduction' in ICRC (ed), *Commentary on the First Geneva Convention* (CUP 2016) 16 [62].

[94] On which see further L Nurick, 'The Distinction between Combatant and Noncombatant in the Law of War' (1945) 39 AJIL 680; EA Korovin, 'Second World War and International Law' (1946) 40 AJIL 742; L Nurick and RW Barrett, 'Legality of Guerrilla Forces Under the Laws of War' (1946) 40 AJIL 563; JAC Gutteridge, 'The Geneva Conventions of 1949' (1949) 26 BYBIL 294; RT Yingling and RW Ginnane, 'The Geneva Conventions of 1949' (1952) 46 AJIL 393.

[95] Similarly Bartels (n 42) 57; Zamir (n 35) 11; T Ferraro and L Cameron, 'Article 2: Application of the Convention', in ICRC (ed), *Commentary on the First Geneva Convention* (CUP 2016) 69–70 [192]–[96] (hereafter Ferraro and Cameron, 'Article 2').

provision in that regard was Common Article 2, the first two paragraphs of which read as follows:

> [T]he present Convention shall apply to all cases of declared war or of any other armed conflict which may arise between two or more of the High Contracting Parties, even if the state of war is not recognized by one of them.
>
> The Convention shall also apply to all cases of partial or total occupation of the territory of a High Contracting Party, even if the said occupation meets with no armed resistance.

Since their adoption, the GCs have gained universal acceptance,[96] supporting the claim that Common Article 2—like most if not all of the rest of the instruments—has become customary international law.[97] Consequently, when the conditions of that provision are met, the entire corpus of the customary law of IAC, together with any treaties that the conflict parties may have ratified, will be activated.[98] It is thus essential to correctly understand the criteria of applicability mandated by Article 2.

To begin with, a key consequence of the wording used by Common Article 2 is that the formal conception of war was replaced by a radically different material conception.[99] In other words, rules of the law of IAC would now come into effect immediately after the first shot was fired,[100] whether or not a war was formally declared or whether the situation was labelled as 'police action' or 'legitimate self-defence'.[101] This is the consequence of including an objectively ascertainable notion of 'armed conflict' next to the more equivocal term 'war' in the text of the provision.[102] In fact, states very rarely admit to being in a state of war, even in situations in which they

[96] ICRC, 'Geneva Conventions of 1949 Achieve Universal Acceptance' (21 August 2006) <www.icrc.org/eng/resources/documents/news-release/2009-and-earlier/geneva-conventions-news-210806.htm>.

[97] See, eg, T Meron, 'The Geneva Conventions as Customary Law' (1987) 81 AJIL 348; *ICRC CIHL Study* (n 23) vol 1, xxiii and xxxvi; J-M Henckaerts, 'The Grave Breaches Regime as Customary International Law' (2009) 7 JICJ 683, 686–88; GD Solis, *The Law of Armed Conflict: International Humanitarian Law in War* (2nd edn, CUP 2016) 88.

[98] C Greenwood, 'The Concept of War in Modern International Law' (1987) 36 ICLQ 283, 295; D Turns, 'The International Humanitarian Law Classification of Armed Conflicts in Iraq since 2003' (2010) 86 International Law Studies 97, 102–03; S Wills, 'The Legal Characterization of The Armed Conflicts in Afghanistan and Iraq: Implications for Protection' (2011) 58 NILR 173, 177; JK Kleffner, 'Scope of Application of International Humanitarian Law' in Fleck *Handbook of International Humanitarian Law* (3rd edn) 44; Zamir (n 35) 48.

[99] L Kotzsch, *The Concept of War in Contemporary History and International Law* (E Droz 1956) 298.

[100] This is the prevailing view in the scholarship: see, eg, JS Pictet (ed) *Geneva Convention IV relative to the Protection of Civilian Persons in Time of War: Commentary* (ICRC 1958) 20–21 (hereafter Pictet, *GC IV Commentary*); Sandoz et al, *APs Commentary* (n 12) 35; Provost (n 9) 250; Kleffner (n 98) 45; A Clapham, 'Concept of International Armed Conflict' in Clapham et al, *Geneva Conventions* (n 9) 16 [38] (hereafter Clapham, 'Concept of IAC'); Ferraro and Cameron, 'Article 2' (n 95) 79 [218]; Zamir (n 35) 53–55; see also *Prosecutor v Delalić et al* (*Čelebići* Trial Judgment) IT-96-21-T (16 November 1998) [184] (juxtaposing IACs and NIACs insofar as the requirements of organization and intensity are concerned); but see C Greenwood, 'Scope of Application of Humanitarian Law' in D Fleck (ed), *The Handbook of International Humanitarian Law* (2nd edn, OUP 2008) 48; ILA Use of Force Committee, Final Report on the Definition of Armed Conflict in International Law (2010) 32; Solis (n 97) 162 (all arguing for a more restrictive view).

[101] JS Pictet (ed), *Geneva Convention I for the Amelioration of the Condition of the Wounded and Sick in Armed Forces in the Field: Commentary* (ICRC 1952) 32.

[102] Kalshoven and Zegveld (n 91) 31.

otherwise acknowledge that IHL applies.[103] Similarly, it is unimportant whether the parties involved recognize each other as independent states.[104] For instance, although the Arab countries did not recognize Israel throughout the Arab-Israeli conflict, both sides accepted that the laws of war applied to the conflict.[105]

Although the matter is not entirely free of controversy, the prevailing view is that there is virtually no threshold requirement of intensity or duration of the conflict.[106] This means that the law of IAC comes into effect with any resort to force between two states,[107] even in the briefest of clashes such as the thirty-minute shootout between the US and Mexico in 1916[108] or the downing of the US Naval pilot Lt Bobby Goodman over Lebanon by Syria in 1983.[109] In summary, whatever the name, the intensity or the duration of the use of force between two or more states, IHL applies.

In addition, the law of IAC may exceptionally come into effect even when states do not resort to force in two specific situations. Firstly, this is the case if a state declares war on another state, but the declaration is not followed by armed hostilities between the parties.[110] Historical examples of practice of this kind have included declarations of war against the Axis powers issued by a number of Latin American countries during the Second World War, as well as those made by several Arab states against Israel in 1967.[111] The fact that a declaration of war triggers the law of armed conflict even if it is not followed by any fighting is a residue of the formal conception of war that had prevailed in international law until 1949.[112]

Secondly, IHL is also triggered by situations that amount to a belligerent occupation even if that occupation is not resisted.[113] Although a definition of occupation is absent from the GCs, it may be found in Article 42 of the 1907 Hague Regulations, which the GCs supplement but do not supersede.[114] According to that provision, a territory is considered occupied when it is actually placed under the authority

[103] For example, the UK denied that its 'military and naval operations' in Falkland Islands after the Argentine invasion in 1982, or 'hostilities against Iraq' in which it 'engaged' in 1991, or again the NATO intervention against Yugoslavia in which it prominently participated in 1999 had amounted to a state of war with any of these states. See Letter from Lord President of the Council, Mr John Biffen, to Mr George Foulkes, MP (20 May 1982), reproduced in (1982) 53 BYBIL, 519–20 (on the UK-Argentine conflict); Statement of British Prime Minister, HC Debs, vol 184, col 375 (28 January 1991) (on the Gulf War); Statement by the Minister of State, Ministry of Defence, HL Debs, vol 605, WA 5-6 (14 June 1999) (on the NATO intervention).

[104] Ferraro and Cameron, 'Article 2' (n 95) 84 [231].

[105] Kleffner (n 98) 48.

[106] See note 100 in this chapter for references to the relevant academic debate.

[107] *Prosecutor v Tadić* (Decision on Jurisdiction) IT-94-1-AR72 (2 October 1995) [70].

[108] Provost (n 9) 250.

[109] See US Department of State, Telegram 348126 to American Embassy at Damascus (8 December 1983), in M Nash (ed), *Cumulative Digest of United States Practice in International Law 1981–1988* (1995) 3456–57 (qualifying the situation as one to which IHL had applied).

[110] cf Common Art 2(1) GCs (referring to 'all cases of declared war'). See, eg, Clapham, 'Concept of IAC' (n 100) 6 [7]; Ferraro and Cameron, 'Article 2' (n 95) 74 [206].

[111] Schindler, 'Different Types of Armed Conflicts' (n 78) 132.

[112] See Section 1.2.1.2.

[113] Common Art 2(2) GCs.

[114] cf Arts 135 GC III and 154 GC IV. With respect to the definition of occupation, this interpretation has also been confirmed in the case law of the ICTY: see *Prosecutor v Naletilić and Martinović* (Trial Judgment) IT-98-34-T (31 March 2003) [215]–[16]; *Prosecutor v Kordić and Čerkez* (Trial Judgment) IT-95-14/2-T (26 February 2001) [339]; *Prosecutor v Prlić et al* (Appeal Judgment) IT-04-74-A (29 November 2017) vol 1 [316]. See further Benvenuti (n 92) 696–97 [23]–[25].

of the hostile army.[115] Thus even if force is not used in acquiring control over another state's territory (as in the cases of the Nazi occupation of Czechoslovakia or Denmark in 1938–40), IHL will apply.[116] By contrast to the first exception, this scenario is thus in line with the material conception of war: the law applies due to the facts on the ground, irrespective of any formal proclamations by the parties.[117]

Finally, the adoption of Additional Protocol I to the Geneva Conventions in 1977 created a legal fiction, extending the application of the norms pertaining to IACs to those internal wars in which 'peoples are fighting against colonial domination and alien occupation and against racist regimes in the exercise of their right of self-determination'.[118] By the inclusion of this provision, the Protocol provided for an *ex lege* internationalization of a class of internal armed conflicts, which will be discussed at greater length later in this work.[119]

1.2.2.2 Non-international armed conflicts

In February 1945, the ICRC announced its goals with respect to the revision of the law of Geneva as threefold: to extend the protection of detained civilians, to improve the enforceability of IHL, and, most importantly for the present purposes, to provide protection to victims of civil wars.[120] As discussed earlier, the law valid at the time did not extend to internal conflicts and states remained generally unconstrained when responding to domestic insurgencies.[121] The view prevailing among states in this regard was fairly straightforward. Prior to the outbreak of an internal conflict, it was considered foolish to give an incentive to potential revolutionaries by assuring them that they would be granted protection equivalent to that of foreign soldiers in international wars.[122] Once a conflict was underway, governments were more than reluctant to recognize the belligerency of their adversaries who were fighting to undermine these governments' authority.[123] For all these reasons, the ICRC's proposal at the outset of the diplomatic conference in Geneva to oblige parties to NIACs to 'implement the provisions' of the Conventions had had very limited prospects of success.[124]

[115] Hague Conventions (n 25) Art 42; see also *Armed Activities on the Territory of the Congo (Democratic Republic of the Congo v Uganda)* (Judgment) [2005] ICJ Rep 116 [172] ('territory is considered to be occupied when it is actually placed under the authority of the hostile army, and the occupation extends only to the territory where such authority has been established and can be exercised').

[116] Pictet, *GC IV Commentary* (n 100) 21; Ferraro and Cameron, 'Article 2' (n 95) 104 [286].

[117] cf Ferraro and Cameron, 'Article 2' (n 95) 105 [288].

[118] Art 1(4) AP I.

[119] See Section 2.4.

[120] F Bugnion, 'From the End of the Second World War to the Dawn of the Third Millennium: The Activities of the ICRC during the Cold War and its Aftermath' (1995) 305 IRRC 207, 211.

[121] See Section 1.2.1.2.

[122] See, eg, Switzerland, *Final Record of the Diplomatic Conference of Geneva of 1949* (Federal Political Department 1949) (hereafter *Final Record*) vol II B, 11 (Greece) (arguing that extending protection to political opponents might 'incite [them] to take up arms against a legitimate government'); ibid 330 (Burma) (criticizing the proposed text of Common Article 3 for being 'an encouragement and an incentive to the insurgents').

[123] Perna (n 42) 30.

[124] cf *Final Record* (n 122) vol I, 47, 61, 73, 113 (draft Common Art 2(4)).

Indeed, the majority of the states present at the conference were not willing to concede what they saw as their sovereign right to maintain law and order in face of potential domestic upheavals.[125] The text proposed by the ICRC was criticized as striking 'at the root of national sovereignty' and as posing a threat to national security.[126] Lawrence Hill-Cawthorne has observed in this regard that the primary concern of many delegations was not so much 'with extending *humanitarian law* to internal conflicts but rather more generally with extending *international law* to intra-state matters'.[127] Among Western states, this legal view was mirrored by political worries that the proposed text could be instrumentalized by the countries of the Soviet bloc in their attempts to destabilize the Western colonial empires.[128] Nonetheless, after weeks of deliberations at the conference, a compromise solution was found.[129] The delegates agreed to limit the number of provisions applicable in civil wars to a bare minimum, resulting in the adoption of the present text of Common Article 3:

In the case of armed conflict not of an international character occurring in the territory of one of the High Contracting Parties, each Party to the conflict shall be bound to apply, as a minimum, the following provisions:

(1) Persons taking no active part in the hostilities, including members of armed forces who have laid down their arms and those placed *hors de combat* by sickness, wounds, detention, or any other cause, shall in all circumstances be treated humanely, without any adverse distinction founded on race, colour, religion or faith, sex, birth or wealth, or any other similar criteria.

To this end, the following acts are and shall remain prohibited at any time and in any place whatsoever with respect to the above-mentioned persons:
(a) violence to life and person, in particular murder of all kinds, mutilation, cruel treatment and torture;
(b) taking of hostages;
(c) outrages upon personal dignity, in particular humiliating and degrading treatment;
(d) the passing of sentences and the carrying out of executions without previous judgment pronounced by a regularly constituted court, affording all the judicial guarantees which are recognized as indispensable by civilized peoples.

(2) The wounded and sick shall be collected and cared for. [...]

Because the article's aim was to impose fundamental humanitarian principles of the Conventions on the belligerents in internal conflicts, it has often been referred

[125] Moir (n 67) 24. [126] *Final Record* (n 122) vol II B, 10 (United Kingdom).
[127] Hill-Cawthorne (n 5) 15 (emphases original).
[128] A Cassese, 'Civil War and International Law' in A Cassese (ed), *The Human Dimension of International Law: Selected Papers of Antonio Cassese* (OUP 2008) 116–17.
[129] For a detailed treatment of the progress of the debates at the diplomatic conference, see Bartels (n 42) 61–64.

to as a 'convention in miniature'[130] or a 'mini-convention'.[131] The International Court of Justice (ICJ) has described its contents as 'elementary considerations of humanity'[132] and as 'general principles of humanitarian law',[133] and held that it was part of the universally binding customary international law.[134] For its part, the ICTY has consistently ruled that Common Article 3 applies as a matter of custom both to NIACs and IACs.[135]

The text of the provision does not, on its face, include a bottom threshold of application, referring only to the existence of an armed conflict 'not of an international character'. Nevertheless, the *travaux préparatoires* indicate[136] and modern-day case-law confirms[137] the generally accepted view that Common Article 3 implies a two-fold requirement of minimum organization and intensity.[138] First, the rebels must be militarily *organized*, the indicators of which include the presence of a command structure, the ability to determine a unified military strategy and speak with one voice, the adherence to military discipline, as well as the capability to comply with IHL.[139] Second, the hostilities must surpass a certain level of *intensity*, for instance when the police forces of the state in question are no longer capable of dealing with the insurrection, and therefore the army has to be mobilized in order to defeat the insurgents.[140] Although the precise application of these criteria depends on the case at hand, the requirement of a certain minimum threshold of application stands in stark contrast to the law of IACs.[141] It also indicates that there is not, at present, a unitary or generic notion of 'armed conflict' of which IACs and NIACs would form

[130] See, eg, *Final Record* (n 122) 326 (Soviet Union); Moir (n 67) 31; L Cameron et al, 'Article 3: Conflicts Not of an International Character' in ICRC (ed), *Commentary on the First Geneva Convention* (CUP 2016) 131 [356] (hereafter Cameron et al, 'Article 3').

[131] See, eg, Kalshoven and Zegveld (n 91) 66; Kleffner (n 98) 69; Zamir (n 35) 62.

[132] *Corfu Channel Case (UK v Albania)* (Merits) [1949] ICJ Rep 4, 22.

[133] *Military and Paramilitary Activities in and against Nicaragua (Nicaragua v US)* (Merits) [1986] ICJ Rep 14 [218].

[134] *Nuclear Weapons* Advisory Opinion (n 8) [79].

[135] *Tadić* Decision on Jurisdiction (n 107) [102]; *Prosecutor v Delalić et al* (*Čelebići* Appeal Judgment) IT-96-21-A (20 February 2001) [138]–[139] and [147]; *Prosecutor v Gotovina* (Trial Judgment) IT-06-90-T (15 April 2011) vol 2 [1671].

[136] See *Final Record* (n 122) 129 (Report drawn up by the Joint Committee and presented to the Plenary Assembly).

[137] See *Tadić* Decision on Jurisdiction (n 107) [70], as applied in *Prosecutor v Tadić* (Trial Judgment) IT-94-1-T (7 May 1997) [562]; *Prosecutor v Limaj, Bala and Musliu* (Trial Judgment) IT-03-66-T (30 November 2005) [84]; *Prosecutor v Haradinaj, Balaj and Brahimaj* (Trial Judgment) IT-04-84-T (3 April 2008) [37]–[60]; *Prosecutor v Boškoski and Tarčulovski* (Trial Judgment) IT-04-82-T (10 July 2008) [175]–[205].

[138] See, eg, Schindler, 'Different Types of Armed Conflicts' (n 78) 147; Kolb and Hyde (n 12) 78; M Sassòli, AA Bouvier, and A Quintin, *How Does Law Protect in War?* (3rd edn, ICRC 2011) vol I, 123; Sivakumaran (n 5) 167–80; L Moir, 'The Concept of Non-International Armed Conflict' in Clapham et al, *Geneva Conventions* (n 9) 404–13 [34]–[61]; Zamir (n 35) 63; Cameron et al, 'Article 3' (n 130) 153–59 [422]–[437].

[139] *Limaj et al* Trial Judgment (n 137) [129]; *Boškoski and Tarčulovski* Trial Judgment (n 137) [199]–[203].

[140] *Limaj et al* Trial Judgment (n 137) [90]; *Boškoski and Tarčulovski* Trial Judgment (n 137) [177].

[141] See text to notes 99–109 in this chapter.

specific subtypes,[142] an issue that gains particular importance with respect to the process of de-internationalization discussed later in this work.[143]

Apart from these minimum requirements, the scope of NIACs under Common Article 3 is fairly broad. In particular, the provision does not establish any requirement as to the nature of the belligerents, and it therefore applies equally to 'vertical' civil wars (confrontations between governmental armed forces and the forces of one or more armed groups) and to 'horizontal' civil wars (confrontations between the forces of several armed groups without the involvement of the government).[144] Moreover, although the provision speaks of conflicts 'occurring *in the territory* of one of the High Contracting Parties', it would be inaccurate to limit the notion of NIACs to intraterritorial situations (sometimes referred to as 'internal armed conflicts').[145] The formulation used in Common Article 3 likely reflects the historical fact that pre-1949, conflicts between a state and a non-state armed group—or those between several such groups—were practically always confined to the territory of a single state.[146] However, modern state practice[147] and the object and purpose of Common Article 3[148] suggest that the law of NIAC applies also to conflicts that cross international borders, as long as they satisfy the minimum criteria outlined previously.[149]

Dealing with the absence of a clear definition of the concept of NIAC was one of the hopes placed on the delegates at the Diplomatic Conference of 1974–77.[150] The states agreed on an applicability provision according to which the newly adopted Second Additional Protocol would:

> apply to all armed conflicts which are not covered by Article 1 of [AP I] and which take place in the territory of a High Contracting Party between its armed forces and dissident armed forces or other organized armed groups which, under responsible command, exercise such

[142] Schindler, 'Different Types of Armed Conflicts' (n 78) 131; D Kritsiotis, 'The Tremors of Tadić' (2010) 43 Isr L Rev 262, 293–99; K Mačák and N Zamir, 'The Applicability of International Humanitarian Law to the Conflict in Libya' (2012) 14 ICLR 403, 407; Akande (n 13) 32; S Sivakumaran, 'Re-envisaging the International Law of Internal Armed Conflict: A Rejoinder to Gabriella Blum' (2011) 22 EJIL 273, 273; M Milanovic and V Hadzi-Vidanovic, 'A Taxonomy of Armed Conflict' in N White and C Henderson (eds), *Research Handbook on International Conflict and Security Law* (Edward Elgar 2013) 269–72; M Milanovic, 'The Applicability of the Conventions to "Transnational" and "Mixed" Conflicts' in Clapham et al, *Geneva Conventions* (n 9) 28–30 [5]–[10] (hereafter Milanovic, '"Transnational" and "Mixed" Conflicts'); Zamir (n 35) 68–69.

[143] See further Section 4.2.1.

[144] Moir (n 138) 397 [13]; Cameron et al, 'Article 3' (n 130) 143 [394].

[145] Moir (n 138) 400–03 [22]–[31].

[146] See Cameron et al, 'Article 3' (n 130) 164 [455].

[147] See, eg, Ecuador, Ministry of Foreign Affairs, Ecuadorian Government Protests Assassination of Raul Reyes in Ecuador (1 March 2008); Germany, Federal Prosecutor General, Targeted Killing in Pakistan case, Case No. 3 BJs 7/12-4, Decision to Terminate Proceedings (23 July 2013) 742; US DoD, *Law of War Manual* (December 2016) [17.1.1.2].

[148] cf Cameron et al, 'Article 3' (n 130) 168 [467].

[149] See further K Mačák, 'Silent War: Applicability of the *Jus in Bello* to Military Space Operations' (2018) 94 International Law Studies 1, 34–36.

[150] See V Potapov, 'Reaffirmation and Development of International Humanitarian Law: An Analysis of Some Key Issues' (1977) 17 IRRC 3, 7–10.

control over a part of its territory as to enable them to carry out sustained and concerted military operations and to implement this Protocol.[151]

This definition of NIAC raises the applicability bar established by Common Article 3 in two main ways. First, it only covers 'vertical' civil wars, as governmental armed forces must be involved in the conflict. Second, it requires the insurgent group to be in control of a discernible part of the state's territory, thereby excluding guerrilla-type violence from its scope.[152] The conditions contained in AP II resemble those required for recognition of belligerency.[153] However, because the full scope of IHL does not come into operation even if these requirements are met, the applicability rules contained in AP II have been portrayed as regrettable[154] and even regressive.[155]

Wide discontent with the stringency of AP II conditions can also be illustrated on the way the states defined NIACs twenty years later for the purposes of the Rome Statute establishing the International Criminal Court (ICC).[156] The drafters deliberately deviated from the definition in Article 1(1) AP II, opting instead for a wording which required only a protracted armed conflict between governmental authorities and organized armed groups or between such groups to exist in order to establish the court's jurisdiction over war crimes committed in a NIAC.[157] It can thus be summarized that the general trigger for the application of the law of NIAC is contained in Common Article 3, while in situations that additionally fulfil the requirements of Article 1(1) AP II and occur in the territory of states that have ratified AP II, the rules of that instrument will also apply.

1.2.3 Convergence and its limits

The adoption of Common Article 3 in 1949 marked the first significant inroad into the otherwise exclusively domestic sphere of regulation of internal conflicts. Because its substance drew from the law of IAC, the provision simultaneously codified the distinction between IACs and NIACs and started the trajectory towards narrowing it.[158] Since then, the development of international law has continued to bring the two legal categories closer to one another. A growing number of international conventions regulating the use of weapons apply equally to both types of conflict.[159]

151 Art 1(1) AP II.

152 For example, in the Guatemalan Civil War, the insurgents were able to carry out sustained and concerted military operations without placing any part of the national territory under their control, which made AP II inapplicable to the conflict. Provost (n 9) 264.

153 See Section 2.5.1.1.

154 Kleffner (n 98) 133.

155 Provost (n 9) 264.

156 Art 8(2)(f) Rome Statute.

157 ibid; see La Haye (n 80) 9.

158 cf Hill-Cawthorne (n 5) 16 ('The new treaty law of non-international armed conflict was . . . modelled on the law applicable in international armed conflict, with the result that, whilst codifying the distinction, the Geneva Conventions partially narrowed it.').

159 See, eg, Convention on the Prohibition of the Development, Production and Stockpiling of Bacteriological (Biological) and Toxin Weapons and on their Destruction (signed 10 April 1972, entered into force 26 March 1975) 1015 UNTS 163, Art 1; Convention on the Prohibition of the Development, Production, Stockpiling and Use of Chemical Weapons and on their Destruction (signed 13 January 1993, entered into force 29 April 1997) 32 ILM 800, Art 1; Convention on the Prohibition of the Use, Stockpiling, Production and Transfer of Anti-Personnel Mines and on their Destruction

Some states expressly declare in their military manuals that they apply IHL to any type of conflict whatever its legal characterization.[160] In addition, the ICTY has held that customary rules governing internal armed conflicts comprise many principles traditionally thought to regulate international conflicts only, including the protection of civilians and civilian objects from hostilities or the prohibition of means and methods of warfare proscribed in IACs.[161] More recently, this has been further corroborated by an extensive study conducted by the ICRC, according to which approximately 90% of customary rules of IHL identified therein applied in both types of conflict.[162]

Still, the distinction between IACs and NIACs has anything but disappeared, in spite of the recurring calls for its elimination.[163] The two types of conflict arise in markedly different ways: while IACs 'would usually be triggered by an armed attack, the evolution of [NIACs] is more likely to follow a path of escalation of internal strife and violence'.[164] Although the adoption of the two Additional Protocols in

(signed 18 September 1997, entered into force 1 March 1999) 2056 UNTS 211, Art 1; Convention on Cluster Munitions (signed 30 May 2008, entered into force 1 August 2010) UN Doc CCM/77, Art 1.

[160] See, eg, US Department of Defense, Directive 2311.01E 'DoD Law of War Program' (9 May 2006) [4.1]; German Ministry of Defence, *ZDv 15/2 Humanitäres Völkerrecht in bewaffneten Konflikten: Handbuch [Humanitarian Law in Armed Conflicts: Manual]* (1992) [211]. The statement in the newest edition of the German manual has since been toned down: see German Ministry of Defence, *ZDv 15/2, Humanitäres Völkerrecht in bewaffneten Konflikten: Handbuch [Humanitarian Law in Armed Conflicts: Manual]* (2013) [210]. Other types of official pronouncements also indicate confluence, including submissions in court proceedings stating that characterization of conflict is of lesser importance because many of the rules have become identical: cf D Turns, 'The "War on Terror" through British and International Humanitarian Law Eyes: Comparative Perspectives on Selected Legal Issues' (2007) 10 New York City Law Review 435, 469–70 (making this point in relation to the State of Israel's submissions in the *Targeted Killings* case); see also Letter from the UK Foreign and Commonwealth Office to author (11 July 2011), on file with author (stating that 'in many cases of armed conflict in which UK forces are engaged, the UK will apply the more developed rules of LOAC applicable to international armed conflicts as a matter of policy'); Letter from the Embassy of the Principality of Monaco to author (10 August 2011), on file with author (stating that Monaco 'doesn't distinguish between international and non-international conflicts'); Letter from the Ministry of Foreign Affairs of the Republic of Latvia to author (15 July 2011), on file with author (stating that 'Latvia does not distinguish between international and non-international armed conflicts applying the law of armed conflicts').

[161] *Tadić* Decision on Jurisdiction (n 107) [127].

[162] *ICRC CIHL Study* (n 23). The study's methodology has not, however, been free from criticism. See, eg, GH Aldrich, 'Customary International Humanitarian Law: An Interpretation on behalf of the International Committee of the Red Cross' (2005) 76 BYBIL 503, 507; J Bellinger and W Haynes, 'U.S. Initial Reactions to ICRC Study on Customary International Law' (2006) 101 AJIL 639; Y Dinstein, 'The ICRC Customary International Humanitarian Law Study' (2006) 82 International Law Studies 99, 101–05; J Bellinger and WJ Haynes, 'A US Government Response to the International Committee of the Red Cross Study on Customary International Humanitarian Law' (2007) 89 IRRC 443, 444–48; D Bethlehem, 'The Methodological Framework of the Study' and I Scobbie, 'The Approach to Customary International Law in the Study', both in E Wilmshurst and S Breau (eds), *Perspectives on the ICRC Study on Customary International Humanitarian Law* (CUP 2007).

[163] See, eg, Stewart (n 16) 348; D Wilmott, 'Removing the Distinction between International and Non-International Armed Conflict in the *Rome Statute of the International Criminal Court*' (2004) 5 MJIL 196; E Crawford, 'Unequal before the Law: The Case for the Elimination of the Distinction between International and Non-International Armed Conflicts' (2007) 20 LJIL 441; K Mastorodimos, 'The Character of the Conflict in Gaza: Another Argument Towards Abolishing the Distinction between International and Non-International Armed Conflicts' (2010) 12 ICLR 437.

[164] Lubell (n 12) 91.

1977 contributed towards the trend of convergence, it also underscored that the two types of conflict remained governed by separate legal frameworks.[165] Similarly, the 1998 Rome Statute, an indicative recent multilateral convention, preserved the distinction in its provisions on war crimes.[166] Furthermore, declarations in military manuals do not necessarily amount to an obligation under international law; norms of this sort may be expressions of state policy, not of *opinio juris*.[167] Even the ICTY emphasized that only some of rules and principles governing IACs have gradually been extended to internal conflicts and that only the 'general essence' of those rules, and not the detailed regulation they may contain, has become applicable to internal conflicts.[168]

In addition, there are notions in the law of IAC, which do not easily square with the reality of NIACs, and which thus might not ever be fully transposable from the former to the latter. In particular, this is the case with the concepts of combatant status and belligerent occupation.[169] The former is a closely guarded prerogative of states and as such it is restricted to conflicts characterized by inter-state hostilities.[170] The latter is predicated on the existence of two enemy states: one in the role of the occupying power, the other as the displaced sovereign.[171] Both of these concepts are of central importance for the present study and they are, accordingly, subject to detailed scrutiny later in the text.[172]

To recapitulate, despite the trend of gradual convergence between the two main types of armed conflict, the distinction is here to stay.[173] As a result, the rights and duties of those engaged in armed conflicts depend to a considerable extent on the exact qualification of the situation at hand. Alison Duxbury has correctly observed that '[o]nly in a system which creates a distinction between the rules that apply in international and internal armed conflict, would the concept of an internationalized armed conflict be considered necessary.'[174] Therefore, having confirmed that the said distinction still persists in IHL, the next section turns to the concept of internationalization.

165 Frits Kalshoven, who had participated in the 1974–77 diplomatic conference, commented that this was 'one of the issues the conferences of the 1970s failed to tackle, leaving us with a dividing line separating the two main categories of armed conflict that we all knew did not reflect reality'. F Kalshoven, 'From International Humanitarian Law to International Criminal Law' (2004) 3 Chinese JIL 151, 158.

166 See Art 8(2) Rome Statute; see also *Prosecutor v Thomas Lubanga Dyilo* (Trial Judgment) ICC-01/04-01/06 (14 March 2012) [539] (confirming the relevance of the IAC/NIAC distinction in IHL).

167 Crawford (n 163) 457; see also Bellinger and Haynes (n 162) 640–41.

168 *Tadić* Decision on Jurisdiction (n 107) [126].

169 See also Section 1.1.1 and particularly notes 12–13 in this chapter and the accompanying text.

170 But see Crawford (n 5) 153–73 (arguing for a universal combatant status applicable in IACs and NIACs alike).

171 But see Sivakumaran (n 5) 529–32 (arguing for an extended applicability of the law of belligerent occupation to NIACs).

172 See Chapters 5–7 and 8–10, respectively.

173 Similarly Wilmshurst (n 35) 500; Milanovic, '"Transnational" and "Mixed" Conflicts' (n 142) 30–31 [10]; Zamir (n 35) 47.

174 A Duxbury, 'Drawing Lines in the Sand: Characterising Conflicts for the Purposes of Teaching International Humanitarian Law' (2007) 8 MJIL 259, 267.

1.3 Concept of Internationalization of Armed Conflicts

1.3.1 Emergence of the term 'internationalization' in international law

The observation that a domestic uprising may grow into hostilities that come within the purview of international law is anything but novel. As discussed earlier, the Swiss scholar Emmerich de Vattel wrote in 1758 that a civil war in which the rebels wield strength sufficient to effectively oppose the sovereign is equivalent to a war between two states under international law.[175]

The phrase 'to internationalize a war', although absent in Vattel's writings, had entered the English language by 1865, when it was first included in Webster's *American Dictionary of the English Language*.[176] It was, however, still used only to denote a change in the factual circumstances rather than to express the transformation of the law applicable to the situation at hand.

In 1901, the international legal scholar Hannis Taylor used the term 'internationalization' in a meaning more relevant for the present purposes. He wrote that a part of state territory that was subject to foreign invasion and occupation would become 'internationalized', meaning that in a district temporarily placed under the control of the foreign army, certain rules of international law would become applicable.[177]

However, it took until the mid-1960s when, against the backdrop of the Vietnam War, a number of publicists started to write about 'international' or 'internationalized' civil wars in the context of the law applicable to such types of violence. For instance, Major Talmadge Bartell argued in 1964 that the 'communist' practice of providing military assistance to insurgents in civil wars had 'internationalized' such conflicts, thus modifying the applicable law.[178] In the same year, Richard Falk wrote that the recognition of belligerency of the insurgents by outside states would render the internal war 'fully internationalized'.[179]

Finally, in 1965, Dietrich Schindler offered the first systematic treatment of conflict internationalization.[180] He referred to internal conflicts, in which outside states provided military assistance to one of the conflict parties, as to 'international civil wars'.[181] He further discussed whether the international law of war should apply to all or only some of the relationships in such conflicts.[182] Schindler's principal contribution was in his use of the term 'internationalization of civil wars'

[175] de Vattel (n 65), book III, ch XVIII, §§292–95; see also text to notes 65–68 in this chapter.

[176] N Webster, *An American Dictionary of the English Language* (G&C Merriam 1865) 707 ('Internationalize, v.t. To make international; to cause to affect or pertain to the mutual relations of two or more nations; as, *to internationalize a war*.') (emphasis added).

[177] H Taylor, *A Treatise on International Public Law* (Callaghan & Co 1901) 556–57. For example, international law would permit the appropriation of public property to prevent it from falling into enemy hands.

[178] TL Bartell, 'Counterinsurgency and Civil War' (1964) 40 North Dakota Law Review 254, 254, 290.

[179] Falk (n 76) 194.

[180] D Schindler, 'Die Anwendung der Genfer Rotkreuzabkommen seit 1949' (1965) 22 ASDI 75, 93–98.

[181] ibid 93 ('[i]nternationale Bürgerkriege').

[182] ibid 94–97.

(*Internationalisierung der Bürgerkriege*)[183] to imply the change in the law applicable to (at least some relationships within) a previously purely internal conflict.

1.3.2 Towards the definition of 'internationalization' in international law

Dietrich Schindler's work and its revised English versions published in 1979[184] and 1982[185] became perhaps the most widely cited sources in the contemporary legal analysis of conflict internationalization. However, a review of the literature reveals an absence of a consensus on the exact meaning and scope of the term. Instead, two views can be said to dominate in the scholarship. On the one hand, many authors, including Schindler, have regarded internationalized conflict as a civil war with some form of outside armed interference.[186] On the other hand, a number of writers have

[183] ibid 98. [184] Schindler, 'Different Types of Armed Conflicts' (n 78) 150–51.

[185] D Schindler, 'International Humanitarian Law and Internationalized Internal Armed Conflicts' (1982) 230 IRRC 255.

[186] See, eg, Schindler, 'Different Types of Armed Conflicts' (n 78) 150 (defining internationalized armed conflicts as 'non-international conflicts in which foreign States or international organizations intervene with armed troops'); H-P Gasser, 'Internationalized Non-International Armed Conflicts: Case Studies of Afghanistan, Kampuchea, and Lebanon' (1983) 33 AULR 145, 145 ('An internationalized non-international armed conflict is a civil war characterized by the intervention of the armed forces of a foreign power.'); R Bierzanek, 'Quelques remarques sur l'applicabilité du droit international humanitaire des conflits armés aux conflits internes internationalisés' in C Swinarski (ed), *Studies and Essays on International Humanitarian Law and Red Cross Principles in Honour of Jean Pictet* (ICRC 1984) 282 ('le phénomène de conflit interne internationalisé: l'intervention d'Etats tiers dans les guerres civiles'); Stewart (n 16) 315 ('the term internationalized armed conflict includes war between two internal factions both of which are backed by different States; direct hostilities between two foreign States that militarily intervene in an internal armed conflict in support of opposing sides; and war involving a foreign intervention in support of an insurgent group fighting against an established government'); APV Rogers, *Law on the Battlefield* (3rd edn, Manchester University Press 2012) 299 ('Sometimes what starts as an internal armed conflict becomes "internationalized" by the military intervention of a state in support of an armed group.'); Pejić (n 35) 84 ('a non-international armed conflict in which a third State or a multinational force intervenes (internationalised non-international conflict)'); S Vité, 'Typology of Armed Conflicts in International Humanitarian Law: Legal Concepts and Actual Situations' (2009) 91 IRRC 69, 71 (considering a conflict to be 'internationalized' in case of 'intervention in a previously existing internal conflict'); T Hoffmann, 'Squaring the Circle? International Humanitarian Law and Transnational Armed Conflicts' in MJ Matheson and D Momtaz (eds), *Rules and Institutions of International Humanitarian Law Put to the Test of Recent Armed Conflicts* (Brill 2010) 218 fn 4 ('The notion of "internationalized non-international armed conflict" ... specifically pertains to civil wars characterized by the intervention of the armed forces of a foreign State.'); Lubell (n 12) 93 (considering internationalized conflicts to mean 'armed conflicts involving a third state as well as internal violence between the government and non-state actors'); E Holland, 'The Qualification Framework of International Humanitarian Law: Too Rigid to Accommodate Contemporary Conflicts' (2011) 34 Suffolk Transnational Law Review 145, 162 ('An "internationalized" conflict exists if there is a non-international armed conflict in which an outside state becomes involved on behalf of the non-state actor.'); KA Johnston, 'Transformations of Conflict Status in Libya' (2012) 17 JCSL 81, 95 (arguing that internationalization occurs 'as a result of the intervention of another state [in a NIAC] on the side of the non-state party'); T Ferraro, 'The ICRC's Legal Position on the Notion of Armed Conflict Involving Foreign Intervention and on Determining the IHL Applicable to This Type of Conflict' (2015) 97 IRRC 1227, 1230 (noting that the ICRC had used the term '"[i]nternationalized internal armed conflict" ... to refer to situations in which one or more third States intervened in a pre-existing armed conflict'); P Muggleton, *Muggleton on the Law of Non-International Armed Conflict* (APCML 2017) 14 ('Internationalised armed conflicts are NIACs that become internationalised due to direct or indirect intervention by an outside state on behalf of an armed group party to the NIAC').

highlighted the 'mixed' or 'hybrid' nature of internationalized conflicts, defining these as conflicts which have both non-international and international elements.[187]

However, it is submitted that neither of these interpretations captures fully the essence and meaning of conflict internationalization. With respect to the first view, this is due to its underinclusiveness. As this study shows, foreign intervention is just one vehicle of transformation from a NIAC to an IAC.[188] The American Civil War of the 1860s or the Yugoslavian Civil War of the 1990s have been, it is argued, prominent examples of internationalized armed conflicts, albeit not on account of external interference.[189] It can thus be said that the first view is unsatisfactory because of its incompleteness *ratione materiae*.[190]

By contrast, the second view, although not principally incorrect, is question-begging and potentially overinclusive. It begs the question which of the supposed international elements must be present in a conflict for it to be considered internationalized. Additionally, it is overinclusive in that it refers to conflicts as 'internationalized' even if they had never been non-international in the first place. For instance, this view would quite illogically characterize a conflict involving two states and a *subsequently* formed non-state armed group as 'internationalized'.[191] This conceptualization should therefore also be rejected.

[187] See, eg, A Roberts, 'Counter-terrorism, Armed Force and the Laws of War' (2002) 44 Survival 7, 16 (' "internationalised civil war" ... is not a formal legal category, but an indication that the rules pertaining to both international and civil wars may be applicable in different aspects and phases of the conflict'); Stewart (n 16) 314 ('internationalized armed conflicts' are 'conflicts that contain both international and non-international elements'); K Dörmann and L Colassis, 'International Humanitarian Law in the Iraq Conflict' (2004) 47 GYIL 293, 313 (describing the conflict in Iraq after 2004 as 'one or possibly several internationalized internal armed conflicts' governed by the law of NIAC); UK Ministry of Defence, *The Manual of the Law of Armed Conflict* (OUP 2004) 16 ('many armed conflicts have at the same time certain aspects which have the character of an internal armed conflict, while other aspects are clearly international'); Crawford (n 163) 446 ('a type of armed conflict that possesse[s] qualities of both international and internal armed conflict... came to be known as "internationalized" armed conflict.'); Arimatsu (n 43) 177 (describing the conflict in Afghanistan after 2002 as 'a non-international armed conflict, albeit internationalized'); R Geiss and M Siegrist, 'Has the Armed Conflict in Afghanistan Affected the Rules on the Conduct of Hostilities?' (2011) 93 IRRC 11, 13–16 (describing the conflict in Afghanistan after 2002 as 'an "internationalized" non-international armed conflict') (internal quotation marks kept); J Odermatt, 'Between Law and Reality: "New Wars" and Internationalised Armed Conflict' (2013) 5 Amsterdam Law Forum 19, 29 (describing 'internationalised armed conflicts' as ' "mixed" conflicts, since they involve both internal and international elements'); MG Janaby, 'The Legal Status of Hezbollah in the Syrian Conflict: An International Humanitarian Law Perspective' (2016) 33 Ariz J Int'l & Comp L 383, 397 ('Internationalized armed conflict has the characteristics of both international and non-international armed conflicts.').

[188] See generally Chapter 2.

[189] See Section 2.5.1 and Section 2.3.1, respectively.

[190] This would also be the case with the small number of publications which equate internationalized armed conflict with one of the other modalities of internationalization. See, eg, H McCoubrey and N White, *International Organizations and Civil Wars* (Dartmouth 1995) 62–63 (considering the term 'internationalized' armed conflicts as covering wars of national liberation only); W Heintschel von Heinegg, 'Introduction' in MN Schmitt and W Heintschel von Heinegg (eds), *The Scope and Applicability of International Humanitarian Law* (Ashgate 2012), vol 1, xi (stating that Art 1(4) AP I recognized 'so-called "internationalized" wars').

[191] For instance, the hostilities between Vietnam and Cambodia (Kampuchea) broke out in May 1975. An insurgent group aligned with Vietnam, the Kampuchean United Front for National Salvation (KUFNS), was formed in Cambodia in December 1978; it invaded Cambodia together with Vietnam the following year. The conflict between Cambodia and Vietnam had been international at least until the Khmer Rouge government was toppled in early 1979. Although the creation of the KUFNS added a

Reflecting some of these criticisms, the ICRC announced in 2015 that it had abandoned the use of the related term 'internationalized internal armed conflict'.[192] Specifically, the ICRC's concern was that the term was 'misleading' because it 'might seem to suggest that a single legal framework—the law of IAC—applies to such situations or that they constitute a third category of armed conflict for which the applicable legal framework is uncertain'.[193] Although the ICRC's position was limited to conflicts involving foreign intervention,[194] its concern about the appropriate terminology can be extended to all modalities of conflict transformation and as such it deserves some attention at this point.

As discussed earlier in this chapter, IHL applies if there is a situation that can be characterized either as an IAC or as a NIAC.[195] There is no 'third category of armed conflict' in that sense and it would indeed be inaccurate to describe internationalized armed conflicts as such.[196] However, it is submitted that the worries about the introduction of a 'third category' are the product of the prevailing *static* approach to conflict qualification, which assesses the legal nature of a conflict in isolation at a particular point in time. Instead, the notion of internationalization is better understood as highlighting the *dynamic* idea of conflict transformation, in other words, the conversion from a NIAC to an IAC.

On the basis of the foregoing, this book defines internationalization as the process of transformation of the legal nature of a prima facie NIAC, which renders the law of IAC applicable to such a conflict. Conflicts that have undergone the process of internationalization in this sense are referred to as 'internationalized armed conflicts'. The process of internationalization is considered in detail in Part I, while the precise application of the law of IAC to internationalized armed conflicts is the subject of Parts II and III of this book.

In addition to the points raised thus far, several final remarks should be made as to the overall strengths of this conceptualization. Firstly, it is consistent with the understanding of the term 'to internationalize' in general language, namely 'to make international'.[197] An internationalized armed conflict is indeed 'made international' insofar as the law to be applied to it is concerned. Secondly, this conceptualization is

non-international element to the existing situation, it could not have internationalized the conflict—it had already been international at the time. See Gasser, 'Internationalized Non-International Armed Conflicts: Case Studies of Afghanistan, Kampuchea, and Lebanon' (n 186) 153–54; *Case of Kaing Guek Eav alias 'Duch'* (Trial Judgment) 001/18-07-2007/ECCC/TC (26 July 2010) [59]–[81] and [423].

192 Ferraro (n 186) 1227. 193 ibid 1251.

194 cf ibid (using the heading 'Terminology used by the ICRC to refer to *armed conflict situations involving foreign intervention*' to introduce the analysis) (emphasis added).

195 See Section 1.2.

196 Similarly, calls for the recognition of a supposed third category of 'transnational armed conflict' or 'extra-state armed conflict' have to acknowledge that such notions are currently without legal basis in positive IHL and that their introduction would necessitate a substantial reform of the existing law. See, eg, RS Schöndorf, 'Extra-State Armed Conflicts: Is There a Need for a New Legal Regime?' (2004) 37 NYU JILP 1, 4–5; GS Corn and ET Jensen, 'Transnational Armed Conflict: A "Principled" Approach to the Regulation of Counter-Terror Combat Operations' (2012) 42 Isr L Rev 46, 50; Milanovic, '"Transnational" and "Mixed" Conflicts' (n 142) 46–47 [68]–[69].

197 See the dictionary definition quoted at note 176 in this chapter.

capable of covering all possible modalities of conflict internationalization and it does not limit itself to foreign intervention in civil wars. Thirdly, it is not overinclusive, as it stresses the process of conflict transformation instead of simply stating the presence of both internal and international elements in a given conflict. There are some examples of academic writing, which have used the concept of internationalization in this sense.[198] It is also the meaning ascribed to it throughout the rest of this book.

[198] See, eg, R Cryer, 'The Fine Art of Friendship: *Jus in Bello* in Afghanistan' (2002) 7 JCSL 37, 43; Crawford (n 5) 15; Milanovic and Hadzi-Vidanovic (n 142) 292–93; Milanovic, '"Transnational" and "Mixed" Conflicts' (n 142) 34–35 [26]; D Kritsiotis, 'War and Armed Conflict: The Parameters of Enquiry' in R Liivoja and T McCormack (eds), *Routledge Handbook of the Law of Armed Conflict* (Routledge 2016) 18–20; Zamir (n 35) 8.

PART I
CONFLICT TRANSFORMATIONS

2

Internationalization

2.1 Introduction

How do internationalized armed conflicts come about? This chapter analyses the ways by which the legal nature of a prima facie non-international armed conflict (NIAC) transforms into an international armed conflict (IAC). It is argued that there are two principal mechanisms through which this result may be brought about.

Firstly, a non-international conflict is internationalized when two independent subjects of international law become engaged against each other as the conflict develops ('standard internationalization'). On the one hand, this may be the effect of an involvement of an *external* actor such as a third state or an international organization by way of military intervention (Section 2.2). On the other hand, this may be the outcome of an *internal* development if the territorial state dissolves during the civil war into two or more successor states (Section 2.3).

Secondly, a conflict may in certain circumstances be internationalized even as the conflict parties maintain their state/non-state asymmetry, as long as the non-state party acquires the requisite legal attributes ('complementary internationalization'). This process may be of an *absolute* nature, as is the case in the so-called 'wars of national liberation' defined in Article 1(4) AP I (Section 2.4), or of a *relative* nature, as in the instances of internationalization by means of recognition of belligerency, special agreements foreseen by Common Article 3, and unilateral declarations (Section 2.5).

2.2 Intervention

Semantically, the term 'international armed conflict' denotes an armed conflict between two nations—or states.[1] The Geneva Conventions (GCs) affirm this

[1] cf also J Bentham, *Introduction to the Principles of Morals and Legislation* (J Burns and HLA Hart eds, Methuen London 1970) 296 (defining the term 'international' as including 'mutual transactions between sovereigns as such'); *Prosecutor v Tadić* (Decision on Jurisdiction) IT-94-1-AR72 (2 October 1995) [70] (holding that an IAC exists 'whenever there is a resort to armed force between States');

understanding and apply only if an armed conflict breaks out 'between two or more of the High Contracting Parties'.[2] The archetypal modality of internationalization will therefore occur when an outside power interferes with a previously internal armed conflict in a way which warrants a change in the classification of the conflict.

Importantly, not every type of interference in an existing conflict amounts to intervention capable of changing its legal nature. For example, an expression of political support or provision of economic aid may well benefit one of the belligerents, but it does not make the outside state a party to the conflict itself.[3] Accordingly, intervention is understood here in its traditional sense as an act, the essence of which is force.[4] In the context of participation in an armed conflict, intervention can be either undertaken with or without the consent of the territorial state. The next two subsections accordingly consider the legal effects of both types of intervention. The final subsection discusses the specific case of intervention by international organizations.

2.2.1 Consensual intervention

2.2.1.1 Historical background

Foreign support of governments beleaguered by domestic revolts has not been uncommon.[5] The Cold War period has seen a number of foreign military interventions to assist the governments in charge of former colonies. The UK came to the aid of President Julius Nyerere of Tanganyika in 1964, after he had lost control of the capital to mutinous army troops.[6] Between 1962 and 1994, France intervened in its former colonies more than a dozen times, typically on the side and with the support of the de jure governments.[7]

The practice has persisted in the twenty-first century, with examples from almost every region of the world. In 2002, the government of the Central African Republic, assisted by the Libyan and Congolese troops, fought off an attempt to seize power

Hamdan v Rumsfeld (2006) 548 US 557, 623 (US Supreme Court) (indirectly describing an IAC as a 'conflict between nations').

[2] Common Art 2(1) GCs.

[3] ICRC, *Conference of Government Experts on the Reaffirmation and Development of International Humanitarian Law Applicable in Armed Conflicts, 24 May–12 June 1971* (ICRC 1971) vol V, 18–19.

[4] See TJ Lawrence, *Principles of International Law* (4th edn, DC Heath 1910) 124.

[5] For more comprehensive analyses of military intervention following a governmental invitation, see L Doswald-Beck, 'The Legal Validity of Military Intervention by Invitation of the Government' (1985) 56 BYBIL 189; G Nolte, *Eingreifen auf Einladung: Zur völkerrechtlichen Zulässigkeit des Einsatzes fremder Truppen im internen Konflikt auf Einladung der Regierung [Intervention upon Invitation: Use of Force by Foreign Troops in Internal Conflicts at the Invitation of a Government under International Law]* (Springer 1999).

[6] D Wippman, 'Military Intervention, Regional Organizations, and Host-State Consent' (1996) 7 Duke J Comp & Int'l L 209, 216.

[7] J Darnton, 'The World; Intervening with Elan and No Regrets' *New York Times* (26 June 1994) <www.nytimes.com/1994/06/26/weekinreview/the-world-intervening-with-elan-and-no-regrets.html>.

led by General François Bozizé.[8] The Sri Lankan government acknowledged (with a few years' delay) that Pakistan's aerial support had been a key factor in the defeat of the Tamil Tigers in 2009.[9] In 2013, France intervened in the Malian conflict, citing government consent as justification for its actions.[10] Russia similarly sought to justify its use of force against Ukraine in 2014 by an alleged invitation issued by the ousted president Viktor Yanukovych.[11] Finally, there are the US-led interventions in Afghanistan (post-2001) and Iraq (post-2003): although both began as military operations against the established governments, as the conflicts unfolded, new sympathetic governments were installed in democratic elections, which then gave their consent to the foreign military presence.[12]

2.2.1.2 Legal nature

It is occasionally contended that conflicts of this kind amount to IACs. If correct, that position implies that a consensual intervention by an outside power internationalizes a pre-existing civil war. It is therefore necessary to examine at this point arguments advanced in support of that view.

Firstly, some argue that a military intervention on the government side can be qualified as a partial occupation without armed resistance from the territorial state, thus triggering the application of the second paragraph of Common Article 2, which provides that the GCs apply 'to all cases of partial or total occupation of the territory of a High Contracting Party, even if the said occupation meets with no armed resistance'.[13] However, this contention is at odds with the definition of occupation given in Article 42 of the Hague Regulations, which stipulates that a territory is occupied when it is 'actually placed under the authority of the hostile army'.[14] Even if the territorial state conceded, unusually, the authority over a part of its territory to an allied third state, the allied army—acting by definition in concert with the established government—cannot be described as 'hostile' to the territorial state.[15] The provision in the GCs was inserted in order to extend protection even to situations

[8] ICG, 'Central African Republic: Anatomy of a Phantom State' (13 December 2007) <www.crisisgroup.org/en/regions/africa/central-africa/central-african-republic/136-central-african-republic-anatomy-of-a-phantom-state.aspx>, at 14.

[9] 'Sri Lanka Thanks Pakistan for Help in Wiping Out Terror' *The Express Tribune* (6 January 2016) <https://tribune.com.pk/story/1022644/sri-lanka-thanks-pakistan-for-help-in-wiping-out-terror>.

[10] Statement by M. François Hollande, President of the Republic, following the Select Defence Council (14 January 2013) <http://basedoc.diplomatie.gouv.fr/exl-doc/FranceDiplomatie/PDF/baen2013-01-14.pdf>.

[11] UN Doc S/PV.7125 (3 March 2014) 3–4.

[12] See also Section 4.3.1 (discussing the question of de-internationalization in the context of these conflicts).

[13] See, eg, JG Stewart, 'Towards a Single Definition of Armed Conflict in International Humanitarian Law: A Critique of Internationalized Armed Conflict' (2003) 85 IRRC 313, 331–32.

[14] Regulations concerning the Laws and Customs of War on Land, Annex to Hague Convention (IV) respecting the Laws and Customs of War on Land (signed 18 October 1907, entered into force 26 January 1910) 205 CTS 277, Art 42 (hereafter Hague Regulations).

[15] But see E Benvenisti, *The International Law of Occupation* (2nd edn, OUP 2012) 59–60 (arguing that the relationship of non-allegiance between the occupier and the occupied population provides a sufficient basis for applying the law of occupation also to occupation of a 'friendly' territory).

not covered by the first paragraph of Common Article 2, such as the Nazi occupation of Czechoslovakia in 1939 or Denmark in 1940, which took place with virtually no armed resistance.[16] Of course, if the territorial state's invitation to intervene or, at least, its consent with the intervention were not validly given,[17] the situation would be more akin to an unresisted occupation. However, in such a situation, the conflict would be internationalized not by the application of Common Article 2(2) *per analogiam*, but rather on account of a third state's military operation in another state's territory without the genuine consent of the latter.[18]

Secondly, some authors argue that an outside intervention so fundamentally transforms the internal conflict that it can no longer be subject to the limited normative framework for NIACs.[19] In this regard, George Aldrich pointed to the Vietnam War (1955–75), in which there were at least four parties to the conflict: South Vietnam as the territorial state, the Vietcong as the local insurgents, and the United States and North Vietnam as the intervening third states. He argued that separating the conflict—which he saw as a 'single armed conflict with two warring sides'—into pairs of sub-conflicts and applying different sets of rules to each was 'practically impossible', highlighting the US practice of according prisoner of war (POW) status to all enemy captives including the Vietcong.[20] However, the central problem with this 'fundamental transformation' argument is that it fails to reconcile with the normative structure underlying the applicability rules of IHL. As stated earlier, Common Article 2 is unequivocal on the requirement that there be two opposing states in order for a conflict to be considered international.[21]

In addition, it is evident from state practice that this understanding has not become reflected in customary international law either. The US practice of granting POW status to all captured fighters in Vietnam was in fact followed expressly as a matter of discretion and policy, and not out of sense of a legal obligation.[22] Recent conflicts characterized by consensual third-state intervention have equally not

[16] JS Pictet (ed), *Geneva Convention IV relative to the Protection of Civilian Persons in Time of War: Commentary* (ICRC 1958) 21 (hereafter Pictet, *GCIV Commentary*); Y Dinstein, *The International Law of Belligerent Occupation* (CUP 2009) 31–32; see also *Legal Consequences of the Construction of a Wall in the Occupied Palestinian Territory* (Advisory Opinion) [2004] ICJ Rep 136 [95].

[17] On validity of consent, see further Doswald-Beck (n 5) 191–92, 251–52; Wippman (n 6) 211–12; Nolte (n 5) 161–62; ILC, Draft Articles on Responsibility of States for Internationally Wrongful Acts, with commentaries Yearbook of the ILC (2001) vol II, part two, 73, commentary to Art 20 [4] (hereafter ILC ASR); T Ferraro and L Cameron, 'Article 2: Application of the Convention', in ICRC (ed), *Commentary on the First Geneva Convention* (CUP 2016) 94–95 (hereafter Ferraro and Cameron, 'Article 2').

[18] M Sassòli, 'Concept and the Beginning of Occupation' in A Clapham, P Gaeta, and M Sassòli (eds), *The 1949 Geneva Conventions: A Commentary* (OUP 2015) 1414 [52]; see also notes 37–47 in this chapter and the accompanying text with respect to cases in which genuine consent was lacking.

[19] See also Chapter 3 (discussing in detail the dilemma between the so-called 'global' and 'mixed' views of conflict internationalization in complex conflict situations characterized by a multiplicity of conflict parties).

[20] GH Aldrich, 'The Laws of War on Land' (2000) 94 AJIL 42, 62–63; see also Annex A of MACV Directive 381-46 (27 December 1967), reproduced in CI Bevans, 'Contemporary Practice of the United States Relating to International Law' (1968) 62 AJIL 754, 766–68.

[21] Although both of these states need not necessarily be directly engaged in fighting each other: see text to notes 51–60 in this chapter.

[22] GS Prugh, *Law at War, Vietnam, 1964–1973* (Department of the Army 1975) 65–66.

been considered as IACs. Despite the foreign intervention in the 2002 conflict in the Central Africal Republic, the International Criminal Court (ICC) confirmed in the *Bemba* case that the situation had remained a NIAC.[23] Similarly, the Sri Lankan government consistently treated its conflict with the Liberation Tigers of Tamil Eelam (LTTE) as a NIAC, notwithstanding the outside assistance it may have received from Pakistan and others.[24] And likewise, France considered that 'dès le début de son intervention sur le sol malien, ... la situation pouvait être qualifiée de "conflit armé non international" de haute intensité'.[25] It may be added that Aldrich's charge of 'practical impossibility' has since been undermined by the case-law of the International Criminal Tribunal for the former Yugoslavia (ICTY), whose decisions have applied different bodies of law to parallel international and internal armed conflicts.[26]

Thirdly, a related argument is that through foreign intervention, the internal armed conflict reaches an intensity equivalent to that of IACs, and thus IHL in its entirety should apply.[27] Putting aside the requirement that two opposing states must normally be engaged in a conflict for it to qualify as an IAC,[28] intensity by itself is not a necessary, or even a sufficient condition for internationalization. In fact, the level of conflict intensity triggering the application of IHL is higher in NIACs than in IACs.[29] For example, despite its limited temporal and geographical ambit, the conflict over the nearly uninhabited Falkland Islands that lasted only eleven weeks in 1982 was governed by IHL in full scope.[30] By contrast, the Rwandan civil war in 1994, during which the whole country descended into vicious interethnic violence resulting in the loss of about 800,000 lives, was described authoritatively in several ICTR decisions as a NIAC.[31] It is thus clear that conflict intensity is an independent variable insofar as internationalization by foreign intervention is concerned.

[23] *Prosecutor v Jean-Pierre Bemba Gombo* (Decision on the Confirmation of Charges, Pre-Trial Chamber II) ICC-01/05-01/08 (15 June 2009) [246].

[24] cf, eg, Sri Lanka, Ministry of Defence, 'Humanitarian Operation: Factual Analysis July 2006–May 2009' (Ministry of Defence, July 2011) 2 [8] ('protracted armed conflict').

[25] 'Garanties prises pour la reconnaissance des soldats menant actuellement des actions au Mali: Réponse du Ministère de la défense publiée dans le JO Sénat' (8 August 2013) <www.senat.fr/questions/base/2013/qSEQ130405720.html>; see also N Guibert, 'Guerre au Mali: que faire des prisonniers djihadistes?' *Le Monde* (8 March 2013) (reporting that the French and Malian authorities entered into an agreement mandating that the detainees be treated humanely, but stopping short of according them POW status; this further confirms that both states considered the situation as a NIAC).

[26] See, eg, *Tadić* Decision on Jurisdiction (n 1) [77]; *Prosecutor v Tadić* (Appeal Judgment) IT-94-1-A (15 July 1999) [84]. See further Section 3.2.1.

[27] cf, eg, D Bindschedler-Robert, 'A Reconsideration of the Law of Armed Conflicts' in *Conferences on Contemporary Problems of International Law: The Law of Armed Conflicts* (Carnegie Endowment for International Peace 1971) 53 (advancing this argument *de lege ferenda*).

[28] See text to note 21 in this chapter. [29] See Section 1.2.2.

[30] See, eg, Letter from the British Ambassador to the UN to the President of the UN Security Council, UN Doc S/15198 (11 June 1982). However, the UK had denied that the 'military and naval operations' amounted to a state of war between the UK and Argentina. See Letter from Lord President of the Council, Mr John Biffen, to Mr George Foulkes, MP (20 May 1982), reproduced in (1982) 53 BYBIL, 519–20.

[31] *Prosecutor v Ntagerura* (Trial Judgment) ICTR-99-46-T (25 February 2004) [74]; *Prosecutor v Akayesu* (Trial Judgment) ICTR-96-4-T (2 September 1998) [621]; *Prosecutor v Semanza* (Decision on Prosecution's Motion for Judicial Notice and Presumptions of Facts Pursuant to Rules 94 and

Finally, it has been argued that an invitation to intervene implies the recognition of belligerency by the issuing government.[32] This argument interprets the invitation as an admission by the territorial state that the rebels' strength is no longer surmountable without assistance, which amounts to recognition of belligerency.[33] Yet this argument must be rejected, too. As will be shown later in a section discussing the doctrine of belligerency, this legal concept is—assuming it has survived in modern international law—of discretionary nature only.[34] It is true that recognition may be tacit: by undertaking certain measures permissible only in an international conflict (such as the proclamation of a naval blockade), a state is in fact tacitly recognizing the belligerency of its opponents.[35] However, a request for outside assistance is a manifestation of state sovereignty and by itself it does not affect the conflict nature. Therefore, the better view is that, under these circumstances, recognition of belligerency is not implied. This approach was also endorsed by government experts in 1971 and 1972 when they rejected an ICRC proposal in favour of conflict internationalization based on the argument of implicit recognition of belligerency.[36]

2.2.1.3 Policy considerations

The analysis presented thus far is not meant to deny that there may be strong *policy* reasons for internationalizing a conflict through foreign intervention in support of the territorial state. In this connection, it has been rightly stated that an invitation may often not be genuine and may be issued by a puppet representative installed or supported by the intervening state prior to any military action.[37] It is widely believed that precisely such an 'invitation' was issued in 1979 to the Soviet Union by Babrak Karmal, an Afghan politician who had not held any official position in the Afghani government at that time.[38] More recently, it was pointed out that the putative Ukrainian invitation to Russia in 2014 had suffered from similar flaws.[39] Another important consideration is that the purpose of the GCs—to protect individuals, not to serve state interests—would be better served if IHL in its entirety applied to

54) ICTR-97-20-T (3 December 2000), Annex A; *Prosecutor v Semanza* (Appeal Judgment) ICTR-97-20-A (20 May 2005) [198].

[32] ICRC, 'Protection of Victims of Non-International Conflicts: Report to the XXIst International Conference of the Red Cross' (1969) 9 IRRC 344, 346; ICRC, *Reaffirmation and Development of the Laws and Customs Applicable in Armed Conflicts: Report* (ICRC 1969) 100–01; Bindschedler-Robert (n 27) 53; T Farer, 'Humanitarian Law and Armed Conflicts: Toward the Definition of "International Armed Conflict"' (1971) 71 Columbia Law Review 37, 69; A Rosas, *The Legal Status of Prisoners of War* (Suomalainen Tiedeakatemia 1976) 286–87.

[33] Bindschedler-Robert (n 27) 53; Farer (n 32) 69.

[34] See Section 2.5.1.3.

[35] See notes 408–09 in this chapter.

[36] See D Schindler, 'International Humanitarian Law and Internationalized Internal Armed Conflicts' (1982) 230 IRRC 255, 259–60.

[37] C Byron, 'Armed Conflicts: International or Non-International?' (2001) 6 JCSL 63, 82.

[38] MW Reisman and J Silk, 'Which Law Applies to the Afghan Conflict?' (1988) 82 AJIL 459, 481; but see A Roberts, 'What Is a Military Occupation?' (1984) 55 BYBIL 249, 278.

[39] J Green, 'Editorial Comment: The Annexation of Crimea: Russia, Passportisation and the Protection of Nationals Revisited' (2014) 1 Journal on the Use of Force and International Law 3, 6.

such conflicts.[40] There is even a pragmatic dimension: states involved in such conflicts may have an incentive to recognize them as IACs in order for members of their armed forces to benefit from combatant status.[41]

However, policy reasons cannot alter the content of a legal norm when that norm is unequivocal.[42] It is submitted that the 'genuineness' (ie, international validity) of an invitation is a fact to be determined by the subject of interpretation and application of the law. Of course, in a given situation, this may be a highly controversial matter, but a potential evidentiary difficulty *in casu* does not suffice to override the text of Common Article 2 which presupposes the presence of two opposing states in an IAC.[43] Similarly, the victim-oriented perspective of the GCs cannot be denied, but any reliance on it for the purposes of interpretation of the rules found therein must 'find[] its limits in the treaty text itself'.[44] As far as the pragmatic reasons mentioned earlier are concerned, states in their capacity as international law-makers are certainly free to attempt to drive the formation of customary law by, for instance, proposing to extend the definition of IAC to consensual interventions. However, the recent practice of states involved in such interventions reveals little will to do so; in fact, available express statements typically qualify situations of this kind as NIACs[45] or at most as 'armed conflicts' without a specific modifier.[46] In sum, if the territorial state consents to the engagement of a third state, it cannot be said that there would be two states pitted in a conflict against one another and the situation must therefore be considered a NIAC.[47]

2.2.2 Non-consensual intervention

2.2.2.1 Meaning of the lack of consent

Broadly speaking, there are two types of intervention in which the consent of the established government is lacking. Firstly, a third state may intervene in support of

[40] cf Byron (n 37) 82–83; JS Pictet (ed), *Geneva Convention III relative to the Treatment of Prisoners of War: Commentary* (ICRC 1960) 23 (hereafter Pictet, *GC III Commentary*).

[41] cf JJ Paust et al, *International Criminal Law* (3rd edn, Carolina Academic Press 2007) 661–62; JJ Paust, 'Self-Defense Targetings of Non-State Actors and Permissibility of U.S. Use of Drones in Pakistan' (2010) 19(2) Journal of Transnational Law & Policy 237, 261.

[42] cf Yearbook of the ILC, 1966, vol II, 219 [6]; ME Villiger, *Commentary on the 1969 Vienna Convention on the Law of Treaties* (Martinus Nijhoff 2009) 428 [14].

[43] cf also Ferraro and Cameron, 'Article 2' (n 17) 80.

[44] Villiger (n 42) 428 [14].

[45] See, eg, T Moore, 'Germany Comes to Terms With Its New War' *Time* (9 April 2010) (noting the German government's view that the situation in Afghanistan constituted a NIAC); *R v Gul* [2012] EWCA Civ 280 [20] (noting the UK government's view that the situation in Afghanistan constituted a NIAC).

[46] cf US DoD, 'Enhancing Security and Stability in Afghanistan: Report to Congress' (December 2016) 9 (stating that '[a]s a matter of international law, the United States remains in an armed conflict against al Qaeda, the Taliban, and associated forces, and against ISIL').

[47] Accord S Vité, 'Typology of Armed Conflicts in International Humanitarian Law: Legal Concepts and Actual Situations' (2009) 91 IRRC 69, 73; D Akande, 'Classification of Armed Conflicts: Relevant Legal Concepts' in E Wilmshurst (ed), *International Law and the Classification of Conflicts* (OUP 2012) 62; D Fleck, 'The Law of Non-International Armed Conflicts' in D Fleck (ed), *The Handbook of International Humanitarian Law* (3rd edn, OUP 2013) 582.

a rebel group acting against the established government. For example, as acknowledged by the ICJ in the *Nicaragua* case, the United States intervened in the internal conflict in Nicaragua on the side of the *contras*, a domestic non-state armed group fighting against the government.[48] In these cases, the lack of consent is due to the hostile involvement of the outside state: the established government can hardly be expected to condone the use of force against itself. If the outside state's armed forces engage in a 'significant and continuous military action' alongside the rebels, the intervening state becomes itself a party to the conflict.[49] As such, the intervention triggers the application of the law of IAC between the territorial state and the intervener.[50]

Secondly, a third state may intervene in a civil war on the territory of another state with no established government. In this situation, sometimes described as a 'failed state' scenario,[51] there is no entity capable of issuing an invitation or granting consent to an outside intervention. Strictly speaking, in such cases the outside state is not fighting against another state, because there are no armed forces that would belong to the territorial state. However, given that the third state is operating militarily in another state's territory without that state's consent to do so, it should be seen as using force against that state.[52]

The resulting situation would once again qualify as an IAC. This is because the key condition for the existence of an IAC, ie, the resort to force between states,[53]

[48] *Military and Paramilitary Activities in and against Nicaragua (Nicaragua v US)* (Merits) [1986] ICJ Rep 14 [81]–[86].

[49] cf *Prosecutor v Rajić* (Rule 61 Decision) IT-95-12-R61 (13 September 1996) [13]; similarly *Prosecutor v Prlić et al* (Appeal Judgment) IT-04-74-A (29 November 2017) vol 1 [267] (considering that outside troops' active participation in an internal conflict alongside the rebels is sufficient to make the intervening state a party to the conflict).

[50] Rosas (n 32) 285; MN Schmitt, CHB Garraway, and Y Dinstein, *The Manual on the Law of Non-International Armed Conflict* (IIHL 2006) [1.1.1(1)]; L Moir, *The Law of Internal Armed Conflict* (CUP 2004) 46; Vité (n 47) 86; Akande (n 47) 57; M Milanovic, 'The Applicability of the Conventions to "Transnational" and "Mixed" Conflicts' in A Clapham, P Gaeta, and M Sassòli (eds), *The 1949 Geneva Conventions: A Commentary* (OUP 2015) 35–37; Ferraro and Cameron, 'Article 2' (n 17) 95; N Zamir, *Classification of Conflicts in International Humanitarian Law: The Legal Impact of Foreign Intervention in Civil Wars* (Edward Elgar 2017) 94; contra R Pinto, 'Les règles du droit international concernant la guerre civile' (1965-I) 114 Recueil des Cours 451, 464–65 (considering that the conflict remains non-international in this case because the underlying political objective of all warring parties remains the same: the overthrow or the retention of the established government).

[51] See, eg, D Thürer, 'The "Failed State" and International Law' (1999) 81 IRRC 731, 733–34; Y Dinstein, 'Concluding Remarks on Non-International Armed Conflicts' in K Watkin and AJ Norris (eds), *Non-international Armed Conflict in the Twenty-first Century* (Government Printing Office 2012) 418 fn 33; E Lieblich, *International Law and Civil Wars: Intervention and Consent* (Routledge 2013) 164.

[52] Accord Rosas (n 32) 285; HP Gasser, 'International Humanitarian Law' in H Haug (ed), *Humanity for All: The International Red Cross and Red Crescent Movement* (P Haupt 1993) 510–11; Y Dinstein, *War, Aggression, and Self-defence* (4th edn, CUP 2005) 245; F Kalshoven and L Zegveld, *Constraints on the Waging of War: An Introduction to International Humanitarian Law* (4th edn, CUP 2011) 221; Akande (n 47) 73–74; Ferraro and Cameron, 'Article 2' (n 17) 93–95; but see, eg, Y Dinstein, *War, Aggression, and Self-defence* (5th edn, CUP 2011) 270 (silently abandoning the position from the previous edition); C Kreß, 'Some Reflections on the International Legal Framework Governing Transnational Armed Conflicts' (2010) 15 JCSL 245, 253–54; N Lubell, *Extraterritorial Use of Force against Non-State Actors* (OUP 2010) 95–96; E Wilmshurst, 'Conclusions' in E Wilmshurst (ed), *International Law and the Classification of Conflicts* (OUP 2012) 484.

[53] cf *Tadić* Decision on Jurisdiction (n 1) [70].

does not require that both states must actually use force; instead, it is sufficient that one state uses force against another state.[54] This interpretation, although not universally accepted in the literature,[55] is further supported by reference to the terms of the UNGA Resolution on Definition of Aggression.[56] That resolution clearly distinguishes between attacks by one state against the *territory* of another state from attacks on the *armed forces* of that state.[57] However, it considers both as possible 'acts of aggression',[58] in other words, forms of armed attack sufficient to trigger the application of the law of IAC.[59] This interpretation finds additional support in the case-law of the ICJ concerning the conflict in the Democratic Republic of the Congo (DRC). Faced with a similar factual pattern, the Court applied the law of IAC to the conduct of the Ugandan army inside the DRC, in spite of the fact that Uganda had not fought against the Congolese state forces.[60]

2.2.2.2 *Direct and indirect intervention*

The focus of the discussion thus far has been on direct forms of intervention, in which the outside state acts in another state's territory through its own armed forces. In these cases, it is submitted, the fact of the third state becoming a party to the conflict brings the law of IAC into force as between the intervening state and the territorial state. However, a third state may also become a party to the conflict even without engaging its forces directly. This is the case if that state acts through a non-state armed group on another state's territory, provided that it wields sufficient control over the group. As confirmed by the ICTY judgment in the *Prlić* case, an outside state may be simultaneously intervening both directly *and* indirectly.[61]

The test used to measure the level of control required to establish an indirect intervention is controversial. The controversy is best illustrated by, and to some extent it can be traced back to, the ICTY's assessment of the nature of the conflict in Bosnia and Herzegovina (1992–95). While the Trial Chamber in *Tadić* concluded that the conflict was not international,[62] the Appeals Chamber in the same case reached the opposite conclusion.[63] Accordingly, the following subsections analyse this case law in detail in order to argue that, firstly, both Chambers had misconstrued

[54] D Akande, 'Clearing the Fog of War? The ICRC's Interpretive Guidance on Direct Participation in Hostilities' (2010) 59 ICLQ 180, 185 fn 24; see further Akande (n 47) 73–79.

[55] See, eg, Kreß (n 52) 253–55; Lubell (n 52) 95–96.

[56] UNGA Res 3314 (XXIX) (Definition of Aggression) (14 December 1974).

[57] ibid, compare Art 3(a) and (b), with Art 3(d). [58] ibid, Art 3, *chapeau*.

[59] cf ICRC, *Model Manual of the Law of Armed Conflict* (ICRC 1999) rule 501. The ICRC considers intentional attacks against targets in the territory of another state as bringing about a situation of armed conflict between the two states irrespective of whether the armed forces of the state under attack are being engaged. See also Ferraro and Cameron, 'Article 2' (n 17) 93–95.

[60] *Armed Activities on the Territory of the Congo (Democratic Republic of the Congo v Uganda)* (Judgment) [2005] ICJ Rep 116 [217]–[20]; but see *Prosecutor v Thomas Lubanga Dyilo* (Trial Judgment) ICC-01/04-01/06 (14 March 2012) [541].

[61] *Prosecutor v Prlić et al* (Trial Judgment) IT-04-74-T (29 May 2013) vol 3 [568]; see also *Prlić* Appeal Judgment (n 49) vol 1 [297] (upholding this finding on appeal).

[62] *Prosecutor v Tadić* (Trial Judgment) IT-94-1-T (7 May 1997) [607].

[63] *Prosecutor v Tadić* (Appeal Judgment) IT-94-1-A (15 July 1999) [162].

the law of state responsibility, and secondly, that a test based on the law of state responsibility is ill-suited for the determination of internationalization of internal conflict by outside intervention. Finally, an alternative test, based on the existence of two parties to the conflict, will be proposed.

2.2.2.3 Indirect intervention in international jurisprudence

2.2.2.3.1 Interpretation of the *Nicaragua* ruling by the *Tadić* Trial Chamber

The ICTY was assessing the nature of the armed conflict in Bosnia and Herzegovina as part of the examination of its jurisdiction over the grave breaches of the GCs allegedly committed by Duško Tadić.[64] As the provisions governing grave breaches are only applicable in IACs,[65] the Trial Chamber examined the relationship between the armed forces of the *Republika Srpska* (*Vojska Republike Srpske* or the VRS, an insurgent entity within Bosnia) and the Federal Republic of Yugoslavia (FRY, the third state closely allied with and supporting the VRS).[66] The Chamber relied on the test of imputability imported from the law on state responsibility, as interpreted by the ICJ in the *Nicaragua* case.[67] While the Trial Chamber did not clearly set out the conditions it deemed to be applying, it cited a passage of the ICJ judgment analysing whether the relationship between the rebels and the third state 'was so much one of dependence on the one side and control on the other' that the rebels could be equated with an organ or an agent of the third state.[68]

In order to determine whether this was the case in *Tadić*, the Chamber required the Prosecution to demonstrate not only the dependence of the VRS on the FRY, but also that the FRY 'exercised the potential for control inherent in that relationship of dependency or that the VRS had otherwise placed itself under the control of the [FRY]'.[69] After determining that the FRY had played a vital role in the establishment, support, and staffing of the VRS, the Chamber narrowed down the question to whether, 'as the [ICJ] required of Nicaragua' (without citing a specific point in ICJ's judgment), the FRY had exercised 'effective control over the operations of the VRS'.[70] It then concluded, on its examination of the facts, that although the two had been 'highly dependent allies', the VRS could not be considered as de facto organs or agents of the FRY and therefore, the Bosnian conflict was not of international nature.[71]

2.2.2.3.2 *Tadić* Trial Judgment assessed against the law of state responsibility

The question of imputability of acts of non-state actors—whether individuals or groups—to a state is addressed by Article 8 of the ILC Articles on state Responsibility:

[64] For commentary on the substance of the case itself, see, eg, MP Scharf, 'Prosecutor v. Tadić: Case No. IT-94-1-T' (1997) 91(4) AJIL 718, 718–21 (regarding the trial judgment) and M Sassòli and LM Olson, 'Prosecutor v. Tadic (Judgement): Case No. IT-94-1-A' (2000) 94(3) AJIL 571, 571–78 (regarding the appeal judgment).

[65] cf also *Tadić* Decision on Jurisdiction (n 1) [81] and *Tadić* Trial Judgment (n 62) [578] fn 56.

[66] *Tadić* Trial Judgment (n 62) [584]–[608].

[67] *Tadić* Trial Judgment (n 62) [585].

[68] ibid [585], citing *Nicaragua* (n 48) [109].

[69] *Tadić* Trial Judgment (n 62) [588].

[70] ibid [595].

[71] ibid [606]–[07].

The conduct of a person or group of persons shall be considered an act of a State under international law if the person or group of persons is in fact acting on the instructions of, or under the direction or control of, that State in carrying out the conduct.

If the influence and control of a state over a non-state actor outgrows these requirements and the latter actor thus becomes indistinguishable from an organ of the said state, the attribution of the non-state actor's conduct will be governed by Article 4(1) ILC ASR. According to that provision, 'conduct of any State organ shall be considered an act of that State under international law'.[72]

Reflecting the logic of these customary[73] norms, in the *Nicaragua* case the ICJ separated the scrutiny of the relationship between a state and a non-state armed group into two complementary legal tests.[74] The first of them has been described variously as the 'agency test',[75] 'strict control test',[76] or 'complete control test'.[77] In it, the Court, in order to determine whether a relationship of agency equivalent to that between a state and its organs had formed, required (1) the rebels to be completely dependent in all fields of activity on the third state, and (2) the outside state to actually make use of that dependence.[78] If these requirements were met, the Court would attribute *all* acts of the rebel group to the outside state.[79]

If (and only if) the criteria of complete dependency were not satisfied, the second test, one of 'effective control', would become applicable as a subsidiary legal test.[80] In this test, only certain acts of the insurgent group would be imputed to the third state.[81] However, it must be shown that the rebels had acted under the third state's instructions or under its effective control.[82] Specifically, this entails that the third state 'must be able to control the beginning of the operation, the way it is carried out, and its end.'[83] Admittedly, the ICJ did not make the relationship of subsidiarity between the two tests explicit in *Nicaragua*. However, it is apparent from the methodology of the scrutiny that it only turned to the 'effective control' test after determining that it could not equate the rebels with a state organ of the outside state in question.[84]

Therefore, it is submitted that the Trial Chamber in *Tadić* misconstrued *Nicaragua* by conflating the two tests and applying them interchangeably to the case at hand. In her dissenting opinion, Presiding Judge McDonald rightly criticized this error[85]

[72] cf also ILC ASR (n 17), commentary to Art 4, 40 [2] (describing Article 4 as a starting point for attribution of conduct to a state).

[73] See, eg, *Case Concerning the Application of the Convention on the Prevention and Punishment of the Crime of Genocide (Bosnia and Herzegovina v Serbia and Montenegro)* (Judgment) [2007] ICJ Rep 43, 202 [385] (re Article 4) and 207–08 [398] (re Article 8) (hereafter *Bosnian Genocide*).

[74] Similarly, see S Talmon, 'The Responsibility of Outside Powers for Acts of Secessionist Entities' (2009) 58 ICLQ 493, 497–503; M Milanovic, 'State Responsibility for Genocide' (2006) 17 EJIL 553, 576–78; *Tadić* Trial Judgment (n 62) (sep and diss op McDonald) [22]–[25]. This interpretation was further confirmed by the ICJ in *Bosnian Genocide* (n 73) [391]–[400].

[75] *Tadić* Appeal Judgment (n 63) [106] (summarizing the prosecution submissions).

[76] Talmon (n 74) 498.

[77] Milanovic (n 74) 576.

[78] *Nicaragua* (n 48) [109].

[79] ibid [116]; see also *Bosnian Genocide* (n 73) [397].

[80] Talmon (n 74) 502; Milanovic (n 74) 577.

[81] *Nicaragua* (n 48) [115].

[82] ibid [115]; *Bosnian Genocide* (n 73) [400].

[83] Talmon (n 74) 503.

[84] *Nicaragua* (n 48) [109]–[115]; see further text to notes 90–94 in this chapter.

[85] *Tadić* Trial Judgment (n 62) (sep and diss op McDonald) [21]–[22].

and argued that the facts of the case had warranted stopping the inquiry after the first test, the application of which had, in her view, already established an agency relationship between the VRS and the FRY.[86]

2.2.2.3.3 Rejection of the *Nicaragua* ruling by the *Tadić* Appeals Chamber

Although it had at its disposal Judge McDonald's analysis as well as the Prosecution's concurring submissions,[87] the Appeals Chamber in the same case rejected that *Nicaragua* had established the two described tests of attribution under the law of state responsibility.[88] Instead, it argued that the ICJ, by its reference to 'effective control' was merely 'spelling out the requirements of the same test'.[89]

It is submitted that this claim of just one general test of attribution is unwarranted. First, the ICJ in *Nicaragua* did indeed use two tests *seriatim*. Only after rejecting that the rebels could be equated with organs of the third state ('agency test')[90] did the Court analyse whether state responsibility could be established based on that state's effective control over the military or paramilitary operations of the rebels ('effective control test').[91] Second, the logic of the rules on state responsibility dictates that even if an entity does not act as an organ of the state (thus establishing attribution under Article 4 ILC ASR), it can still incur subsidiary responsibility for acts under direction or control of that state (Article 8 ILC ASR). Finally, despite the perhaps 'somewhat unclear'[92] and 'not always ... straight'[93] line of reasoning adopted by the ICJ in the *Nicaragua* case, the same Court expressly confirmed the two-test interpretation in the *Bosnian Genocide* case.[94]

Nevertheless, the Appeals Chamber insisted that the ICJ had applied a single threshold for attribution, namely one of 'effective control'.[95] It then proceeded to criticize this test as defying the logic of the system of international law on state responsibility.[96] The Chamber saw the purpose of the law of state responsibility as preventing states from acting through individuals and shedding responsibility whenever these individuals breached international law.[97] It concluded that, due to the hierarchy and structure of authority present in organized armed groups as opposed to individuals and 'unorganised groups',[98] a lower standard of 'overall control' should be used to determine state responsibility for acts of organized groups:

> In order to attribute the acts of a military or paramilitary group to a State, it must be proved that the State wields overall control over the group, not only by equipping and financing the group, but also by coordinating or helping in the general planning of its military activity.[99]

The two elements apparent from this test—supporting and co-ordinating—were further elaborated on in later cases before the ICTY.[100] As the law stands today, the

[86] ibid [298]. [87] Cf *Tadić* Appeal Judgment (n 63) [111]. [88] ibid [112].
[89] ibid [112]. [90] *Nicaragua* (n 48) [109]–[110]. [91] ibid [115].
[92] *Tadić* Appeal Judgment (n 63) [114]. [93] ibid [108].
[94] cf *Bosnian Genocide* (n 73) [391]–[93], [399]–[400].
[95] *Tadić* Appeal Judgment (n 63) [112]. [96] ibid [124]. [97] ibid [117].
[98] ibid [120]. [99] ibid [131].
[100] See, in particular, *Prosecutor v Kordić and Čerkez* (Trial Judgment) IT-95-14/2-T (26 February 2001) [115]; *Prosecutor v Kordić and Čerkez* (Appeal Judgment) IT-95-14/2-A (17 December

test requires the intervening state (1) to provide the armed group with financial and training assistance, military equipment, and/or operational support, and (2) to participate in the organization, co-ordination, or planning of military operations with the armed group.[101]

2.2.2.3.4 Assessment of the novel standard proposed by the *Tadić* Appeal Judgment

By introducing this new standard of 'overall control', the Appeals Chamber created the possibility that a state would be held responsible for the conduct of groups that retained a significant degree of independence and were not subject to operational control and instruction. The Chamber claimed that this standard was supported by the practice of states regarding attribution of conduct of military or paramilitary groups to states.[102] However, as noted by Sassòli and Olson, the practice actually referred to in the judgment consisted mainly of cases in which a state was held responsible for armed groups acting on its own territory, which was a very different factual pattern to that in the *Tadić* case.[103]

Even putting aside the doubtful customary provenance of the new test, it is clear that by its introduction, the Appeals Chamber purported to lower the bar required for the attribution of conduct under Article 8 ILC ASR.[104] In doing so, the Chamber not only stretched the connection that must exist between the conduct of a state's organs and its international responsibility 'almost to a breaking point',[105] but it also, it is submitted, departed from the logic behind the interplay of Articles 4 and 8 ILC ASR, thereby allowing attribution of acts well beyond what a state should answer for on the international plane.[106] However, it is submitted that in order to establish the nature of the conflict, the ICTY need not have dealt with the question of state responsibility at all.

The ICJ in *Nicaragua* did not apply the law of state responsibility to determine the nature of the conflict in Nicaragua. It dealt with issues of state responsibility in an unrelated part of the judgment and never connected the two issues[107]—this connection was first made by the ICTY Trial Chamber in *Tadić*.[108] The Trial Chamber was mute on why it turned to the law on state responsibility. The Appeals Chamber

2004) [361]; *Prosecutor v Naletilić and Martinović* (Trial Judgment) IT-98-34-T (31 March 2003) [198]; *Prlić* Trial Judgment (n 61) vol 1 [86(a)].

101 *Prosecutor v Mladić* (Trial Judgment) IT-09-92-T (22 November 2017) vol 3 [3014]; *Prlić* Appeal Judgment (n 49) vol 1 [282]; cf also Talmon (n 74) 506.

102 *Tadić* Appeal Judgment (n 63) [124] et seq.

103 M Sassòli and LM Olson, 'The Judgment of the ICTY Appeals Chamber on the Merits in the *Tadic* Case' (2000) 82 IRRC 733, 740.

104 cf *Tadić* Appeal Judgment (n 63) [124] (referring to a 'lower degree of control').

105 *Bosnian Genocide* (n 73) [406].

106 cf also Akande (n 47) 60 ('A State should only be held to be legally responsible for acts which are really its own').

107 cf *Nicaragua* (n 48) [109], [115] (state responsibility), and [219] (conflict nature); see also T Meron, 'Classification of Armed Conflict in the former Yugoslavia: *Nicaragua*'s Fallout' (1998) 92 AJIL 236, 241; Milanovic (n 74) 578–79 fn 129 (commenting that the fact that 'the relevant parts of the *Nicaragua* judgment are separated by more than a hundred paragraphs is an obvious indication').

108 *Tadić* Trial Judgment (n 62) [585].

attempted to fill this gap and justify its approach by claiming that IHL lacked unique criteria for determining whether a group of individuals is 'under the control of a state'.[109] Because of this supposed absence of *lex specialis*, the Appeals Chamber turned to the *lex generalis* comprised of the norms of state responsibility laid down in general international law.[110]

However, this reliance on the law of state responsibility is erroneous. As Milanović rightly put it, 'international humanitarian law is in no way *lex specialis* to the law of state responsibility'.[111] The Appeals Chamber's analysis is thus marred by a misunderstanding of the distinction between primary and secondary rules of international law.[112] While the nature of an armed conflict is determined by the primary rules of international law systematically belonging to the subdiscipline of IHL,[113] the question of state responsibility is determined by the secondary rules of international law, which govern whether international law obligations have been violated and determine the consequences of such violations.[114] Therefore, the ICTY's proposal of the 'overall control' test is unpersuasive insofar as the determination of the requisite degree of control under Article 8 is concerned. Broadly for these reasons, it was also rejected by the ICJ in the *Bosnian Genocide* case.[115]

2.2.2.4 Decoupling the law of state responsibility from conflict qualification under IHL

Rather than borrowing from the regime of state responsibility, IHL must be capable of determining its applicability within the framework of its own norms.[116] In doing so, it is not concerned with the *subjective* question of responsibility for the conduct of states; its sole aim is to adjudge the *objective* question whether two opposing states are parties to an armed conflict.[117] This is best assessed not by examining whether a third state can be held internationally responsible for the acts of a rebel group against the territorial state, but by focusing on whether a state has used force through a non-state group. This is because, apart from few exceptions,[118] it is only through the use of force that an IAC comes about.[119]

[109] *Tadić* Appeal Judgment (n 63) [98]. [110] ibid [98].

[111] Milanovic (n 74) 587; but see Ferraro and Cameron, 'Article 2' (n 17) 96.

[112] cf also O de Frouville, 'Attribution of Conduct to the State: Private Individuals', in J Crawford, A Pellet, and S Olleson (eds), *The Law of International Responsibility* (OUP 2010) 270; H Tonkin, *State Control over Private Military and Security Companies in Armed Conflict* (CUP 2011) 118–19; J Crawford, *State Responsibility: The General Part* (CUP 2013) 153.

[113] cf Akande (n 47) 60.

[114] ILC, 'Report of the Commission to the General Assembly: Document A/8010/Rev.1', Yearbook of the ILC, 1970, vol II, 271, 306 [66(c)].

[115] cf *Bosnian Genocide* (n 73) [403]–[06].

[116] cf also Milanovic, '"Transnational" and "Mixed" Conflicts' (n 50) 36–37.

[117] Contra Ferraro and Cameron, 'Article 2' (n 17) 99 [271] (arguing that the test to be used 'must avoid a situation where some acts are governed by the law of international armed conflict but cannot be attributed to a State').

[118] See Section 1.2.2.1 (discussing occupation without armed resistance as one of the triggers of IAC).

[119] See also *Tadić* Appeal Judgment (n 63) (sep op Shahabuddeen) [7]–[14] and [24].

Although the terminology of the use of force is reminiscent of the *jus ad bellum*, it bears emphasis that the interpretation advanced here is not meant as a *renvoi* to that area of the law, either.[120] Rather, the notion of (armed) force should be interpreted in the specific context of IHL as a separate branch of international law.[121] In this regard, an IHL-specific definition suggested recently by Noam Zamir is particularly instructive: 'the term "armed force" should be understood as an act . . . that is either intended or likely to cause physical or mental injury, unnecessary suffering, death or damage to property to the adversary forces or to protected persons'.[122] This definition situates the concept of armed force in the normative context of IHL and thus provides an appropriate starting point for the qualification of an originally internal conflict involving the participation of an outside state.

Manifestly, the conduct of a non-state armed group engaged in a NIAC against the established government brings about at least some of the consequences listed in Zamir's definition. The remaining question therefore concerns the necessary level of involvement by an outside state that will amount to an act intended or likely to cause these outcomes. It is submitted that, in this regard, the two elements of the 'overall control' test provide a suitable and applicable yardstick.

If an outside state only supports the rebels materially or logistically (the first step of the test), it cannot yet be said to be using force through them for the purposes of IHL. True, its involvement may amount to a violation of the principle of non-intervention[123] or, in certain cases, such as when the support in question entails arming and training of the rebels, even a violation of the *jus ad bellum*.[124] Nonetheless, it would be inaccurate to speak of a direct causal connection between the act of supporting the insurgents and the relevant outcomes for IHL purposes such as injury, death, damage, or destruction occasioned by the insurgent forces.[125] Support of this kind thus does not make the outside state a party to the conflict at hand.[126] This interim conclusion is also bolstered by the practice of states in modern conflicts. For example, although several third states provided material and logistical support to the Syrian opposition groups in the early phases of the ongoing Syrian

[120] But see Akande (n 47) 62 ('In order to determine whether there is a use of force by one State against another we must turn to those aspects of the *ius ad bellum* that determine this question.').

[121] cf also N Lubell, 'The War (?) against Al-Qaeda' in E Wilmshurst (ed), *International Law and the Classification of Conflicts* (OUP 2012) 432–33 (highlighting the need to separate the questions of conflict qualification under IHL from those of possible violations of the *jus ad bellum*).

[122] Zamir (n 50) 58–59.

[123] cf *Nicaragua* (n 48) [228], [292(3)]; MN Schmitt (ed), *Tallinn Manual 2.0 on the International Law Applicable to Cyber Operations* (CUP 2017) 381 [5] (hereafter *Tallinn Manual*).

[124] cf *Nicaragua* (n 48) [228]. This further demonstrates that the notion of the use of force may carry different meanings under IHL and the *jus ad bellum*. Within the context of the latter body of law, arming and training of non-state actors in another state's territory may amount to a prohibited use of force against that state. cf ibid ('the arming and training of the *contras* can certainly be said to involve the threat or use of force').

[125] cf Zamir (n 50) 58–59 (discussing the causal requirements that must be met in order for specific conduct to qualify as the use of armed force under IHL).

[126] See, eg, *Tallinn Manual* (n 123) 381–82 [6] (in the context of cyber operations, 'merely taking measures to maintain rebel access to the national cyber infrastructure' or 'the provision of cyber attack tools' would not suffice to internationalize a conflict).

civil war, there was no evidence that either those states or the Syrian government considered this support to have turned the situation into an IAC.[127]

Accordingly, it is only when an outside state additionally participates in organizing and co-ordinating rebels within another state's territory (the second step of the 'overall control' test) that its involvement amounts to a use of force against the latter state.[128] This is because at this point, the third state's involvement is directly causally related to the consequences of the insurgents' conduct. The outside state thus becomes a belligerent party to a conflict against the territorial state.[129] Because from this point onwards two states are engaged against each other, the situation must thenceforth be qualified as an IAC. Nevertheless, it may well be that the rebels preserve a degree of independence to the extent that they would not be considered the state's de facto organs or entities effectively controlled by it for the purposes of determining state responsibility.[130] This proposed test thus maintains a conceptual separation between questions of conflict qualification under IHL and the standard of attribution under the law of state responsibility.

The proposed test for the internationalization of armed conflicts involving non-consensual outside intervention has several important advantages. Firstly, unlike the test of 'effective control', it is realistic in its requirements and capable of practical application. It is noteworthy in this regard that the two prominent cases in which the 'effective control' standard was applied by the ICJ have both resulted in a negative finding.[131] In fact, the ICRC has described the latter test as being 'almost impossible to prove'.[132] By contrast, the 'overall control' standard has been relied on successfully for nearly two decades by the ICTY and other international courts.[133]

[127] See Report of the Independent International Commission of Inquiry on the Syrian Arab Republic, UN Doc A/HRC/21/50 (16 August 2012) [19] (noting the provision of 'communication and material support to anti-Government armed groups' by outside states); ibid, Annex II [3] (qualifying the situation as a NIAC and noting that that view was supported by the Syrian government); see also Zamir (n 50) 129–30 fns 68–69.

[128] cf *Nicaragua* (n 48) [228]. The required degree of support may be disentangled from the question of 'control' altogether: *participation* in organization and co-ordination is not equivalent to *control* and thus, to some extent, the notion of 'overall control' is a misnomer. German domestic courts used in their analysis of the nature of the Yugoslavian conflict a test that did not refer to control, yet would—in the opinion of this author—result in the same determination as the 'overall control' test. For example, in *Jorgić*, the Higher Regional Court of Appeal of Düsseldorf required a 'close personal, organisational and logistical interconnection' between the intervening state (FRY) and the insurgent group (VRS) to hold that, after 19 May 1992, the conflict in Bosnia and Herzegovina had been international. The judgment was not published; for the reference see Talmon (n 74) 514 fn 130.

[129] See, eg, *Tallinn Manual* (n 123) 382 [6] (in the context of cyber operations, 'providing specific intelligence on cyber vulnerabilities that renders particular rebel cyber attacks possible' suffices for conflict internationalization).

[130] cf *Nicaragua* (n 48) [292(9)].

[131] *Nicaragua* (n 48); *Bosnian Genocide* (n 73). But see L Cameron and V Chetail, *Private Military and Security Companies under Public International Law* (CUP 2013) 213 (advancing a novel interpretation of the *Nicaragua* case, according to which the conduct of the UCLAs was in fact deemed by the ICJ to have been under the effective control of the US).

[132] Ferraro and Cameron, 'Article 2' (n 17) 99 fn 124.

[133] See, eg, *Tadić* Appeal Judgment (n 63) [145]; *Prosecutor v Aleksovski* (Appeal Judgment) IT-95-14/1-A (24 March 2000) [134]; *Prosecutor v Delalić et al* (*Čelebići* Appeal Judgment) IT-96-21-A (20 February 2001) [26]; *Naletilić and Martinović* Trial Judgment (n 100) [184]; *Kordić and Čerkez* Appeal Judgment (n 100) [307]; *Prlić* Appeal Judgment (n 49) vol 1 [238]; *Prosecutor v Brima et al* (Trial

This observation leads to the second advantage, which is that the endorsement of this test for the purposes of conflict qualification maintains the soundness of the international jurisprudence produced since *Tadić*. The precedential value of dozens of judgments relying on the 'overall control' test cannot be overstated and its preservation is a strong consideration by itself. At the same time, decoupling the test from the law of state responsibility serves to resolve the supposed dispute between the ICTY and ICJ by endorsing a compromise solution without the need for 'winners' or 'losers'.[134]

Thirdly, it is submitted that the conceptual separation of the two tests is a value in itself. It has been rightly noted in this regard that 'it is conceptually inappropriate for secondary rules of attribution to determine the scope of application of the primary rules of IHL'.[135] The two sets of rules serve different purposes in international law and it is unnecessary to conflate them.[136] In fact, the ICTY Appeals Chamber's original approach of proposing the 'overall control' test as the correct standard of attribution under Article 8 ILC ASR has been prominently described as a prime example of 'institutional struggles' between international courts and, as such, evidence of the so-called fragmentation of international law.[137] Finding an appropriate 'drawer' for each of the approaches within the 'wardrobe' of international law thus additionally serves to alleviate these worries about the fragmentation of the law.

2.2.3 Intervention by international organizations

Post-Second World War practice shows that international organizations can also be the means of outside interference in an internal armed conflict. This type of interference primarily includes peace-keeping and peace-enforcement operations mandated by the United Nations (UN). Moreover, regional organizations such as the ECOWAS, NATO, or EU have also intervened in internal conflicts on several occasions. These operations come in a wide variety and only some of them have the potential to transform the nature of a conflict. This section begins by analysing those situations that clearly lack this potential, either because the intervention is not of sufficient intensity or because it is consensual. It then focuses on those types of intervention by international organizations which may internationalize the underlying conflict, and distinguishes in that regard between the two main models of control over the intervening forces that have emerged in modern practice.

Judgment) SCSL-04-16-T (20 June 2007) [251]; *Lubanga* Trial Judgment (n 60) [541]; *Prosecutor v Germain Katanga* (Trial Judgment) ICC-01/04-01/07 (7 March 2014) [1178].

134 Both courts have labelled the analyses of the other institution as 'unpersuasive', leading to an impasse that cannot be institutionally resolved given the absence of hierarchy among international judicial institutions. See *Tadić* Appeal Judgment (n 63) [115]; *Bosnian Genocide* (n 73) [404].

135 Milanovic, '"Transnational" and "Mixed" Conflicts' (n 50) 36 [31].

136 See also M Spinedi, 'On the Non-Attribution of the Bosnian Serbs' Conduct to Serbia' (2007) 5 JICJ 829, 835–36.

137 See, eg, M Koskenniemi and P Leino, 'Fragmentation of International Law? Postmodern Anxieties' (2002) 15 LJIL 553, 564–67.

2.2.3.1 Intensity and consent criteria

2.2.3.1.1 Sufficient intensity

Classic peace-keeping operations based on the consent of all parties to the conflict and limited in their mandate to refrain from the use of force except in self-defence[138] cannot be said to trigger the application of IHL in and of themselves. For instance, the 2008–09 EU military operation in Chad and the Central African Republic (Operation EUFOR Tchad/RCA) was to operate as a non-belligerent force, unaligned with any of the conflict parties and tasked with the protection of civilians and facilitation of the delivery of humanitarian aid.[139] Such a multinational force does not become a party to the conflict and its personnel do not become combatants.[140] In addition to the domestic law of the territorial state, the troops' conduct may be governed by rules agreed by the dispatching international organization and contributing countries.[141] However, rules of IHL do not apply unless and until the troops engage in combat exceeding the use of force in individual self-defence.[142] As the international organization stays outside of the armed conflict, its legal qualification as a NIAC remains unchanged for the purposes of application of IHL.

2.2.3.1.2 Consent of the territorial state

Even if a multinational force intervenes without the consent of one or more of the insurgent groups operating in the territory of a state, the nature of the conflict does not change as long as force is used with the consent of the state. Similarly to third-state intervention in support of the established government, the extension of consent over the actions undertaken by the international organization rules out conflict internationalization.[143] Because the two subjects of international law are not acting against each other, the conflict remains internal, unless the insurgents can elevate their status by some other means.[144]

[138] cf E Suy, 'Peacekeeping Operations' in RJ Dupuy (ed), *A Handbook on International Organizations* (Springer 1988) 379.

[139] UNSC Res 1778 (25 September 2007) [6(a)]; Council Joint Action (EU) 2007/677/CFSP of 15 October 2007 on the European Union military operation in the Republic of Chad and in the Central African Republic [2007] OJ L279/21; Council Joint Action (EU) 2009/795/CFSP of 19 October 2009 repealing Joint Action 2007/677/CFSP on the European Union military operation in the Republic of Chad and in the Central African Republic [2009] OJ L283/61.

[140] cf *Prosecutor v Sesay et al* (Trial Judgment) SCSL-04-15-T (2 March 2009) [233] (holding that the protection of peacekeepers as civilians does not cease if they only use armed force in exercising their right to individual self-defence).

[141] See, eg, Report of the Special Committee on Peacekeeping Operations and its Working Group, Annex (Revised Draft Model Memorandum of Understanding), UN Doc A/61/19/Rev.1 (2008) 39–46.

[142] Convention on the Safety of United Nations and Associated Personnel (signed 9 December 1994, entered into force 15 January 1999) 2051 UNTS 363, Art 2(2) *a contrario; Sesay* Trial Judgment (n 140) [233]; *Prosecutor v Bahar Idriss Abu Garda* (Decision on the Confirmation of Charges, Pre-Trial Chamber I), Pre-Trial Chamber I, ICC-02/05-02/09 (8 February 2010) [83].

[143] See Section 2.2.1.

[144] But see ICRC, 'Expert Meeting on Multinational Peace Operations: Report' (2003) <www.icrc.org/eng/assets/files/other/icrc_002_0912.pdf>, at 11.

2.2.3.2 *Internationalizing forms of intervention*

The remaining modality of internationalization through outside intervention by an international organization is that through 'peace-enforcement' operations initiated by international organizations without the consent of the territorial state and with a mandate to use force to achieve the mission's aims.[145] The only international body authorized to conduct such operations at the global level is the UN acting through the Security Council under Chapter VII of the UN Charter. Although the Charter originally foresaw the creation of a permanent international army placed at the disposal of the Security Council, this has not materialized in reality.[146] Hence, the Council instead acts by authorizing individual states to undertake military enforcement measures within the limits of a specifically granted mandate.[147]

Similarly, regional enforcement action may lawfully be undertaken only with the Security Council's authorization.[148] Nevertheless, on several occasions regional organizations have used force on the territory of a third state without that state's consent or a prior Security Council authorization. For example, in 1991 ECOWAS intervened in the Liberian civil war in order to stop the violence and restore law and order in Liberia;[149] and in 1999 NATO intervened against the governmental forces of the Federal Republic of Yugoslavia with the purported aim to 'prevent an overwhelming humanitarian catastrophe' resulting from the ethnic cleansing of the Albanian ethnic minority in Kosovo.[150] The legality of such actions is a question of *jus ad bellum* and as such it falls beyond the scope of this work. For greater clarity, the ensuing analysis focuses on UN operations; however, the described principles would, unless otherwise specified, apply to other international organizations as well.[151]

145 As stated previously, international forces that were not originally mandated to engage in hostilities may still become involved in fighting, either on their own initiative or in self-defence against an outside attack. Such a case would also be treated according to the principles discussed in this section.

146 cf Charter of the United Nations (signed 26 June 1945, entered into force 24 October 1945) 1 UNTS XVI, Art 43 (hereafter UN Charter); see further N Krisch, 'Article 43' in B Simma (ed), *The Charter of the United Nations: A Commentary* (3rd edn, OUP 2012), vol II, 1354–56 [9]–[13] (noting some limited progress but concluding that on the whole the provision 'remains far from implementation').

147 See further, eg, C Gray, *International Law and the Use of Force* (4th edn, OUP 2018) 262–340.

148 UN Charter, Art 53(1); see further M Akehurst, 'Enforcement Action by Regional Agencies' (1967) 42 BYBIL 175; J Bröhmer, G Ress, and C Walter, 'Article 53' in B Simma (ed), *The Charter of the United Nations: A Commentary* (3rd edn, OUP 2012), vol II, 1487–89 [26]–[30]; for the opposing view see, eg, J Levitt, 'Humanitarian Intervention by Regional Actors in Internal Conflicts: The Cases of ECOWAS in Liberia and Sierra Leone' (1998) 12 Temp Int'l & Comp LJ 333. Discussion of the legality or otherwise of the so-called humanitarian intervention is beyond the scope of this work.

149 ECOWAS Standing Mediation Committee, Decision A/DEC.1/8/90, on the Cease-fire and Establishment of an ECOWAS Cease-fire Monitoring Group for Liberia, Banjul, Republic of Gambia (7 August 1990), reproduced in M Weller, *Regional Peace-keeping and International Enforcement: The Liberian Crisis*, vol 6 (Grotius Publications 1994) 67–68.

150 UN Doc S/PV.3988 (24 March 1999) 12 (United Kingdom).

151 cf also UNSC Res 1327 (13 November 2000), Annex, at 2 (urging regional and subregional organizations to comply with IHL while they are engaged in peacekeeping operations).

There are essentially two models of command and control (C2) structure in international peace enforcement operations.[152] The command authority and operational control[153] may remain with the troop-contributing states as was the case in the 1950–53 Korean War (military forces from individual states were placed under the unified command of the United States[154]) or in the 1991 Gulf War (states responding to the Iraqi invasion of Kuwait acted individually under the authorization of the Security Council[155]). Alternatively, command and control over multinational forces may rest with the international organization as it did in the United Nations Operation in the Congo (ONUC) in 1961[156] or in the Somali operation UNOSOM after it was endowed with enforcement powers in 1993.[157] In the former model, the sending states qualify as conflict parties for the purposes of IHL; in the latter, the UN becomes a conflict party itself.[158]

2.2.3.2.1 International troops subject to command and control of contributing states

In the first model, the responsibility for the national contingents' conduct remains with the states. Even with the authorization of the Security Council, a national force retains the status of an organ of the sending state.[159] According to Article 7

[152] Noam Zamir additionally identifies a hybrid third model, in which states exercise their joint control over their armed units *through* a given international organization: see Zamir (n 50) 185–88. For the purposes of the present study, such arrangements (typical particularly for interventions under the aegis of NATO) fall under the first model described later as long as the sending states maintain command authority and operational control over their respective forces. In such cases, the sending states and the international organization in question may be jointly responsible for the conduct of these armed units. Nonetheless, it is the states who should be seen as the parties to the conflict at hand, and thus the analysis presented in the next subsection concerning the first model applies equally to these situations.

[153] See R Murphy, *UN Peacekeeping in Lebanon, Somalia and Kosovo: Operational and Legal Issues in Practice* (CUP 2007) 115–16 (defining the notions of command and control).

[154] UNSC Res 84 (7 July 1950); see also R Baxter, 'Constitutional Forms and Some Legal Problems of International Military Command' (1952) 29 BYBIL 325, 335.

[155] UNSC Res 678 (29 November 1990).

[156] UNSC Res 143 (14 July 1960) (establishing the ONUC); UNSC Res 161 (21 February 1961) (authorizing the ONUC to use force).

[157] UNSC Res 751 (24 April 1992) (establishing the UN operation in Somalia); UNSC Res 814 (26 March 1993) (expanding its mandate acting under Chapter VII of the UN Charter); Report of the Commission of Inquiry Established pursuant to Security Council Resolution 885 (1993) to Investigate Armed Attacks on UNOSOM II Personnel which Led to Casualties Among Them, UN Doc S/1994/653 (24 February 1994) 26 [125] (reporting that 'a virtual war situation' between the UN forces in Somalia and domestic armed militias occurred over the course of four months). In practice, however, '[m]any major operations undertaken under the United Nations flag and in the context of UNOSOM's mandate were totally outside the command and control of the United Nations'. ibid 45 [244].

[158] The following text justifies this position with reference to the law governing the international responsibility of states and international organizations. It should be reiterated that IHL is capable of determining its applicability within the framework of its own norms and that, when determining the legal nature of armed conflicts, it is not concerned with the subjective question of responsibility (see Section 2.2.2.4). The analysis of the norms governing international responsibility is undertaken here in order to identify the entity that should properly be seen as the relevant conflict party. In other words, the following text looks into the control over the forces in question in order to determine who should be considered as the intervening third party: is it the contributing states, or the authorizing international organization?

[159] cf ILC ASR (n 17), Art 4.

of the Draft Articles on the Responsibility of International Organizations, the responsibility would shift to the organization only if the international body exercised 'effective control' over the force's conduct.[160] However, in this model such control is precluded by the fact that command authority and operational control remains with the sending states.[161]

Admittedly, the European Court of Human Rights (ECtHR) took the contrary view in its 2007 judgment in the *Behrami and Saramati* case.[162] The Court held that even the conduct of national forces acting with UN authorization, but outside of the UN chain of command, was attributable to the UN.[163] It considered, inter alia, whether detaining the applicant on the Kosovo Force (KFOR) commander's orders fell within the Court's jurisdiction *ratione personae*[164] and it eventually found the case inadmissible, due to the UN not being a party to the ECHR.[165] The Court did consider the criterion of 'effective control' in Article 7 ILC DARIO as applicable,[166] but it nevertheless held that while the KFOR had 'operational command', the 'ultimate authority and control' was retained by the Security Council.[167] Therefore, any conduct of the KFOR performed in the furtherance of the Security Council's authorization was attributable to the UN only.[168]

The European Court was widely criticized both for its reasoning and the decision it had made.[169] For the present purposes, it suffices to say that the Court wrongly applied—or failed to apply—the 'effective control' standard built into Article 7 ILC DARIO. As the ILC noted in response to the ECtHR's ruling, 'when applying the criterion of effective control, "operational" control would seem more significant than "ultimate" control, since the latter hardly implies a role in the act in question'.[170] When the Security Council gives mandate for an operation but has no actual control over the troops' conduct, responsibility for such conduct lies with the

160 ILC, Draft Articles on the Responsibility of International Organizations, with commentaries, Yearbook of the ILC (2011) vol II, part two, Art 7 (hereafter ILC DARIO).

161 See also G Porretto and S Vité, 'The Application of International Humanitarian Law and Human Rights to International Organisations', Research Papers Series No 1, Centre Universitaire de Droit International Humanitaire (2006) 28; M Milanovic and V Hadzi-Vidanovic, 'A Taxonomy of Armed Conflict' in N White and C Henderson (eds), *Research Handbook on International Conflict and Security Law* (Edward Elgar 2013) 277; Zamir (n 50) 180.

162 *Behrami and Behrami v France, Saramati v France, Germany and Norway* (App nos 71412/01 & 78166/01) (2007) 45 EHRR 85 (ECtHR).

163 ibid [132]–[41]. 164 ibid [72], [121]. 165 ibid [144]–[52].

166 ibid [31]–[32]. The text of the ruling speaks of Article 5, but the provision was later renumbered, first to Article 6, and finally to Article 7 (used throughout the main text of this study).

167 ibid [133]–[34]. 168 ibid [141].

169 See, eg, A Sari, 'Jurisdiction and International Responsibility in Peace Support Operations: The *Behrami* and *Saramati* Cases' (2008) 8(1) HRLR 151; M Milanovic and T Papić, 'As Bad as It Gets: The European Court of Human Rights *Behrami and Saramati* Decision and General International Law' (2009) 58 ICLQ 267; see also ILC DARIO (n 160), commentary to Art 7, 23–24 [10] fn 115.

170 ILC DARIO (n 160), commentary to Art 7, 23 [10]; see also ILC, 'Seventh Report on Responsibility of International Organizations' by Mr Giorgio Gaja, Special Rapporteur, UN Doc A/CN.4/610 (27 March 2009) 9 [26]; but see A Cassese, 'The *Nicaragua* and *Tadić* Tests Revisited in Light of the ICJ Judgment on Genocide in Bosnia' (2007) 18 EJIL 649, 667.

contributing states. It is submitted, therefore, that to the extent that *Behrami and Saramati* suggests otherwise, it was wrongly decided.[171]

Since the sending state retains the responsibility over the conduct of the contingent under its command authority and operational control, it is that state that is also a party to the conflict, not the organization authorizing the mission.[172] This conclusion is also consonant with the existing official statements, which confirm that states consider their international obligations to extend to the troops under their command and control.[173] Hence, under the first model of command and control structure, whether a given conflict is internationalized (or not) will depend on the application of the principles and rules applicable to third-state intervention.[174]

2.2.3.2.2 International troops subject to command and control of international organizations

In the second model, the responsibility for the conduct of armed forces is vested with the international organization, which acts as a separate legal entity distinct from its troop-contributing member states. The UN possesses a separate legal personality under international law[175] and it is responsible for acts carried out by its organs;[176] these principles may also be extended to other organizations acting in situations of armed violence. Furthermore, international organizations bear responsibility for organs or agents placed at their disposal by third states or international organizations.[177] Although a state's military force is normally considered to be that state's organ under the law of international responsibility,[178] the functional link between that state and its troops is severed when the troops are actually placed under the UN command.[179] While some powers, especially those of disciplinary and criminal nature, are likely to remain with the contributing state,[180] troops commanded by

[171] See also *Al-Jedda v UK* (App no 27021/08) (2011) 53 EHRR 23 (ECtHR) [80]–[84] (holding that an authorization granted by the UNSC does not by itself result in all conduct undertaken on the basis of this authorization being attributable to the UN and not to the troop-contributing states). Regrettably, the Court did not dispense of the criticism of its ruling in *Behrami* and satisfied itself with holding that neither the 'effective control test' nor the 'ultimate authority and control test' would have been met on the facts of the case. See ibid [84].

[172] Similarly Akande (n 47) 65; Milanovic and Hadzi-Vidanovic (n 161) 278; Zamir (n 50) 184.

[173] See, eg, Dutch Minister of Defence, Note to the Senate on Legal aspects of military deployment, Kamerstukken I 2003/2004 29200 X, C (28 April 2004), reproduced in (2005) 36 NYBIL, 348–49; Agreement concerning the service with the United Nations Peace-Keeping Force in Cyprus of the national contingent provided by the Government of Canada (signed 21 February 1966, deemed to have taken effect from 13 March 1964) 555 UNTS 120 [10]. The relevant text is identical to that of the agreements concluded between the UN and the other seven contributing states (Austria, Australia, Denmark, Finland, New Zealand, Sweden, and UK). See also further examples of practice referred to in Zamir (n 50) 185 fns 53–55.

[174] See Section 2.2.2.

[175] *Reparation for Injuries Suffered in the Service of the United Nations* (Advisory Opinion) [1949] ICJ Rep 174, 179.

[176] *Difference relating to Immunity from Legal Process of a Special Rapporteur of the Commission on Human Rights* (Advisory Opinion) [1999] ICJ Rep 62 [66]; see also ILC DARIO (n 160), commentary to Art 3, 13 [3].

[177] ILC DARIO (n 160), Art 7.

[178] ILC ASR (n 17), Art 4.

[179] cf also Zamir (n 50) 178 and 191.

[180] See M Bothe, 'Peacekeeping' in B Simma (ed), *The Charter of the United Nations: A Commentary* (3rd edn, OUP 2012), vol 1, 1190–91; ILC DARIO (n 160), commentary to Art 7, 20 [1].

the UN are subject to its effective control.[181] As a result, the key functional link between an armed force and the contributing state is replaced by a novel link between the force and the UN and, consequently, the force's conduct is attributable to the UN.[182] Troops under the UN chain of command are in a position equivalent to that of UN organs, which has in principle been accepted by the UN itself.[183] Therefore, if the UN uses force through these troops, it becomes a party to the conflict.[184]

The remaining issue is to establish whether an international organization becoming a party to a previously internal armed conflict internationalizes the conflict in terms of the applicable rules of IHL. In order to answer this question, it is first necessary to deal with the objection that due to its privileged position, the UN cannot be subject to the same rules of conduct in war as ordinary belligerents. Then, the next step is to consider whether an international organization may be subject to the law of IAC as it was codified by the GCs, given the prima facie restrictive text of those treaties.

The argument that the UN should be subject to a privileged set of rules or none at all due to its distinct nature and the higher moral ground of its operations has been made repeatedly virtually since the organization was established. Among the early prominent proponents, Hersch Lauterpacht opined that due to its dignity and purpose, 'the collective enforcement of the basic instrument of organized international society [ie, the UN Charter] ... should rank in a category different from war' (thus dissociating it from the application of the laws of war).[185] A committee of the American Society of International Law, which counted Hans Kelsen among its six members, ostensibly led by the same rationale, suggested in 1952 that the UN should not be bound by all laws of war but only *choose* those rules that 'fit its purposes'.[186] In the model agreement with the troop-contributing states issued in the early 1990s, the UN still insisted that it would only observe the 'principles and spirit' of IHL in peacekeeping operations.[187] Notably, in 1999, Kofi Annan as the UN

[181] But cf ILC DARIO (n 160), commentary to Art 7, 22 [8] (noting situations in practice in which, in spite of the formal placement of national contingents under the UN command, these persisted in seeking orders from their home authorities).

[182] ILC DARIO (n 160), commentary to Art 7, 22 [9]. But see, eg, *Attorney-General v Nissan* [1970] AC 179 (House of Lords) 223 per Lord Pearce.

[183] ILC, Responsibility of International Organizations: Comments and Observations Received from International Organizations, UN Doc A/CN.4/545 (25 June 2004) 17–18.

[184] This conclusion is also supported by international practice. See Agreements providing for compensation of damage arising from the conduct of the ONUC forces in the Congo, concluded by the UN with Belgium (535 UNTS 197), Greece (565 UNTS 3), Italy (588 UNTS 197), Luxembourg (585 UNTS 147), and Switzerland (564 UNTS 193); Report of the UN Secretary General: Administrative and Budgetary Aspects of the Financing of United Nations Peacekeeping Operations, UN Doc A/51/389 (20 September 1996) 6 [17]; ILC, Responsibility of International Organizations: Comments and Observations Received from International Organizations, UN Doc A/CN.4/545 (25 June 2004) 17; Dutch Minister of Defence, Note to the Senate on Legal aspects of military deployment, Kamerstukken I 2003/2004 29200 X, C (28 April 2004), reproduced in (2005) 36 NYBIL, 348–49.

[185] H Lauterpacht (ed), *Oppenheim's International Law* (7th edn, Longmans 1952) 224–25.

[186] Report of Committee on Study of Legal Problems of the United Nations, 'Should the Law of War Apply to United Nations Enforcement Action?' (1952) 46 ASIL Proceedings 216, 220.

[187] Model Agreement between the United Nations and Member States Contributing Personnel and Equipment to United Nations Peace-Keeping Operations: Report of the Secretary-General, UN Doc A/46/185 (23 May 1991) [28].

Secretary-General avoided such sweeping terms in a non-binding bulletin on the observance of IHL by the UN forces.[188] Nevertheless, the essence of his proclamation was very much in line with the view of Lauterpacht and Kelsen propounded half a century earlier—the UN chose which norms it deemed applicable to its own operations:

> The fundamental principles and rules of international humanitarian law *set out in the present bulletin* are applicable to United Nations forces when in situations of armed conflict they are actively engaged therein as combatants, to the extent and for the duration of their engagement. They are accordingly applicable in enforcement actions, or in peacekeeping operations when the use of force is permitted in self-defence.[189]

Although the rules listed in the same bulletin represent the main principles of IHL and exceed the protection given in Common Article 3, they still lack the comprehensiveness of the full body of law applicable to IACs.[190]

It is submitted that an exemption from the full application of IHL for one party to the conflict, no matter how noble its aims or dignified its purpose, would significantly diminish the other party's incentive to follow the same norms. Indeed, as Lauterpacht himself observed in a later publication:

> it is impossible to visualize the conduct of hostilities in which one side would be bound by the rules of warfare without benefiting from them and the other side would benefit from the rules of warfare without being bound by them.[191]

Instead of furthering the humanitarian aims of the UN, such an approach would conflate unacceptably the *jus ad bellum* with the *jus in bello*,[192] contravene the principle of equal application of IHL which stands at the core of this body of law,[193] and risk triggering a race to the bottom insofar as the applicability of humanitarian norms is concerned.

Moreover, exempting the UN as such from the full application of IHL would violate the legal maxim *nemo plus juris transferre potest quam ipse habet* (no one can transfer a greater right than he has himself). In the area of IHRL, the ECtHR held expressly that states may not absolve themselves from their responsibility under human rights conventions by establishing international organizations and transferring to them competences that had originally belonged to the concerned states.[194] It is submitted that a similar logic applies to the rules of IHL. Under Common Article 1 and

[188] Secretary-General's Bulletin, 'Observance by United Nations forces of international humanitarian law', UN Doc ST/SGB/1999/13 (6 August 1999).

[189] ibid, s 1 (emphasis added).

[190] See also I Shearer, 'Rules of Conduct During Humanitarian Intervention' (2002) 78 International Law Studies 71, 77.

[191] H Lauterpacht, 'The Limits of the Operation of the Law of War' (1953) 30 BYBIL 206, 242.

[192] cf AP I, preamble (IHL applies 'without any adverse distinction based on the nature or origin of the armed conflict or on the causes espoused by or attributed to the Parties to the conflict').

[193] For a general summary of the principle and its contemporary significance, see A Roberts, 'The Equal Application of the Laws of War: A Principle under Pressure' (2008) 90 IRRC 931; for its relevance to internationalized armed conflicts, see Section 6.2.2.

[194] *Waite and Kennedy v Germany* (App no 26083/94) (1999) 30 EHRR 261 (ECtHR) [67]; *Bosphorus v Ireland* (App no 45036/98) (2006) 42 EHRR 1 (ECtHR) [154].

the corresponding norms of customary international law, states are bound to respect the full extent of IHL 'in all circumstances'.[195] Therefore, they cannot skirt its application in situations of peace enforcement by transferring their power to use force onto an international organization they themselves established—this would amount to attributing to the UN a power which its constituent states did not possess.[196] Hence, the argument that the scope of the rules applicable to the UN forces should significantly differ from those applicable to states flouts the precepts of IHL and general international law alike, and must be rejected. The fact that the UN (or any other such entity) possesses the material capacity to become party to an armed conflict gives rise to its subjective capacity to be bound by IHL.[197]

Finally, the UN is a subject of international law[198]— albeit of derivative nature and with limited legal capacity[199]—that may, by virtue of its establishing document, participate in armed conflicts.[200] As the organization can be a party to a conflict in a way analogous to that of third states, its involvement duly transforms the legal nature of an internal conflict. True, textually the conflict does not occur between two 'High Contracting Parties' to the GCs as required by Common Article 2(1) simply because the UN is not a party to the GCs.[201] However, there are several interpretive routes which suggest that the treaty text is not an insurmountable obstacle in this regard.

Firstly, the UN may be subsumed under the generic term 'Power' used by Common Article 2(3) in reference to a conflict party which is not a party to the GCs.[202] Under this interpretation, provided the UN expressly accepts and applies the provisions of the GCs, it would thereby internationalize the conflict to which it was a party.[203] Notably, a declaration of this kind was issued by the UN with respect to its presence

[195] See also *Nicaragua* (n 48) [220] (confirming that the obligation to respect and to ensure respect for the Conventions derives not only from the Conventions themselves, but is also part of international customary law).

[196] cf also TD Gill, 'Legal and some Political Limitations on the Power of the UN Security Council to Exercise its Enforcement Powers under Chapter VII of the Charter' (1995) 26 NYBIL 33, 82 (making a similar argument in relation to Security Council's obligation to respect humanitarian law in military enforcement action); A Reinisch, 'Developing Human Rights and Humanitarian Law Accountability of the Security Council for the Imposition of Economic Sanctions' (2001) 95 AJIL 851, 858 (making a similar argument in relation to the Security Council's obligation to respect human rights and humanitarian law in adopting economic sanctions).

[197] T Ferraro, 'IHL Applicability to IOs Involved in Peace Operations' (2012) 42 Proceedings of the Bruges Colloquium 15, 17.

[198] *Reparation for Injuries* (n 175) 178.

[199] cf *Legality of the Use by a State of Nuclear Weapons in Armed Conflict* (Advisory Opinion) [1996] ICJ Rep 66, 78 [25].

[200] cf UN Charter, Art 42.

[201] Ferraro and Cameron, 'Article 2' (n 17) 80 fn 47.

[202] cf Common Art 2(3) GCs (stipulating that states parties shall be bound by the Conventions even in relation to a non-party power if it 'accepts and applies the provisions thereof').

[203] However, it is controversial whether the UN may qualify as a 'power' under Common Article 2(3): compare, eg, D Schindler, 'The Different Types of Armed Conflicts According to the Geneva Conventions and Protocols' (1979) 163 Recueil des Cours 117, 130; F Seyersted, *United Nations Forces in the Law of Peace and War* (AW Sijthoff 1966) 350 and 383 (both in favour); with D Shraga, 'The United Nations as an Actor Bound by International Humanitarian Law' (1998) 5(2) International Peacekeeping 64, 67; M Zwanenburg, *Accountability Of Peace Support Operations* (Martinus Nijhoff 2005) 136–37 (both against).

in the Congo in 1962.[204] Accordingly, the UN may unilaterally trigger the application of the law of IAC with respect to conflicts in which it intervenes.

However, in many situations, such proclamations have not been made and will not be forthcoming. The second possible interpretive route is thus to construe Common Article 2(1) broadly—taking into account the humanitarian aim underlying both the conventional norms of IHL and the UN Charter—to include hostilities between a High Contracting Party (the non-consenting territorial state) and an international organization entrusted with maintaining collective security by states who are all High Contracting Parties themselves.[205] On that basis, the UN would be seen as a party to an IAC governed by the GCs even without a previously made declaration under Common Article 2(3).

Thirdly, even on a strict interpretation of the treaty terms,[206] the UN should at the very least be considered a party to an IAC governed by customary IHL.[207] For the purposes of conflict internationalization, the resulting legal situation would be the same even under this fallback solution. In other words, the intervention of the UN forces would trigger the applicability of the law of IAC and thus internationalize the underlying conflict.

In sum, on the basis of the foregoing it can be concluded that as long as the command and control over the intervening forces rests with the UN—as it largely did during the peace enforcement operations in the Congo (1961) and Somalia (1993)[208] —such conflicts should properly be seen as internationalized in the sense proposed by this book.[209]

2.3 Dissolution

This section focuses on the effects of the original NIAC and examines to what extent they can bring about internationalization without the involvement of

[204] See Letter from the UN Secretary-General to the ICRC reproduced in (1962) 2 IRRC 29, 29. This public communication followed a series of appeals made to the UN by the ICRC, demanding the widest possible application of IHL to UN operations. See, eg, Letter from President of ICRC to UN Secretary-General (8 November 1961), ICRC Archives, BAG 202-223-003.

[205] See further K Mačák and N Zamir, 'The Applicability of International Humanitarian Law to the Conflict in Libya' (2012) 14 International Community Law Review 403, 416–18.

[206] cf, eg, Ferraro and Cameron, 'Article 2' (n 17) 80 fn 47 ('[i]nternational organizations cannot be signatories of the Geneva Conventions and thus cannot become High Contracting Parties').

[207] Mačák and Zamir (n 205) 416 fn 84; Milanovic and Hadzi-Vidanovic (n 161) 278; Milanovic, '"Transnational" and "Mixed" Conflicts' (n 50) 40 [46]; M Zwanenburg, 'United Nations and International Humanitarian Law' in R Wolfrum (ed), *Max Planck Encyclopedia of Public International Law* (OUP 2008) <www.mpepil.com> (updated October 2015), [6]; Ferraro and Cameron, 'Article 2' (n 17) 80 fn 47; Zamir (n 50) 175.

[208] See notes 156–57 and the accompanying text in this chapter.

[209] cf also Seyersted (n 203) 212–14 (arguing that the UN intervention in the Congo civil war constituted an IAC between the UN and the Katangese forces); K Okimoto, 'Violations of International Humanitarian Law by United Nations Forces and their Legal Consequences' (2003) 6 YIHL 199, 217–18 (arguing that the UN forces in the Congo and in Somalia were subject to the law of belligerent occupation); Akande (n 47) 69 (arguing that the hostilities between the UN forces and the Congolese armed forces amounted to an IAC).

any external forces. Eruption and escalation of hostilities during an internal armed conflict often produce effects domestically and abroad which may transform the conflict's nature, rendering rules governing international conflicts applicable to the situation. This section examines, in particular, the effects of dissolution of a state on whose territory the conflict is underway and the destabilizing effect an armed conflict may have on its surrounding region.

2.3.1 Disintegration

In addition to contest over control or power within a state, one of the most frequent causes of internal conflict is a struggle of a non-state actor for independence from the central government. If the insurgents succeed, and a new state emerges while the conflict is still underway (which has happened during some of the decolonization wars), the nature of that conflict changes. It is no longer an internal armed conflict between the insurgents and the established government, but rather an IAC between two sovereign states. Similarly, an internal armed conflict may evolve into an IAC if—instead of one state seceding from another—a state dissolves into two or more independent states (the leading example here is the former Yugoslavia).

It is generally accepted that state secession is a legally neutral act (neither legal nor illegal) and that only its consequences have legal significance from the perspective of international law.[210] Internationalization of an armed conflict may conceivably be one of those consequences—provided that the secession is successful and a new state is formed before the end of the hostilities.[211] As illustrated by the *Åland Islands* case,[212] pre-1945 international law required the seceding state-to-be to govern its territory effectively and with sufficient stability before it could be recognized as a state.[213] By implication, the original state would have either abandoned the armed struggle for the seceded territory or would have been defeated militarily.[214] As a result, those aspiring to independence could not achieve it until after the armed conflict had ended—whether by reaching a peace agreement or through the defeat of the parent state's forces.

Control over territory still is, in principle, a precondition for a claim to statehood in international law.[215] However, after the Second World War, in several internal

[210] H Lauterpacht, *Recognition in International Law* (CUP 1947) 8; J Crawford, *The Creation of States in International Law* (2nd edn, OUP 2006) 390; but see, eg, J Dugard and D Raič, 'The Role of Recognition in the Law and Practice of Secession' in MG Kohen (ed), *Secession: International Law Perspectives* (CUP 2006) 102–04. In its 2010 advisory opinion on Kosovo, the ICJ refused to discuss the legality of state secession: cf *Accordance with International Law of the Unilateral Declaration of Independence in respect of Kosovo* (Advisory Opinion) [2010] ICJ Rep 141 [56].

[211] cf also Akande (n 47) 43; Milanovic, '"Transnational" and "Mixed" Conflicts' (n 50) 35 [27]; Ferraro and Cameron, 'Article 2' (n 17) 84 [231].

[212] *Åland Islands Case* (1920) League of Nations Official Journal Spec Supp 3, 9 (holding that Finland did not become a state 'until a stable political organisation had been created' which was in 'May, 1918, [when] the civil war ended').

[213] Crawford (n 210) 383; see also WV Harcourt, *Letters by Historicus on Some Questions of International Law* (Macmillan 1863) 9.

[214] cf Crawford (n 210) 382 (stating that third states could only recognize a seceding territory as a state if 'there was no real likelihood of the previous sovereign reasserting its position').

[215] ibid 59.

armed conflicts the independence of the emerging state was generally recognized well before the end of the conflict and thus before stability and permanence of control could be established.[216] These conflicts generally belong to two broad categories, namely (1) state secession in the decolonization context, and (2) irreversible state dissolution.[217] With regard to these two categories, whether or not the conflict parties recognize one another as a state is irrelevant for the purposes of conflict qualification under IHL.[218]

2.3.1.1 State secession of self-determination units

To begin with, state practice shows that a state can emerge during an ongoing internal conflict, if the emerging entity is a distinct political unit to which the principle of self-determination applies (a 'self-determination unit').[219] It should be noted that if Article 1(4) of Additional Protocol I was applicable to such a situation, the conflict would be internationalized already by virtue of the legal fiction stipulated in that provision, irrespective of whether a new state would successfully form or not.[220] However, for reasons described later in this work, the application of Article 1(4) AP I in practice has so far been extremely limited.[221]

Nevertheless, the emergence of new states during national liberation wars has alleviated the need for a legal fiction that two entities with full international personality are involved in the conflict. A good example in this regard is Guinea-Bissau's struggle for independence from Portugal (1963–74). The liberation movement of Guinea-Bissau emerged in 1963 and by the end of 1973, it had achieved effective control over most (but not all) of the territory. At that point, it had also been recognized as a state by forty states and the UN General Assembly.[222] The conflict between the rebels and the parent state continued for a few more months until Portugal finally pledged to recognize Guinea-Bissau's independence in August 1974. However,

[216] It is a matter of controversy whether recognition by third states is constitutive of statehood under international law. Throughout this book, it is presumed that if the objective conditions of statehood are met, recognition serves only as evidence of legal status. However, if recognition is entirely or nearly entirely lacking in relation to a specific entity, eg, the Turkish Republic of Northern Cyprus or historically the South African Bantustan states, such an entity's claim to statehood is severely undermined as it would not be able to demonstrate its capacity to enter into relations with other states, which is one of the customary conditions of statehood, as reflected in the Montevideo Convention. This is the perspective from which the presence or absence of third-state recognition is considered in the following text. See further Crawford (n 210) 27; Dugard and Raič (n 210) 98–99; Montevideo Convention on the Rights and Duties of States (signed 26 December 1933, entered into force 26 December 1934) 165 LNTS 19, Art 1.

[217] The following analysis draws on James Crawford's authoritative overview of state practice in relation to state secession, updated with respect to post-2006 practice. cf Crawford (n 210) 383–418.

[218] Ferraro and Cameron, 'Article 2' (n 17) 84 [231]; but see Section 2.3.1.3 (on the theoretical possibility that the parent state accepts the statehood of a seceding unit).

[219] On the term 'self-determination unit', see Crawford (n 210) 115–21, 124–28.

[220] See Section 2.4.

[221] See Section 2.4.3 and Section 2.4.5.

[222] UNGA Res 3061 (XXVIII) (Illegal Occupation by Portuguese Military Forces of Certain Sectors of the Republic of Guinea-Bissau and Acts of Aggression Committed by Them Against the People of the Republic) (2 November 1973) [1].

Guinea-Bissau's statehood was widely believed to have been established well before then.[223]

Although the traditional requirements of stability and permanence, as the corollaries of the principle of territorial integrity, may not be fully met in cases such as Guinea-Bissau's, state practice indicates that these are trumped by the principle of self-determination. Consequently, in such situations, a state may emerge while a conflict is still underway.[224] In practice, this outcome has been contingent on the reaction of third states. Thus, in the example discussed in this section, the recognition of third states had affirmed Guinea-Bissau's statehood prior to Portugal's concession of defeat.

The applicable criteria for state recognition (popular support and territorial control) are analogous to those for recognition of belligerency. James Crawford's suggestion that in such cases, recognition of statehood might have replaced recognition of belligerency[225] may be welcomed as a potential contribution to the confluence of the rules on modalities of internationalization.[226] However, it should be noted that the process of decolonization is now considered to be complete (perhaps with the exception of Western Sahara).[227] Since the principle of self-determination of peoples gained prominence primarily in this specific context,[228] and its validity in the post-decolonization period is a matter of controversy,[229] this mode of internationalization will in the future likely be sporadic to non-existent.

2.3.1.2 Irreversible state dissolution

Outside of the context of self-determination struggles, the only type of situation in which new states emerge during an internal conflict is in cases of irreversible state dissolution complemented by the extinction of the parent state, such as the dissolution of Yugoslavia in the early 1990s.[230] Before examining the salient features of this case, a distinction needs to be made between irreversible dissolution and situations in which the parent state continues to exist.

Successful unilateral secessions against the wishes of the parent state have been very scarce in the period after the Second World War.[231] Perhaps the only universally

[223] Crawford (n 210) 386 and sources cited therein. [224] ibid 387. [225] ibid.

[226] See further Section 2.5.1 (discussing recognition of belligerency as a self-standing modality of internationalization).

[227] cf E Benvenisti, *The International Law of Occupation* (2nd edn, OUP 2012) 171–72.

[228] cf *Legal Consequences for States of the Continued Presence of South Africa in Namibia (South West Africa) notwithstanding Security Council Resolution 276* (1970) (Advisory Opinion) [1971] ICJ Rep 16, 31; *Western Sahara* (Advisory Opinion) [1975] ICJ Rep 12, 31.

[229] cf G Simpson, 'The Diffusion of Sovereignty: Self-Determination in the Post-Colonial Age' (1996) 32 Stan J Int'l L 255; K Knop, *Diversity and Self-Determination in International Law* (CUP 2002) 18; J Castellino, 'International Law and Self-Determination', in C Walter, A von Ungern-Sternberg, and K Abushov (eds), *Self-Determination and Secession in International Law* (OUP 2014) 30.

[230] For previous attempts to define dissolution in this sense in international law, see, eg, Vienna Convention on Succession of States in Respect of State Property, Archives and Debts (signed 8 April 1983, not yet in force) UN Doc A/Conf 117/14, Art 18; ILC Articles on Nationality of Natural Persons in Relation to the Succession of States, UN Doc A/54/10 (3 April 1999), Art 22.

[231] Crawford (n 210) 390.

accepted exception in this regard is the case of Bangladesh.[232] By 1973, Bangladesh had been recognized as state by over 100 states and admitted to the Commonwealth, while facing continued opposition from Pakistan.[233] (Bangladesh's statehood was only recognized by Pakistan in February 1974.[234]) However, Bangladesh only achieved attributes of statehood and broad state recognition well *after* the close of hostilities, which had ended already in December 1971.[235]

A more recent, but also more controversial, case is the one of Kosovo's unilateral declaration of independence (UDI) in 2008.[236] Nevertheless, even if Kosovo was considered to have gained independence from Serbia and, consequently, statehood,[237] this would still have happened long after the end of the armed conflict between the Kosovo Liberation Army and the Serbian-Yugoslavian armed forces in 1999.[238]

Another potential recent example is the situation of Palestine. One may certainly make a plausible case in favour of Palestinian statehood, especially following the UN General Assembly vote to grant it 'non-member observer State status' in 2012.[239] This is generally understood as the General Assembly's recognition of Palestine as a sovereign state.[240] Moreover, it has been said that the prevailing view among states and scholars is now in favour of considering Palestine as an independent state.[241] Nonetheless, as is the case with many other aspects of the Israeli/Palestinian conflict, this view is certainly not universally accepted.[242] In any event, even if Palestine has by now become a state, it would be erroneous to consider this to be the result of *secession* from a parent state. Israel is not the parent state vis-à-vis Palestine; it may at best be considered as the occupying power exercising control over the occupied Palestinian territories[243] (which have been repeatedly described as 'territories with a

[232] cf JJA Salmon, 'Naissance et Reconnaissance du Bangladesh' in J Tittel (ed), *Multitudo legum, lex unum: Mélanges en honneur de Wilhelm Wengler* (Interrecht 1973) vol I, 467–90; Crawford (n 210) 140–43 and 390; J Dugard, *The Secession of States and Their Recognition in the Wake of Kosovo* (Brill 2013) 187–91.

[233] Dugard and Raič (n 210) 121–22; but see J Vidmar, 'Palestine and the Conceptual Problem of Implicit Statehood' (2013) 12 Chinese JIL 19, 25–26 and 30.

[234] E Tepper, 'The New Pakistan: Problems and Prospects' (1974) 47 Pacific Affairs 56, 59 fn 2b.

[235] Dugard and Raič (n 210) 121–22.

[236] Assembly of Kosovo, 'Kosovo Declaration of Independence' (17 February 2008) <www.assembly-kosova.org/?cid=2,128,1635>.

[237] cf Vidmar (n 233) 30 (considering Kosovo to be an example of an entity with ambiguous legal status: '[f]or some it is a State, for others it is not') (internal footnotes omitted).

[238] The 2010 ICJ advisory opinion concluded only that the UDI issued two years earlier did not violate any applicable rule of international law. The opinion expressly excluded the question whether or not Kosovo had achieved statehood following the UDI. *Kosovo* Advisory Opinion (n 210) [51], [123(3)].

[239] UNGA Res 67/19 (Status of Palestine in the United Nations) (4 December 2012) [2].

[240] See, eg, E Kontorovich, 'Israel/Palestine: The ICC's Uncharted "Territory"' (2013) 11 JICJ 979, 979–80.

[241] See, eg, A Zimmermann, 'Palestine and the International Criminal Court Quo Vadis?' (2013) 11 JICJ 303, Y Ronen, 'Israel, Palestine and the ICC: Territory Uncharted but Not Unknown' (2014) 12 JICJ 7, 8–9 fn 4–5; cf Whitman, 'Palestine's Statehood and Ability to Litigate in the International Court of Justice: Comment' (2013) 44 California Western International Law Journal 73, 77–87; K Ambos, 'Palestine, UN Non-Member Observer Status and ICC Jurisdiction' (6 May 2014) <www.ejiltalk.org/palestine-un-non-member-observer-status-and-icc-jurisdiction/>.

[242] See, eg, JHH Weiler, 'Differentiated Statehood? "Pre-States"? Palestine@the UN' (2013) 24 EJIL 1, 3–4; Vidmar (n 233) 40–41.

[243] *Wall* (n 16) [78].

controversial international status'[244]). However, Israel has never been the territorial sovereign with regard to these territories.[245] Therefore, even assuming *arguendo* that Palestine has emerged as an independent state during the Israeli-Palestinian armed conflict, it would in any event not be an example of a successful secession from a parent state in the sense discussed here.

In sum, it appears that no state has ever achieved statehood during an armed conflict if the parent state continued to exist after the war. It may thus be concluded that in the present state of the law, such situations would not be internationalized by way of state disintegration. Rather, in the absence of other internationalizing factors, they should be viewed as situations to which the law of NIAC continues to apply.

Conversely, in cases of irreversible dissolution of the parent state, the issue of consent given by that state becomes irrelevant.[246] Logically, if a conflict leads to the destruction of the central authority which would speak on behalf of the former state, the consent of that state cannot be plausibly solicited. This impossibility of granting consent distinguishes the situation of complete state breakdown from a mere unilateral secession, as was the case of Bangladesh and, perhaps, Kosovo.[247] The obvious and (in spite of the ICTY's oft-cited but unsubstantiated statement suggesting otherwise[248]) so far the only example of the former in the post-1945 practice is the breakdown of the Socialist Federal Republic of Yugoslavia (SFRY).

Although the hostilities in Yugoslavia ended with the Dayton Peace Agreement in November 1995,[249] Member States of the European Community (the predecessor of today's European Union) had recognized the statehood of the newly emergent states of Slovenia, Croatia, Macedonia, and Bosnia and Herzegovina much earlier.[250] For the most part, these instances of recognition occurred already between December 1991 (Germany's unilateral recognition of Slovenia and Croatia) and December 1993 (EU Member States' recognition of Macedonia).[251] Significantly, in *Tadić*, a trial chamber of the ICTY accepted expressly the international nature of the conflict between the SFRY successor states (Bosnia and Herzegovina on the one side, and

[244] M Bothe, KJ Partsch, and WA Solf, *New Rules for Victims of Armed Conflicts: Commentary on the Two 1977 Protocols Additional to the Geneva Conventions of 1949* (Martinus Nijhoff 1982) 51–52; Roberts (n 38) 254–55; Ferraro and Cameron, 'Article 2' (n 17) 115 [325].

[245] Benvenisti (n 227) 203–04; Crawford (n 210) 434; but see, eg, M Koskenniemi, 'Occupied Zone: A Zone of Reasonableness' (2008) 41 Isr L Rev 13, 29–40 (arguing that the gradual extension of Israeli jurisdiction to the occupied territories has resulted in the Israeli authorities exercising sovereign powers in a functional way).

[246] Crawford (n 210) 418.

[247] This distinction is not new to international law: cf Vienna Convention on Succession of States in Respect of Treaties (signed 23 August 1978, entered into force 6 November 1996) 1946 UNTS 3, Arts 34–35.

[248] *Tadić* Appeal Judgment (n 63) [166] ('in modern inter-ethnic armed conflicts such as that in the former Yugoslavia, *new States are often created during the conflict* and ethnicity rather than nationality may become the grounds for allegiance.') (emphasis added).

[249] Bosnia and Herzegovina-Croatia-Yugoslavia, General Framework Agreement for Peace in Bosnia and Herzegovina with Annexes (entered into force 14 December 1995) (1996) 35 ILM 75.

[250] See also Crawford (n 210) 395–401.

[251] See further R Caplan, *Europe and the Recognition of New States in Yugoslavia* (CUP 2005) 15–48.

Serbia and Montenegro on the other) 'from the beginning of 1992', affirming that by that point they must have each acquired independent statehood.[252]

In summary, the conditions of stability and permanence, insofar as these may have been required in the past, have in the case of the breakup of Yugoslavia given way to an overriding concern for the effectiveness of international law. It is submitted that this is the correct outcome. Indeed, in the absence of a central government acting on behalf of the predecessor state, the continuation of hostilities between the new states should not stand in the way of their taking on duties and responsibilities within the international community.

2.3.1.3 Acceptance by parent state

Besides these two rare categories of cases, it is possible to conceive of an even more exceptional and a virtually theoretical modality of internationalization. Specifically, the predecessor state could accept and recognize the statehood of the emerging entity. If that entity fulfilled the objective criteria of statehood, its existence as a state would be affirmed by the parent state's recognition, despite there still being a situation of armed conflict between the two. However, this possibility is very likely only of theoretical nature given that the struggle for independence is typically the actual cause of the internal conflict. Even if the incumbent state did desire to elevate the insurgents' status, it would most certainly prefer a mode less damaging to its territorial integrity, such as recognition of belligerency[253] or an agreement based on Common Article 3 of the GCs.[254]

2.3.2 Destabilization

Far too frequently, armed violence spreads like contagion, with little consideration given to territorial borders that may lie in its way. A civil war occasions a state of lawlessness which may extend beyond the state where the war had originated. Governmental and insurgent armed forces may temporarily make use of the neighbouring states' territories for tactical reasons. Outside states may decide to support one of the parties to the conflict with the aim to protect their national interests. Fighting may erupt outside the borders of the state of origin, but along the same ethnic lines as in the original conflict. Yet, all of these forms of regional destabilization can be subsumed under one of the other modalities of internationalization—or easily distinguished from them.[255]

[252] *Tadić* Trial Judgment (n 62) [569]; see also *Prosecutor v Slobodan Milošević* (Decision on Motion for Judgment of Acquittal) IT-02-54-T (16 June 2004) [85]–[115]; *Prlić* Appeal Judgement (n 49) vol 1 [247].

[253] See Section 2.5.1.

[254] See Section 2.5.2.

[255] Use of force in another state's territory without its consent renders the conflict international (see Section 2.2.2.1). Outside support of armed forces fighting a civil war depends on the object and the intensity of the support (see Sections 2.2.2.2–2.2.2.4). Finally, an eruption of parallel fighting along the same ethnic lines but without a further cross-border element would not change the nature of any of the conflicts—legally speaking they would be independent of each other.

What remains is the case of regional destabilization due to massive refugee flows. For instance, in 1994 the Tutsi-dominated insurgent group Rwandan Patriotic Front (RPF) took control of Rwanda and stopped an unprecedented genocide perpetrated mainly by Rwandan Hutus against Tutsis. Hutu civilians in Rwanda, fearing reciprocal violence, fled to eastern Zaire (now the Democratic Republic of the Congo) in the hundreds of thousands. Their arrival polarized the relatively harmonious relations between Zairian Hutus and Tutsis, led to the further persecution of the local Tutsis, and finally to a spike in interethnic violence in Zaire, destabilizing the region for years to come.[256]

Although the flow of refugees does not per se export violence across borders, it has been suggested that it can internationalize the armed conflict at the source of such migration. Writing expressly in the context of applicability of IHL, Emily Crawford put 'the flow of refugees from a war zone across state borders' on par with foreign intervention as a possible mode of conflict internationalization.[257] The observation that cross-border displacement of populations brings about conflict internationalization is found also in the work of other scholars and documents of international organizations.[258] Although these other texts have used a rather more flexible understanding of 'internationalization' of armed conflicts, their existence justifies the further exploration of this question.

Large population movements caused by internal strife adversely affect countries surrounding the unstable state. The UN Group of Governmental Experts on International Co-operation to Avert New Flows of Refugees, established by the General Assembly in 1981,[259] observed that flows of refugees

> may affect the political and social stability, as well as the economic development, of the receiving States, and also carry adverse consequences for the economies of the countries of origin and entire regions, thus endangering international peace and security.[260]

One of the members of the same UN expert group, Luke Lee, wrote at around the same time that because endangering international peace and security violates Article 1 and Chapter VII of the UN Charter, 'an act generating refugee flows' must be seen as an internationally wrongful act which activates the international responsibility of the state concerned.[261] As a result, even an internal conflict producing refugees

256 SK Lischer, *Dangerous Sanctuaries: Refugee Camps, Civil War, and the Dilemmas of Humanitarian Aid* (Cornell University Press 2005) 14.

257 E Crawford, 'Unequal before the Law: The Case for the Elimination of the Distinction between International and Non-International Armed Conflicts' (2007) 20 LJIL 441, 446 fn 23.

258 See, eg, NM Blokker and M Kleiboer, 'The Internationalization of Domestic Conflict: The Role of the UN Security Council' (1996) 9 LJIL 7, 32; JN Abuodha, 'Sovereignty with Responsibility: A Critical Analysis of State Sovereignty in the context of International Humanitarian Intervention in Internal Conflicts' (2007) 1 Kenya Law Review 252, 260; United Nations Secretary-General's Report on the Protection of Civilians in Armed Conflict, UN Doc S/2001/331 (30 March 2001) [28].

259 UNGA Res 36/148 (International Co-operation to Avert New Flows of Refugees) (16 December 1981) [4].

260 UNGA, International Co-operation to Avert New Flows of Refugees, UN Doc A/41/324 (13 May 1986), Annex, 16 [63].

261 L Lee, 'Toward a World Without Refugees: The United Nations Group of Governmental Experts on International Co-operation to Avert New Flows of Refugees' (1986) 57 BYBIL 317, 331–32.

should be elevated to the international plane, permitting outside states to respond individually or collectively.[262] In a similar vein, India attempted to justify its 1971 invasion of East Pakistan (now Bangladesh) as a response to 'a kind of aggression', namely Pakistan's instigation of the exodus of over ten million refugees from that territory:

> If aggression against another foreign country means that it strains its social structure, that it ruins its finances, that it has to give up its territory for sheltering the refugees ... what is the difference between that kind of aggression and the other type, the more classical type, when someone declares war[?][263]

Extending this line of argument, it could be averred that the effects of refugee flows on other states remove the internal conflict from the *domaine réservé* of one state, thereby rendering the conflict international in nature and triggering the application of the whole body of IHL. One can see that this type of reasoning could influence the qualification of several modern conflicts and particularly the ongoing armed conflict in Syria (2011–), which has already occasioned the flight of over five million refugees to the neighbouring countries and beyond.[264]

Accordingly, both the premise and the extension of the argument must be examined. Lee assumes the international responsibility of the state for refugee displacements. However, even in an internal armed conflict involving the state's military—a state organ under Article 4 ILC ASR[265]—it is unlikely that the population displacement could be traced back to a single 'act generating refugee flows'.[266] Mass population movements are complex phenomena resulting from a multitude of interlinked and independent causes, including, inter alia, the conduct of the non-state party (or parties) to the conflict. It would often be difficult if not impossible to isolate the exact act attributable to the state in order to trigger its international responsibility.[267] The argument that refugee flows are potentially a vehicle of conflict internationalization was further undermined by the fact that no other member of the international community supported the Indian-invented notion of 'refugee aggression'.[268]

Nevertheless, even if refugee flows did invoke the international responsibility of the state concerned, internationalization of the armed conflict for the purposes of IHL would not follow. The Security Council has already considered purely internal conflict situations to be a threat to peace and international security yet there is no doubt that these continued to be non-international for the purposes of IHL (provided none of the other factors of internationalization were applicable, of course).[269]

[262] ibid 332.

[263] UN Doc S/PV.1606 (4 December 1971) 15 [161] (India).

[264] UNHCR, 'Global Trends: Forced Displacement in 2016' (19 June 2017) <www.unhcr.org/5943e8a34.pdf>, at 3.

[265] cf ILC ASR (n 17), commentary to Art 4, 40 [6].

[266] cf Lee (n 261) 331.

[267] cf *Prosecutor v Milutinović et al* (Trial Judgment) IT-05-87-T (26 February 2009), vol 3, 13–17 (demonstrating the difficulty in identifying causality in the context of migration flows allegedly triggered by the military action in Kosovo).

[268] The UN 'Definition of Aggression', adopted only three years later by the General Assembly, does not mention the act generating refugee flows (or any variant thereof) among the defined acts of aggression. See UNGA Res 3314 (XXIX) (Definition of Aggression) (14 December 1974), Art 3.

[269] See UNSC Res 794 (3 December 1992) (considering that 'the magnitude of the human tragedy caused by the conflict in Somalia' constitutes a threat to international peace and security). The conflict

More crucially, this study has repeatedly emphasized that, in principle, for a conflict to be internationalized, two states must be involved in the conflict against each other. Even though other states are affected by refugee flows, and sometimes greatly so, as the Rwandan-Zairian and the Syrian examples so aptly demonstrate, this does not by itself transform the affected third states into parties to the original internal armed conflict. Furthermore, the legal nature of a conflict marked by population displacement does not differ from other internal armed conflicts in terms of the underlying motivation behind states' reluctance to extend the rules governing international conflicts to non-international ones, namely the 'fear' (in the words of the ICRC) that the observance of these rules would interfere with the government's lawful prerogative to suppress a revolt.[270] On the basis of the foregoing, it can thus be concluded that in contemporary international law, refugee flows do not internationalize internal armed conflicts for the purposes of application of IHL.

2.4 Wars of National Liberation

In 1977, at the terminal stage of decolonization, states party to Additional Protocol I to the Geneva Conventions carved out a category of internal conflicts and, by way of legal fiction, proclaimed it international in nature. Article 1(4) of the new Protocol stipulated that 'armed conflicts which peoples are fighting against colonial domination and alien occupation and against racist regimes in the exercise of their right of self-determination' fall within the material scope of the instrument, which was otherwise limited to IACs.[271] In theory, this provision was meant to internationalize qualifying conflicts in the territories of states parties to the Protocol without the need for any further international element. In reality, the provision was heavily criticized for its political and subjective nature and has seen very limited, if any, application in practice.

2.4.1 Historical context

Strictly as a matter of descriptive accuracy, one could well attach the label 'wars of national liberation' already to the eighteenth-century armed struggles motivated by nationalist passions such as the Corsican insurrection against the Genoese (1729–36) or, indeed, the American War of Independence (1775–83).[272] However, the term only gained its legal valence in the process of decolonization in the 1960s and 1970s.[273] During that period, developing countries were stepping up their demands

in Somalia—at least until the SC authorized in 1993 the UN forces operating there to use enforcement powers (see note 157 in this chapter)—is considered to be an example par excellence of a NIAC. See, eg, Moir (n 50) 39; R Provost, *International Human Rights and Humanitarian Law* (CUP 2002) 267.

[270] See Pictet, *GC III Commentary* (n 40) 44.

[271] cf AP I, title ('Protocol Additional to the Geneva Conventions of 12 August 1949, and relating to the Protection of Victims of *International Armed Conflicts*') (emphasis added).

[272] SC Neff, *War and the Law of Nations* (CUP 2005) 206.

[273] DW Glazier, 'Wars of National Liberation' in R Wolfrum (ed), *Max Planck Encyclopedia of Public International Law* (OUP 2008) <www.mpepil.com> (updated May 2009) [1].

that wars waged for the purpose of 'national liberation' be subject to the full scope of IHL.[274] The concept of national liberation found its legal basis in the principle of self-determination, which had been enshrined in Article 1(2) of the UN Charter[275] and which was further developed by the 1970 Friendly Relations Declaration.[276] The latter even specifically referred to forcible resistance against colonial powers as an exercise of the right to self-determination.[277]

At the same time, wars of national liberation were increasingly seen by a variety of international actors as conflicts with a just cause.[278] However, although liberation movements were often eager to apply the rules of IHL,[279] they lacked the appropriate legal mechanism to do so.[280] For example, during the Algerian war of independence (1954–62), the Provisional Government of the Algerian Republic submitted a declaration of accession to the GCs to Switzerland as the depositary of the GCs.[281] Switzerland, however, declined to regard the accession as effective, citing the lack of international recognition for the provisional government.[282]

The demands culminated during the 1974–77 Diplomatic Conference in Geneva, at which a broad coalition consisting mostly of developing states pressed for the extension of the GCs to wars of national liberation.[283] Although Article 1(4) of Protocol I was adopted with the aim to resolve this problem and provide for such

[274] See UNGA Res 2105 (XX) (Implementation of the Declaration on the Granting of Independence to Colonial Countries and Peoples) (20 December 1965) [10]; UNGA Res 2621 (XXV) (Programme of Action for the Full Implementation of the Declaration on the Granting of Independence to Colonial Countries and Peoples) (12 December 1970) [3(6)(a)]; UNGA Res 3103 (XXVIII) (Basic Principles of the Legal Status of the Combatants Struggling against Colonial and Alien Domination and Racist Regimes) (12 December 1973), Art 3.

[275] UN Charter, Art 1(2) (listing, as one of the purposes of the UN, the development of 'friendly relations among nations based on respect for the principle of equal rights and *self-determination of peoples*') (emphasis added).

[276] UNGA Res 2625 (XXV) (Declaration on Principles of International Law Concerning Friendly Relations and Co-operation among States in accordance with the Charter of the United Nations) (24 October 1970), Annex, [1(5)] (hereafter Friendly Relations Declaration).

[277] ibid.

[278] See, eg, G Ginsburgs, '"Wars of National Liberation" and the Modern Law of Nations: The Soviet Thesis' (1964) 29(4) Law and Contemporary Problems 910, 932–33; ICRC, *Conference of Government Experts on the Reaffirmation and Development of International Humanitarian Law Applicable in Armed Conflicts, 24 May–12 June 1971* (ICRC 1971) vol V ('Protection of Victims of Non-International Armed Conflicts') 28; Bothe et al (n 244) 40.

[279] See, eg, SWAPO, 'Namibia and the International Rule of Law', CONF.DAKAR/NDH/76/IV/a (International Institute of Human Rights 1976) 9 ('the Namibian Liberation Army must—and does—comply with the laws of and customs of war as set out, in particular, in the Geneva Conventions of 1949').

[280] See, eg, J Dugard, 'International Terrorism and the Just War' (1977) 12 Stanford Journal of International Studies 21, 33.

[281] Algerian Provisional Government, Instruments of Accession of the Algerian Republic to the Geneva Conventions of August 12, 1949 (11 April 1960), reproduced in M Bedjaoui, *Law and the Algerian Revolution* (International Association of Democratic Lawyers 1961) 199; see further ibid 183–84 for the specific mechanism through which the declaration was transmitted to Switzerland.

[282] Switzerland, 'Algerien und die Genfer Abkommen' ['Algeria and the Geneva Conventions'], Neue Zürcher Zeitung (28 July 1960) 3, cited in S Talmon, *Recognition of Governments in International Law: With Particular Reference to Governments in Exile* (OUP 1998) 123–24 fn 37.

[283] Switzerland, *Official Records of the Diplomatic Conference on the Reaffirmation and Development of International Humanitarian Law Applicable in Armed Conflicts, Geneva (1974–1977)* (Federal Political Department 1978) vol VIII, CDDH/I/SR.13, 97–102 (hereafter *Official Records*).

a legal mechanism, its wording gave rise to further controversy in at least three important areas, which are considered in the following subsections.

2.4.2 Material scope of application

To begin with, it is unclear from the drafters' choice of wording to which conflicts this provision actually applies. The subject of the clause, 'peoples' is undefined in the Protocol and one would search in vain for a generally accepted definition elsewhere in international law.[284] Although the term appears in several provisions of the UN Charter, its meaning in that instrument varies from a synonym for 'states' in the preamble to simply 'inhabitants' with respect to non-self-governing territories regulated by Chapter XI.[285] The text of Article 1(4) AP I thus regrettably brings about interpretive ambiguity already at the point of identifying who is supposedly endowed with rights and duties as a party to this type of conflict.

It has been suggested that the provision covers any 'internal conflict ... directed towards self-government',[286] but such an interpretation likely goes too far. It is recalled that Article 1(4) AP I specifically requires that the 'peoples' must be engaged in the conflict in question 'in the exercise of their right of self-determination'.[287] The entity in question thus must be a beneficiary of the right of self-determination as understood in the UN Charter and the Friendly Relations Declaration.[288] Although, as stated previously, the Charter is not particularly helpful in this regard, the Declaration expressly bestows this right upon peoples living under colonial domination.[289] Some groups, such as the populations of Western Sahara or East Timor, have thus been subsequently designated by the ICJ as 'peoples' in this sense without any notable opposition or controversy.[290] All of this indicates that Article 1(4) AP I applies only if the territorial state acts in violation of the principle of equal rights and self-determination of peoples stipulated in the Declaration, evidenced by the absence of 'a government representing the whole people belonging to the territory without distinction as to race, creed or colour'.[291] By contrast, armed groups that fight against an established government which is representative of the whole people remain subject to the law of NIAC.[292]

284 cf Y Sandoz, C Swinarski, and B Zimmermann (eds), *Commentary on the Additional Protocols of 8 June 1977 to the Geneva Conventions of 12 August 1949* (ICRC 1987) 52 [103] (hereafter Sandoz et al, *APs Commentary*).

285 See, eg, Art 73 UN Charter.

286 LC Green, 'Low-Intensity Conflict and the Law' (1997) 3 ILSA Journal of International & Comparative Law 493, 503.

287 Art 1(4) AP I. 288 ibid. 289 Friendly Relations Declaration (n 276) [1(5)].

290 See *Western Sahara* (n 228) [70]; *East Timor (Portugal v Australia)* (Judgment) [1995] ICJ Rep 90 [31]. See also text to notes 303–05 and 342–44 in this chapter (concerning the qualification of the conflict in Western Sahara).

291 Friendly Relations Declaration (n 276) [1(5)]; accord Schindler (n 203) 137; HA Wilson, *International Law and the Use of Force by National Liberation Movements* (Clarendon Press 1988) 166; F Kalshoven, 'The Diplomatic Conference on Reaffirmation and Development of International Humanitarian Law Applicable in Armed Conflicts, Geneva, 1974–1977' in F Kalshoven (ed), *Reflections on the Law of War: Collected Essays* (Martinus Nijhoff 2007) 196; see also Sandoz et al, *APs Commentary* (n 284) 54–55 [108]–[13].

292 Bothe et al (n 244) 52; Wilson (n 291) 167.

A further limitation is provided by the requirement that the conflict must be waged for one of the three specifically listed purposes included in Article 1(4) AP I. Specifically, the 'peoples' in question must be fighting against 'colonial domination', 'alien occupation', or 'racist regimes'. Unfortunately, the phraseology chosen by the drafters leaves much to be desired in terms of legal certainty. 'Colonial domination' and 'racist regimes' are hardly neutral terms[293] and have frequently been used as tools of international politics rather than as terms of legal precision.[294] In particular, any objective definition of the term 'racist regimes' remains elusive as it is unclear what level or form of racial discrimination present in a state would justify such designation.[295]

The term 'alien occupation' is also problematic, although, as will be seen later, it is likely the only one of the three that is capable of application in practice. To begin with, the choice of words is misguiding because the majority of possible situations of belligerent occupation had already been included in the ambit of Common Article 2(2). It may be recalled that that provision triggers the application of the law of IAC 'in all cases of partial or total occupation of the territory of a High Contracting Party'.[296] There are likely only two remaining types of occupation that may be outside of the scope of Common Article 2(2) and, therefore, potentially within the meaning of 'alien occupation' under Article 1(4) AP I.

Firstly, the occupied territory could conceivably belong to a state not party to the GCs. However, today this is at best a theoretical possibility given that the GCs have already achieved universal ratification.[297]

Secondly, the term may be taken to refer to the occupation of 'territories of controversial international status',[298] in other words those territories that had not been subject to effectively established sovereignty of a state prior to their occupation.[299] In today's reality, such unclear status can probably only be ascribed to, respectively, the Occupied Palestinian Territories[300] and Western Sahara.[301] As far as the former is concerned, Article 1(4) AP I does not in any event apply to the Israeli-Palestinian conflict due to the fact that Israel is not a state party to the Protocol.[302] Conversely,

[293] But see Bothe et al (n 244) 49 (suggesting that 'there are no problems' with the interpretation of the term 'colonial domination'); Wilson (n 291) 167 (suggesting that the term 'colonial domination' 'presents the least difficulty').

[294] For example, in 1975 the UNGA based its determination that 'zionism is a form of racism' upon an observation that a racist regime operated in the occupied Palestine. This determination was only revoked in 1991. UNGA Res 3379 (XXX) (Elimination of All Forms of Racial Discrimination) (10 November 1975); UNGA Res 46/86 (Elimination of Racism and Racial Discrimination) (16 December 1991).

[295] Wilson (n 291) 167.

[296] Common Art 2(2) GCs.

[297] ICRC, 'States Party to the Following International Humanitarian Law and Other Related Treaties' (14 December 2017) <https://ihl-databases.icrc.org/applic/ihl/ihl.nsf/vwTreaties1949.xsp>.

[298] Bothe et al (n 244) 50; but see Ferraro and Cameron, 'Article 2' (n 17) 114–15 [323]–[27] (arguing that the occupation of territories with unclear international status equally falls within the scope of Common Article 2(2)).

[299] cf Ferraro and Cameron, 'Article 2' (n 17) 114 [323] (suggesting that on this interpretation, a 'territory over which the sovereignty of a State has [not] been effectively established' would fall outside of the scope of GC IV).

[300] See further Schindler (n 203) 138.

[301] See further Wilson (n 291) 167–68.

[302] cf ICRC, 'States Party' (n 297) 4; but see, eg, UNGA Res ES-10/14 (8 December 2003) preambular para 8 ('Reaffirming the applicability of the Fourth Geneva Convention as well as Additional

that obstacle no longer exists with respect to the latter conflict, ie, the one between Morocco and the Polisario Front in Western Sahara, given that Morocco had acceded to AP I on 3 June 2011.[303] Accordingly, in 2015 Switzerland acting as the depositary of the Protocol seemed to accept that '[l]e Front POLISARIO lutte contre le Maroc en tant que puissance occupant étrangère'.[304] Yet, the practical impact of that recognition remains limited. Morocco immediately denounced the depositary's decision and objected in strong terms to the application of Article 1(4) AP I to the situation in Western Sahara; in fact, it went so far as to claim that there was not even a situation of an armed conflict between itself and the Polisario Front.[305]

The possibility for politicization is further aggravated by the fact that there is no independent entity with the power to decide whether the criteria have been met.[306] Proposals to endow either the UN General Assembly or the Security Council with the general power to determine the legal nature of armed conflicts have not been brought to fruition.[307] In addition, several states stated in reservations entered at time of their ratification of the Protocol that the legitimacy of the authority representing a people engaged in a war of national liberation should be recognized by a regional intergovernmental organization.[308] However, even for these states the absence of such recognition would only have bearing on the validity of an Article 96(3) declaration (discussed in Section 2.4.3) and not on the applicability of IHL as such.[309] In practical terms, the decision as to whether the Article 1(4) criteria had been met thus falls on the depositary of the Protocol who must decide whether to accept any such declaration or not. However, as the example of Western Sahara amply demonstrates, the depositary's decision will likely remain hotly contested by the relevant actors.

Protocol I to the Geneva Conventions to the Occupied Palestinian Territory, including East Jerusalem') (footnotes omitted).

303 cf ICRC, 'States Party' (n 297) 4.

304 Switzerland, 'Déclaration unilatérale du Front POLISARIO d'application des Conventions de Genève et de leur premier Protocole additionnel dans son conflit avec le Maroc' (25 June 2015, completed and updated 30 June 2015) 2 (internal memorandum, on file with author). The memorandum contains the legal reasoning on the basis of which the depositary decided to accept the Article 96(3) declaration issued by the Polisario Front. See also Switzerland, 'Notification to the Governments of the States Parties to the Geneva Conventions of 12 August 1949 for the Protection of War Victims' (26 June 2015) <www.eda.admin.ch/content/dam/eda/fr/documents/aussenpolitik/voelkerrecht/geneve/150626-GENEVE_en.pdf>, at 1 (notifying the states parties to the GCs of the acceptance of the declaration).

305 Communication by the Kingdom of Morocco (30 June 2015), annexed to Switzerland, 'Notification to the Governments of the States Parties to the Geneva Conventions of 12 August 1949 for the Protection of War Victims' (9 July 2015) <www.eda.admin.ch/content/dam/eda/fr/documents/aussenpolitik/voelkerrecht/geneve/150709-GENEVE-avec-ann_e.pdf>, at 2.

306 cf also Ferraro and Cameron, 'Article 2' (n 17) 78 [214].

307 R Bierzanek, 'Quelques remarques sur l'applicabilité du droit international humanitaire des conflits armés aux conflits internes internationalisés' in C Swinarski (ed), *Studies and Essays on International Humanitarian Law and Red Cross Principles in Honour of Jean Pictet* (ICRC 1984) 289–90.

308 See A Roberts and R Guelff (eds), *Documents on the Laws of War* (3rd edn, OUP 2000) 501 [7] (Belgium), 503 [L] (Canada), 506 [15] (Ireland), and 507 [4] (South Korea).

309 J Gaudreau, 'The Reservations to the Protocols Additional to the Geneva Conventions for the Protection of War Victims' (2003) 85 IRRC 143.

It can thus be concluded that the terms used in Article 1(4) AP I are highly ambiguous and leave considerable uncertainty as to the exact material scope of this provision.[310] The rule has accordingly been subject to heavy criticism for its subjectivity and vagueness by a number of Western countries, including Canada,[311] West Germany,[312] the UK,[313] the US,[314] the Netherlands,[315] and Switzerland.[316] The US has even cited this provision as one of the reasons for rejecting the Protocol in its entirety.[317]

2.4.3 Temporal scope of application

Further difficulties are posed by the inclusion in Article 96(3) AP I of a mechanism, through which the authority representing a people engaged in a war of national liberation may undertake to apply the GCs and the Protocol. The text of the provision is as follows:

> The authority representing a people engaged against a High Contracting Party in an armed conflict of the type referred to in Article 1, paragraph 4, may undertake to apply the Conventions and this Protocol in relation to that conflict by means of a unilateral declaration addressed to the depositary. Such declaration shall, upon its receipt by the depositary, have in relation to that conflict the following effects:
>
> (a) the Conventions and this Protocol are brought into force for the said authority as a Party to the conflict with immediate effect;
> (b) the said authority assumes the same rights and obligations as those which have been assumed by a High Contracting Party to the Conventions and this Protocol; and
> (c) the Conventions and this Protocol are equally binding upon all Parties to the conflict.

The chosen wording raises the question of the exact moment of conflict internationalization. Is it immediately when conditions set out in Article 1(4) AP I are met (automatic application), or only after a valid Article 96(3) declaration has been

[310] See further Wilson (n 291) 168 (explaining that the terms used in Article 1(4) were in actual facts 'words taken from United Nations resolutions and tailor-made for Portugal, Israel, and South Africa').

[311] Canada, Legal Bureau, Letter (2 May 1974), reproduced in (1975) 13 Canadian Yearbook of International Law, 337–38.

[312] *Official Records* (n 283) vol VI, CDDH/SR.36, 61.

[313] BA Wortley, 'Observations on the Revision of the 1949 Geneva "Red Cross" Conventions' (1983) 54 BYBIL 143, 145.

[314] Letter of Transmittal from President Ronald Reagan (29 January 1987), reproduced in (1987) 81 AJIL 910, 911; see also US DoD, *Law of War Manual* (December 2016) 77 [3.3.4].

[315] Netherlands, Minister for Foreign Affairs, Letter to Parliament (18 May 1987), Bijl. Hand. I 1986/87-18277 (R 1247) No 38b, reproduced in (1988) 19 NYBIL 381.

[316] Switzerland, Conseil fédéral, Report of 18 February 1981 (Message du Cons. Féd. à l'Ass. Féd., du 18 février 1981, concernant les Protocoles additionnels aux Conventions de Genéve, FF 1981 I 973), reproduced in (1982) 39 ASDI, 143–44.

[317] Letter of Transmittal from President Ronald Reagan (29 January 1987), reproduced in (1987) 81 AJIL 910, 911; but see GS Corn, 'Thinking the Unthinkable: Has the Time Come to Offer Combatant Immunity to Non-State Actors?' (2011) 22 Stanford Law & Policy Review 253, 276 (arguing that the internationalization of wars of national liberation by way of Article 1(4) AP I was only a 'subsidiary concern' for the US, whereas the extension of the definition of combatants in the Protocol was the 'more important' issue).

made (conditional application)?[318] The drafting history of the provision is ambiguous, with several countries speaking in favour of the former interpretation,[319] while others endorsed the latter.[320]

It might be thought that an interpretation according to which Article 1(4) AP I applies automatically would leave little incentive for a putative liberation movement to actually issue a declaration under Article 96(3) AP I.[321] In other words, if the declaration is not a necessary precondition triggering the law of IAC, then what motivation would the movement have to issue one? However, an assessment of modern practice reveals that attempts to issue Article 96(3) declarations have in fact been made on multiple occasions, including by the African National Congress (1980),[322] possibly the Palestinian Liberation Organization (1989),[323] the National Democratic Front of the Philippines (1996),[324] and the Polisario Front (2015).[325] Interestingly, it was only the last mentioned declaration made by the Polisario Front that was accepted by the depositary; all others had either not even been addressed to the depositary[326] or had been rejected for failing to meet the necessary criteria.[327] Be that as it may, this practice demonstrates that a liberation movement's decision to issue an Article 96(3) declaration may be motivated by factors other than the desire to internationalize the underlying conflict. These may include the goal to clarify the

318 The latter interpretation is supported, *inter alia*, by the authors of the UK military manual: see UK Ministry of Defence, *The Manual of the Law of Armed Conflict* (OUP 2004) [3.4.2(c)]. See also LC Green, *The Contemporary Law of Armed Conflict* (3rd edn, Manchester University Press 2008) 80.

319 cf *Official Records* (n 283) vol IX, CDDH/I/SR.67, 364 [57] (Norway); ibid 366 [77] (Mexico); ibid CDDH/I/SR.68, 372 [14] (Syria); ibid vol VI, CDDH/SR.46, Annex, 364 (Canada).

320 cf *Official Records* (n 283) vol IX, CDDH/I/SR.68, 369 [1] (Federal Republic of Germany); ibid vol VI, CDDH/SR.46, Annex, 372 (Federal Republic of Germany); ibid 379–80 (Japan); ibid 387 (United Kingdom).

321 See Wilson (n 291) 169–70.

322 ANC, 'Declaration of Intent by the African National Congress' (28 November 1980), reproduced in (1981) 21 IRRC 20.

323 ICRC, 'Palestine and the Geneva Conventions' (1990) 30 IRRC 64; see further Green (n 318) 134 fn 43 (interpreting the statement as an Article 96(3) declaration); but see Switzerland, 'Note of Information to Governments' (13 September 1989), reproduced in ICRC, 'Palestine and the Geneva Conventions' (*op cit*) 64–65 (interpreting the statement as a putative instrument of accession issued by an entity whose statehood was disputed: 'the Swiss Government . . . is not in a position to decide whether this communication can be considered as an instrument of accession' due to 'the uncertainty within the international community as to the existence or non-existence of a State of Palestine'). Switzerland as the depositary of the Conventions and their Protocols finally accepted the accession of the 'State of Palestine' to these instruments in 2014: cf Switzerland, 'Notification to the Governments of the States parties to the Geneva Conventions of 12 August 1949 for the Protection of War Victims' (10 April 2014) <www.eda.admin.ch/content/dam/eda/fr/documents/aussenpolitik/voelkerrecht/geneve/140410-GENEVE_e.pdf>.

324 NDFP, 'Declaration of Undertaking to Apply the Geneva Conventions of 1949 and Protocol I of 1977' (5 June 1996) <www.ndfp.org/ndfp-declaration-of-undertaking-to-apply-the-geneva-conventions-of-1949-and-protocol-i-of-1977>.

325 Polisario Front, Letter to the Federal Ministry of Foreign Affairs of Switzerland (21 June 2015) <http://theirwords.org/media/transfer/doc/declarationofficielle_polisariofront_2015-f426d1a96a4465 affd1f87e794374b06.pdf>.

326 cf ANC, 'Declaration of Intent' (n 322) 20 (noting that the declaration was 'handed to the President of the ICRC' by the President of the ANC).

327 cf Switzerland, 'Déclaration unilatérale' (n 304) 2 ('C'est la première fois qu'il reçoit une telle déclaration remplissant tous ces critères').

legal relationship between the conflict parties, but also simply the movement's aim to influence the international public opinion in its favour.

Therefore, it is submitted that it is better to view internationalization to occur already at the moment when Article 1(4) conditions are met. This interpretation is also supported by the clear text of Article 96(3) AP I, which expressly provides that acceptance of the declaration by the depositary brings the GCs and the Protocol into force 'for the said authority' only.[328] This implies that the effects on the territorial state arise independently of such a declaration. Moreover, modern IHL is based on a clear rejection of any requirement of reciprocity of application.[329] A state should thus not be allowed to argue that the law of IAC does not apply to a situation, which otherwise fulfills the Article 1(4) criteria, only because its adversary failed to issue an Article 96(3) declaration.[330]

It can thus be summarized that a war of national liberation should be considered internationalized as soon as fighting in the sense of Article 1(4) AP I erupts. The primary effect of a valid Article 96(3) declaration is to modify the status of the national liberation movement, making it formally a party to the internationalized conflict.[331] The movement will also thereby assume the same rights and obligations as those held by a state party to the Protocol.[332] However, no further action by the territorial state is required; in fact, under this interpretation it is bound by the law of IAC even if it rejects the Article 96(3) declaration issued by its adversary as Morocco did in 2015.[333]

2.4.4 Effect on the legal status of the liberation movement

To say that an Article 96(3) declaration may modify the status of the liberation movement raises the question whether such outcome is actually permitted in the legal framework of the Protocol. Like the questions concerning the scope of Article 1(4) AP I discussed in the previous two subsections, this matter is also not free from controversy.

On the one hand, Article 4 AP I provides that the application of the Protocol shall not affect the legal status of the parties to the conflict. It is in line with this provision that, by virtue of its participation in an Article 1(4) conflict, a national liberation movement certainly does not become a 'state', a party to the GCs or the Protocol, or an entity otherwise endowed with full international legal personality.[334] The logic of

[328] Art 96(3)(a) AP I.

[329] Fleck (n 47) 583–84; see also J-M Henckaerts and L Doswald-Beck (eds), *Customary International Humanitarian Law* (CUP 2005) rule 140.

[330] But see Kalshoven and Zegveld (n 52) 155 (endorsing the conditional interpretation and defending it as an instance of 'positive reciprocity' permitted by the law: 'I am bound to respect the law because you undertake to do so too').

[331] Art 96(3)(a) AP I.

[332] Art 96(3)(b) AP I.

[333] See Communication by the Kingdom of Morocco (3 July 2015) (n 305).

[334] But see Section 9.2.3 (demonstrating that NLMs may be seen as benefiting from limited legal personality).

Article 96(3) AP I also dictates that a declaration under that provision may only be made by a non-state entity.[335]

On the other hand, the proposition that application of the Protocol would have no effect whatsoever on the legal status of the insurgents is impossible to uphold. To begin with, it transforms the status of movement members who meet further requirements stipulated by the Protocol[336] from internationally irrelevant 'fighters'[337] to 'combatants' entitled to an array of rights under the GCs and the Protocol.[338] Additionally, as stated earlier, the Protocol expressly provides that after a valid Article 96(3) declaration is received by the depositary, the movement becomes 'a Party to the conflict with immediate effect', assuming 'the same rights and obligations as those assumed by a High Contracting Party'.[339] In other words, the legal status of the movement and its members is fundamentally altered, putting it on par with the territorial state in terms of its rights and duties under IHL.

2.4.5 Evaluation

It appears that the practical impact of Article 1(4) AP I has been inversely proportional to the amount of discussion and controversy it had generated at the time of its drafting in Geneva. This is no doubt in large part due to the fact that wars of national liberation were a 'temporally and geographically limited phenomenon'.[340] It has subsequently even been suggested that the provision would 'never be applied' and that it amounted to 'a dead letter'.[341]

While Article 1(4) AP I may have been languishing for a long time, the events surrounding the Polisario Front's declaration in 2015 appear to have breathed new life into the provision. The decision of the depositary to accept the declaration[342] coupled with the near-universal recognition of the people of Western Sahara's right to self-determination[343] strengthen the case for considering the situation in Western Sahara as an armed conflict internationalized by way of Article 1(4) AP I.[344]

At the same time, the continuing criticism of the provision by states not party to the Protocol[345] suggests that it has not acquired the force of customary international

[335] Similarly Switzerland, 'Déclaration unilatérale' (n 304) 2. [336] AP I, Arts 43–44.

[337] Understood in the sense of para 1.1.2 of Schmitt, Garraway, and Dinstein (n 50).

[338] Green (n 318) 80. See further Section 7.3. [339] AP I, Art 96(3)(a)–(b).

[340] DE Graham, 'The 1974 Diplomatic Conference on the Law of War: A Victory for Political Causes and a Return to the "Just War" Concept of the Eleventh Century' (1975) 32 Washington & Lee Law Review 25, 53.

[341] GH Aldrich, 'Prospects for United States Ratification of Additional Protocol I to the 1949 Geneva Conventions' (1991) 85 AJIL 1, 7.

[342] Switzerland, 'Notification' (n 304).

[343] See, in particular, UNGA Res 2229 (XXI) (Question of Ifni and Spanish Sahara) (20 December 1966); *Western Sahara* (n 229) [70]; UNGA Res 34/37 (21 November 1979); Case C-104/16 P, *Council of the European Union v Front Polisario* (CJEU, 21 December 2016) [87]–[106].

[344] But see Communication by the Kingdom of Morocco (3 July 2015) (n 305).

[345] See, eg, US, Memorandum submitted in *United States v Shakur*, 690 F Supp 1291 (SDNY 1988), reproduced in M Nash Leich (ed), *Cumulative Digest of United States Practice in International Law 1981–1988* (Department of State 1995) vol III, 3441.

law.[346] Its potential application in the future thus remains limited to conflicts involving states which have ratified the Protocol.[347] However, even with respect to these situations, interpretive difficulties resulting from the vague and subjective nature of the terms used by the provision will continue to provide further obstacles to its application in practice.[348] Therefore, it appears that it is still true that even if Article 1(4) AP I 'opens a Pandora's box at all, it is an unexpectedly small one'.[349]

2.5 Recognition of Belligerency, Unilateral Declarations, and Special Agreements

Along with states, insurgents are sometimes described as the 'traditional' subjects of international law.[350] However, unlike states, insurgents possess only a limited legal capacity marked by the transience of their existence: they either prevail in the civil strife and transform into a fully-fledged state, or they lose and disappear from the international scene.[351] A state may, however, by its attitude and conduct towards the rebels elevate their international legal standing *inter partes* by at least three distinct legal mechanisms: (1) recognition of belligerency, (2) conclusion of a special agreement under Common Article 3 of the Geneva Conventions, and (3) unilateral decision by the territorial state.[352] This, it is argued, has the effect that can be characterized as *relative internationalization*: treating the insurgents as equals to the acting state internationalizes the conflict in question primarily with an effect on the insurgents and the recognizing state.

[346] Accord JK Kleffner, 'Scope of Application of International Humanitarian Law' in D Fleck (ed), *The Handbook of International Humanitarian Law* (3rd edn, OUP 2013) 46; Dinstein (n 51) 408; S Sivakumaran, *The Law of Non-International Armed Conflict* (OUP 2012) 216; contra A Cassese, 'Wars of National Liberation and Humanitarian Law' in A Cassese (ed), *The Human Dimension of International Law: Selected Papers of Antonio Cassese* (OUP 2008) 106–08; Glazier (n 273) [15].

[347] cf Glazier (n 273) [15] (opining that since AP I has been ratified by over 85% of the existing states, its Article 1(4) is 'statistically likely to apply to any future conflict that otherwise qualifies').

[348] Recent examples include the situation in Western Sahara (discussed earlier) and the conflict between the Turkish state armed forces and the Kurdish armed group PKK (*Partiya Karkerên Kurdistan*, Kurdistan Workers' Party). In spite of the PKK's claims of acting in the exercise of the right to self-determination, Germany stated that it viewed the situation as a NIAC and that Article 1(4) remained inapplicable. See Reply by the Federal Government to the written question submitted by Bundestag member Vera Wollenberger and the parliamentary party of the Alliance 90/Greens (7 September 1994), reproduced and translated in M Sassòli, AA Bouvier, and A Quintin, *How Does Law Protect in War?* (3rd edn, ICRC 2011) vol III, 2288–90.

[349] Wilson (n 291) 168.

[350] See, eg, A Cassese, *International Law* (2nd edn, OUP 2005) 71–72 and 127–31; M Herdegen, *Principles of International Economic Law* (OUP 2016) 27; E Fahey, 'Introduction: Framing the Actors of Postnational Rule-Making' in E Fahey (ed), *The Actors of Postnational Rule-Making: Contemporary Challenges of European and International Law* (Routledge 2016) 8; MN Shaw, *International Law* (8th edn, CUP 2017) 195.

[351] See, eg, P Malanczuk, *Akehurst's Modern Introduction to International Law* (7th edn, Routledge 2002) 104; Cassese (n 350) 70–71.

[352] cf WA Solf, 'Commentator on the subject of Non-International Armed Conflicts' (1982) 31 AULR 927, 931.

2.5.1 Recognition of belligerency

2.5.1.1 Existence in contemporary law

According to the rule of traditional customary law outlined by Oppenheim in 1906,

> any State can recognise insurgents as a belligerent Power, provided (1) they are in possession of a certain part of the territory of the legitimate Government; (2) they have set up a Government of their own; and (3) they conduct their armed contention with the legitimate Government according to the laws and usages of war.[353]

At that time, recognition of belligerency was considered as 'a very modern addition to International Law',[354] although the concept can be traced all the way back to the American War of Independence (1775–83).[355] A century later, the tables have turned and many now contend that the rule has fallen into complete or 'virtual' *desuetude*.[356] It has been argued in response that *desuetude* does not apply to customary international law,[357] but this proposition is not generally accepted.[358]

Happily, although not always prominent, instances of practice do exist even now. Authors usually cite the American Civil War (1861–65)[359] or the Boer War (1899–1902)[360] as the last episodes of recognized belligerency.[361] In fact, these were only

[353] L Oppenheim, *International Law: A Treatise* (Longmans, Green & Co. 1905 & 1906) vol II, 86; see also L Oppenheim, *International Law: A Treatise* (2nd edn, Longmans, Green & Co. 1912) vol II, 92 (using an identical wording except for replacing the modal verb 'can' for 'may').

[354] AS Hershey, *The Essentials of International Public Law* (Macmillan 1912) 121.

[355] cf F Bugnion, '*Jus ad Bellum, Jus in Bello* and Non-International Armed Conflicts' (2003) 6 YIHL 167, 178.

[356] See, eg, RR Oglesby, *Internal War and the Search for Normative Order* (Martinus Nijhoff 1971) 100; R Higgins, 'International Law and Civil Conflict' in E Luard (ed), *The International Regulation of Civil Wars* (New York University Press 1972) 171; Doswald-Beck (n 5) 252; J Crawford, 'First Report on State Responsibility', UN Doc A/CN.4/490 and Adds 1-6 (1998) [270]; Provost (n 269) 279; R Kolb, *Ius contra bellum: Le droit international relatif au maintien de la paix* (2nd edn, Helbing Lichtenhahn 2009) 326; E David, *Principes de droit des conflits armés* (5th edn, Bruylant 2012) 138; A Sanger, 'The Contemporary Law of Blockade and the Gaza Freedom Flotilla' (2010) 13 YIHL 397, 424–25; L Hill-Cawthorne, *Detention in Non-International Armed Conflict* (OUP 2016) 13; see also R Baxter, 'Ius in Bello Interno: The Present and Future Law' in JN Moore (ed), *Law & Civil War in the Modern World* (Johns Hopkins University Press 1974) 520; A Cullen, *The Concept of Non-International Armed Conflict in International Humanitarian Law* (CUP 2010) 8 fn 2; Moir (n 50) 41; D Guilfoyle, 'The Mavi Marmara Incident and Blockade in Armed Conflict' (2011) 81 BYBIL 1, 192.

[357] I Scobbie, 'Gaza' in E Wilmshurst (ed), *International Law and the Classification of Conflicts* (OUP 2012) 303–04 ('desuetude ... applies only to treaties'); Akande (n 47) 50 (endorsing Scobbie's view).

[358] ME Villiger, *Customary International Law and Treaties: A Study of Their Interactions and Interrelations, with Special Consideration of the 1969 Vienna Convention on the Law of Treaties* (Brill 1985) 32–33; E Milano, *Unlawful Territorial Situations in International Law: Reconciling Effectiveness, Legality And Legitimacy* (Martinus Nijhoff 2006) 232; J Wouters and S Verhoeven, 'Desuetudo' in R Wolfrum (ed), *Max Planck Encyclopedia of Public International Law* (OUP 2008) <www.mpepil.com> (updated November 2008) [13]–[16]. I am grateful to Douglas Guilfoyle for drawing my attention to the controversy at the heart of the claim referred to in the main text.

[359] H McCoubrey and N White, *International Organizations and Civil Wars* (Dartmouth 1995) 7; YM Lootsteen, 'The Concept of Belligerency in International Law' (2000) 166 MLR 109, 110.

[360] Gasser (n 52) 559; E La Haye, *War Crimes in Internal Armed Conflicts* (CUP 2008) 14 fn 87.

[361] A less well-known occurrence was the Costa Rican recognition of the state of belligerency between itself and the Rivas-Walker regime since 1856, acknowledged in the arbitral award in the case

the last instances, in which the *territorial state* was (uncontroversially) seen as having recognized insurgents challenging its authority.[362] Instances of *third-state* recognition have been rare in the period following the Second World War but not non-existent.[363] In particular, Nicaraguan Sandinistas were recognized by the member states of the Andean Group (1979);[364] El Salvadorean rebels by France and Mexico (1981);[365] and the Colombian insurgent group FARC by Venezuela (2008).[366] At times, other more ambiguous cases of recognition by third states have been put forward as further instances of state practice in this sense.[367]

It is submitted that the argument that the doctrine of belligerency has been superseded by other provisions of IHL governing NIACs (such as either Common Article 3 or Additional Protocol II)[368] is also problematic. With respect to Common Article 3, this argument implies that the law applicable to internal armed conflicts ('*jus in bello interno*') would be limited to this provision, which would have replaced the customary norms pertaining to the recognition of belligerency.[369] In a similar vein, it has been argued that even if recognition of belligerency were to occur, only 'common Article 3 and not the Conventions as a whole will apply to the conflict.'[370]

of *Accessory Transit Company v Costa Rica*. See *Accessory Transit Company v Costa Rica* (Decision of the Umpire, Commander Bertinatti) (1862) 29 RIAA 78, 80.

362 It has been said that the 'declaration of war' issued by the Nigerian government to the secessionist state of Biafra in 1967 amounted to a recognition of belligerency. C Zorgbibe, 'Sources of the Recognition of Belligerent Status' (1977) 17 IRRC 111, 114. However, Sivakumaran has argued that the declaration 'was not intended in that manner by the parent state'. Sivakumaran (n 346) 17. While establishing intent is notoriously difficult with respect to proclamations issued by states and should not be seen as determinative with respect to the effects of such statements, at the very least it can be said that the Biafran case is not generally accepted as a clear recognition of belligerency by the territorial state.

363 Contra, eg, Sivakumaran (n 346) 19.

364 Joint Declaration of the Foreign Ministers of Member States of the Cartagena Agreement on the Situation in Nicaragua (16 June 1979), reproduced in R Nieto Navia, '¿Hay o no hay conflicto armado en Colombia?' (2008) 1 Anuario Colombiano de Derecho Internacional 139, 147.

365 Joint Franco-Mexican Declaration on El Salvador, reprinted in Information Bulletin of the Political-Diplomatic Commission of the FMLN-FDR (16 October 1981) 4.

366 Venezuelan President Hugo Chavéz's proposal that the FARC and a smaller rebel group ELN be recognized as belligerents was supported on 17 January 2008 by the Venezuelan National Assembly in a 'near unanimous vote' by a resolution to grant the FARC belligerent status. C Kraul, 'Chavez Keeps Up Campaign to Get Rebels Off Terrorist List' *Los Angeles Times* (20 January 2008).

367 See, eg, *Namibia* Advisory Opinion (n 228) (sep op Ammoun) 92 (arguing that '[t]he recognition by the United Nations of the legitimacy of the Namibian people's struggle against the South African aggression [was] nothing less than a recognition of belligerency'); J Dugard, 'SWAPO: The *Jus ad Bellum* and the *Jus in Bello*' (1976) 93 South African Law Journal 144, 156 (arguing that the recognition of the Namibian liberation movement SWAPO as 'the authentic representative of the Namibian people' by the UNGA might be seen as a recognition of belligerency); S Foster Halabi, 'Traditions of Belligerent Recognition: The Libyan Intervention in Historical and Theoretical Context' (2012) 28 AUILR 321, 373–90 (considering that the recognition of Libya's NTC by France, Italy, Qatar, US, and UK may have amounted to a recognition of belligerency in the traditional sense).

368 See, eg, Provost (n 269) 279–80; W Heintschel von Heinegg, 'Introduction' in MN Schmitt and W Heintschel von Heinegg (eds), *The Scope and Applicability of International Humanitarian Law* (Ashgate 2012), vol 1, xiv.

369 A Roberts and R Guelff (eds), *Documents on the Laws of War* (OUP 1982) 12–13. Compare, however, with the most recent edition of the book: Roberts and Guelff (n 308) 23–24.

370 Moir (n 50) 41–42.

In response, while the ICRC commentaries to the GCs are admittedly equivocal on this point,[371] in its remarks to National Red Cross societies issued immediately after the conference, the ICRC expressly stated that the application of Common Article 3 is independent of any potential recognition of belligerency.[372] More importantly, the text of Common Article 3 does not exclude other norms from being applied to internal armed conflicts; on the contrary, its *chapeau* stipulates that the following provisions should be applied 'as a minimum' only.[373] In addition, at the 1949 Diplomatic Conference in Geneva, the Australian delegation proposed that recognition of belligerency should be considered as a prerequisite for Common Article 3 to apply.[374] However, this proposal was rejected in the drafting process, and thus the two legal categories maintained their mutual independence in the post-1949 period.[375] In sum, internal conflicts to which Common Article 3 applies may still be internationalized by way of recognition of belligerency,[376] as long as the more stringent conditions for recognition are met.[377]

The argument about the recognition of belligerency being superseded by the law of NIAC appears slightly stronger with respect to Additional Protocol II. The threshold of applicability of this instrument encapsulated in Article 1(1) can be said to 'mirror' closely conditions associated with belligerency.[378] It is thus arguable that states parties to Protocol II have agreed that when these conditions are met, the conflict is to be regulated by the Protocol and internationalization by way of recognition of belligerency would thus be excluded.

Nevertheless, the rules on recognition remain relevant at least for states *not* party to Protocol II.[379] Furthermore, the Protocol's applicability is triggered automatically when the conditions in Article 1(1) AP II are met, irrespective of any further action or assent of the parties to the conflict. This provision does not rule out the possibility

[371] Compare Pictet, *GC IV Commentary* (n 16) 36 with Pictet, *GC III Commentary* (n 40) 38. The new 2016 Commentary does not clarify this issue either: cf L Cameron et al, 'Article 3: Conflicts Not of an International Character' in ICRC (ed), *Commentary on the First Geneva Convention* (CUP 2016) 133–34 [360]–[61] (hereafter Cameron et al, 'Article 3').

[372] ICRC, *The Geneva Conventions of August 12, 1949: Analysis for the use of National Red Cross Societies* (ICRC 1950), vol II, 8.

[373] Common Art 3 GCs; see also Schindler (n 203) 5 ('According to Art. 3, common to all four Conventions, certain minimum rules of humanity apply to all "armed conflicts not of an international character", *regardless of any recognition of belligerency*') (emphasis added); S Radin, 'The Current Relevance of the Recognition of Belligerency' in M Matthee et al (eds), *Armed Conflict and International Law: In Search of the Human Face* (TMC Asser 2013) 134 ('Common Article 3 was intended to provide minimum guarantees in an attempt to fill gaps in protection during internal conflicts, in recognition of the doctrine of belligerency's failure to do so').

[374] Switzerland, *Final Record of the Diplomatic Conference of Geneva of 1949* (Federal Political Department 1949) vol II B, 121 (hereafter *Final Record*).

[375] See ibid, vol II B, 129 (citing 'enormous practical difficulties').

[376] cf Dinstein (n 16) 34 (noting that the applicability of Common Article 3 is 'not contingent on any recognition of belligerency' and that upon recognition, the conflict has to be treated as if it were an IAC).

[377] Accord Radin (n 373) 130–35.

[378] Lootsteen (n 359) 128; see also Aldrich (n 20) 60; but see Radin (n 373) 135–36.

[379] See Lootsteen (n 359) 128–30. By the end of 2017, 168 states had ratified AP II. Non-ratifying states include India, Iran, Iraq, Israel, Pakistan, Somalia, Turkey, and the US. See ICRC, 'States Party' (n 297).

that when these requirements are met—and Protocol II is thus applicable—a state could in addition recognize the rebels as belligerents, thereby internationalizing the conflict *inter se*.[380]

Again, this position is supported by a closer examination of the *travaux préparatoires*. At the 1974–77 diplomatic conference, the Egyptian delegate (and later a prominent international judge) Georges Abi-Saab stated that in situations in which a recognition of belligerency was granted, 'there would be no need for a Protocol II, because, according to general international law, the whole body of the law of war would then apply.'[381] This statement remained unopposed at the conference.[382]

On the basis of the foregoing, it can thus be summarized that the doctrine of recognition of belligerency has not been replaced by either the GCs or their Additional Protocols.

2.5.1.2 Relative nature

The effects of recognition of belligerency are in principle limited to the relationship between the recognizing state and the recognized entity. Because the act of recognition transforms the nature of a conflict between specific actors, the result can be described as *relative internationalization*. This is, it is submitted, a consequence of the nature of international legal obligations. Due to the horizontal structure of the international community and the equality of its members as subjects of international law, a novel international obligation may in principle arise only on the basis of *consent* of the concerned state(s).[383] Internationalization of a conflict imposes on both the territorial and an outside state a host of new obligations. For the territorial state, this means that after recognition, rules of IHL are triggered as between the conflict parties. For an outside state, rights and duties of neutrality become applicable.

The relative nature of internationalization by recognition of belligerency is obvious in cases where belligerency is recognized by a third state. For example, during the First World War, the Allied Powers recognized the Polish National Army fighting for Poland's independence against Russia. Nevertheless, the Permanent Court of

[380] See also Radin (n 373) 136 (concluding that 'APII constitutes a category of conflict separate from one where belligerency is recognized').

[381] *Official Records* (n 283) vol VIII, CDDH/I/SR.24, 235 [31] (Egypt).

[382] cf ibid, vol VIII, CDDH/I/SR.24, 238–39.

[383] See, eg, L Oppenheim, *International Law: A Treatise* (2nd edn) (n 353) vol I, 17; *Lotus Case (France v Turkey)* (Merits) [1927] PCIJ Rep Series A No 10, 18; see also Shaw (n 351) 7–8. Shaw accepts the importance of the role of consent in international law but points out the flaws in accepting it as the sole basis for obligation in international law. For instance, if a state 'withdraws' its consent to a rule of international law, the rule does not become optional or non-binding for the state in question. On the contrary, if the state acted upon its decision, it would be in breach of the particular rule. The reliance on consent for the purposes of the argument in the main text is, however, more limited and consistent with Shaw's view. The present author views the absence of state consent (for example, in the form of acknowledgement of a status of belligerency) as preventing in principle the emergence of an obligation directly affecting the non-consenting state (such as obligations stemming from the transformed nature of conflict triggered by the recognition). The specific application of this principle is demonstrated in the following text.

International Justice (PCIJ) later held in the *Upper Silesia* case that this recognition had no effect with respect to Germany, which 'had no share in the transaction'.[384] Therefore, the legal effect of the recognition is solely in relation to the recognizing state, with respect to whom the insurgents are then accorded the same 'war status' as the parent state.[385] However, their status with respect to other states (and *a fortiori* to the parent state) would not be affected.[386] Nevertheless, as pointed out by Baxter, widespread recognition of belligerency by third states would put pressure on the government in power to recognize the insurgents, as well.[387] The recognizing state consequently becomes subject to the rights and duties of neutrality with respect to both belligerent parties.[388]

If recognition is granted by the territorial state, the relative nature of internationalization is less evident. Of course, the primary effect of recognition is indeed *inter partes*: both parties will be subject to the norms of IHL applicable to IACs. However, recognition is also thought to activate rights and duties of neutrality with respect to third states.[389] It is submitted that it is preferable to regard recognition as a demonstration of a view that a conflict is to be treated as international, implying the *intention* to impose duties and confer rights of neutrality on the concerned outside states.[390] Although in principle the outside states are free to disagree with this view,[391] in practice they are unlikely to do so given the significance of the act of recognition issued by the established government.[392] In sum, recognition of belligerency is relative in that it affects only the relationship between the recognizing state and the recognized group; yet in practice, recognition given by the territorial state has typically been respected by outside states as well.[393]

2.5.1.3 Discretionary nature

Finally, it is necessary to consider whether the recognizing state is free to do so, or whether there is a duty to recognize in specific situations. In this regard, Lauterpacht argued in 1947 in favour of obligatory recognition in case the customary conditions were met. Notably, he proposed a fourth condition to complement the three set out here,[394] namely that circumstances must exist 'which make it necessary for

[384] *Case concerning certain German interests in Polish Upper Silesia* (Germany v Poland) (Merits) [1926] PCIJ Rep Series A No 7, 28.

[385] GG Wilson, *Handbook of International Law* (West Publishing Company 1910) 41.

[386] Wilson (n 385) 41; see also H Kelsen, *Principles of International Law* (Rinehart 1952) 291; Sandoz et al, *APs Commentary* (n 284) 1321 [4346]; Zorgbibe (n 362) 113; Clapham (n 130) 22 [56]; Cameron et al, 'Article 3' (n 371) 133 [361].

[387] Baxter (n 356) 518; accord Zorgbibe (n 362) 113.

[388] WE Hall, *A Treatise on International Law* (AP Higgins ed, 7th edn, Clarendon Press 1917) 30; Kelsen (n 386) 291; see also Institute of International Law, Resolution concerning Rights and Duties of Foreign Powers and Their Ressortissants towards Established and Recognized Governments in Case of Insurrection (8 September 1900), Art 7.

[389] Cameron et al, 'Article 3' (n 371) 134 [361] fn 26.

[390] cf Hall (n 388) 30.

[391] In which case, for example, they retain a right not to respect blockades established by the insurgents. Institute of International Law (n 388), Art 5(2).

[392] cf Lauterpacht (n 210) 247.

[393] cf also Neff (n 272) 266.

[394] See text to note 353 in this chapter.

outside states to define their attitude by means of recognition of belligerency'.[395] Lauterpacht argued that recognition of belligerency was declaratory of facts (four conditions for recognition) but constitutive of rights and obligations (for the insurgent group and for third states).[396] On this view, recognition must be viewed as taking place in fulfilment of a legal duty and not as an act of policy guided only by the interests of the state concerned.[397] Lauterpacht perceived this process as collective and believed it should be further developed by conferring upon an international authority the power to determine whether the requirements of recognition of belligerency exist in a given case.[398]

However, the argument for obligatory recognition suffers from two key weaknesses. The first problem is that the argument is circular in nature. Defining, as it does, one of the factual conditions for belligerency as the existence of circumstances *necessitating* recognition only restates the desired outcome, namely that recognition is obligatory if the applicable conditions are met. Secondly (and more importantly), Lauterpacht's argument is at odds with actual practice. Not only has the international recognizing authority that he had desired never come about, but states have also very rarely granted recognition to insurgents despite the abundance of internal armed conflicts in modern history. Even in the period when recognitions of belligerency were more common than today, there were instances in which such recognition was not given for political reasons, in spite of the fact that the rebels in question had met the conditions under customary law. An example of the kind was the US government's decision not to recognize the Cuban insurgents as belligerents during the third Cuban revolution of 1895–98.[399] Nevertheless, even supposing that there once had been a conception of obligatory recognition of belligerency in international law, the development of customary law after the Second World War has eliminated it. Hence, internationalization by way of recognition of belligerency is better seen as discretionary in nature.[400]

It might be asked why a state, if it was not legally compelled to do so, would voluntarily decide to recognize belligerency in a particular case. Indeed, the paucity of practice suggests that most of the time, states have considered that it would be

[395] Lauterpacht (n 210) 176; see also H Wheaton, *Elements of International Law* (Dana's 8th edn, Little, Brown & Co. 1866) 29–30 fn 15 (stating that recognition may only be issued if the third state's 'own rights and interests are so far affected as to require a definition of its own relations to the parties' as otherwise it would be premature and may be regarded as an unfriendly act).

[396] Lauterpacht (n 210) 253. [397] ibid. [398] ibid 253–55.

[399] See MW Hazeltine, 'What Shall be Done about Cuba?' (1896) 163 The North American Review 731, 789 (demonstrating that the Cuban rebels had met the requisite conditions for recognition); W McKinley, 'First Annual Message' (6 December 1897) <www.presidency.ucsb.edu/ws/index.php?pid=29538> ('I regard the recognition of the belligerency of the Cuban insurgents as now *unwise, and therefore inadmissible*. Should that step hereafter be deemed wise as a measure of right and duty, the Executive will take it.') (emphasis added); but see Lauterpacht (n 210) 182–83 (suggesting that the true reason for the US refusal to recognize the belligerency of the Cuban rebels was the lack of sufficient cohesion on their part necessary to establish stable governmental agencies).

[400] cf also Cameron et al, 'Article 3' (n 371) 133 [360] fn 24 (noting that Lauterpacht's 'was not a generally held view'); Neff (n 272) 264 (suggesting that the prevailing view came to be that if the criteria for recognition of belligerency were met, states were permitted to recognize belligerency, but they were not compelled to do so).

'unwise' or otherwise unnecessary to extend such recognition.[401] Yet, there may be situations, in which either the territorial state or third states might consider it in their interest to recognize the belligerency of a given group of insurgents. In this regard, territorial states might be motivated by a desire, for example, to avoid the international responsibility for acts done in the insurgent territory;[402] to secure a better treatment of their own forces by the enemy;[403] or to subject third states to the law of neutrality with respect to the conflict.[404] Additionally, third states may consider it expedient to grant recognition in order to express their support for the cause espoused by the rebels;[405] to define precisely their relations to the conflict parties;[406] or to promote the goal of securing compliance with IHL by the conflict parties.[407]

Nonetheless, the discretionary nature of recognition of belligerency is an issue separate from the necessity of explicit recognition. The majority of the cases of recognition by the territorial state have been, in fact, tacit and evident only from the use of measures permissible only in international conflict.[408] For instance, the US blockade against the Confederate States in 1861 was, in the words of the US Supreme Court, 'official and conclusive evidence' that the Civil War was a conflict between the established government and a recognized belligerent.[409] Nevertheless, President Lincoln's decision to impose the blockade was discretionary, which was also duly recognized by the same court.[410] Analogously, if the ongoing armed violence between Israel and the Hamas-controlled Gaza Strip had originated as a NIAC,[411] the naval

[401] cf, eg, US Grant, 'Seventh Annual Message' (7 December 1875) <www.presidency.ucsb.edu/ws/index.php?pid=29516> ('I regard the accordance of belligerent rights [to the Cuban insurgents] still to be as unwise and premature as I regard it to be'); W McKinley, 'First Annual Message' (6 December 1897) <www.presidency.ucsb.edu/ws/index.php?pid=29538> ('I regard the recognition of the belligerency of the Cuban insurgents as now unwise, and therefore inadmissible.'); JW Garner, 'Recognition of Belligerency' (1938) 32(1) AJIL 106, 110–13 (noting the UK government's position that although the situation in the context of the civil war in Spain had met the customary criteria, the government had considered it expedient to deny recognition).

[402] See Wheaton (n 395) 37; see also US Grant, 'Special Message' (13 June 1870) <www.presidency.ucsb.edu/ws/?pid=70164> ('The parent Government becomes relieved from responsibility for acts done in the insurgent territory'); contra Lauterpacht (n 210) 247–50.

[403] See Moir (n 50) 10.

[404] cf Neff (n 272) 260–61; see also US Grant, 'Special Message' (13 June 1870) <www.presidency.ucsb.edu/ws/?pid=70164> ('The parent Government ... acquires the right to exercise against neutral commerce all the powers of a party to a maritime war.').

[405] cf Moir (n 50) 8.

[406] cf Wheaton (n 395) 29–30 fn 15.

[407] cf Lauterpacht (n 210) 227.

[408] Sandoz et al, *APs Commentary* (n 284) 1320–21 [4345]; E Riedel, 'Recognition of Belligerency' in R Bernhardt (ed), *Encyclopedia of Public International Law* (1982), vol 3, 48; see further Wilson (n 385) 43; Hershey (n 354) 120 fn 16; A Cullen, 'Key Developments Affecting the Scope of Internal Armed Conflict in International Humanitarian Law' (2005) 183 Military Law Review 66, 75; Radin (n 373) 127–28. In addition, third-state recognition could also have been implicit: by acting as neutrals, in other words, by applying the law of neutrality, third states could 'convert' an internal conflict into a 'true civil war'. Neff (n 272) 261–62; see also ibid 267 for further examples of practice.

[409] *Prize Cases* (1862) 67 US 2, 670 (US Supreme Court).

[410] ibid 670.

[411] The question of classification of the conflict in Gaza is controversial and falls beyond the scope of this study. One view consistent with the analysis presented here is that following the physical withdrawal of the Israeli forces from Gaza in 2005, Israel's belligerent occupation of Gaza has ended; since Gaza was not an independent state nor a territory belonging to any other sovereign, the conflict between it and Israel would consequently have been a NIAC. See Y Shany, 'Faraway, So Close: The Legal

blockade imposed by Israel on Gaza in 2007 could also be described as an implicit recognition of Hamas's belligerency, lending further contemporary relevance to the doctrine.[412]

2.5.2 Unilateral declarations and special agreements

While recognition of belligerency is limited by stringent conditions as to the conduct and control exercised by the insurgents, parties to an internal conflict not meeting these requirements may declare their willingness to apply some or all of the rules applicable in IACs.[413] Although not all unilateral acts give rise to international legal obligations, acts given in public and with the intention to be bound are universally considered to imply obligation for the acting entity.[414] A declaration to apply a certain set of rules during an armed conflict is by definition issued in public and, unless stated otherwise, manifests the intention to be bound by these rules; therefore, it can be concluded that it will in principle be binding on the issuing entity.

Insurgent groups have issued such declarations on multiple occasions, be it in anticipation of reciprocal treatment, international prestige, or enhanced discipline within their own ranks.[415] Provided that the insurgent group has a sufficiently cohesive and hierarchical structure, which makes it possible for it to actually comply with its declaration, this undertaking should be considered binding on the group in question.[416] Although an insurgent group only enjoys a limited legal capacity in international law,[417] it is submitted that such a self-imposed restriction on permissible war conduct is a quintessential example of an act within this capacity. Accordingly, it should be seen as binding on the group as a matter of international law.

Status of Gaza after Israel's Disengagement' (2005) 8 YIHL 369. For a more detailed treatment of the legal qualification of the conflict see, eg, Scobbie, 'Gaza' (n 357) 280–316.

[412] See, eg, Scobbie, 'Gaza' (n 357) 301 (arguing that the imposition of the blockade served to internationalize the conflict); but see Radin (n 373) 147 (noting that the imposition of a blockade serves as a relevant indicator only insofar as blockades are not considered to apply in NIACs); Guilfoyle (n 356) 191–94 (arguing that the law is unclear as to whether blockades are available under the law of NIACs).

[413] cf M Sassòli and LM Olson, 'The Relationship Between International Humanitarian and Human Rights Law Where It Matters: Admissible Killing and Internment of fighters in Non-International Armed Conflicts' (2008) 90 IRRC 599, 623 (highlighting the similarity between the doctrine of recognition of belligerency and Common Article 3 agreements and encouraging the application of the law of IAC by analogy in NIACs).

[414] See *Nuclear Tests Case (New Zealand v France)* (Judgment) [1974] ICJ Rep 253, 267; ILC Guiding Principles Applicable to Unilateral Declarations of States Capable of Creating Legal Obligations (2006) UN Doc A/61/10, principle 1.

[415] For a detailed list of such declarations, see, eg, I Detter, *The Law of War* (2nd edn, CUP 2000) 186; ML Mack and J Pejić, *Increasing Respect for International Humanitarian Law in Non-international Armed Conflicts* (ICRC 2008) 20; Geneva Call, 'Their Words: Directory of Armed Non-State Actor Humanitarian Commitments' (online database) <http://theirwords.org>.

[416] cf Detter (n 415) 189; A Roberts and S Sivakumaran, 'Lawmaking by Nonstate Actors: Engaging Armed Groups in the Creation of International Humanitarian Law' (2012) 37 YJIL 107, 141–43.

[417] Peter Malanczuk, *Akehurst's Modern Introduction to International Law* (7th edn, Routledge 2002) 104; Cassese (n 350) 71–72.

Similarly, a government engaged in a civil war may agree to apply the law of IAC to the insurgents. This has happened on multiple occasions, although the states concerned usually emphasized that they did so only as a matter of policy, implying their refusal to consider themselves bound by such decisions. For instance, the US Military Command in Vietnam decided in 1966 to treat all captured enemy soldiers as POWs.[418] The Nigerian government followed a similar policy in the 1967–70 civil war.[419] Likewise, Israel, despite its position that GCs do not apply de jure to the Occupied Palestinian Territories,[420] has consistently declared that it applies the provisions of GC IV within the territories de facto.[421] In order for such a proclamation to rise to the level of international obligation, the issuing government would have to state its intention to be bound by the declaration 'in clear and specific terms'.[422] Accordingly, in *Mrkšić*, the ICTY Appeals Chamber held that various statements of the Yugoslavian National Army to the effect that the GCs would apply to the treatment of the ethnically Croatian POWs in Vukovar in 1991 gave rise to the actual applicability of these instruments as a matter of law.[423]

Whether the norms in question are applied as a matter of law or policy, the practical difference is often minimal. For political reasons, states tend to observe declarations delimiting the permissible conduct in hostilities. This is because such declarations are issued as concessions to the opposing party, typically with the aim to induce it to reciprocal conduct or to improve the perception of the issuing state by the international public opinion; their violation would thus serve little practical utility. Hence, it is submitted that even a clear expression of the state's intention to be bound would not decrease that state's actual room for manoeuvre after issuing the declaration. In addition, it would also improve legal certainty for all actors involved. Nevertheless, it may well be that international criminalization on the basis of such extensions of applicability of IHL as seen in the *Mrkšić* case serves as a countervailing incentive for the military commanders concerned.

Provided that the binding declarations are comprehensive and entail a proclamation that the declaring entity will apply the full body of IHL to the conflict at hand, one may again speak of relative internationalization of a conflict. If a declaration

418 MACV Directive Number 381-11 (5 March 1966), reproduced in Prugh (n 22) 127–31. The practice to treat captured enemy soldiers as POWs in Indochinese conflicts dates back to the Franco-Vietnamese war (1946–54). On the basis of the French-declared intention to respect the spirit and 'insofar as the particular conditions of the struggle in Indochina permit it', the letter of the GCs, the ICRC even argued that the conflict—otherwise seen as a decolonization war—was international. See Letter from Director of ICRC to the Swiss Ministry of Foreign Affairs (27 January 1954), ICRC Archives, BAG 202-223-001.

419 Solf (n 352) 929–30.

420 But see Switzerland, 'Notification' (10 April 2014) (n 323) (accepting the accession of the 'State of Palestine' to the GCs).

421 The described Israeli legal position was first outlined by the then-Attorney General Meir Shamgar in 1971. M Shamgar, 'The Observance of International Law in the Administered Territories' (1971) 1 Israel Yearbook on Human Rights 262, 263–66. It was rejected by the ICJ in 2004. *Wall* (n 16) [90]–[101].

422 ILC Guiding Principles Applicable to Unilateral Declarations of States Capable of Creating Legal Obligations (2006) UN Doc A/61/10, principle 7.

423 *Prosecutor v Mrkšić et al* (Appeal Judgment) IT-95-13/1-A (5 May 2009) [69].

of this kind is made only by one party to the conflict, its legal effect differs from recognition of belligerency in that the declaration is only binding on the issuing entity. However, if both parties make concordant declarations or even enter into an express agreement to apply the law of IAC,[424] the legal effects are analogous to those of a situation, in which the territorial state, but not third states, grants a recognition of belligerency. The conflict would in such a case be internationalized between the parties to the extent agreed.[425]

It might be questioned to what extent this position aligns with the material conception of armed conflict as one of the central features of modern IHL.[426] The new ICRC commentary to the GCs suggests that this conception requires that conflict qualification 'must be based solely on the prevailing facts demonstrating the *de facto* existence of hostilities between the belligerents'.[427] Similarly, a trial chamber of the ICTY held in the *Blaškić* case that 'the parties to the conflict may not agree between themselves to change the nature of the conflict'.[428] All of this may suggest that the subjective will of the parties, whether expressed in parallel declarations or a dedicated agreement, should not be considered as sufficient in itself to modify the legal qualification of the conflict between them.[429]

However, the ruling in *Blaškić* was given in response to an argument, advanced by the defence in the case, that the the text of an agreement between the belligerents in central Bosnia supposedly evidenced that the situation had been a NIAC.[430] If the defence had succeeded in this argument, a range of rules would have had to be deemed inapplicable to the situation.[431] It is unlikely that the ICTY would have objected to the parties agreeing instead to abide by the more onerous norms of the law of IAC.[432] The better view thus is that the parties may not 'contract out' of a particular normative framework which would otherwise be binding on them,[433] but may certainly 'contract in' and accept additional obligations, even to the extent of internationalizing the conflict in question *inter se*.

Such result is additionally encouraged by Common Article 3(3), which requires the parties to a conflict to endeavour to bring into force, by means of special

[424] Two concordant declarations issued by the parties to an internal conflict should be treated as equivalent to an express agreement between them. cf Schindler (n 203) 148; cf also J Toman, *The Protection of Cultural Property in the Event of Armed Conflict* (UNESCO 1996) 216 (endorsing the same interpretation in the context of the protection of cultural property during NIAC).

[425] See also Cameron et al, 'Article 3' (n 371) 286 [852] fn 805 (noting, as an example of parallel unilateral declarations of this kind those made by the government of the DRC and the non-state armed group M23 in December 2013).

[426] On which see Section 1.2.2.1.

[427] Ferraro and Cameron, 'Article 2' (n 17) 76 [211].

[428] *Prosecutor v Blaškić* (Trial Judgment) IT-95-14-T (3 March 2000) [82].

[429] See also *Milutinović* Trial Judgment (n 267) [125] ('The existence of an armed conflict does not depend upon the views of the parties to the conflict.').

[430] *Blaškić* Trial Judgment (n 428) [78]–[80]. [431] cf ibid [74].

[432] cf ibid [82] (commending the ICRC—which was instrumental in mediating the preparation of the agreement in question—for attempting 'to provide the best possible protection to civilians and persons placed *hors de combat* whilst the war unfolded around them').

[433] G Mettraux, *International Crimes and the Ad Hoc Tribunals* (OUP 2005) 59.

agreements, norms pertaining to IACs.[434] The drafting history of the provision reveals that states had indeed considered it desirable that conflict parties in NIACs be allowed to augment the scope of the applicable law by means of such agreements.[435] Many agreements of this kind have been entered into by conflict parties in internal armed conflicts around the world, including in the Yemen (1963),[436] ex-Yugoslavia (1992),[437] Sudan (2002),[438] and Nepal (2006).[439] These agreements certainly may not derogate from the applicable IHL so as to lessen the protection under the law.[440] On the contrary, if a special agreement provides for the full application of the law of IACs, it should be seen as internationalizing the conflict as between the parties to the agreement.[441]

2.6 Evaluation

A NIAC transforms into an IAC if certain legal conditions are met. This chapter has sought to show that several distinct sets of such conditions have developed in international law. Hence, the notion of 'internationalized armed conflicts' cannot be equated with only one of these modalities. On the contrary, that concept encompasses conflicts internationalized through outside intervention; by way of state dissolution; through a legal fiction set out in Article 1(4) AP I; and on a relative basis.

The former two forms of internationalization bring about the 'standard' Common Article 2 situation of two or more states (or, more precisely, independent subjects of international law) being involved in an armed conflict. This may either be the result of (1) a direct or indirect intervention by an *external* actor such as a state or

[434] See Common Art 3(3) GCs ('The Parties to the conflict should further endeavour to bring into force, by means of special agreements, all or part of the other provisions of the present Convention.'); see also Hague Convention for the Protection of Cultural Property in the Event of Armed Conflict (signed 14 May 1954, entered into force 7 August 1956) 249 UNTS 240, Art 19(2) (containing a similar encouragement to parties to NIACs 'to bring into force, by means of special agreements, all or part of the other provisions of' that Convention).

[435] *Final Record* (n 374) vol II B, 79 (USSR); ibid 120–24 (Seventh Report drawn up by the Special Committee of the Joint Committee).

[436] ICRC, *Annual Report 1963* (ICRC 1964) 16–17; see also K Boals, 'The Relevance of International Law to the Internal War in Yemen' in RA Falk (ed), *The International Law of Civil War* (Johns Hopkins Press 1971) 315.

[437] Agreement on the Application of IHL between the Parties to the Conflict in Bosnia and Herzegovina (22 May 1992), UN Doc S/25824, Annex (12 May 1993) 3 (confirming that the GCs and AP I were 'fully applicable' in the conflict).

[438] Agreement between the Government of the Republic of Sudan and the Sudan People's Liberation Movement to Protect Non-Combatant Civilians and Civilian Facilities from Military Attack (31 March 2002) <http://peacemaker.un.org/sudan-protection-civilians2002>.

[439] The Code of Conduct for Ceasefire agreed between the Government of Nepal and the CPN (Maoist), Gokarna, (25 May 2006) <http://peacemaker.un.org/nepal-25pointceasefire2006>.

[440] Common Art 3(1) GCs (mandating that 'each Party to the conflict shall be bound to apply, *as a minimum*' the provisions of the article) (emphasis added); Cameron et al, 'Article 3' (n 371) 287 [854].

[441] But see Cameron et al, 'Article 3' (n 371) 289 [860] (arguing that the conclusion of special agreements does not imply recognition of belligerency nor signify that the non-state party to the agreement possesses full international legal personality).

an international organization, or of (2) an *internal* development occasioning the dissolution of the territorial state.

The latter two forms are complementary and stem from the development of treaty and customary rules, which proclaim certain intra-state conflicts as (or as equivalent to) IACs. These are (3) the so-called 'wars of national liberation', a rarely-if-ever applied legal category, originally designed to transform internal conflicts into IACs on an *absolute* basis; and (4) instances of *relative* internationalization effected by means of recognition of belligerency, unilateral declarations, and special agreements under Common Article 3.

3

Complex Conflict Situations

3.1 Introduction

Armed conflicts are complex phenomena characterized by a plethora of causes, contributing factors, and conflicting interests. This is true even for the most binary of conflicts, in which two parties only resort to violence in order to achieve a pursued aim. However, the situation gets exponentially more complicated by the entry of every additional independent conflict party, creating the potential for mutual interdependence, alliances, and tension. That raises a crucial legal question for the present study. Specifically, if the entry of a third party results in, or is a factor in, conflict internationalization (under one of the forms discussed in Chapter 2), what effect does it have on the law applicable to such situations?

The plurality of parties implies a plurality of potential conflict relationships. For example, since the mid-1990s, an ongoing internal armed conflict had existed in Afghanistan between the de facto Taliban government and the insurgent group Northern Alliance.[1] The intervention of US-led coalition forces following the 9/11 attacks in 2001 meant that a range of new actors entered the conflict scene. Should the mutual relationships between each of these actors be considered separately, as 'mini-conflicts' of sorts, or did an overarching single international armed conflict (IAC) come into existence after the attacks from abroad commenced?

More complex situations are also conceivable. Consider, for instance, the situation in the Democratic Republic of the Congo (DRC) following the assumption of power by Laurent Kabila in 1998. The country was plagued by several separate cases of armed hostilities, some of which appeared to have been purely internal in nature, such as the tribal conflict between the Balendu and the Bahema.[2] By contrast, others were marked by heavy foreign involvement. For example, the

[1] See, eg, LR Blank and BR Farley, 'Characterizing United States Operations in Pakistan: Is the U.S. Engaged in an Armed Conflict?' (2010) 34 Fordham Int'l Law Journal 151, 179; F Hampson, 'Afghanistan 2001–2010' in E Wilmshurst (ed), *International Law and the Classification of Conflicts* (OUP 2012) 242–43.

[2] Report on the Situation of Human Rights in the Democratic Republic of the Congo, submitted by the Special Rapporteur, Mr Roberto Garretón, in accordance with Commission on Human Rights Resolution 2000/15, UN Doc E/CN.4/2001/40 (1 February 2001) 15 [31] (hereinafter Garretón Report); but see also ibid 36 [154] (noting that it was 'incitement by Ugandan soldiers' that had triggered this conflict). For a more detailed discussion of the situation in the DRC after 1998, see text to notes 71–82 in this chapter.

most formidable rebel group, the Rally for Congolese Democracy (RCD), was assisted in its struggle against the Kinshasa government by no fewer than three regional powers, including Burundi, Rwanda, and Uganda.[3] Yet others were conflicts fought by outside states against their insurgents in the Congo's territory, such as Angola's civil war between the ruling government and the UNITA rebel forces.[4] In total, it is widely accepted that between 1998 and 2003, nine states and around twenty armed groups were involved in what became known as the Second Congo War, or the Great War of Africa.[5] How should such situations be assessed? Should internationalization of one conflict have a bearing on other conflicts in the same territory?

The analysis in this chapter focuses principally on conflicts internationalized by foreign intervention. This is in part because intervention, by definition, results in the eponymous 'complex conflict situation'; in other words, a situation characterized by the participation of more than two conflict parties.[6] Moreover, in much of the relevant scholarly discourse, the question of coexistence of several conflicts in one state territory is typically treated as an aspect of qualification of situations marked by an outside armed intervention.[7] However, it is certainly conceivable for other modalities of internationalization to evolve to encompass several conflict parties acting concurrently.[8] For example, the process of state dissolution may see one of the newly formed states locked in simultaneous hostilities against a non-state actor in its own territory and against another new state: arguably, this was the fact pattern in Bosnia and Herzegovina after 1992.[9] Similarly, an armed group whose belligerency was recognized by the territorial government may additionally face armed opposition from within its own ranks: consider the historical example of the Second Boer War (1899–1902), during which hundreds of so-called 'joiners' abandoned the Boers and formed irregular and regular units supporting the British forces.[10] Accordingly, the following analysis should be taken to apply *mutatis mutandis* to all internationalized armed conflicts with more than two belligerent parties.

[3] US Department of State, Democratic Republic of Congo Country Report on Human Rights Practices for 1998 (26 February 1999) 1; Garretón Report (n 2) 14 [22].

[4] Garretón Report (n 2) 48.

[5] Garretón Report (n 2) 2; Roberto Garretón, Report for the International Criminal Court, Document ICC 01/04-01/06 <www.icc-cpi.int/RelatedRecords/CR2015_15041.PDF> 10.

[6] On outside intervention as a modality of internationalization, see Section 2.2.

[7] See, eg, S Sivakumaran, *The Law of Non-International Armed Conflict* (OUP 2012) 222–25; M Milanovic, 'The Applicability of the Conventions to "Transnational" and "Mixed" Conflicts' in A Clapham, P Gaeta, and M Sassòli (eds), *The 1949 Geneva Conventions: A Commentary* (OUP 2015) 35–39 [29]–[41]; N Zamir, *Classification of Conflicts in International Humanitarian Law: The Legal Impact of Foreign Intervention in Civil Wars* (Edward Elgar 2017) 98–111.

[8] On those modalities of internationalization, see Sections 2.3–2.5.

[9] See further Section 2.3.1.2.

[10] A Wessels, 'Afrikaners at War' in J Gooch (ed), *The Boer War: Direction, Experience and Image* (Routledge 2013) 99–100.

3.2 The Apparent Choice: 'Global' Versus 'Mixed' Approach

The dilemma presented by complex conflict situations is often described as a choice between a 'global' and a 'mixed' characterization of situations of armed violence.[11] The global approach argues that a foreign military intervention 'transforms' or 'contaminates' any ongoing non-international armed conflict(s) (NIAC(s)) in the target state's territory.[12] Consequently, once internationalization has taken place, the law of IAC will apply 'globally' to all the conflict parties and in the entire territory of the state in question.[13]

By contrast, under the mixed approach, the said intervention would not have any effect on the nature of the ongoing conflicts.[14] The individual conflicts would continue to exist in parallel and the law of IACs would *only* apply to the relationship between the intervening state and the target state.[15] As a logical extension of this view, each conflict pair should be assessed separately, with a number of legally separate conflicts potentially co-existing in one state's territory.[16]

It is submitted that international humanitarian law (IHL) does not actually present an 'either-or' dilemma of this type. The two positions are reconcilable. In this chapter, they are also referred to as the 'pure' variants; the chapter also suggests that a 'hybrid', more nuanced approach should be adopted that combines the elements of both 'pure' approaches. It thus begins by deconstructing the pros and cons of the 'pure' approaches, considering the global approach first and the mixed approach second, and then it proposes the 'hybrid' model as a workable alternative.

3.2.1 Pure global view and the geographical scope of applicability of IHL

The most logical starting point with respect to assessing the 'pure global' approach is in the question of the geographical scope of applicability of IHL. Perhaps if the rules require the law to apply to the *whole* territory of the conflict parties, it could be argued that the entry of an outside power extinguishes the law of NIACs and replaces it with the law of IACs with effect for that territory.[17] If that were the case, by way of an example, the NATO intervention against the government of Libya in 2011—undoubtedly an IAC—should be seen as triggering the application of the

[11] See, eg, JG Stewart, 'Towards a Single Definition of Armed Conflict in International Humanitarian Law: A Critique of Internationalized Armed Conflict' (2003) 85 IRRC 313, 333–35; T Hoffmann, 'Squaring the Circle? International Humanitarian Law and Transnational Armed Conflicts' in MJ Matheson and D Momtaz (eds), *Rules and Institutions of International Humanitarian Law Put to the Test of Recent Armed Conflicts* (Brill 2010) 242–45; KA Johnston, 'Transformations of Conflict Status in Libya' (2012) 17 JCSL 81, 98–102; Zamir (n 7) 98–103.

[12] cf Hoffmann (n 11) 230; Zamir (n 7) 98.

[13] cf Johnston (n 11) 98; L Cameron et al, 'Article 3: Conflicts Not of an International Character' in ICRC (ed), *Commentary on the First Geneva Convention* (CUP 2016) 146 [403].

[14] cf Johnston (n 11) 100.

[15] cf Hoffmann (n 11) 243; Zamir (n 7) 98.

[16] cf Milanovic (n 7); Cameron et al (n 13) 147 [406].

[17] See, eg, *Prosecutor v Aleksovski* (Trial Judgment) IT-95-14/1-T (25 June 1999) (diss op Rodrigues) [19]–[20].

law of IACs as regards all conflict parties in Libya's territory, including the rebel forces that were operating from Benghazi at the time.

What is the geographical scope of application of the rules of IHL as enshrined in the Geneva Conventions? The 1969 Vienna Convention on the Law of Treaties (VCLT), most of which is considered to be reflective of customary law,[18] only establishes a residual rule:[19] according to its Article 29, a treaty is binding upon each party in respect of its 'entire territory' unless a different intention appears from the treaty or is otherwise established.[20] (All proposals to include a general rule concerning the extraterritorial application of treaties were rejected as problematic and unsatisfactory during the drafting process of the VCLT.)[21] The Geneva Conventions and their First Additional Protocol do not, however, contain a general clause about their territorial scope, and a close examination of their provisions uncovers a spectrum of possible solutions.

Some of the provisions seem to apply due to their nature in the immediate theatre of operations only. For instance, the targeting rules cannot, by definition, apply elsewhere. If a conflict party designates a new target outside of the existing combat zone, the act of its designation merely extends the combat zone to encompass that target as well. By contrast, some provisions apply irrespective of territorial considerations.[22] For example, persons deprived of their liberty by one of the conflict parties do not lose their protection if they are transported outside of the territory in which combat operations are being conducted.[23] Although the defeat of the *Afrika Korps* in Northern Africa during the Second World War was followed by the removal of hundreds of thousands of German POWs into the United States, it was never suggested that their status was affected by their transfer.[24] So how do we determine to what territory the rules of IACs apply?

An attempt to answer this question authoritatively appeared in the first case before the International Criminal Tribunal for the former Yugoslavia (ICTY). In *Tadić*, the Appeals Chamber of the ICTY faced a very practical problem that the accused could only be held accountable for certain crimes if they had been committed within

[18] S Rosenne, *The Law of Treaties: A Guide to the Legislative History of the Vienna Convention* (Brill 1970) 91; M Akehurst, 'Custom as a Source of International Law' (1974–75) 47 BYBIL 1, 46–47; ME Villiger, *Commentary on the 1969 Vienna Convention on the Law of Treaties* (Martinus Nijhoff 2009) 27 [63]; A Aust, *Modern Treaty Law and Practice* (3rd edn, CUP 2013) 10–11.

[19] A Aust, *Handbook of International Law* (2nd edn, CUP 2010) 81; Villiger (n 18) 392 [6].

[20] Vienna Convention on the Law of Treaties (concluded 23 May 1969, entered into force 27 January 1980) 1155 UNTS 331, Art 29 (hereafter VCLT).

[21] ILC, Draft Articles on the Law of Treaties with commentaries, Yearbook of the ILC (1966) vol II, 213–14 [5].

[22] See further K Schöberl, 'The Geographical Scope of Application of the Conventions' in Clapham et al (n 7) 74–75 [19]–[20].

[23] See, eg, Art 46(3) GC III (requiring the detaining power to ensure the safety of POWs during their transfer by sea); JS Pictet (ed), *Geneva Convention III relative to the Treatment of Prisoners of War: Commentary* (ICRC 1960) 553 (noting that the Article 118(4)(b) GC III requirement for the detaining power to bear the costs of repatriation extends to localities outside of that power's territory as long as these are under its authority).

[24] See AP Krammer, 'German Prisoners of War in the United States' (1976) 40 Military Affairs 68, 72. Notably, many former inmates were so impressed by the treatment they had received in the POW camps that they decided to stay after the war and apply for US nationality.

the context of an armed conflict.[25] The Chamber thus felt the need to clarify the legal landscape as well as to address the defendant's 'ingenious'[26] argument that there was no armed conflict in the Prijedor region where his alleged crimes were said to have taken place because the Bosnian Serbs had managed to take control of it without any active combat.[27] Accordingly, it stated that IHL applies 'from the initiation' of an armed conflict 'in the whole territory of the warring States or, in the case of internal conflicts, the whole territory under the control of a party' until peace is re-established.[28] This way it was able to conclude that IHL applied even with respect to crimes committed in prison camps for civilians, located in the Prijedor region far away from the theatre of hostilities.[29]

With respect to IACs, the Appeals Chamber based its assessment on textual and teleological reasons. Textually, it relied on Article 6 GC IV and Article 3(b) AP I in support of the proposition that IHL applies throughout the territories of the conflict parties.[30] Both of these provisions contain language to the effect that the Conventions and AP I shall cease to apply 'in the territory of Parties to the conflict' on the general close of military operations.[31] The Chamber's obvious, although unstated, inference was that if the rules are supposed to cease to apply in the parties' territory at a certain point in time, they must have applied across that territory before that moment.

Although possibly superficially appealing, this interpretation has to be rejected if the context of the norms on temporal application of the Conventions and the Protocol is carefully examined. The said provisions use the phrase 'in the territory of Parties to the conflict' to differentiate this general case of application of the norms to the conflict itself, from a special case of their application to occupied territories.[32] In occupied territories, the rules dissociate the end of application of IHL from the close of hostilities.[33] As demonstrated by the examples of the Occupied Palestinian Territories since 1967, or of the Japanese occupation of Singapore after the Second World War, occupation may end years after the military operations are over.[34] In such cases, the occupier will continue to exercise governmental functions in the

[25] cf Statute of the International Criminal Tribunal for the former Yugoslavia, UN Doc S/RES/827 (25 May 1993) (last amended 7 July 2009), Arts 2, 3, and 5.

[26] APV Rogers, *Law on the Battlefield* (2nd edn, Manchester University Press 2005) 219.

[27] cf *Prosecutor v Tadić* (Decision on Jurisdiction) IT-94-1-AR72 (2 October 1995) [66] (hereafter *Tadić* Decision on Jurisdiction).

[28] *Tadić* Decision on Jurisdiction (n 27) [70]. [29] ibid. [30] ibid [68].

[31] Art 6(3) GC IV; Art 3(b) AP I.

[32] See further J Grignon, 'The Geneva Conventions and the End of Occupation' in Clapham et al (n 7) 1576–86.

[33] cf Art 6(3) GC IV ('In the case of occupied territory, the application of the present Convention shall cease one year after the general close of military operations; however, the Occupying Power shall be bound, for the duration of the occupation, to the extent that such Power exercises the functions of government in such territory, by the provisions of [enumerated articles].'); Art 3(b) AP I ('in the case of occupied territories, [the application shall cease] on the termination of the occupation, except, in either circumstance, for those persons whose final release, repatriation or re-establishment takes place thereafter. These persons shall continue to benefit from the relevant provisions of the Conventions and of this Protocol until their final release repatriation or re-establishment.').

[34] See, eg, Y Dinstein, *International Law of Belligerent Occupation* (CUP 2009) 116–17.

occupied territory.[35] The drafters had therefore considered it desirable to continue to hold the occupying state bound by IHL in order to safeguard the protection of the persons in its power.[36] These provisions, therefore, determine the temporal scope of application of the treaty instruments—nothing more and nothing less.[37] The rules 'switch off' the application of the Geneva Conventions (GCs) in the territory of the conflict parties, regardless of whether they had been 'switched on' everywhere in that territory in the first place. The ICTY Appeals Chamber's textual interpretation therefore appears to be incorrect.

Teleologically, the Chamber reasoned that 'the very nature of the Conventions—particularly Conventions III and IV—dictates their application throughout the territories of the parties to the conflict; any other construction would substantially defeat their purpose'.[38] Although the Chamber did not go into any further detail, its position appears to be that the Conventions could not achieve their main purpose—the protection of the victims of war[39]—if they did not apply to these persons. However, here the Chamber mistakenly used the vehicle of application *ratione loci* to achieve an aim properly served by application *ratione personae*. It has been shown that some provisions (such as those setting out the parties' obligations towards detainees) need to apply even outside of the territory of the warring parties in order to safeguard the protection of the victims of war foreseen by the GCs.[40] It is submitted that the correct approach is to address the problem via the personal scope of application of IHL rules. Moreover, the absence of a reference to application *ratione loci* in IHL treaties is not a coincidence: the drafters had expressly discussed the possibility with respect to AP I and agreed that such a reference would be too restrictive and would not add to the clarity of the instrument.[41] The purpose referred to by the Appeals Chamber is better served if these rules are considered applicable to persons and relationships with a nexus to the IHL-triggering armed conflict.[42]

In relation to internal armed conflicts, the Chamber held that the aim of protection of those taking no active part or no longer taking part in the hostilities (Common Article 3) and of all those affected by an armed conflict (Article 2(1) AP II) suggested 'a broad geographical scope' extending beyond the actual hostilities.[43] Although it highlighted in passing the 'war nexus' requirement[44] proposed earlier, which would suggest using a *ratione personae* lens, in the end it settled for a strictly

[35] On the meaning of 'functions of government' in Art 6 GC IV, see Grignon (n 32) 1580–81.

[36] cf JS Pictet (ed), *Geneva Convention IV relative to the Protection of Civilian Persons in Time of War: Commentary* (ICRC 1958) 62–63; Y Sandoz, C Swinarski, and B Zimmermann (eds), *Commentary on the Additional Protocols of 8 June 1977 to the Geneva Conventions of 12 August 1949* (ICRC 1987) 68 [154]–[56] (hereafter Sandoz et al, *APs Commentary*).

[37] See also T Ferraro, 'Determining the Beginning and End of an Occupation under International Humanitarian Law' (2012) 94 IRRC 133, 156 fn 72.

[38] *Tadić* Decision on Jurisdiction (n 27) [68].

[39] cf JS Pictet (ed), *Geneva Convention I for the Amelioration of the Condition of the Wounded and Sick in Armed Forces in the Field: Commentary* (ICRC 1952) 14 ('The discussions [at the 1949 diplomatic conference] were dominated throughout by a common horror of the evils caused by the recent World War and a determination to lessen the sufferings of war victims.').

[40] See text to note 23 in this chapter.

[41] Sandoz et al, *APs Commentary* (n 36) 138 [413].

[42] Similarly Schöberl (n 22) 75.

[43] *Tadić* Decision on Jurisdiction (n 27) [69].

[44] ibid [69].

geographical criterion of applicability, namely that IHL was to apply 'in the whole territory under the control of a party'.[45] This conclusion is liable to criticism on at least two grounds.

Firstly, as shown earlier, applying a territorial lens to persons and relationships affected by armed conflicts is unhelpful as it obfuscates the reality that it is not their geographical location but rather their connection (or nexus) to the conflict that makes the rules of IHL relevant to them. Moreover, similarly to the rules applicable in IACs, the drafting history of AP II indicates that the omission of a criterion *ratione loci* was deliberate;[46] in the words of the International Committee of the Red Cross (ICRC) commentary, 'the applicability of the Protocol follows from a criteria [*sic*] related to persons, and not to places.'[47] The strictly geographical approach endorsed by the Appeals Chamber may also lead to counterintuitive results in situations where hostilities are limited to specific parts of the territories held by the parties: for example, this was the case in the civil war of Sri Lanka (1983–2009), which took place mainly in the northern and eastern regions of the country.[48]

Second, the limiting proviso that the territory in question must be 'under the control of a party' was unsubstantiated by any analysis, unparalleled with the requirements pertaining to IACs, and it raised further uncertainty as to the level of control required.[49] Accordingly, in the judgments of the ICTY's sister tribunal, the ICTR, Trial Chambers have usually acknowledged the *Tadić* decision, but then omitted the control requirement.[50] Likewise, in *Niyonteze*, one of the few domestic judgments to grapple with this issue, the Swiss Military Appeals Tribunal expressly acknowledged that the norms governing NIACs apply beyond 'le front ou le contexte géographique étroit du théâtre effectif des opérations de combats'.[51] Even the ICTY has been quite liberal in applying the requirement that had originated in its own case law. For example, in *Milutinović et al* it held five official representatives of Serbia criminally responsible for the crimes of deportation and forcible transfer as crimes against humanity committed against Kosovo Albanian civilians.[52] The Trial Chamber was satisfied that the elements of the crimes were fulfilled by a Serbian-orchestrated campaign of violence and intimidation in Kosovo, without inquiring in depth whether each of the villages from which the civilians had fled was actually under the control

[45] ibid [70].

[46] Switzerland, *Official Records of the Diplomatic Conference on the Reaffirmation and Development of International Humanitarian Law Applicable in Armed Conflicts, Geneva (1974–1977)* (Federal Political Department 1978) CDDH/I/SR.22, 211 [47]–[48] (hereafter *Official Records*).

[47] Sandoz et al, *APs Commentary* (n 36) 1360 [4490].

[48] Schöberl (n 22) 75 fn 53.

[49] See L Arimatsu, 'Territory, Boundaries and the Law of Armed Conflict' (2009) 12 YIHL 157, 187–88.

[50] See, eg, *Prosecutor v Akayesu* (Trial Judgment) ICTR-96-4-T (2 September 1998) [635]–[636]; *Prosecutor v Kayishema and Ruzindana* (Trial Judgment) ICTR-95-1-T (21 May 1999) [182]–[183]; *Prosecutor v Rutaganda* (Trial Judgment) ICTR-96-2-T (6 December 1999) [101]–[102]; *Prosecutor v Musema* (Trial Judgment) ICTR-96-13-T (27 January 2000) [283]; *Prosecutor v Bagilishema* (Trial Judgment) ICTR-95-1A-T (7 June 2001) [101]; *Prosecutor v Semanza* (Trial Judgment) ICTR-97-20-T (15 May 2003) [367].

[51] *Niyonteze v Public Prosecutor* (26 May 2000) (Switzerland, Tribunal militaire d'appel 1A) 32.

[52] *Prosecutor v Milutinović et al* (Trial Judgment) IT-05-87-T (26 February 2009) vol 3 [1208]–[1212].

of the Serbian forces.[53] By contrast, it did state that there was a nexus between the crimes and the armed conflict in question.[54]

In summary, it is suggested that the ICTY's holding from *Tadić* need not be considered incorrect insofar as it is taken to mean that provisions of IHL *may* apply in the whole territory of the conflict parties. This is undoubtedly correct: if the facts on the ground are closely related to the hostilities and fall within the subject matter of IHL rules, then IHL will apply to the affected persons and relationships.[55] In the ICTY's ensuing jurisprudence, this is also how the rules of applicability were interpreted, with emphasis placed on the war nexus, not on the geographical location.[56] Similarly, the ICRC as the guardian of IHL interprets its mandate to relate to situations of armed conflict, which it understands as covering 'the entire territory of the parties to a conflict *as far as the protection and assistance of the victims of that conflict are concerned*'.[57]

However, it would be incorrect to conclude that an outbreak of an armed conflict in the territory of a state triggers the application of IHL relative to that type of conflict across the entire state territory, without regard to the actual reach of the ongoing conflict. Persons unaffected by and unrelated to the conflict fall outside the scope of IHL even if they find themselves in the territory of the state engaged in the conflict in question.[58] This interpretation also prevents counterintuitive and outright absurd outcomes. In addition to the example of the Sri Lankan conflict mentioned earlier,[59] reference has been made in this regard to the provision of humanitarian relief to victims of natural disasters occurring in the territory of a state involved in an armed conflict, but at a great distance from and with no relationship to existing hostilities.[60] For example, the criticized strict geographical approach would require that 'any relief provided to the United States in the immediate aftermath of Hurricane Katrina in August 2005 would have been primarily governed by IHL'.[61] But that would surely amount to an impractical and absurd outcome and should be rejected as such.

[53] *Milutinović* Trial Judgment (n 52) vol 2 [1179]–[1262].

[54] ibid [1180].

[55] Similarly Arimatsu (n 49) 189; Schöberl (n 22) 83 [36].

[56] See, eg, *Prosecutor v Stakić* (Trial Judgment) IT-97-24-T (22 March 2006) [342]; *Prosecutor v Kunarac et al* (Appeal Judgment) IT-96-23&IT-96-23/1-A (12 June 2002) [57]–[58]; *Prosecutor v Mrkšić et al* (Trial Judgment) IT-95-13/1-T (27 September 2007) [423]; *Prosecutor v Mladić* (Trial Judgment) IT-09-92-T (22 November 2017) vol 3 [3015]–[3016]; *Prosecutor v Prlić et al* (Appeal Judgment) IT-04-74-A (29 November 2017) vol 1 [232].

[57] Agreement on the Organization of the International Activities of the Components of the International Red Cross and Red Crescent Movement (signed 26 November 1997) (1998) 38 IRRC 159, Art 5(1)(a) (emphasis added).

[58] The requirement of a connection with the conflict does not mean that the conflict must be the only cause of the situation in which these persons find themselves. For example, there is no reason why victims of natural disasters whose plight was *exacerbated* by the armed conflict should not be covered by IHL provisions on humanitarian relief. See also D Gavshon, 'The Applicability of IHL in Mixed Situations of Disaster and Conflict' (2009) 14 JCSL 243, 248 (reaching the same conclusion on the basis of a teleological analysis of Part II of GC IV). In terms of formal logic, it is sufficient for the conflict to be a contributing cause; it need not be a complete or a necessary cause of the situation at hand. Conversely, as explained in the main text, IHL does not apply to persons whose conduct or situation is entirely unrelated to an ongoing armed conflict, irrespective of their geographical location.

[59] See text to note 48 in this chapter.

[60] Gavshon (n 58) 247.

[61] ibid.

A crucial upshot of the analysis presented thus far is that it excludes one variant of the pure global approach that would have all conflicts transformed to international solely on the basis of territorial applicability of IHL. Its rejection means that an outbreak of an IAC does not automatically affect all relationships in a state's territory. The next step to consider, then, is whether the addition of this international element might transform the nature of all *conflict* relationships. If that was the case, the pure global approach could still be plausible insofar as this effect would make the law of IAC applicable to these conflicts. Accordingly, the following section considers policy arguments advanced in favour of such legal transformation.

3.2.2 Blanket nature of the pure global view

There are some strong reasons militating in favour of the use of the pure global view, including the improved ease and consistency of application. Before moving on to the analysis of these individual reasons, it bears emphasizing that the argument in favour of the pure global view is of a general nature. Put differently, it maintains that as long as several conflicts co-exist in one state's territory, their legal nature will always change to international once an IAC breaks out in that territory, irrespective of the mutual relationships between individual conflicts.

It is submitted that this variant of the global approach should also be rejected. Applying such a standard for determination of the conflict nature is too sweeping and it ignores the often more nuanced reality on the ground. Proponents of this view admittedly portray its blanket nature as a key advantage. They argue that application of the same norms to all conflict situations is easier[62] and consistent.[63] Although this may be true, upon closer inspection, neither of these reasons actually proves convincing.

Firstly, in a similar context, Marco Sassòli rightly rejects the ease or difficulty of conflict qualification as irrelevant: 'the fact that a situation is difficult to qualify under existing law is, except for first-year students, no argument to apply a new, easy solution'.[64] Lawyers often have to put up with the application of complex norms to complex facts and while the simplification of application may be an expedient goal *de lege ferenda*, it cannot in and of itself serve as a justification to create a new meta-rule of application. Therefore, in practice, it may be necessary to apply 'different

[62] Report of the Commission of Experts established pursuant to Security Council Resolution 780 (1992), UN Doc S/25274 (10 February 1993) [45]; Final Report of the Commission of Experts established pursuant to Security Council Resolution 780 (1992), UN Doc S/1994/674 (27 May 1994) [44]; *Aleksovski* Trial Judgment (n 17) (diss op Rodrigues) [23] (embracing the cited report of the Commission of Experts); Hoffmann (n 11) 244; Johnston (n 11) 101; Sivakumaran (n 7) 224.

[63] *Aleksovski* Trial Judgment (n 17) (diss op Rodrigues) [27]; S Vité, 'Typology of Armed Conflicts in International Humanitarian Law: Legal Concepts and Actual Situations' (2009) 91 IRRC 69, 86; E David, *Principes de droit des conflits armés* (5th edn, Bruylant 2012) 178.

[64] M Sassòli, 'The Legal Qualification of the Conflicts in the Former Yugoslavia: Double Standards or New Horizons for International Humanitarian Law?' in S Yee and W Tieya (eds), *International Law in the Post-Cold War World: Essays in Memory of Li Haopei* (Routledge 2001) 330.

legal regimes ... to persons deprived of their liberty by either the non-State armed group or the intervening State'.[65]

Secondly, the call for consistency is laudable in principle but mistaken in this context. It originally appeared in Judge Rodrigues's dissent in *Aleksovski* where he seemed to argue for two kinds of consistency: the consistency of protection of 'victims of similar acts' and the consistency of judicial determination of conflict nature in such complex situations.[66] However, the risk of inconsistency in both of these senses is an inevitable consequence of the existence of a distinction between international and non-international armed conflicts in IHL.[67] As long as there is a legal distinction between IACs and NIACs, there will be some glaring discrepancies in the protection of victims of acts that are 'similar' or even identical—except for the type of armed conflict in which they occur.[68] The possibility of various trial chambers reaching different conclusions as to the conflict nature, alluded to by Judge Rodrigues, is definitely not a desirable outcome.[69] However, it must be acknowledged that it results from the chambers' primary responsibility to determine and assess the facts before them.[70]

In addition, the blanket nature of the global view may result in absurd outcomes. The complex situation in the Congo during the Great War of Africa between 1998 and 2003 is a case in point. After Laurent Kabila took power in the capital Kinshasa, large parts of the country descended into violence.[71] The new president's weak hold on power was perceived by many regional actors as an opportunity to profit from the country's vast natural resources.[72] Kabila's government was directly challenged by at least two separate rebel movements. The RCD was established in Goma on the Rwandan-Congolese border with significant Rwandan support and was engaged in the most serious clashes with the government forces.[73] The Movement for the Liberation of the Congo (MLC) operated with Ugandan support in the northern Equateur province.[74] In addition to these confrontations for domination

[65] Cameron et al (n 13) 147 [405]. On the legal framework applicable to detention in NIACs, see generally L Hill-Cawthorne, *Detention in Non-International Armed Conflict* (OUP 2016).

[66] *Aleksovski* Trial Judgment (n 17) (diss op Rodrigues) [27]; see also David (n 63) 178.

[67] K Mačák and N Zamir, 'The Applicability of International Humanitarian Law to the Conflict in Libya' (2012) 14 ICLR 403, 413–14; see also Zamir (n 7) 102.

[68] This has been criticized on numerous occasions. See, eg, E Crawford, 'Unequal before the Law: The Case for the Elimination of the Distinction between International and Non-International Armed Conflicts' (2007) 20 LJIL 441; Y Sandoz, 'Foreword' in J-M Henckaerts and L Doswald-Beck (eds), *Customary International Humanitarian Law* (CUP 2005) vol 1, xxii; Stewart (n 11) 313 and references cited therein. However, these arguments are properly made *de lege ferenda*, not with respect to the *lex lata* to be applied to existing conflicts. See also D Schindler, 'The Different Types of Armed Conflicts According to the Geneva Conventions and Protocols' (1979) 163 RdC 117, 138–39.

[69] cf *Aleksovski* Trial Judgment (n 17) (diss op Rodrigues) [27].

[70] See, eg, *Prosecutor v Tadić* (Appeal Judgment) IT-94-1-A (15 July 1999) [64].

[71] See generally F Reyntjens, *The Great African War: Congo and Regional Geopolitics, 1996–2006* (CUP 2009) 194–231.

[72] See further UNSC, Final Report of the Panel of Experts on the Illegal Exploitation of Natural Resources and Other Forms of Wealth of the Democratic Republic of the Congo, UN Doc S/2002/1146 (16 October 2002) 28–29 [149]–[154].

[73] R Lemarchand, *The Dynamics of Violence in Central Africa* (University of Pennsylvania Press 2009) 217.

[74] ibid.

over the DRC, several 'wars within the war' (a term coined by Filip Reyntjens[75]) continued at their own pace. One of them was the conflict between the Bahema and the Balendu ethnic groups in the Ituri region. Although there is evidence that Uganda fuelled the conflict by supporting the Bahema,[76] these clashes predated the Second Congo War and they have been authoritatively described as 'classical ethnic confrontations over power and assets (land)' localized in Ituri.[77]

A persuasive case can be made in support of the internationalized nature of the conflict between the RCD and the Congolese government. The RCD was established in 1998 with significant Rwandan support and there is strong evidence that its operations were co-ordinated from Kigali.[78] This would suffice for the two crucial components of the test for internationalization by intervention proposed elsewhere in this work—essentially, support and co-ordination[79]—to be met.[80] But it would be absurd to claim that by the same token, *all* conflicts occurring in the Congolese territory simultaneously (the UN Special Rapporteur spoke of no less than nine)[81] should automatically be considered international, too. Perhaps the Ugandan support for the Bahema was of a nature and intensity that would turn it into a conflict party operating against the Balendu without the territorial state's consent.[82] This would have also triggered the applicability of the law of IACs for the conflict parties. But to claim that the Rwandan involvement with the RCD in Goma by itself affected the legal nature of the conflict in Ituri would amount to divorcing the law from the facts on the ground.

This logic equally undermines the broader claim of the proponents of the 'pure' global view that following internationalization, all conflicts in a given state's territory should be seen as a single 'global' international conflict. In fact, it is conceivable that several conflicts come about in one state's territory, but they nevertheless have an insignificant or no mutual relationship.[83] Especially in states blessed with vast territories or cursed with a complicated position in the region, this plurality of mutually independent armed conflicts is often a fact. For instance, Russia's short but

75 Reyntjens (n 71) 207.

76 See Garretón Report (n 2) 36 [154].

77 Reyntjens (n 71) 216; see further Lemarchand (n 73) 235–36; 'DRC: IRIN Focus on Hema-Lendu conflict' *IRIN* (15 November 1999) <www.africa.upenn.edu/Hornet/irin_111599b.html> (citing a humanitarian source as stating that '[i]t started as a land issue, but it has now become a conflict over power and money').

78 Lemarchand (n 73) 217; Reyntjens (n 71) 195.

79 See Section 2.2.2.4.

80 cf L Arimatsu, 'The Democratic Republic of the Congo 1993–2010' in E Wilmshurst (ed), *International Law and the Classification of Conflicts* (OUP 2012) 174, 178 fn 154 (accepting the possibility that RCD/Goma was acting under the overall control of Rwanda, but noting that a conclusion to that effect would be 'dependent on the evidence').

81 Garretón Report (n 2) 3.

82 But see *Prosecutor v Germain Katanga* (Trial Judgment) ICC-01/04-01/07 (7 March 2014) [1219]–[1228] (holding that between January and May 2003, the period material for that case, the DRC's consent to Ugandan military operations on its territory precluded the application of the law of IAC to the hostilities in question).

83 Similarly, armed hostilities could break out between two or more non-state armed groups in an occupied territory, but without the occupying power being involved in the fighting. See A Paulus and M Vashakmadze, 'Asymmetrical War and the Notion of Armed Conflict: A Tentative Conceptualization' (2008) 91 IRRC 95, 115; L Moir, 'The Concept of Non-International Armed Conflict' in Clapham et al (n 7) 397 [14].

heated border conflict with Georgia in 2008 overlapped in time with its much more long-winded domestic confrontation with the Chechen separatists.[84] Similarly, during the first phase of a guerrilla war launched against Peru by the armed group *Sendero Luminoso* (Shining Path) in the south of the country in the 1980s, a short-lived international confrontation over the control of disputed border territory flared up between Peru and Ecuador in the north.[85] In neither of these cases was it seriously suggested that IHL would require for the simultaneously occurring conflicts to be considered as somehow merged or subsumed under one another.

In sum, it is submitted that the law must recognize the possibility of states being engaged in several discrete conflicts simultaneously. It should not be interpreted as joining such conflicts artificially. Because in such situations internationalization does not affect *all* conflicts in a given state's territory, the pure global view of internationalization must be rejected.

3.2.3 Artificiality of the pure mixed view

For the proponents of the pure mixed view, the existence of an outside intervention does not change anything in relation to the law applicable to the ongoing internal conflict. The relationship between the intra-territorial parties is governed by the law of NIACs irrespective of the extent and nature of involvement of the outside power. According to this view, only the hostile relationship between the intervening state and the target state is governed by the law of IACs.

This extreme form of legal compartmentalization is easily rejected. It has been shown elsewhere in this work that internationalization of a previously internal armed conflict can be brought about by an outside state's involvement of a certain extent and nature in that conflict.[86] If this involvement meets the twin requirements of support of the insurgents and participation in their organization, co-ordination, or planning of military operations, then the outside state may be said to be using force against the territorial state indirectly *through* the proxy of the local insurgents.[87]

If the insurgent group submits itself to the command and control of the outside state (or, in certain circumstances, an intervening international organization[88]), thus relinquishing its autonomy, it would be illogical to insist on decoupling the conflict into its international and non-international strands. Following the Yugoslavian army's withdrawal from Bosnia in May 1992, the Bosnian Serb faction of the army was formally renamed and reconstituted as a separate militia, the Army of *Republika Srpska* (*Vojska Republike Srpske*, VRS).[89] However, on the facts established by the ICTY, the VRS never acquired independence of its operations, it acted in pursuance of the military goals formulated in Belgrade, and remained subject to a chain of military command leading up to the General Staff of the Yugoslavian army.[90] Accordingly, since May 1992 the Federal Republic of Yugoslavia (FRY) was

[84] See, eg, ICRC, *Annual Report 2008* (ICRC 2009) 264.
[85] See GM Lauderbaugh, *The History of Ecuador* (Greenwood 2012) 142.
[86] See Section 2.2.2. [87] See Section 2.2.2.4. [88] See Section 2.2.3.
[89] RC Nation, *War in the Balkans, 1991–2002* (Strategic Studies Institute 2003) 157.
[90] *Tadić* Appeal Judgment (n 70) [152].

using force against Bosnia and Herzegovina through the VRS. Because the VRS did not operate as an autonomous actor and because any separate military activities of the FRY in Bosnia and Herzegovina were of ancillary nature,[91] it is submitted that there only existed one conflict in the territory of Bosnia and Herzegovina at the relevant time. It follows that a single conflict should be governed by one body of law applicable to armed conflicts. As the FRY's involvement internationalized the conflict following the principles described previously, this applicable body must be the law of IAC.[92]

The artificiality of dividing conflicts into isolated segments is also highlighted by academic writings and the positions of some states.[93] Attempting to do so may also lead to operational difficulties and highly impractical results where the conflict parties are particularly intertwined.[94] Yet, although cases like the Bosnian example from mid-1990s certainly do not lend themselves to this segmentation, this argument should not be taken too far.[95] As shown in Section 3.2.2, several discrete conflicts may coexist in one state's territory. In such instances, it would indeed be artificial *not* to consider them separately and to join in law what in reality remains separate.[96] Importantly, this is also reflected in some recent expressions of *opinio juris* by states.[97]

To sum up, the existence of situations of internationalized conflict which cannot be plausibly divided into international and non-international 'sub-conflicts' confirms that the pure mixed view must also be rejected. Such situations must be treated as a single IAC with three parties: the territorial state on the one side, and the outside state and the armed group it is assisting on the other.

3.3 Spectrum, Not a Choice: Introducing the Hybrid Model

Due to the complex nature of contemporary conflicts, it is difficult to speak of the existence in one state territory either, on the one hand, of two or more conflicts that are entirely separate and unrelated (thus clearly justifying the mixed approach) or, on the other hand, of one evidently single indivisible conflict (thus clearly justifying the global approach). In reality, complex conflict situations typically fall somewhere in between. Conflict parties, in-state and foreign, use armed violence in varying degrees in the individual conflict pairs and affect, to a certain extent, the remaining

[91] ibid [151(iii)]. [92] See also ibid [162] (reaching an equivalent conclusion).

[93] T Meron, 'Classification of Armed Conflict in the Former Yugoslavia: *Nicaragua*'s Fallout' (1998) 92 AJIL 236, 238 ('to divide [a conflict] into isolated segments to exclude the application of the rules of international armed conflict would be artificial'), referring to *Prosecutor v Tadić* (Amicus Curiae Brief Presented by the Government of the United States) IT-94-1-T (25 July 1995) 28.

[94] Johnston (n 11) 101.

[95] Contra A McDonald, 'The Year in Review' (1998) 1 YIHL 121 ('[w]ith the increase in the number of internal and internationalized armed conflicts is coming greater recognition that a strict division of conflicts into internal and international is scarcely possible, if it ever was').

[96] cf C Greenwood, 'International Humanitarian Law and the *Tadic* Case' (1996) 7 EJIL 265, 271.

[97] See, eg, UK Ministry of Defence, *The Manual of the Law of Armed Conflict* (OUP 2004) 16 [1.33.6]; US DoD, *Law of War Manual* (December 2016) 74 [3.3.1.2].

conflict pairs by doing so. It is submitted that it is the degree of armed violence used and the extent to which it affects the other conflict pairs that determines whether the conflict pairs should be considered separately (mixed approach) or together (global approach). As this model combines the elements of both supposed opposite views, it is presented as a hybrid model. In order for this model to be workable, it must opt for one of the approaches as the baseline and then provide a framework which allows determining at what point the baseline approach gives way to the other one.

An examination of the states' positions expressed during the drafting history of the Additional Protocols to the Geneva Conventions strongly supports the position that the conflict pairs coexisting in a state's territory should initially be considered separately. First, in the run-up to the diplomatic conference of 1974–77, the ICRC's proposal that foreign military assistance should trigger the full applicability of IHL was rejected twice[98] and eventually dropped from the final draft of the Additional Protocols.[99] This refusal should be seen as an expression of a clear view of the international community that outside military assistance per se does not modify the nature of the conflict at hand. However, the government experts seemed to be unanimous in their opinion that the relationship between the opposing states should be governed by the provisions applicable to IACs.[100] This position thus left it entirely conceivable that an originally internal conflict with some foreign involvement would be governed by two sets of rules: those applicable to, respectively, IACs and NIACs.

Second, during the diplomatic conference itself, a number of government delegations expressed their concern that rules governing IACs should not be projected into the domestic sphere. The delegates were worried that such application might encroach on the sovereignty of the afflicted states, or even become the pretext for external armed intervention.[101] These anxieties were reflected in the outcome of the conference, which preserved the existence of two types of conflict in international law, international and non-international, and clarified the thresholds of their applicability.[102] State views apparent from the preparatory works on the Additional Protocols thus indicate that rules governing IACs were considered to be only

[98] See ICRC, *Conference of Government Experts on the Reaffirmation and Development of International Humanitarian Law Applicable in Armed Conflicts: Report on the Work of the Conference* (ICRC 1971) [290]–[308] (hereafter *Conference of Government Experts 1971*); ICRC, *Conference of Government Experts on the Reaffirmation and Development of International Humanitarian Law Applicable in Armed Conflicts, Second Session: Report on the Work of the Conference* (ICRC 1972) vol 1 [2.332]–[2.353] (hereafter *Conference of Government Experts 1972*).

[99] See further D Schindler, 'International Humanitarian Law and Internationalized Internal Armed Conflicts' (1982) 230 IRRC 255, 259–60; HP Gasser, 'Internationalized Non-International Armed Conflicts: Case Studies of Afghanistan, Kampuchea, and Lebanon' (1983) 33 AULR 145, 146–47; Zamir (n 7) 35–36.

[100] *Conference of Government Experts 1971* (n 98) [301(1)]; *Conference of Government Experts 1972* (n 98) vol 1 [2.347].

[101] See, eg, *Official Records* (n 46) vol VIII, CDDH/I/SR.22, 206 [25]–[27] (Germany); 212 [58] (Vietnam); CDDH/I/SR.23, 221 [33] (Romania); 223 [45] (Italy); CDDH/I/SR.24, 231 [14] (Mexico); 234 [28]–[29] (Egypt).

[102] See Art 1(3)–(4) AP I; Art 1 AP II; see further Section 1.2.2 and Section 4.2.1.

applicable to inter-state resort to force.[103] As the mixed approach recognizes this distinction and allows for a differentiated application of the law, it is submitted that it should be used as the baseline.[104]

Still, it must be recognized that, at a certain point on the spectrum, the use of force by the outside intervener and the rebels it supports becomes so indistinguishable that it is impossible to speak of separate conflicts anymore. As always, the exact location of this 'tipping point' may be difficult to determine. In this regard, it is helpful to consider potential scenarios that demonstrate the extent to which the conflict pairs existing in the territory of a state may be mutually intertwined. They are presented in the increasing order of mutual interrelation, from independence to unity.

Firstly, conflicts occurring especially in states with vast territories may be entirely unrelated. For example, in 2010, India was plagued by localized conflicts over the territorial control of the geographically distant and separate states of Assam and Kashmir, with no known mutual overlap or interaction.[105]

Secondly, the conflicts may affect each other indirectly without there being any alignment or assistance between the conflict parties from across the conflict pairs. Consider, for example, the situation in Sudan in the period between 2003 and 2005. The government of Sudan was concurrently involved in a long-standing conflict of declining intensity with the separatist South as well as in newly flared up fighting against two local armed groups in Darfur.[106] The individual non-state parties fought on different fronts and had little known direct interaction, but they may have affected each other indirectly by relying on the same natural resources and by triggering population movement across the territory of Sudan.[107]

Thirdly, the conflicts may affect each other directly by having mutual strategic significance, albeit without actual assistance or co-ordination between the individual conflict parties. This can be achieved, for instance, when the parties to different conflicts are engaging a common enemy, which results in considerable relative relief for one or each of them. In its early stages, the 2011 conflict in Libya appeared to fit this muster, when the NATO-led intervention targeted solely the Gaddafi government forces, without directly assisting the rebels operating from Benghazi.[108] Still, NATO

[103] Accord Zamir (n 7) 39–46. On the exception for wars of national liberation provided for in Art 1(4) AP I, see Section 2.4.

[104] cf also Milanovic (n 7) 46 [67].

[105] Uppsala Conflict Data Program, 'UCDP Conflict Encyclopedia' (Uppsala University, 2011) <www.ucdp.uu.se>.

[106] See further, eg, S Basha, 'Sudanese Civil Wars: Multiple Causes, Multiple Parties – One "Comprehensive" Agreement?' in B Raftopoulos and K Alexander (eds), *Peace in the Balance: The Crisis in the Sudan* (Institute for Justice and Reconciliation 2006) 7–22.

[107] See, eg, ICRC, *Annual Report 2003* (ICRC 2004) 95–98; ICRC, *Annual Report 2004* (ICRC 2005) 102–06.

[108] See, eg, NATO, 'Press Briefing on Libya' (13 May 2011) <www.nato.int/cps/en/natolive/opinions_74038.htm> ('The NATO mandate does not give us any authority to decide on sides at a NATO level. The operational activities that are being carried out, as I've said, are to protect the civilian population. Any relationship with pro- or anti-Qadhafi forces is beyond this forum for myself at this stage.').

air strikes offered significant relief to the rebels as the Libyan state army had to split its attention and resources into two different combat zones.[109]

Fourthly, the relationship between the parties to the separate conflicts may be one of mutual support without it reaching the level of joint organization, co-ordination, or planning of military operations. This support may take various forms, from financial assistance, to the provision of training and advice, to the supplies of military equipment and arms. These forms of support were a common, if mostly covert, form of waging the so-called 'proxy wars' in the Cold War period. For instance, the US funded training and arms for the guerrillas known as the *Khampas*, who fought the Chinese government in Tibet during and after the 1959 uprising.[110]

Fifthly, the level of mutual assistance and support between the conflict parties may develop to provide the outside party a role in the making of strategic and tactical decisions as to how to engage the common enemy. The aligned conflict parties can thus be said to participate jointly in the organization, co-ordination, or planning of their military operations. The conflict in Libya in 2011 apparently developed in this way: between April and May, reports emerged that the rebels and NATO had established a 'joint operations centre' to co-ordinate the preparation of individual forces' military operations conducted on land and from air.[111]

Sixthly, one of the aligned conflict parties may be acting entirely through the other one, without it being actively present with its own forces on the ground. In such a situation, the two parties are still separate entities, but one of them is subordinated to the other to the extent that the hierarchically superior party controls the operations of the inferior party. As a result, the shared enemy is actually fighting against one independent force only. For example, in the Bosnian Civil War in 1992, this was the case with the Serbian support of the Bosnian Serb militias, the VRS.[112]

Finally, on the opposite end of the spectrum starting from total independence is the seventh possible scenario: unity. Allied conflict parties may eventually merge and become a single warring faction in the conflict, subjected to one leadership and one hierarchical command structure, thus turning the former non-state party into an organ of the third state.[113] Accordingly, here there will remain a single conflict pair,

109 See further Mačák and Zamir (n 67) 413–23.

110 D Norbu, *China's Tibet Policy* (Curzon Press 2001) 268 ff.

111 M Chmaytelli and PS Green, 'Libya Rebels, NATO Don't Have Joint Operations, Official Says' *Bloomberg* (16 April 2011) <www.bloomberg.com/news/2011-04-16/libya-rebels-nato-don-t-have-joint-operations-official-says.html> (confirmation by the rebels and denial by NATO); B Waterfield, 'Libya: British Military Advisers Set Up "Joint Operations Centre" in Benghazi' *The Telegraph* (18 May 2011) <www.telegraph.co.uk/news/worldnews/africaandindianocean/libya/8521977/Libya-British-military-advisers-set-up-joint-operations-centre-in-Benghazi.html> (confirmation by the UK).

112 See *Prosecutor v Tadić* (Trial Judgment) IT-94-1-T (7 May 1997) (sep and diss op McDonald) [14] ('the Federal Republic of Yugoslavia (Serbia and Montenegro) essentially depleted its own army to establish the VRS to carry out effectively the war effort in Bosnia and Herzegovina without significant overt involvement of the [FRY].'); contra Trial Chamber view in the same judgment at [606] (believing the two were mere allies); but see *Tadić* Appeal Judgment (n 70) [152] (effectively supporting Judge McDonald's view). See also text to note 91 in this chapter (noting the ancillary role played by the Yugoslav army units in Bosnia and Herzegovina at that time).

113 ILC, Draft Articles on Responsibility of States for Internationally Wrongful Acts, with commentaries, Yearbook of the ILC (2001) vol II, part two, 40, Art 4 (hereafter ILC ASR); see also *Case Concerning the Application of the Convention on the Prevention and Punishment of the Crime of Genocide*

namely between the erstwhile shared enemy and the newly unified conflict party. One may think in this regard, for example, of those partisan groups fighting the Nazis in the occupied Eastern European countries at the end of the Second World War, which were incorporated in the Soviet Red Army upon its progress across the continent towards the heart of the Reich.[114]

It follows from the criticism of the 'pure' approaches[115] that scenario 1 (utterly disconnected conflicts in one state's territory) is best served by the mixed approach, whereas scenario 7 (one single conflict due to the parties' merger) is best served by the global approach. Where does, however, the latter replace the former on this proposed spectrum of situations? Where do we draw the line?

It is submitted that the dividing point is represented by the moment at which the two parties can be said to be using force together.[116] This, on the one hand, requires more than mere complicity as understood in the International Law Commission's Articles on State Responsibility (ILC ASR), that is, more than mere provision of aid or assistance,[117] embodied in scenario 4. Although under the law of state responsibility, each of the two entities might be responsible for a wrongful act resulting from their complicity, for the purposes of conflict qualification the two remain autonomous.[118] Their respective confrontations with the territorial state should thus still be considered as separate armed conflicts in line with the baseline mixed view.

On the other hand, the requirement of a joint use of force is not equivalent with the demand that the insurgent group be subordinated to the intervening state, or even subjected to one line of command.[119] It suffices that the two entities participate in the organization, co-ordination, or planning of their military activities. In such a case, neither of the parties can be said to be using force autonomously. Their activities have become sufficiently intertwined to justify the conclusion that 'a single armed conflict is being fought, albeit with multiple actors participating in it'.[120]

In summary, the dividing line lies on the border between scenario 4 and scenario 5. The use of operational autonomy as a distinguishing criterion is sufficiently nuanced to provide for a solution to the conundrum presented at the outset of this chapter. Situations in which the mutual effect of the conflict pairs is insufficient to disrupt the parties' autonomy should be seen as instances of separate uses of force, and thus as separate armed conflicts. But once the autonomy of the aligned conflict parties has been sacrificed, their use of force against the common enemy should be seen

(Bosnia and Herzegovina v Serbia and Montenegro) (Judgment) [2007] ICJ Rep 43, 204–05 [391]–[392] (holding that entities that act in 'complete dependence' on the third state may be equated with an organ of that state).

114 See EM Howell, *The Soviet Partisan Movement 1941–1944* (6th edn, Merriam Press 2006) 230.

115 See Sections 3.2.1–3.2.3.

116 On the IHL-specific notion of force, see Section 2.2.2.4.

117 cf ILC ASR (n 113) Art 16. Note that this provision formally applies to inter-state relations only. On the possibility that a non-state analogue will develop in international law, see M Jackson, *Complicity in International Law* (OUP 2015) 214–16.

118 On the conceptual separation between IHL and the law of state responsibility, see Section 2.2.2.4.

119 cf *Prlić* Appeal Judgment (n 56) vol 1 [284] (holding that in order to establish overall control, it is not necessary to find that the outside state 'maintained the ultimate decision-making authority and command over each and every military operation').

120 Sivakumaran (n 7) 224.

as a joint effort, enclosing all three relevant parties in a single IAC. In practice, much will, of course, depend on the assessment of the facts.

For instance, the autonomy of the KLA vis-à-vis NATO during the 1999 conflict was a key contentious point among academics writing about the conflict. On the one hand, Greenwood highlighted that the relations between NATO and the KLA were not 'sufficiently close' for the conflict between the KLA and the FRY to be considered part of the IAC between the NATO states and the FRY.[121] On the other hand, Ronzitti considered it possible that the KLA was so close to the NATO forces and, in fact, subjected to the control of NATO, that it did not represent an autonomous conflict party.[122] Without taking a position on the Kosovo conflict, it appears that the model presented here produces answers that are in alignment with the casuistic analysis found in academic writing, which further affirms its broader workability.

3.4 Evaluation

Internationalization of conflicts marked by a plurality of conflict parties brings about a dilemma for the application of IHL. It is clear that the law of IAC becomes applicable to such situations—that is the essence of internationalization, after all—but to what extent? Does it apply to all conflict parties, or only to those that are full-fledged states? James Stewart lamented that this dilemma entailed a choice 'between a theory that cannot work and a practice that is not justified'.[123] This author respectfully disagrees. There is a third way.

The hybrid model proposed in this chapter responds to the academic criticism and provides an answer to Stewart's choice that is both justifiable and workable. It is justified as it takes duly into consideration the states' reluctance to extend the rules governing IACs to internal situations. It only triggers the application of this body of law to the conflict 'globally' when the use of force by the individual conflict parties, external and internal, can no longer be distinguished.

It is also workable as it provides clear rules determining the nature of complex conflict situations on the basis of assessment grounded in real historical examples. The model does not force either an artificial segmentation of a conflict characterized by a joint use of force, or an overarching application of the same body of law to discrete conflict situations. Although in the form presented here it focuses on the triangular relationship between the territorial state, a third state, and an in-state armed group, its method is easily scalable to more complex situations as each of the conflict pairs can be assessed on this basis separately.

[121] C Greenwood, 'The Applicability of International Humanitarian Law and the Law of Neutrality to the Kosovo Campaign' (2002) 78 International Law Studies 35, 45–46.

[122] N Ronzitti, 'Commentary' (2002) 78 International Law Studies 35, 114.

[123] Stewart (n 11) 335.

4
De-internationalization

4.1 Introduction

Although the focus of this book is on the process and consequences of internationalization of armed conflicts, a consideration of the reverse phenomenon of de-internationalization is also in order. As understood here, it denotes a process by which an erstwhile international armed conflict (IAC) transforms in nature into a non-international armed conflict (NIAC). This process has been described in the literature as either 'de-internationalization' or 'internalization' of armed conflicts.[1] The former of the two terms is used here as it is considered slightly more accurate than the other one. Indeed, as discussed earlier, not every NIAC is necessarily 'internal' in nature.[2] Hence, it is more appropriate to speak of de-internationalization when what is meant is a process by which a given situation ceases to be characterized as an IAC and is transformed into a NIAC as a matter of law.

The examination of the process of de-internationalization is apposite for several main reasons. Firstly, in the complex reality of modern armed conflicts, the legal qualification of a particular situation may evolve in both directions. As Chapter 2 shows, an armed contestation that begins as a NIAC may acquire additional characteristics, which necessitate its requalification as an IAC. However, the reverse may be (and frequently is) the case, too. The dynamic perspective that this book adopts

[1] K Mačák and N Zamir, 'The Applicability of International Humanitarian Law to the Conflict in Libya' (2012) 14 ICLR 403, 423–29; M Milanovic and V Hadzi-Vidanovic, 'A Taxonomy of Armed Conflict' in N White and C Henderson (eds), *Research Handbook on International Conflict and Security Law* (Edward Elgar 2013) 281–82; R Kolb, *Advanced Introduction to International Humanitarian Law* (Edward Elgar 2014) 116–17; M Milanovic, 'The End of Application of International Humanitarian Law' (2014) 96 IRRC 163, 182–83 (hereafter Milanovic, 'End of Application'); M Milanovic, 'The Applicability of the Conventions to "Transnational" and "Mixed" Conflicts' in A Clapham, P Gaeta, and M Sassòli (eds), *The 1949 Geneva Conventions: A Commentary* (OUP 2015) 31–34 (hereafter Milanovic, ' "Transnational" and "Mixed" Conflicts'); N Zamir, *Classification of Conflicts in International Humanitarian Law: The Legal Impact of Foreign Intervention in Civil Wars* (Edward Elgar 2017) 157–69; P Muggleton, *Muggleton on the Law of Non-International Armed Conflict* (APCML 2017) 18.

[2] See Section 1.2.2.2.

requires a closer look on both possible trajectories between the two principal static categories of conflict qualification under international humanitarian law (IHL).[3]

Secondly, if a conflict is de-internationalized, the sum total of rules of IHL that applies to it will inevitably decrease.[4] Despite the general trend of convergence between the two main types of armed conflict, some notions and associated norms have not traversed the IAC/NIAC divide.[5] Therefore, persons fighting on behalf of the conflict parties may no longer be able to benefit from combatant immunity and prisoner of war status, both of which are IAC-specific concepts.[6] Moreover, at least on the currently prevailing view,[7] parties to the conflict may thereafter be left without the legal authority to detain under IHL and may need to seek an alternative legal basis in order to justify the continued detention of persons in their power.[8] In short, understanding at what moment an IAC becomes a NIAC (if at all) is thus an essential ingredient of any attempt to precisely and accurately apply the law to the facts of modern conflicts.

This directly leads to the third reason, which concerns the accountability for violations of IHL committed during the conflicts in question. It is true that following the 1995 *Tadić* decision on jurisdiction[9] and the subsequent adoption of the Rome Statute in 1998,[10] the notion of war crimes today includes a wide range of serious violations of IHL applicable to NIACs.[11] However, the categories of war crimes in IACs and NIACs, respectively, are still far from identical and quite a few forms of conduct criminalized in IACs remain *praeter legem* in NIACs.[12] Moreover, the requirement of a 'nexus' with an armed conflict is much more difficult to establish

[3] See Chapter 1 and particularly Section 1.3.2.

[4] In a few rare areas, it is the law of NIAC that offers greater protection than the law of IAC. See S Sivakumaran, *The Law of Non-International Armed Conflict* (OUP 2012) 68–69 (contrasting the rules from both legal regimes concerning the restrictions on the recruitment of child soldiers, the prohibition on deportation, and the protection of works and installations containing dangerous forces). Moreover, in some situations qualifying as IACs, protections under international human rights law (IHRL) may be diminished through claims that specific rules of IHL operate as the *lex specialis*, whereas such claims would be unavailable in NIACs. This is particularly the case with respect to the procedural rules applicable to internment: see L Hill-Cawthorne, *Detention in Non-International Armed Conflict* (OUP 2016) 227–28.

[5] See further Section 1.2.3.

[6] See Art 43(2) AP I; Art 4A GC III.

[7] See, eg, AS Deeks, 'Administrative Detention in Armed Conflict' (2009) 40 Case W Res J Int'l L 403, 413; P Rowe, 'Is There a Right to Detain Civilians by Foreign Armed Forces During a Non-International Armed Conflict?' (2012) 61 ICLQ 697; E Debuf, *Captured in War: Lawful Internment in Armed Conflict* (2013) 451–88; G Rona, 'Is There a Way Out of the Non-International Armed Conflict Dilemma?' (2015) 91 International Law Studies 32, 35–45; Hill-Cawthorne (n 4) 66–76; Milanovic, 'End of Application' (n 1) 183.

[8] But see K Mačák, 'A Needle in a Haystack? Locating the Legal Basis for Detention in Non-International Armed Conflict' (2015) 45 IYHR 87 (arguing that the legal basis for detention in NIAC is inherent in customary IHL).

[9] *Prosecutor v Tadić* (Decision on Jurisdiction) IT-94-1-AR72 (2 October 1995) [134].

[10] Rome Statute of the International Criminal Court (opened for signature 17 July 1998, entered into force 1 July 2002) 2187 UNTS 90 (hereafter Rome Statute).

[11] See further, eg, R O'Keefe, *International Criminal Law* (OUP 2015) 126–28.

[12] See, eg, Arts 8(2)(a)(vii) Rome Statute (war crime of unlawful confinement); Art 8(2)(b)(xiv) Rome Statute (war crime of declaring abolished, suspended, or judicially inadmissible the rights and actions of nationals of the hostile party); Art 85(4)(b) AP I (war crime of unjustifiably delaying the repatriation of POWs or civilians).

with respect to conduct in NIACs owing to the particular characteristics of this class of conflicts.[13] What is more, states are under a positive duty to search for and bring to trial or extradite alleged perpetrators of 'grave breaches' of the Geneva Conventions[14] and Additional Protocol I,[15] a category of crimes limited to IACs.[16] No corresponding *obligation* exists in NIACs;[17] at most it can be said that an emerging customary law norm *empowers* states to do so with respect to identical conduct in NIACs.[18] In short, a transformation of the conflict nature has a profound effect on achieving accountability for criminal conduct in armed conflicts.

Finally, identifying the tipping point at which a conflict undergoes de-internationalization may have wide political consequences. Of course, at times political considerations will translate into the relevant actors' desire to avoid legal qualification altogether,[19] or even to deny that an armed conflict exists at all.[20] However, an acknowledgement that a conflict has indeed transformed into a NIAC may also open the doors for the belligerents to consider politically expedient steps which may speed up the process of conflict termination and post-conflict recovery. In particular, the law of NIAC positively encourages the granting of amnesties at the end of the conflict.[21] Therefore, the correct identification of the threshold of de-internationalization may in some cases also be politically desirable.

4.2 Conceptualizing De-internationalization

This section aims to provide a conceptualization of the notion of de-internationalization in international law. Firstly, this requires an assessment of the relationship between IAC and NIAC as separate legal categories. The section argues that the two are not subtypes of a supposed overarching generic concept of 'armed conflict' and that it is therefore inaccurate to view de-internationalization as a process by which an IAC 'loses' its international character. Rather, both IAC and NIAC are independent legal notions and for a situation to transform from the former to the latter, the conditions precedent for the existence of a NIAC must always be met. Secondly, the section argues that for a conflict transformation to qualify as de-internationalization, the situation must be characterized by the identity of the relevant parties before and after the transformation and by the continuity of the hostilities in question. If these requirements are not met, the transformed situation

[13] See further A Cassese et al (eds), *Cassese's International Criminal Law* (3rd edn, OUP 2013) 77–78.

[14] Arts 49(2)/50(2)/129(2)/146(2) GC I/II/III/IV.

[15] Art 85(1) AP I.

[16] *Tadić* Decision on Jurisdiction (n 9) [80]–[84].

[17] MC Bassiouni, *International Criminal Law* (3rd edn, Brill 2008) vol 1, 510.

[18] See, eg, T Meron, *The Humanization of International Law* (Martinus Nijhoff 2006) 137; L Moir, 'Grave Breaches and Internal Armed Conflicts' (2009) 7 JICJ 763, 784; Cassese (n 13) 71.

[19] See Milanovic and Hadzi-Vidanovic (n 1) 256.

[20] See, eg, UK Ministry of Defence, *The Manual of the Law of Armed Conflict* (OUP 2004) 386 [15.3.1] (hereafter *UK Military Manual*). For specific examples of state practice denying the existence of armed conflicts in their territories, see Sivakumaran (n 4) 200–01.

[21] Art 6(5) AP II.

needs to be qualified anew and may amount to a discrete NIAC or even fall outside the scope of IHL.

4.2.1 De-internationalization and the notion of 'armed conflict'

In order to understand the process of de-internationalization, a clarification is needed of the recurring misunderstanding as to the relationship between the start and end point of this transformation. The labels used for these termini, IAC and NIAC, suggest they are both species of a larger genus, a supposed 'AC' or (to write out the acronym in full) an 'armed conflict'. To some extent, the language of Common Article 3 feeds this misunderstanding, given that it only contains a non-definition[22] of a NIAC, seemingly formulated in residual terms: 'armed conflict not of an international character'.[23] On the face of it, the provision thus suggests that if an armed conflict is not international, it must be non-international, with nothing in between.[24] If that was the correct understanding, then a legal analysis of the nature of a particular hostile situation would begin by assessing whether or not it amounts to an 'armed conflict', and only then whether it is one that is 'international', or not.[25] However, such approach is without basis in the existing *lex lata*.[26]

To begin with, international law does not define anywhere 'armed conflict' in its supposedly generic meaning.[27] Even the most widely accepted case-law definition promulgated by the ICTY in its 1995 *Tadić* decision actually defines each of the two categories separately: '[A]n armed conflict exists whenever there is a resort to armed force between states *or* protracted armed violence between governmental authorities and organized armed groups or between such groups within a State'.[28] The text before the highlighted 'or' defines an IAC; the text that follows defines a NIAC.[29]

As discussed in Chapter 1, the two categories have different thresholds of application, the most notable difference being that in order for a NIAC to come about, the violence between conflict parties must reach a certain minimum level of intensity.[30] Therefore, as a matter of law it is inaccurate to speak of an 'armed conflict' as if it was a generic concept.[31] Rather, both IAC

---

22 Sivakumaran (n 4) 156.

23 Common Art 3 GCs.

24 See, eg, GS Corn and ET Jensen, 'Transnational Armed Conflict: A "Principled" Approach to the Regulation of Counter-Terror Combat Operations' (2012) 42 Isr L Rev 46, 54; Kolb (n 1) 108; L Moir, 'The Concept of Non-International Armed Conflict' in Clapham et al (n 1) 396–97 [12].

25 D Kritsiotis, 'The Tremors of Tadić' (2010) 43 Isr L Rev 262, 294; Milanovic, '"Transnational" and "Mixed" Conflicts' (n 1) 29 [5].

26 But see, eg, ILA, Committee on the Use of Force, Final Report on the Meaning of Armed Conflict in International Law (2010) 3 fn 7 (considering that its mandate 'was to report on the *general definition of armed conflict*') (emphasis added). For a succinct and convincing critique of this methodology, see, eg, A Clapham, 'Concept of International Armed Conflict' in Clapham et al (n 1) 13 [31].

27 cf also ME O'Connell, 'Defining Armed Conflict' (2008) 13 JCSL 393, 393 (noting that, as of 2005, 'no widely accepted definition of armed conflict was recognized by international law scholars').

28 *Tadić* Decision on Jurisdiction (n 9) [70] (emphasis added).

29 See further Kritsiotis (n 25) 267–70.

30 See Sections 1.2.2.1–1.2.2.2.

31 The approach in other disciplines may be (and is) different. See, eg, in the context of peace research, P Wallensteen, 'What's in a War? Insights from a Conflict Data Program' in ME O'Connell (ed), *What Is War?: An Investigation in the Wake of 9/11* (Martinus Nijhoff 2016) 266 (relying on a 'generic

and NIAC are separate legal categories and one is not a mere inversion of the other.[32]

This has important implications for the present discussion. Because there is no generic concept of 'armed conflict', an IAC does not become de-internationalized simply by 'losing' its international character.[33] Instead, a transformation from IAC to NIAC means not only that a given situation no longer meets the criteria of the former, but also that it must now meet the criteria of the latter.[34] This poses some additional legal complications, but these are not insurmountable.

To say that a situation used to be an IAC but now is no longer logically implies that in the meantime the IAC in question must have ended. However, the end of an IAC ordinarily triggers several important obligations of conflict parties. These include the duty to release and repatriate prisoners of war;[35] a parallel duty to release civilian internees;[36] and a separate obligation to clear, remove, or destroy various explosive devices including mines, booby-traps, and explosive remnants of war.[37] This raises a question whether all of these obligations apply also in case the hostilities continue, but their legal qualification changes, ie, as in the case of de-internationalization. It is submitted that such interpretation—requiring, for example, that persons detained during the IAC would need to be released and then, if necessary, re-detained as part of the new NIAC[38]—would lead to manifestly impractical or even absurd outcomes.[39] It could be said that if such outcomes were required by the law, then this would be a powerful argument against the availability of de-internationalization altogether.[40]

definition of armed conflict', according to which 'an armed conflict is a contested incompatibility which concerns government and/or territory where the use of armed force between two parties, of which at least one is the government of a state, results in at least 25 battle-related deaths').

32 S Sivakumaran, 'Re-envisaging the International Law of Internal Armed Conflict: A Rejoinder to Gabriella Blum' (2011) 22 EJIL 273, 273; Milanovic, '"Transnational" and "Mixed" Conflicts' (n 1) 30 [8]–[10].

33 But see, eg, S Breau and M Aronsson, 'Drone Attacks, International Law, and the Recording of Civilian Casualties of Armed Conflict' (2012) 35 Suffolk Transnational Law Review 255, 274 ('the conflict therefore lost its international character and fell into the realm of long-standing, non-international armed conflict'); see also S Wills, 'The Legal Characterization of the Armed Conflicts in Afghanistan and Iraq: Implications for Protection' (2011) 58 NILR 173, 174 (using the formulation 'requalification of an armed conflict *downwards* to non-international') (emphasis added).

34 Mačák and Zamir (n 1) 407.

35 Art 118(1) GC III.

36 Art 133(1) GC IV.

37 Protocol on Prohibitions or Restrictions on the Use of Mines, Booby-Traps and Other Devices as amended on 3 May 1996 annexed to the Convention on Prohibitions or Restrictions on the Use of Certain Conventional Weapons which may be deemed to be Excessively Injurious or to have Indiscriminate Effects (signed 3 May 1996, entered into force 3 December 1998) 2048 UNTS 93, Art 10(1) (hereafter CCW Protocol II); Protocol on Explosive Remnants of War to the Convention on Prohibitions or Restrictions on the Use of Certain Conventional Weapons which may be deemed to be Excessively Injurious or to have Indiscriminate Effects (signed 28 November 2003, entered into force 12 November 2006) 2399 UNTS 100, Art 3(2) (hereafter CCW Protocol V).

38 cf, eg, Amnesty International, 'Guantánamo and Beyond: The Continuing Pursuit of Unchecked Executive Power' (13 May 2005) <www.amnesty.org/download/Documents/84000/amr510632005en.pdf> 12.

39 cf JB Bellinger, III, 'Legal Issues in the War on Terrorism—A Reply to Silja N. U. Vöneky' (2007) 8 German Law Journal 871, 872 fn 7.

40 See further Mačák and Zamir (n 1) 427–28.

However, on closer scrutiny, it is apparent that the relevant provisions are not contingent on a formal end of an IAC. Instead, the formulations used in these rules to specify their triggering point speak instead of 'the cessation of active hostilities'[41] or 'the close of hostilities'.[42] Unlike the legal question of termination of an IAC, whether hostilities survive is a question of fact.[43] Because active hostilities do not cease in the process of de-internationalization,[44] the preferred interpretation is that these end-of-conflict obligations do not activate at the point of conflict transformation. Rather, it is submitted that these duties, even though they originate in the law of IAC, remain dormant through conflict transformation and only come in play once all hostilities (now part of the transformed NIAC) have ceased. This interpretation is in line with modern practice[45] as well as with the logic of the rules in question.[46]

4.2.2 Conflict transformations and de-internationalization

Not all conflict transformations qualify as de-internationalization in the sense that this term is used in this work. To begin with, de-internationalization is not synonymous with any regime change or reversal of political inclinations in one of the warring states. Changes of this kind, albeit primarily non-legal in nature, may indeed have an impact on the legal qualification of a given situation. For instance, a belligerent occupation governed by the law of IAC may end if the territorial sovereign expresses its consent with the continued presence of the occupying forces in its territory. Provided that the attendant hostilities do not continue any further and that the consent is genuine,[47] the conflict between the two states will end at that point.[48] This is because the territorial state's consent obviates the belligerent relationship between the two former conflict parties, which brings the original IAC to its end.[49] It is difficult to identify a clear real-world example of this precise factual pattern, but a possible candidate may be the expression of consent by the newly formed state of Bangladesh with the presence of Indian forces in its territory in 1971.[50] In any

41 Art 118(1) GC III; Art 10(1) CCW Protocol II; Art 3(2) CCW Protocol V.

42 Art 133(1) GC IV.

43 See, eg, JS Pictet (ed), *Geneva Convention IV relative to the Protection of Civilian Persons in Time of War: Commentary* (ICRC 1958) 514–15 (hereafter Pictet, *GC IV Commentary*); *UK Military Manual* (n 20) 205 [8.169].

44 See Section 4.2.2. 45 See Bellinger (n 39) 872 fn 7.

46 See, eg, US DoD, *Law of War Manual* (December 2016) [9.37.2]; *UK Military Manual* (n 20) 205.

47 See also Sections 2.2.1.2–2.2.1.3 for a more detailed discussion of the legal and policy considerations relating to the genuineness of consent with foreign military presence in a state's own territory.

48 T Ferraro and L Cameron, 'Article 2: Application of the Convention', in ICRC (ed), *Commentary on the First Geneva Convention* (CUP 2016) 110 [306] (hereafter Ferraro and Cameron, 'Article 2').

49 But see J Grignon, 'The Geneva Conventions and the End of Occupation', in Clapham et al (n 1) 1586–87 [24] (arguing that an agreement between the occupied and occupying powers proclaiming an end to occupation would be without legal effect if it deprived persons living in the occupied territory of their protections under the law of belligerent occupation); see also Art 47 GC IV ('Protected persons who are in occupied territory shall not be deprived, in any case or in any manner whatsoever, of the benefits of the present Convention ... by any agreement concluded between the authorities of the occupied territories and the Occupying Power').

50 See E Benvenisti, *The International Law of Occupation* (2nd edn, OUP 2012) 67 and 188–91.

event, the absence of continued hostilities means the conflict terminates altogether. Therefore, there is no surviving conflict which could be described as a NIAC and thus logically no de-internationalization to speak of.

Furthermore, de-internationalization presumes then continuity of conflict. Consider, for instance, the sequence of events in the Horn of Africa around the turn of the century. In 1998, an international conflict broke out between the two neighbouring countries—Ethiopia and Eritrea.[51] This conflict ended with a peace agreement signed in December 2000 in Algiers.[52] After April 2007, Ethiopia was embroiled once again in an armed conflict, this time an internal conflict between the government forces and the so-called Ogaden National Liberation Front (ONLF).[53] Although an IAC was followed by a NIAC in the territory of Ethiopia, this is not enough to speak of de-internationalization. The reason for that is that when hostilities end 'with a degree of stability and permanence', as they did following the 2000 peace agreement between the two countries, the IAC in question is terminated.[54] The post-2007 conflict should be seen as a separate NIAC and thus not one to which the analysis in this chapter applies.

Similarly, de-internationalization is contingent on the continuity of conflict parties. Even if the hostilities do not cease following the end of the original IAC, we can only speak of conflict de-internationalization if there is an identity of belligerents throughout the conflict transformation. By way of an example, consider a situation in which an IAC between two states terminates with the withdrawal of the occupying forces of one state from the territory of another. Immediately afterwards, a non-state armed group with no material link to the outside state commences fighting against the territorial government—perhaps because its members perceive the situation as a window of opportunity to take on an enemy weakened by the previous conflict. Whatever the precise motivations of the parties may be, it would again be inaccurate to speak of de-internationalization in this context. This is because the new situation would not result from a transformation of the original conflict but rather it would amount to a new, unrelated armed contestation. Its legal qualification would thus have to be assessed as a new conflict against the usual criteria for the existence of a NIAC.[55]

A more complex situation arises if one slightly expands and modifies the last-mentioned scenario. Assume, for example, that the occupier would retain its control over a part of the other state's territory, and thus the original IAC would continue. Additionally, a new non-state armed group would now emerge from the occupied territory and start fighting against the occupying state. This is, of course, what happened in many countries occupied by Nazi Germany during the Second World War

[51] See further SD Murphy, 'The Eritrean-Ethiopian War (1998–2000)' in T Ruys and O Corten (eds), *The Use of Force in International Law: A Case-Based Approach* (OUP 2018).

[52] Agreement between the Government of the State of Eritrea and the Government of the Federal Democratic Republic of Ethiopia, UN Doc A/55/686–S/2000/1183 (signed 12 December 2000).

[53] ICRC, *Annual Report 2009* (ICRC 2010) 130.

[54] cf Ferraro and Cameron, 'Article 2' (n 48) 101 [277].

[55] See Section 1.2.2.2.

after partisan groups had formed in the occupied territories.[56] It is submitted that in such circumstances, the conflict would not be de-internationalized because of the continuity of the original IAC. De-internationalization presupposes a transformation in the conflict nature; but here the original conflict would clearly persist.[57] Whether the new relationship between the occupier and the resistance forces should be seen as a separate NIAC or as a part of the ongoing IAC will depend on the linkage between the conflict parties, which is a question analysed in detail elsewhere in this book.[58]

4.3 Modalities of De-internationalization

The previous section showed that de-internationalization is consistent with the conceptualization of IAC and NIAC as separate independent legal categories (and not as species of an overarching generic supercategory of 'armed conflict') and that it is contingent on the continuity of hostilities and the identity of conflict parties throughout the transformation of the conflict in question. It thus remains to be seen what modalities of this process exist in modern international law. Accordingly, the present section assesses the potential types of de-internationalization in the order parallel to that in which modalities of internationalization were examined in Chapter 2. However, as will become apparent, not every form of internationalization can be said to have a corresponding form of de-internationalization.

4.3.1 Regime change and outside intervention

As shown earlier in this work, the exact constellation of conflict parties in a conflict marked by an outside intervention is crucial for its legal characterization.[59] If an outside power intervenes on the side of the government embroiled in a civil war, the situation remains a NIAC.[60] As a matter of *factual* description, the presence of the intervening forces surely amounts to an 'international element',[61] but it does not suffice for the *legal* internationalization of the conflict.[62] By contrast, if the outside power intervenes on the side of the rebels (or, more precisely, of the relevant armed non-state actor), then a certain nature and intensity of the intervention will indeed

[56] See, eg, *The Hostages Trial, List et al* (Judgment) (19 February 1948) (1949) 8 Law Reports of Trials of War Criminals 34 (US MT) 55–59 (discussing the conduct and status of partisan groups in the Nazi-occupied territories in Greece and Yugoslavia).

[57] It is controversial whether the territory in which such fighting breaks out should still be considered occupied. See further Section 10.2.2.

[58] See Chapter 3. [59] See Sections 2.2.1–2.2.2. [60] See Section 2.2.1.2.

[61] cf A Roberts, 'What Is a Military Occupation?' (1984) 55 BYBIL 249, 278; M Sassòli, 'Transnational Armed Groups and International Humanitarian Law' [2006] Program on Humanitarian Policy and Conflict Research at Harvard University, Occasional Paper Series 1, 5; O Engdahl, 'A Rebuttal to Eric David' (2013) 95 IRRC 667, 667.

[62] Contra, eg, R Pinto, 'Les règles du droit international concernant la guerre civile' (1965-I) 114 RdC 451, 464–65.

transform the conflict in question into an IAC.[63] But what if this constellation changes later on during the conflict?

To be sure, there are scenarios that result in the de-internationalization of such conflicts and which are either not particularly controversial or which may be resolved by reference to the analysis in the preceding chapters. An example of the former would be the complete withdrawal of all foreign intervening forces from the target state.[64] In such circumstances, any conflict that would still carry on in the said territory could only be described as a NIAC.[65] As the ICC held in a decision in the *Lubanga* proceedings, that was precisely the case with respect to the surviving hostilities in the Congolese province of Ituri after Uganda's full withdrawal in 2003.[66] The reason for such requalification is that after the foreign forces withdraw, one can no longer speak of a resort to armed force *between* states, which is a pre-requisite for the existence of an IAC.[67]

For an example of the latter type of scenario, consider a falling out between the intervening state and the rebels who had hitherto fought jointly against the territorial government. If, as a result of this development, the non-state party regained its operational autonomy,[68] the conflict would undergo a partial de-internationalization. This is because the emancipation of the non-state actor would reinstate separate armed conflicts between the involved parties. Specifically, the relationship between the government and the newly autonomous rebels would now be governed by the law of NIAC, whereas the relationship between the outside power and the territorial government would retain its classification as an IAC.[69]

The most problematic outstanding situation is one in which the 'domestic' conflict parties switch sides during an ongoing outside intervention. In other words, due to a regime change in the state in question, the former rebels become the government, while the former government is relegated to the role of a non-state armed group. As we shall see, there is a strong presumption in international law against

[63] See further Section 2.2.2.

[64] Mačák and Zamir (n 1) 424.

[65] *Prosecutor v Delalić et al* (*Čelebići* Trial Judgment) IT-96-21-T (16 November 1998) [215] (noting that 'the nature of the armed conflict' would be 'changed by the withdrawal of the external forces involved'); *Prosecutor v Aleksovski* (Trial Judgment) IT-95-14/1-T (25 June 1999) (diss op Rodrigues) [17] (emphasizing the need for the genuineness of the withdrawal, as opposed to a formal retreat without corroborative evidence of its effectiveness).

[66] *Prosecutor v Thomas Lubanga Dyilo* (Decision on the Confirmation of Charges, Pre-Trial Chamber I) ICC-01/04-01/06 (29 January 2007) [220] (holding that, 'as a result of the presence of the Republic of Uganda as an occupying power', the situation in Ituri in the Congo between 2002 and 2003 was an IAC until 'the date of the effective withdrawal of the Ugandan army') and [235]–[37] (finding that after Uganda's withdrawal, the hostilities in Ituri amounted to a NIAC). For the sake of completeness, it should be noted that the *Lubanga* Trial Chamber later 'change[d] the legal characterisation of the facts to the extent that the armed conflict *relevant to the charges* was non-international in character' (emphasis added). However, this does not affect the analysis in the main text given that the Chamber acknowledged the possible existence of a separate prior IAC (unrelated to the charges in the case) between the DRC and Uganda. See *Prosecutor v Thomas Lubanga Dyilo* (Trial Judgment) ICC-01/04-01/06 (14 March 2012) [565]–[66].

[67] cf *Tadić* Decision on Jurisdiction (n 9) [70].

[68] See further Section 3.3.

[69] ibid.

de-internationalization in such cases. However, it may occur and likely has occurred in several recent conflict situations, including Afghanistan and Iraq.[70]

The competing policy considerations at play in such situations are well understood.[71] On the one hand, international law's concern for effectiveness dictates that new realities on the ground also be recognized by the law.[72] In other words, the law should not insist that a government long-since removed from power still is the valid representative of the state—with the situation remaining an IAC—simply because it had been *in situ* at the moment of intervention.[73] On the other hand, the law should also not encourage the setting up of friendly puppet governments whose consent would then allow the intervener to unilaterally transform the conflict into a NIAC.[74] As Milanovic noted, this was the *modus operandi* of Nazi Germany during the Second World War[75]—and few would agree that international law should legitimate such measures.[76] But how do we strike a balance between these competing considerations?

The answer, it is submitted, lies in the strict application of the IHL criteria for the existence of a NIAC and, subsequently, general international law requirements for government effectiveness. First, it is imperative that the situation following the regime change must still meet the twin requirements of organization and intensity.[77] If it does not, the surviving situation does not qualify as a NIAC and thus there is no de-internationalization of which to speak.[78] Although it is true that some of the

[70] For the analysis of the transformation of the conflict in Afghanistan, see text to notes 97–103 in this chapter. On Iraq, see, eg, Zamir (n 1) 166–68; MN Schmitt, 'Iraq (2003 onwards)' in E Wilmshurst (ed), *International Law and the Classification of Conflicts* (OUP 2012) 369–75.

[71] See, in particular, Mačák and Zamir (n 1) 427–28; Milanovic and Hadzi-Vidanovic (n 1) 280; Milanovic, '"Transnational" and "Mixed" Conflicts' (n 1) 32 [19]; Zamir (n 1) 159–60.

[72] On the role of effectiveness in international law, see generally H Kelsen, *Principles of International Law* (Rinehart 1952) 414–19; J Wildeman, 'The Philosophical Background of Effectiveness' (1977) 24 NILR 335; E Milano, *Unlawful Territorial Situations in International Law: Reconciling Effectiveness, Legality And Legitimacy* (Martinus Nijhoff 2006) 21–54.

[73] Similarly Zamir (n 1) 159.

[74] In fact, such a unilateral transformation is precluded by Article 47 GC IV, which mandates that protected persons in an occupied territory shall not be deprived of the protections under the Fourth Convention by any occupation-related changes introduced into the institutions or government of that territory. The main implication of the rule is that 'it must be possible for the Convention to be applied to [these persons] in its entirety, even if the Occupying Power has introduced changes in the institutions or government of the occupied territory'. Pictet, *GC IV Commentary* (n 43) 274. Therefore, the installation of a new government by the occupying power would be without effect as to the legal qualification of the conflict, given that de-internationalization would bring about a significant reduction of the legal protections available to the occupied population. See also Grignon (n 49) 1587 [25] (arguing that Art 47 GC IV amounts to a 'safeguard against the establishment of a "puppet" government'); Ferraro and Cameron, 'Article 2' (n 48) 85 [233] (arguing that the nature of the armed conflict would not change if a new government was instituted by an occupying power). However, in reality, the problem will always be of evidentiary nature, because no occupier will readily admit to having installed a puppet government and will instead likely insist that any such government came to power in a democratic and representative process.

[75] Milanovic, '"Transnational" and "Mixed" Conflicts' (n 1) 32 [19].

[76] See, eg, MW Reisman and J Silk, 'Which Law Applies to the Afghan Conflict?' (1988) 82 AJIL 459, 481 (arguing that IHL should apply in full to the post-1979 conflict in Afghanistan because the 'invitation' to the Soviet Union to enter Afghanistan had been illegitimate).

[77] See Section 1.2.2.2.

[78] See Section 4.2.2.

indicators developed in the case law may be more difficult to apply 'in reverse',[79] for the most part the law is clear. With respect to the requirement of organization, this means that if the deposed government disintegrates and the forces it once used to control are no longer bound together by an effective command structure, it would not qualify as an 'organized armed group' necessary for the existence of a NIAC.[80] Similarly, if the original government's defeat brings about a stabilization of the situation such that either all armed confrontations cease[81] or that there are, at most, isolated or sporadic acts of violence,[82] the intensity of the conflict would be insufficient to support a finding of a NIAC.[83] By contrast, if the surviving situation did hypothetically qualify as a NIAC, the next question to consider is whether the regime change as such would be recognized by international law.

The legal qualification of a situation marked by a regime change falls to be determined by reference to rules of general international law concerning the representation of states on the international plane.[84] Because states are juridical abstractions, they can only act through their organs or agents.[85] The foremost among them—and indeed, an organ of which every state can only have one at any given time[86]—is the government, in other words, 'the depository of the State's sovereignty, exclusively entitled in international law to represent that State in its international relations and to exercise its sovereign rights'.[87] Therefore, the central question is whether the political event of regime change means that the supposed new government also becomes a new government from the perspective of international law.

Whether a particular entity is a government or not depends on its effectiveness.[88] In this regard, international law is based on a strong presumption of effectiveness in favour of the original government.[89] Given 'the status quo orientation of the

[79] R Bartels, 'From *Jus In Bello* to *Jus Post Bellum*: When do Non-International Armed Conflicts End?' in C Stahn, JS Easterday, and J Iverson (eds), *Jus Post Bellum* (OUP 2014) 309.

[80] See *Prosecutor v Haradinaj, Balaj and Brahimaj* (Trial Judgment) IT-04-84-T (3 April 2008) [65]–[68] and [89] (prior to the establishment of a centralized command structure, the Kosovo Liberation Army did not qualify as an 'organized armed group'); *Prosecutor v Boškoski and Tarculovski* (Trial Judgment) IT-04-82-T (10 July 2008) [287] and [291] (prior to the establishment of an effective command structure, the ethnic Albanian National Liberation Army in Macedonia did not qualify as an 'organized armed group').

[81] L Cameron et al, 'Article 3: Conflicts Not of an International Character' in ICRC (ed), *Commentary on the First Geneva Convention* (CUP 2016) 176 [491].

[82] ibid 176 [489] and 177 [494].

[83] But see Zamir (n 1) 162 (suggesting that an IAC would transform into a NIAC also in cases where the former government 'has ceased to assert its authority' and where 'its armed resistance is practically hopeless or purely nominal'). It is submitted that such situations would not meet the criterion of intensity and as such would not amount to a NIAC.

[84] Accord Zamir (n 1) 152.

[85] J Crawford and S Olleson, 'The Character and Forms of International Responsibility' in M Evans (ed) *International Law* (4th edn, OUP 2014) 453.

[86] *Case of Charles J Jansen v Mexico* (1868) 29 RIAA 159, 184.

[87] S Talmon, *Recognition of Governments in International Law: With Particular Reference to Governments in Exile* (OUP 1998) 67.

[88] RY Jennings and A Watts (eds), *Oppenheim's International Law* (9th edn, Longman 1992) vol 1, 150–51; J Crawford (ed), *Brownlie's Principles of Public International Law* (8th edn, OUP 2012) 151–52; Ferraro and Cameron, 'Article 2' (n 48) 85 [234]; MN Shaw, *International Law* (8th edn, CUP 2017) 336–40.

[89] H Lauterpacht, *Recognition in International Law* (CUP 1947) 93; Zamir (n 1) 155–56.

international system'[90] and the 'conservative nature of international law',[91] this is perhaps not too surprising. But at what point is the presumption overturned? The traditional position, stated concisely by Lauterpacht in 1947, was that 'so long as the lawful government, however adversely affected by the fortunes of the civil war, remains within national territory and asserts its authority, it is presumed to represent the State as a whole'.[92] Under this interpretation, the presumption would only give way at the point when the resistance offered by the former government became 'ostensibly hopeless or purely nominal'.[93]

The problem with reliance on this traditional interpretation is twofold. First, the wording of Lauterpacht's test would likely preclude de-internationalization altogether. If the defeat of the government progresses so far that its resistance has been reduced to being 'ostensibly hopeless or purely nominal',[94] the situation would by the same token fall below the threshold of intensity required for the existence of a NIAC.[95] As such, the regime change could bring about the end of an IAC (provided the relevant requirements for the end of the conflict were met[96]), but not its transformation to a NIAC.

This leads directly to the second layer of the problem, which is that Lauterpacht's test is very clearly at odds with modern state practice. The best example in this regard is the conflict in Afghanistan after 2001. The conflict clearly began as an IAC between the international coalition of states and the Taliban as the de facto[97] government of Afghanistan.[98] In June 2002, however, a new government led by President Hamid Karzai was established and soon received virtually universal international recognition.[99] The continued presence of the allied forces on the Afghan territory was based on the consent granted by the Afghan authorities.[100] There is little doubt[101] that the Taliban continued (and, at the time of writing, continues) to offer resistance far in excess of what could be described as 'ostensibly hopeless or

[90] BR Roth, *Governmental Illegitimacy in International Law* (Clarendon Press 1999) 151.

[91] O Taylor, 'Reclaiming Revolution' (2011) 22 Finnish Yearbook of International Law 259, 269.

[92] Lauterpacht (n 89) 93. [93] ibid 94. [94] ibid.

[95] See, eg, ICC, OTP, Report on Preliminary Examination Activities 2013 (November 2013) <www.icc-cpi.int/OTP%20Reports/otp-report-2013.aspx> [129] (observing that because the confrontations between the *Urabeños* non-state armed group and other conflict parties were 'not sufficiently intense', the group did not qualify as a party to the conflict in Colombia).

[96] See generally Milanovic, 'End of Application' (n 1) 170–78.

[97] Only three states had recognized the Taliban as the *de jure* government of Afghanistan prior to 2001: Pakistan, Saudi Arabia, and the United Arab Emirates. R Wolfrum and CE Philipp, 'The Status of the Taliban: Their Obligations and Rights under International Law' (2002) 6 Max Planck UNYB 559, 575 fn 75.

[98] See, eg, F Hampson, 'Afghanistan 2001–2010' in E Wilmshurst (ed), *International Law and the Classification of Conflicts* (OUP 2012) 251.

[99] See UNSC Res 1419 (26 June 2002) [3] (welcoming the election of Hamid Karzai as the President of Afghanistan).

[100] See Military Technical Agreement between the International Security Assistance Force (ISAF) and the Interim Administration of Afghanistan (4 January 2002), (2002) 41 ILM 1032, Arts I(2) and IV; Afghanistan Compact (1 February 2006) <www.nato.int/isaf/docu/epub/pdf/afghanistan_compact.pdf> 3.

[101] But see Zamir (n 1) 165.

purely nominal'.[102] Yet, there is a clear international consensus that after June 2002, the situation in Afghanistan transformed into a NIAC.[103]

The point at which the former rebels gain effectiveness as the new government must therefore lie elsewhere than where the traditional doctrine put it. It is sometimes suggested that the external recognition received by a putative new government is a *constitutive* factor in this regard: in other words, that if the authority achieves broad recognition (sometimes in combination with other factors), it *becomes* the government.[104] However, such suggestions impermissibly invert the causal chain. An entity may be recognized as a government because it is effective—but it does not become effective because it is recognized.[105] (On the contrary, premature recognition of an entity that has not yet achieved effectiveness amounts to a violation of the principle of non-intervention and is therefore an internationally wrongful act against the state in question.[106]) To accept the inverse approach would infuse the determination of a conflict nature with political and subjective considerations that necessarily undergird each state's decision to recognize or not.[107] As such, it is incompatible with the requirement that IHL's scope of applicability must be determined on the basis of objective and factual criteria[108] and it should therefore be rejected.[109]

It is submitted that the better approach is to inquire instead whether the new government has acquired such level of effectiveness that its status as a government cannot be denied any longer. In Henkin's pithy shorthand: 'A régime that is a Government

[102] For the situation in Afghanistan after the regime change, see Report of the Secretary-General: The Situation in Afghanistan and its Implications for International Peace and Security, UN Doc A/56/1000–S/2002/737 (11 July 2002) [61]; Report of the Secretary-General: The Situation in Afghanistan and its Implications for International Peace and Security, UN Doc A/57/762–S/2003/333 (18 March 2003) [24]. For the situation in 2017, see Report of the Secretary-General: The Situation in Afghanistan and its Implications for International Peace and Security, UN Doc A/71/932–S/2017/508 (15 June 2017) [14]–[16].

[103] See, eg, Letter from Philip Spoerri, ICRC Legal Adviser to the UK House of Commons (Select Committee on International Development) (20 December 2002) <https://publications.parliament.uk/pa/cm200203/cmselect/cmintdev/84/84ap09.htm> (noting the 'unanimous recognition by the entire community of States' of the new government and qualifying the post-June situation in Afghanistan as a NIAC).

[104] Milanovic and Hadzi-Vidanovic (n 1) 281; Milanovic, 'End of Application' (n 1) 182; Milanovic, '"Transnational" and "Mixed" Conflicts' (n 1) 34 [24]; J Serralvo, 'Government Recognition and International Humanitarian Law Applicability in Post-Gaddafi Libya' (2016) 18 YIHL 3, 23.

[105] See also Talmon (n 87) 271 ('Recognition as the manifestation of a subjective opinion on the legal status of an authority can be neither constitutive of its objective legal status under international law nor declaratory of government status if the authority in question does not qualify for government status under international law in the first place.').

[106] Lauterpacht (n 89) 95; PK Menon, 'Some Aspects of the Law of Recognition: Part III: Recognition of Governments' (1990) 68 Revue de droit international, de sciences diplomatiques, politiques et sociales 157, 159; Jennings and Watts (n 88) 143–44.

[107] Mačák and Zamir (n 1) 427; Zamir (n 1) 161.

[108] See, eg, *Boškoski and Tarculovski* Trial Judgment (n 80) [174]; ILA, Committee on the Use of Force, Final Report on the Meaning of Armed Conflict in International Law (2010) 33; Ferraro and Cameron, 'Article 2' (n 48) 76–77 [210]–[12].

[109] For a more detailed critique of the de-internationalization test originally proposed by Milanovic and Hadzi-Vidanovic and reproduced in Milanovic's later writings, see Mačák and Zamir (n 1) 425–27; see also Zamir (n 1) 160–62.

in fact is a Government in law.'[110] A government is effective in this sense (ie, it is 'a Government in fact') if it is capable of exercising state functions both internally and externally.[111] The internal dimension of effectiveness entails, in particular, that the purported government exercises control over the state's territory, including its capital, and that it is able to continuously maintain law and order there.[112] The external dimension comprises the maintenance of international relations with other states on behalf of the state in question.[113] Again, this is a matter separate from recognition: as Justice Taft held in the 1923 *Tinoco* arbitration, so long as an administration is effective, it is the valid government of a state even if it remains unrecognized by others.[114] The same applies in wartime situations; 'no formal recognition of a particular regime as the Government of an enemy State is necessary'.[115]

In practice, in contested situations, the presumption in favour of the original government should serve as the starting point of the inquiry. However, the moment at which the new government is seen as effective by modern international law comes earlier than only after its enemy's position has been reduced to hopelessness. Rather, if the new authority is in control of the state territory as well as of the machinery of the state (internal dimension) and, at the same time, capable of maintaining relations with third states (external dimension), it should be assumed to be the effective government, thereby de-internationalizing the conflict in question. Until the moment when these facts emerge with reasonable clarity, the starting presumption will necessitate the conclusion that the original government remains the government from the perspective of international law, and the situation remains an IAC.

This interpretation is supported by modern practice. Consider the aforementioned example of the conflict in Afghanistan. Although the Taliban continued its resistance after June 2002, it is reasonably clear that the new government had soon thereafter acquired and kept control of the vast majority of Afghanistan's territory and its state apparatus.[116] Equally, it has maintained effective relations with outside states, as confirmed by the fact of its international recognition[117] as well as by actual agreements it concluded on behalf of Afghanistan with other states.[118] That

[110] L Henkin, 'International Law: Politics, Values and Functions: General Course on Public International Law' (1989–IV) 216 RdC 9, 33.

[111] P Daillier, M Forteau, and A Pellet, *Droit international public* (8th edn, LGDJ 2009) 417; Ferraro and Cameron, 'Article 2' (n 48) 85 [234]; Serralvo (n 104) 16–17.

[112] G Hafner, 'Present Problems of the Use of Force in International Law' (2009) 73 Annuaire de l'Institut de droit international 299, 397–98; S Talmon, 'Recognition of Opposition Groups as the Legitimate Representative of a People' (2013) 12 Chinese JIL 219, 232–33; Ferraro and Cameron, 'Article 2' (n 48) 85 [234]; see also Roth (n 90) 183–84 (discussing the importance of the maintenance of control over the state capital).

[113] D Geldenhuys, *Contested States in World Politics* (Palgrave Macmillan 2009) 11; Ferraro and Cameron, 'Article 2' (n 48) 85 [234].

[114] *Awards in the Tinoco Arbitration* (1923) 1 RIAA 369, 380–81.

[115] Y Dinstein, 'Comments on War' (2004) 27 Harvard Journal of Law and Public Policy 877, 888.

[116] See Report of the Secretary-General: The Situation in Afghanistan and its Implications for International Peace and Security, UN Doc A/57/762–S/2003/333 (18 March 2003), section II.A (Consolidation of Government Authority).

[117] See UNSC Res 1419 (26 June 2002) [3] (welcoming the election of Hamid Karzai as the President of Afghanistan).

[118] See, eg, Kabul Declaration on Good Neighbourly Relations, signed by the Transitional Administration of Afghanistan and the Governments of China, the Islamic Republic of Iran, Pakistan,

the conflict in Afghanistan has been universally described as a NIAC since at least June 2002 is therefore consistent with the Karzai government being viewed as the effective government of the country.

The events in Libya in 2011 offer a useful contrasting example. During the course of that year, rebels fighting against the Gaddafi regime united themselves in the so-called National Transitional Council (NTC).[119] Although the NTC received a degree of external recognition while the conflict was still underway,[120] this was far from universal, and many states insisted it was not the effective government of the country.[121] Similarly, the extent of the NTC's internal control remained contested at least until the capture and death of Muammar Gaddafi in October 2011.[122] The new regime thus did not gain effectiveness early enough[123] and therefore, the conflict between Libya and the intervening states remained an IAC until the close of military operations at the end of that month.[124] Again, this is in line with the legal position taken at the time by the actors involved in the conflict, all of whom had treated the situation as an IAC until the end of the hostilities.[125]

4.3.2 State unification?

The reverse process to state disintegration[126] is state unification, sometimes also referred to as the uniting of states.[127] The process of unification is generally understood as involving 'the disappearance of two or more sovereign States and, through their uniting, the creation of a new State'.[128] It is, of course, theoretically imaginable that

Tajikistan, Turkmenistan, and Uzbekistan (22 December 2002), reprinted in UN Doc S/2002/1416 (24 December 2002), annex.

119 Reuters, 'Anti-Gaddafi Figures Say Form National Council' (27 February 2011).

120 See, eg, UK, Announcement: Libyan Charge d'Affaires to be Expelled from UK (27 July 2011) <www.gov.uk/government/news/libyan-charge-d-affaires-to-be-expelled-from-uk>; US, Statement by the President on Libya (22 August 2011) <https://obamawhitehouse.archives.gov/the-press-office/2011/08/22/statement-president-libya>; Russia, Statement by the Russian Ministry of Foreign Affairs (1 September 2011) <www.mid.ru/en/foreign_policy/news/-/asset_publisher/cKNonkJE02Bw/content/id/196598>.

121 See, eg, UN Doc A/66/PV.2 (16 September 2011), 8–9 (Venezuela); ibid 9 (Cuba); ibid 11 (Angola).

122 See, eg, Arab Organization for Human Rights, Report of the Independent Civil Society Fact-Finding Mission to Libya (January 2012) [202] (reporting that in mid-September 2011, Gaddafi forces recaptured the western part of Sirte from the NTC-led forces).

123 A transitional government was only installed in November 2011. ICRC, *Annual Report 2011* (ICRC 2012) 136.

124 See R Norton-Taylor, 'NATO Ends Military Operations in Libya', *The Guardian* (31 October 2011) <www.theguardian.com/world/2011/oct/31/nato-ends-libya-rasmussen>; NATO, '"We Answered the call": The End of Operation Unified Protector' (31 October 2011) <www.nato.int/cps/en/natohq/news_80435.htm>.

125 See, eg, US, *Law of Armed Conflict Deskbook* (5th edn, US Army 2015) 43; UN Human Rights Council, Report of the International Commission of Inquiry on Libya, UN Doc A/HRC/19/68 (2 March 2012), Annex I, [21]; see further Zamir (n 1) 157 and 168–69.

126 See Section 2.3.1.

127 See, eg, Vienna Convention on Succession of States in respect of Treaties (signed 23 August 1978, entered into force 6 November 1996) 1946 UNTS 3, Arts 31–33.

128 Report of the International Law Commission on the work of its twenty-fourth session, UN Doc A/8710/Rev.1 (1972) 286 [2].

two states involved in an IAC would merge while the hostilities would continue as a NIAC in the newly formed single state. However, as this section shows, such a course of events would run against the fundamental principle of international law on the illegality of territorial acquisition by force. Therefore, it is submitted that de-internationalization by state unification is unavailable in the current state of international law.

The principle of non-acquisition of territory by force has been endorsed by a number of UN Security Council and General Assembly resolutions.[129] In the 2005 *Wall* Advisory Opinion, the ICJ described this principle as a corollary of the prohibitions on the threat or use of force incorporated in the UN Charter and confirmed its customary nature.[130] Furthermore, it has been recently reaffirmed by the reaction of the international community to the purported annexation of Crimea by Russia in 2014.[131] Crucially, any creation of a new unified state (and, *a fortiori*, an annexation of the entire territory of one state by another) during ongoing armed hostilities would manifestly amount to acquisition of territory by force.[132] As such, it would be without effect in international law, including any supposed legal requalification of the nature of the conflict in question.[133]

It is instructive to compare the hypothetical scenario described thus far with the actual sequence of events in the Persian Gulf in 1990–91. As is well known, Iraq invaded Kuwait on 2 August 1990[134] and several days thereafter declared 'the unity of Iraq and Kuwait' as a purportedly single country.[135] If this annexation had been recognized as a lawful merger of the two states while the original conflict would continue, the situation could indeed be described as de-internationalization of the initial IAC between Iraq and Kuwait.[136] Instead, the Iraqi attack was subject to

[129] See, eg, UNSC Res 242 (22 November 1967) preambular [2]; UNSC Res 252 (21 May 1968) preambular [6]; UNSC Res 582 (24 February 1986) preambular [6]; UNGA Res 2625 (XXV) (Declaration on Principles of International Law Concerning Friendly Relations and Co-operation among States in accordance with the Charter of the United Nations) (24 October 1970) [1] (hereafter Friendly Relations Declaration); UNGA Res 47/121 (18 December 1992) preambular [14].

[130] *Legal Consequences of the Construction of a Wall in the Occupied Palestinian Territory* (Advisory Opinion) [2004] ICJ Rep 136 [87].

[131] See UNGA Res 68/262 (27 March 2014) [6]; see further T Grant, *Aggression Against Ukraine: Territory, Responsibility, and International Law* (Palgrave Macmillan 2015) 64 ('[t]he predominant view among States was that the purported annexation of Crimea is unlawful and is not to be recognized') and 71 (noting that even those states that did not actively reject the annexation, 'were by no means supportive of [it]').

[132] See also Third Report on State Responsibility, by Mr James Crawford, Special Rapporteur, UN Doc A/CN.4/507 (4 August 2000) 23 [410] ('States may not recognize as lawful, for example, a unilateral acquisition of territory procured by the use of force, even if the use of force was arguably lawful.').

[133] See also *South West Africa cases (Ethiopia v South Africa; Liberia v South Africa)* (Judgment) [1966] ICJ Rep 6, 418 (diss op Jessup) ('It is a commonplace that international law does not recognize military conquest as a source of title.').

[134] See generally M Weller, *Iraq and the Use of Force in International Law* (OUP 2010) 12–58.

[135] UN Doc S/PV.2934 (9 August 1990) 46 (Iraq) ('the Iraqi Revolutionary Command Council decided to restore to our country the portion taken away from it, thus re-establishing the eternal, indestructible unity of our country.... My Government reaffirms that the unity of Iraq and Kuwait is indestructible').

[136] There is no doubt that Kuwait considered the situation as amounting to an IAC. See, eg, statement of the Kuwaiti Government of 2 August 1990 quoted in UN Doc S/PV.2932 (2 August 1990),

virtually universal condemnation.[137] Moreover, in its Resolution 662, the Security Council expressly decided that the 'annexation of Kuwait by Iraq under any form and whatever pretext has no legal validity, and is considered null and void'.[138] It can thus be inferred that the situation was generally treated as a continuing IAC between Iraq and Kuwait.[139] Additionally, within months, an international coalition was assembled under the leadership of the United States with the imprimatur of the Security Council.[140] The coalition forces undertook aerial and ground military operations against Iraq and succeeded in expelling it from Kuwait within a brief period in early 1991.[141] There can be no doubt that despite the Iraqi initial proclamation of 'unity', the situation had remained an IAC at all stages between August 1990 and April 1991, when a ceasefire was finally agreed by the conflict parties.[142] If anything, the reaction of the international community amounts to an implicit rejection of any idea of conflict de-internationalization by way of state unification.

Other examples of practice, where unification was contemplated by states that had previously been embroiled in conflict, confirm this interpretation. For instance, the Joint Communiqué on Basic Principles of National Unity agreed by the North and South Koreas in 1972 expressly affirmed that unification was to be 'achieved by peaceful means, without recourse to the use of arms against the other side'.[143] Similarly, in the 1973 Paris Peace Agreement, North and South Vietnam agreed that '[t]he reunification of Vietnam shall be carried out step by step through peaceful means on the basis of discussions and agreements between North and South Vietnam, without coercion or annexation by either party'.[144] Clearly, even if both concerned states do wish to unite, one of the fundamental preconditions before the unification can proceed is that any pre-existing IAC between them will have terminated.[145] It can thus be summarized that in the present state of international law, a situation of ongoing hostilities between two states precludes their lawful unification

6 (Kuwait) ('Iraq occupied Kuwait at dawn today.'); UN Doc S/PV.2939 (14 September 1990) 78 (Kuwait) (referring to 'the continued Iraqi occupation of Kuwait').

137 See, eg, UN Doc S/PV.2932 (2 August 1990), 13 (United States); ibid 16 (Colombia); ibid 17 (Canada); ibid 18 (France); ibid 19 (Malaysia); ibid 21 (United Kingdom); ibid 22 (Finland); ibid 23 (USSR); ibid 23 (China).

138 UNSC Res 662 (9 August 1990) [1].

139 cf also S Lyons, 'Naval Operations in the Gulf' in P Rowe (ed) *The Gulf War 1990–91 in International and English Law* (Routledge 1993) 141 ('That there was an international armed conflict between Iraq and Kuwait was not in dispute').

140 See UNSC Res 678 (29 November 1990) [2].

141 '1991: Iraqi troops flee Kuwait City' *BBC On This Day* (26 February 1991) <http://news.bbc.co.uk/onthisday/hi/dates/stories/february/26/newsid_4716000/4716868.stm>.

142 See UNSC Res 687 (8 April 1991) [33]; UN Doc S/22456 (6 April 1991) 7.

143 Joint statement of the North and the South of Korea (4 April 1972), in (1972) 2(3) Journal of Contemporary Asia 334, 334 para. 1(ii).

144 Agreement on Ending the War and Restoring Peace in Vietnam (Paris, 27 January 1973), reprinted in The Department of State Bulletin, vol LXVIII (12 February 1973) 169–88, Art 15.

145 The possibility that both states would give valid consent to unification while hostilities between them were underway is in any event purely hypothetical. Even if the belligerents shared the aim of uniting in one state, it is most unlikely that they would agree on the terms of unification without first bringing the armed contestation to an end. See similarly Section 2.3.1.3 (discussing the possibility that a state would accept and recognize the statehood of one of its parts during a mutual war of secession).

and, consequently, any attendant de-internationalization of the original IAC between the two belligerents.

4.3.3 Wars of national liberation

Although it has been said that wars of national liberation were a 'temporally and geographically limited phenomenon',[146] the decision of Switzerland to accept an Article 96(3) AP I declaration by the Polisario Front in June 2015 has breathed new life into this hitherto dormant legal category.[147] Provided that an armed conflict is internationalized when fighting in the sense of Article 1(4) AP I erupts, is it possible for this process to be reversed later and for a conflict previously classified as a war of national liberation to be de-internationalized?

The answer to this question can be inferred from the material scope of application of Article 1(4) AP I.[148] It is recalled that the provision internationalizes *ex lege* 'armed conflicts in which peoples are fighting against colonial domination and alien occupation and against racist regimes in the exercise of their right of self-determination'.[149] As mentioned previously, only such forms of conflict transformation which leave an ongoing situation of armed hostilities may be categorized as falling under the notion of de-internationalization.[150] Therefore, the crux of the question is whether it is possible that one of the conditions precedent for the applicability of Article 1(4) AP I would no longer be met while, at the same time, the underlying hostilities would continue.

There are two sides to this equation. Firstly, by definition, any war of national liberation in the sense of Article 1(4) AP I must feature a people fighting in exercise of its right to self-determination as a belligerent party. Clearly, if the territorial state were to extend sufficient rights to those represented by a national liberation movement pursuant to their internal self-determination, this would normally bring the conflict to an end. For example, the belligerent parties could agree on an inclusive constitutional process through which the people in question would be able to pursue its political, economic, social, and cultural development.[151] This would not de-internationalize, but rather terminate, the conflict as it could not be said anymore that the non-state party was engaged in 'fighting' against the parent state. If

[146] DE Graham, 'The 1974 Diplomatic Conference on the Law of War: A Victory for Political Causes and a Return to the "Just War" Concept of the Eleventh Century' (1975) 32 Washington & Lee Law Review 25, 53.

[147] Switzerland, 'Notification to the Governments of the States parties to the Geneva Conventions of 12 August 1949 for the Protection of War Victims' (26 June 2015) <www.eda.admin.ch/content/dam/eda/fr/documents/aussenpolitik/voelkerrecht/geneve/150626-GENEVE_en.pdf>, at 1 (notifying the states parties to the GCs of the acceptance of the declaration). See also Section 2.4.5.

[148] See generally Section 2.4.2.

[149] Art 1(4) AP I.

[150] See Section 4.2.2.

[151] cf *Secession of Quebec, Re, Reference to Supreme Court*, [1998] 2 SCR 217 (20 August 1998) [126] ('The recognized sources of international law establish that the right to self-determination of a people is normally fulfilled through internal self-determination—a people's pursuit of its political, economic, social and cultural development within the framework of an existing state.').

hostilities were to break out again at a later stage, the situation would then have to be qualified anew.

It is less clear what the consequences would be if the territorial state did ostensibly make such an offer, but the representatives of the people engaged in the conflict would reject it and carry on fighting. It could be argued that the offer by itself puts an end to the former denial of the right to self-determination and thus any continuing hostilities would no longer meet the Article 1(4) AP I conditions and should thereafter be seen as a NIAC between the same conflict parties. However, the better view is that such an offer would still be insufficient grounds for conflict de-internationalization, as otherwise the decision about the legal nature of the conflict would be left in the hands of one party only. Rather, the question whether the right to self-determination of a people has been fulfilled is an objective one and should be assessed on a case-by-case basis. In sum, developments concerning the right to self-determination of a people engaged in an Article 1(4) AP I conflict may terminate that conflict, but do not transform it into a NIAC.

The second side of the equation concerns the qualifiers in Article 1(4) AP I relating to the nature of the state party to the conflict and the potential for these to be affected in a given case by regime change or other internal constitutional developments. It is recalled that Article 1(4) AP I requires that the people in question must be fighting against 'colonial domination', 'alien occupation', or 'racist regimes'.[152] It has been observed earlier that the three categories are imprecise and ambiguous.[153] However, even supposing that a given situation could fairly be described as falling within one of these scenarios, it is unclear what change would have to happen in order for such a conflict to be de-internationalized.

As far as the first two of the three categories are concerned, this is because they are both inextricably intertwined with the existence of hostilities and, as such, with an armed conflict per se. In other words, the only way in which a colonial domination or an alien occupation (in the sense of this provision) can be terminated is through the withdrawal of armed forces of the state in question. This is because the essence of dominating or occupying another is in the exertion of one's power by force over that another. If that state of affairs ends, so does the underlying conflict, and thus there is logically no remaining space for de-internationalization.

The remaining category is that of 'racist regimes'. It is certainly imaginable that a regime, once described as racist, will be removed or transformed at one point and a more benign government will replace it ie one that would no longer discriminate against its subjects on the basis of their race, ethnicity, or a similar criterion. It can also be imagined that the hostilities would nonetheless continue in spite of this regime change. Consider, for example, that the conflict between the government of South Africa and the African National Congress (ANC) would persist beyond the end of apartheid in the early 1990s.[154] It could then be argued that such a

[152] Art 1(4) AP I. [153] See Section 2.4.2.

[154] In reality, the ANC announced in August 1990 that it was unilaterally suspending all armed actions. See 'Pretoria Minute' (6 August 1990), <http://peacemaker.un.org/sites/peacemaker.un.org/files/ZA_900806_The%20Pretoria%20Minute.pdf> [3].

situation would no longer be subsumed under Article 1(4) AP I, given that the new government would no longer be a racist regime, which would have the effect of de-internationalizing any surviving conflict. However, it is submitted that such an interpretation of the material scope of Article 1(4) AP I would be inordinately narrow.

It should not be forgotten that the concept of a 'racist regime' is a mirror requirement for the struggle being described as one fought in the exercise of the right to self-determination.[155] The 1970 Friendly Relations Declaration,[156] which is expressly acknowledged in the text of Article 1(4) AP I, can be instructive in this regard. The Declaration made it clear that a state which 'possessed of a government representing the whole people belonging to the territory without distinction as to race, creed or colour' was to be seen as conducting itself in compliance with the right to self-determination.[157] Therefore, if the racist regime was removed and the entire population would now be included 'in the political process which leads to the formation of the government',[158] the Article 1(4) AP I struggle should be viewed as terminated. If any hostilities persisted past that point, it could no longer be said that the non-state party represented a people fighting in exercise of its right to self-determination. Rather, any groups continuing the fighting would have to be assessed anew against the criteria of the existence of a NIAC.[159] But it would be inaccurate to speak of de-internationalization in such a case: the effective removal of the racist regime would end the Article 1(4) AP I conflict and break any continuity between the conflict parties.[160]

4.3.4 Recognition of belligerency, special agreements, and unilateral declarations

As discussed in Chapter 2, recognition of belligerency only internationalizes the conflict as between the recognizing state and the recognized non-state armed group.[161] Is it possible for this process to be reversed? It should be noted that the effects of recognition may be brought to an end in a number of ways, most of which would not de-internationalize the conflict. In particular, if the recognized belligerent is 'utterly defeated', as the case may be,[162] the conflict as such comes to an end, and thus there is no surviving situation that could be described as a NIAC. The same applies, logically, to a hypothetical decisive victory by the non-state actor such that would bring about a complete cessation of hostilities.[163] In such circumstances, the recognition does not need to be withdrawn (although

[155] See further Section 2.4.2. [156] Friendly Relations Declaration (n 129).
[157] Friendly Relations Declaration (n 129) [7].
[158] M Bothe, KJ Partsch, and WA Solf, *New Rules for Victims of Armed Conflicts: Commentary on the Two 1977 Protocols Additional to the Geneva Conventions of 1949* (Martinus Nijhoff 1982) 49.
[159] See Section 1.2.2.2. [160] See Section 4.2.2. [161] See Section 2.5.1.2.
[162] cf Lauterpacht (n 89) 350 ('a recognized belligerent may be utterly defeated').
[163] cf Shaw (n 88) 346 ('Recognition of belligerency will naturally terminate with the defeat of either party').

it certainly may be[164]) because the close of hostilities makes it inoperative *ipso facto*.[165]

However, it is conceivable that although the conflict continues, one or more of the customary conditions for recognition will no longer be met.[166] Lauterpacht allowed expressly for the possibility that 'the parties to the struggle ceased to conduct themselves in accordance with the rules of warfare' (condition 3) and considered it a permissible grounds for withdrawal of recognition.[167] But it is equally possible that the previously recognized belligerent would lose all territorial control (condition 1), or that the government it had set up would become completely ineffective (condition 2). In any of these situations, the previously recognizing state would be free (though not obliged[168]) to withdraw its previously granted recognition.[169] In fact, the right of states to do so was expressly recognized by a 1900 resolution of the Institute of International Law.[170] Stephen Neff noted in this connection that in practice, 'problems [with withdrawal of recognition] never actually arose, doubtless due to the rarity of recognition of belligerency in state practice'.[171] In any event, a withdrawal of this kind would de-internationalize the conflict as between the relevant parties.

It is more doubtful whether the effects of unilateral declarations and/or special agreements that had brought about relative internationalization could similarly be reversed at will. It is true that permitting such reversals would seem to be in line with the respect for the autonomy of conflict parties. After all, if policy reasons may lead a state to agree to apply the law of IAC to the insurgents, then a change in its policy could logically remove its willingness to do so.[172] However, once a conflict is subject to the full range of the law of IAC, this body of law entails also the strict obligation not to enter into any special agreement which would adversely affect the situation of protected persons.[173] Any agreement to requalify the conflict as a NIAC (and *a fortiori* a unilateral declaration purporting to do so) would inescapably 'diminish the protections afforded by the Conventions'[174] and as such be

[164] Jennings and Watts (n 88) 176.

[165] See, eg, H Lauterpacht, 'De Facto Recognition, Withdrawal of Recognition, and Conditional Recognition' (1945) 22 BYBIL 164, 184 fn 2, citing UK, Opinion of the Law Officers (29 April 1869) (F.0. 83/2299) (taking the view that it was not necessary to revoke an executive order that had enjoined neutrality on all British subjects in Japan, as with the end of hostilities there, the order 'cease[d] to be operative for want of parties, to whom it would be applicable').

[166] See Section 2.5.1.1 for a discussion of the traditional criteria for belligerency.

[167] Lauterpacht (n 165) 184.

[168] On which see Section 2.5.1.3.

[169] But see, eg, Ti-Chiang Chen, *The International Law of Recognition* (Praeger 1951) 260 ('while recognition is revocable, the revocation must be conceived not as an arbitrary act of policy, but as one of application of international law') (of states); Talmon (n 87) 234 ('Legal recognition may only be withdrawn upon a change in the factual circumstances') (of governments).

[170] Institute of International Law, Resolution concerning Rights and Duties of Foreign Powers and Their Ressortissants towards Established and Recognized Governments in Case of Insurrection (8 September 1900) Art 9.

[171] SC Neff, *War and the Law of Nations* (CUP 2005) 268.

[172] See further Section 2.5.2.

[173] Arts 6/6/6/7 GC I/II/III/IV.

[174] cf L Cameron, 'Article 6: Special Agreements' in ICRC (ed), *Commentary on the First Geneva Convention* (CUP 2016) 355 [978] (hereafter Cameron, 'Article 6').

without legal effect.[175] Moreover, 'an extra layer of protection'[176] is provided by the fact that, to the extent that such agreements or declarations purported to derogate from IAC rules which amount to *jus cogens*, they would be rendered void.[177] As stated earlier, although conflict parties may 'contract in' and thus accept additional obligations, including through internationalizing the conflict *inter se*,[178] they may not 'contract out' of a particular normative framework which would be otherwise binding on them.[179]

4.4 Evaluation

De-internationalization of armed conflicts is more than simply a reversal of the process of internationalization. This chapter has demonstrated that some modalities of internationalization cannot be reverted at all, while others contain at least a presumption against de-internationalization. It is submitted in conclusion that this is not a flaw, but rather a strength, of the law as it stands today. After all, re-qualifying a former IAC as a NIAC automatically brings about a substantial reduction in the protections afforded to those people who stand to be harmed by it the most.[180] As such, de-internationalization is in principle in stark contrast with the object and purpose of much of IHL.[181] Therefore, the legal tests identified in this chapter should be applied with utmost caution. For the same reason, in case doubt remains as to the qualification of a situation at hand, it is advisable to err against de-internationalization and assume that the situation remains an IAC.[182]

[175] T Meron, 'The Humanization of Humanitarian Law' (2000) 94 AJIL 239, 252; see also *Prosecutor v Tadić* (Trial Judgment) IT-94-1-T (7 May 1997) [583].

[176] Cameron, 'Article 6' (n 174) 356 [979].

[177] See Vienna Convention on the Law of Treaties (concluded 23 May 1969, entered into force 27 January 1980) 1155 UNTS 331, Art 53; ILC Guiding Principles Applicable to Unilateral Declarations of States Capable of Creating Legal Obligations (2006) UN Doc A/61/10, principle 8.

[178] See Section 2.5.2.

[179] See also G Mettraux, *International Crimes and the Ad Hoc Tribunals* (OUP 2005) 59.

[180] But see note 4 in this chapter (referring to the few areas in which the law of NIAC offers greater protection than the law of IAC).

[181] cf, eg, Ferraro and Cameron, 'Article 2' (n 48) 79 [216] (describing the object and purpose of IHL as the protection of those who are not or no longer taking part in the hostilities during armed conflict); K Okimoto, 'The Relationship between *Jus Ad Bellum* and *Jus In Bello*' in M Weller (ed), *The Oxford Handbook of the Use of Force in International Law* (OUP 2015) 1214 (arguing that 'since the object and purpose of IHL is to alleviate the suffering of individuals during armed conflict, any attempts at curtailing its application … [are] contrary to that object and purpose'); *Prosecutor v Tadić* (Appeal Judgment) IT-94-1-A (15 July 1999) [168] (holding that Art 4 GC IV, 'if interpreted in the light of its object and purpose, is directed to the protection of civilians *to the maximum extent possible*') (emphasis added).

[182] cf C Byron, 'Armed Conflicts: International or Non-International?' (2001) 6 JCSL 63, 84–85 (arguing on similar grounds for a reversal of the burden of proof in criminal proceedings faced with the question whether a conflict has changed from an IAC to a NIAC); but see *Prosecutor v Delalić et al* (*Čelebići* Appeal Judgment) IT-96-21-A (20 February 2001) [45]–[46] (holding that a presumption against de-internationalization would be inappropriate in the context of criminal proceedings).

PART II
COMBATANT STATUS

5

Historical Development

5.1 Introduction

Perhaps one day battlefield robots, auto-piloted UAVs, and self-replicating cyber viruses will completely remove the need for the presence of the 'human factor' in armed conflicts. Until that day comes, the determination of who may legitimately participate in an armed conflict is going to remain a key legal exercise in international humanitarian law (IHL).

In a 'classic' international armed conflict (IAC), where armies of two independent states meet on the battlefield, this determination is based on the distinction between combatants and civilians. Combatants are authorized to participate directly in hostilities, whereas civilians generally are not. Importantly, the reverse is also true: combatants may normally be made the object of attack, whereas civilians are granted a general protection from the dangers arising from military operations.

A crucial difference between such 'classic' conflicts and internationalized armed conflicts, then, is in the nature of the conflict parties. Irrespective of the specific way in which the internationalization process may occur, at its outset at least one of the parties necessarily is a non-state actor. It may have since transformed into a full-fledged state, although this qualification will likely remain contested while the conflict remains underway. Alternatively, it may have remained a non-state actor but with significant new links to an outside state or an international organization.

The general understanding in the literature is that members of non-state armed groups do not normally benefit from combatant status.[1] Therefore, the aim of Chapters 5, 6, and 7 is to explore the extent to which this position needs to be

[1] See, eg, GH Aldrich, 'Customary International Humanitarian Law: An Interpretation on behalf of the International Committee of the Red Cross' (2005) 76 BYBIL 503, 507; A Rogers, 'Combatant Status' in E Wilmshurst and S Breau (eds), *Perspectives on the ICRC Study on Customary International Humanitarian Law* (CUP 2007) 117; R Kolb and R Hyde, *An Introduction to the International Law of Armed Conflicts* (Hart 2008) 69; A Paulus and M Vashakmadze, 'Asymmetrical War and the Notion of Armed Conflict: A Tentative Conceptualization' (2009) 91 IRRC 95, 116; E Crawford, *The Treatment of Combatants and Insurgents Under the Law of Armed Conflict* (OUP 2010) 79; N Lubell, *Extraterritorial Use of Force Against Non-State Actors* (OUP 2010) 139; W Banks, 'Toward an Adaptive International Humanitarian Law: New Norms for New Battlefields' in W Banks (ed), *New Battlefields/Old Laws: Critical Debates on Asymmetric Warfare* (Columbia University Press 2011) 6; S Sivakumaran, *The Law of Non-International Armed Conflict* (OUP 2012) 71; K Ipsen, 'Combatants

adapted against the reality and legal nature of internationalized armed conflicts. Overall, these chapters argue that most fighters belonging to most non-state armed groups in most types of internationalized armed conflicts should, in fact, be considered eligible for combatant status.

This chapter makes the first step of that argument by analysing the historical development of the regulation of combatancy. In doing so, it demonstrates that, contrary to more sceptical views, international humanitarian law (IHL) IHL has for decades enabled certain classes of non-state actors access to combatant status. Chapter 6 and Chapter 7 then consider the theoretical and practical ramifications of granting combatant status to members of parties to modern-day internationalized armed conflicts.

5.2 Before 1949

5.2.1 Pre-modern times: before the concept of combatancy

In pre-modern times, the right to participate in war was not subject to strict legal criteria. Little need was felt to regulate who was allowed to take part in hostilities. In this regard, Cicero simply stated that 'it is not lawful for one who is not a soldier to fight [against] the enemy'.[2] But the category of 'soldiers' was open-ended, contingent on the will of the sovereign, and unconstrained by specific legal rules.[3] As late as at the time of Vattel's writing, it was common that 'immediately on a declaration of war, every man became a soldier', and thus whole adult male populations of the contesting territorial units engaged in the resulting armed struggle.[4] Alternatively, in more stratified societies characterized by feudal structures, participation in combat was seen as the honourable duty of the noblemen,[5] whereas serfs and slaves were often not expected to take part in fighting.[6] Either way, little consideration was given to the plight of the non-fighting population who often became the target of

and Non-Combatants' in D Fleck (ed), *The Handbook of International Humanitarian Law* (3rd edn, OUP 2013) 85; A Clapham, 'Concept of International Armed Conflict' in A Clapham, P Gaeta, and M Sassòli (eds), *The 1949 Geneva Conventions: A Commentary* (OUP 2015) 11 [22]; L Hill-Cawthorne, *Detention in Non-International Armed Conflict* (OUP 2016) 18; Y Dinstein, *The Conduct of Hostilities under the Law of International Armed Conflict* (3rd edn, CUP 2016) 41; GD Solis, *The Law of Armed Conflict: International Humanitarian Law in War* (2nd edn, CUP 2016) 201.

[2] Cicero, *On Duties* (MT Griffin and EM Atkins eds, CUP 1991) 16.

[3] cf SC Neff, *War and the Law of Nations* (CUP 2005) 208.

[4] E de Vattel, *The Law of Nations or the Principles of Natural Law* (J Chitty tr, 1758), book III, ch II, §9.

[5] FL Ganshof, *Feudalism* (3rd edn, Harper & Row 1964) 87 (discussing the obligation to provide 'military service as a mounted knight' as part of the duty of *auxilium* owed by a vassal to his feudal lord). The 'military classes' were bound by a nascent legal system, the medieval law of arms (*jus militare*), which can be considered one of the roots of the international law of war. GIAD Draper, 'The Status of Combatants and the Question of Guerrilla Warfare' (1971) 45 BYBIL 173, 173–75.

[6] See, eg, Y Diallo, 'African Traditions and Humanitarian Law' (1976) 16 IRRC 387, 392–93 (mapping out West African traditions that confirm this trend even in the twentieth century).

indiscriminate attacks of the assaulting army.[7] In these circumstances, the need for the delineation of the entitlement to participate in hostilities was not felt as pressing.

This observation is paralleled by a closer reading of the works of the classical international legal scholars. These did contain, admittedly, traces underlying the principle of distinction, which were often linked to these writers' moral and religious instincts. For example, Francisco de Vitoria argued that 'the deliberate slaughter of the innocent is never lawful in itself'.[8] Similarly, Hugo Grotius wrote that 'the bidding of mercy, if not of justice' required that 'no action be attempted whereby innocent persons may be threatened with destruction'.[9] However, classical works published before the nineteenth century did not go much beyond stating this fundamental principle and they did not, in particular, attempt to define who the 'non-innocent' persons were who could therefore lawfully participate in hostilities.[10] For example, even in a section tellingly entitled 'Who may be classed under the term combatants', Grotius actually discussed a different issue, namely when safe-conducts granted to the army could be extended to its senior officers.[11] At most, one could infer a partial answer to this question from Grotius's views on who should be spared during wartime,[12] but this analysis still did not extend to the identification of any specific criteria of combatancy.

5.2.2 Dawn of modernity: the landscape starts to change

The legal landscape started to change with the advent in Europe of the Age of Enlightenment. In his landmark work *The Social Contract*, Jean-Jacques Rousseau expressed the important idea that war was a relation 'not between man and man, but between State and State'.[13] The object of the war, thus understood, was to defeat the enemy state, and to achieve this aim, it sufficed to subdue that state's armed forces.[14] The period of the early nineteenth century marked the general acceptance of the notion of war no longer as the domain of feudal rulers or city-states, but rather as an

[7] See, eg, GP Noone, 'The History and Evolution of the Law of War Prior to World War II' (2000) 47 Naval L Rev, 181 ('Genghis Khan would punish a city for fighting against him by killing every inhabitant—men, women, and children regardless of combatant or non-combatant status.'); see further ME O'Connell, 'Historical Development and Legal Basis' in Fleck (n 1) 17; Neff (n 3) 204–06.

[8] F de Vitoria, *De Indis and De Jure Belli* (JP Bate tr, 1557), vol I, book VI, §35. Vitoria expressly mentioned Exodus 23 and Deuteronomy 20 as the authorities for this claim.

[9] H Grotius, *The Law of War and Peace in Three Books* (FW Kelsey tr, 1625), book III, ch XI, 8.

[10] LC Green, *The Contemporary Law of Armed Conflict* (3rd edn, Manchester University Press 2008) 102–04.

[11] Grotius (n 9), book III, ch XXI, §10. See also Green (n 10) 104.

[12] Grotius listed children, women, old men, and persons 'whose manner of life is opposed to war', including priests, writers, farmers, and merchants. Grotius (n 9), book III, ch XI, 2, 9–12; see also F Kalshoven, 'Grotius' Jus in Bello, with Special Reference to Ruses of War and Perfidy' in F Kalshoven (ed), *Reflections on the Law of War* (Martinus Nijhoff 2007) 332–33 (referring to these views as an illustration of 'Grotian moral justice').

[13] J-J Rousseau, *The Social Contract* (1762, GDH Cole tr, Cosimo 2008) 19.

[14] Rousseau (n 13) 20; see also O'Connell (n 7) 19–20; but see L Oppenheim, *The Future of International Law* (OUP 1921) 62–63 (warning against a too-broad reading of Rousseau and arguing that even non-combatants are in a 'passively hostile position' vis-à-vis the enemy state and that they may therefore lawfully become the object of coercive measures taken by that state's armed forces).

instrument of national policy.[15] Sparked by the writings of humanitarians such as Henry Dunant, who wrote a searing memoir about the aftermath of the 1859 Battle of Solferino,[16] the international public opinion increasingly focused on the plight of the victims of wars.[17] After Dunant unsuccessfully attempted to visit German fighters interned in Paris during the 1870 Franco-German war,[18] he reportedly understood that 'victims of a conflict, particularly those who took up arms to defend their country although not members of a regular army, could be protected only if the concept of belligerent (and hence of prisoner of war) were clearly defined'.[19]

Legal instruments of the time paid a growing amount of attention to this issue. The first codification of the laws of armed conflict, the 1863 Lieber Code,[20] referred expressly to the distinction between combatants and non-combatants and stipulated that non-combatants had 'to be spared in person, property, and honor as much as the exigencies of war will admit'.[21] The Code did not contain a definition of a lawful combatant, but a limited understanding of this concept could be drawn from two of its provisions. Article 57 stated that '[s]o soon as a man is armed by a sovereign government and takes the soldier's oath of fidelity, he is a belligerent'.[22] By contrast, Article 155 described non-combatants as the 'unarmed citizens of the hostile government'. The Lieber Code thus affirmed the important distinction between unarmed civilians and armed soldiers.[23]

The Lieber Code quickly became influential abroad and many European nations used it as a basis for their own military instructions.[24] In addition, the 1860s marked the adoption of two additional ground-breaking international instruments of the laws of war: the 1864 Geneva Convention dedicated to the protection of persons wounded in wars[25] and the 1868 Declaration of St Petersburg prohibiting exploding bullets below 400 grams.[26] However, these legal documents likewise did not address the challenge identified by Henry Dunant and he thus launched an initiative for the

[15] Crawford (n 1) 49. [16] H Dunant, *A Memory of Solferino* (ICRC 1862).

[17] JS Pictet, *Development and Principles of International Humanitarian Law* (Martinus Nijhoff 1985) 26.

[18] Y de Pourtales and R Durand, 'Henry Dunant, Promoter of the 1874 Brussels Conference' (1975) 15 IRRC 61, 65–66.

[19] ibid 66.

[20] See Section 8.2.2 for a more detailed discussion of the historical background to this codification.

[21] Instructions for the Government of Armies of the United States in the Field, prepared by Francis Lieber, General Orders No 100 (24 April 1863) Arts 22 (protection of non-combatants) and 155 (principle of distinction) (hereafter Lieber Code).

[22] Today, the noun 'belligerent' is normally used to refer to a party to an armed conflict, not to an individual fighter.

[23] See Rogers (n 1) 103–04; but see R Giladi, 'A Different Sense of Humanity: Occupation in Francis Lieber's Code' (2012) 94 IRRC 81, 112 (putting forward an alternative view that Lieber considered 'the whole citizenry of the belligerents as enemies' and thus 'directly rejected Rousseau's doctrine').

[24] L Friedman (ed), *The Law of War: A Documentary History* (Random House 1972) vol 1, 152.

[25] Geneva Convention for the Amelioration of the Condition of the Wounded in Armies in the Field (signed 22 August 1864, entered into force 22 June 1865), reproduced in D Schindler and J Toman (eds), *The Laws of Armed Conflicts* (3rd edn, Martinus Nijhoff 1988) 279–83.

[26] Declaration Renouncing the Use, in Time of War, of Explosive Projectiles Under 400 Grammes Weight, Saint Petersburg (entered into force 11 December 1868), reproduced in Schindler and Toman (n 25) 101–04.

organization of an international conference tasked with the preparation of a comprehensive code on the regulation of war.[27]

5.2.3 Brussels Declaration: the first definition of combatant status

The Brussels Conference of 1874 was attended by the delegates of 15 European powers.[28] During the conference, a divide between larger military states and their smaller, weaker counterparts was beginning to show and it reportedly occasioned a considerable stalling of the diplomatic process.[29] On the one hand, the great powers of the period, like Germany and Russia, were anxious to limit the privilege of lawfully taking part in hostilities to a narrowly defined class of army soldiers clad in state uniforms.[30]

On the other hand, small states like Belgium and the Netherlands shared the concern that any regulation should not deprive them of their ability to rely on mass forms of resistance in case of foreign invasion.[31] They therefore demanded that combatant status not be limited to members of regular armies but that it should also extend to resistance fighters defending their home state.[32]

In the end, the delegates succeeded in formulating a 'somewhat muddled compromise'[33] in the form of Article 9 of what became known as the Brussels Declaration of 1874.[34] That provision thus contained the first international attempt to formulate a definition of combatant status. It appeared under the heading 'Who should be recognized as Belligerents Combatants and Non-Combatants':

The laws, rights, and duties of war apply not only to armies, but also to militia and volunteer corps fulfilling the following conditions:

1. That they be commanded by a person responsible for his subordinates;
2. That they have a fixed distinctive emblem recognizable at a distance;
3. That they carry arms openly; and
4. That they conduct their operations in accordance with the laws and customs of war.

In countries where militia constitute the army, or form part of it, they are included under the denomination 'army'.[35]

[27] de Pourtales and Durand (n 18) 66–77 (detailing Dunant's efforts in the preparation of the conference).

[28] Schindler and Toman (n 25) 25.

[29] Friedman (n 24) 152; Neff (n 3) 208–09.

[30] F Kalshoven, 'The Diplomatic Conference on Reaffirmation and Development of International Humanitarian Law Applicable in Armed Conflicts, Geneva, 1974–1977' in F Kalshoven (ed), *Reflections on the Law of War* (Martinus Nijhoff 2007) 194; Neff (n 3) 208.

[31] WJ Ford, 'Resistance Movements in Occupied Territory' (1956) 3 NILR 355, 355; Kalshoven (n 30) 194.

[32] SE Nahlik, 'A Brief Outline of International Humanitarian Law' (1984) 24 IRRC 187, 200; Neff (n 3) 208; GIAD Draper, 'The Legal Classification of Belligerent Individuals' in MA Meyer and H McCoubrey (eds), *Reflections on Law and Armed Conflicts* (Kluwer 1998) 197–99.

[33] Neff (n 3) 208.

[34] Brussels Declaration Concerning the Laws and Customs of War (27 August 1874), reproduced in Schindler and Toman (n 25) 27–34 (hereafter Brussels Declaration).

[35] Brussels Declaration (n 34) Art 9.

Although the Brussels Declaration was never ratified due to the lack of general will to accept it as a binding agreement,[36] its content was highly influential in the following development of the law of armed conflict.[37] The text of Article 9 of the Declaration was reproduced virtually without modification in the Hague Regulations of 1899 and 1907.[38] It was then incorporated in the 1929 Geneva Convention on the Treatment of Prisoners of War by way of a *renvoi* to the 1907 Regulations.[39]

There is no doubt that in the late-nineteenth and early-twentieth centuries, the prevailing paradigm of international law was based on state sovereignty and that the government delegates participating at the international conferences considered the rules they adopted to apply in the context of inter-state warfare only,[40] possibly complemented by situations of recognized belligerency.[41] Nevertheless, it is worth noting that in the adopted form, the provision originating at the 1874 Brussels Conference and confirmed at The Hague in 1899 and 1907 accorded combatant status to fighters belonging to potentially non-state entities described as 'militias' and 'volunteer corps'.[42] These were, to be sure, understood by the delegates to be acting to defend their home state against foreign invaders,[43] but the adopted text

[36] J Goldblat, *Arms Control: The New Guide to Negotiations and Agreements* (SAGE 2002) 279; J Gardam, *Necessity, Proportionality and the Use of Force by States* (CUP 2004) 51; K Göcke, 'Brussels Declaration (1874)' in R Wolfrum (ed), *Max Planck Encyclopedia of Public International Law* (OUP 2008) <www.mpepil.com> (updated October 2009) [7].

[37] cf Hague Convention (II) with Respect to the Laws and Customs of War on Land (signed 29 July 1899, entered into force 4 September 1900) 32 Stat 1803, TS 403 (hereafter Hague Convention II (1899)), preamble (confirming the inspiration of the drafters by the 'views which are enjoined at the present day, as they were twenty-five years ago at the time of the Brussels Conference in 1874, by a wise and generous foresight').

[38] Regulations Respecting the Laws and Customs of War on Land, Annex to Hague Convention (II) (1899) (n 37) Art 1; Regulations Respecting the Laws and Customs of War on Land, Annex to Hague Convention (IV) respecting the Laws and Customs of War on Land (signed 18 October 1907, entered into force 26 January 1910) 205 CTS 277, Art 1 (hereafter Hague Regulations). The only difference of more than syntactical import was the inclusion of the words 'or volunteer corps' in the last sentence of the provision, which signified the parties' understanding that in addition to militias, even volunteer corps could be integrated within a state army.

[39] Geneva Convention Relative to the Treatment of Prisoners of War (signed 27 July 1929, entered into force 19 June 1931) 118 LNTS 343, Art 1(1) ('The present Convention shall apply . . . [t]o all persons referred to in Articles 1, 2 and 3 of the [Hague] Regulations . . . , who are captured by the enemy').

[40] See, eg, JB Scott, *The Hague Peace Conferences of 1899 and 1907* (Johns Hopkins Press 1909) 27, citing the following passage by William Ladd as outlining 'the actual program of the Hague Conferences': '[it] is to have *nothing to do with the internal affairs of nations, or with insurrections, revolutions, or contending factions of people or princes*, or with forms of government, but solely to concern themselves with the intercourse of nations in peace and war'. W Ladd, *An Essay on A Congress of Nations* (Whipple and Damrell 1840) 16 (emphasis added).

[41] See R Bartels, 'Timelines, Borderlines and Conflicts: The Historical Evolution of the Legal Divide between International and Non-international Armed Conflicts' (2009) 91 IRRC 35, 47 (arguing that the concept of belligerency strengthened, rather than undermined, the sovereignty-based approach); see also Section 2.5.1.

[42] The interpretation that these terms were intended to cover units not under direct control of states, and thus non-state actors, is confirmed by the inclusion of the final sentence of the provision, which draws a distinction between militias *lato sensu* (to be seen as part of the 'army' of the state) and *stricto sensu* (only these had to fulfil the four conditions). On this distinction in the context of the 1949 Geneva Conventions, see Section 5.3.1.

[43] cf Scott (n 40) 528–30.

did not require any specific connection linking these units to a particular State.[44] In fact, a requirement of subordination of these units under a 'general command' was proposed in the first draft of the Declaration, but it was then removed following the submission of the Austrian-Hungarian delegate who had argued that such an attachment would be 'rare' in practice.[45] Revealingly, the delegates in 1874 may have been more apprehensive of the reality of contemporary warfare than their counterparts a century later. As discussed in Chapter 7, a similar requirement in Article 43(1) AP I that forces be subjected to a 'command responsible' to a conflict party may actually prevent many actors in internationalized conflicts from meeting the Protocol's criteria of combatancy.[46]

5.3 After 1949

5.3.1 Geneva Convention III: expansion of the concept of combatancy

The reality of the Second World War confirmed the emergence of a new type of armed non-state actors with an unresolved legal status. All across Europe, so-called partisan movements engaged the Nazi German armed forces to contest for control over territories attacked or occupied by the *Wehrmacht*. Understandably, the partisans demanded to be treated as lawful combatants, but the German practice in this respect was far from consistent. They accorded prisoner-of-war (POW) treatment to some partisan units but denied it to most.[47] Postwar commentary was divided on the question whether partisans, as groups engaged in armed resistance in occupied territories, could qualify at all for combatant status.[48] Several decisions of war crime tribunals accepted that the partisans would have qualified as combatants if they had met the four criteria required by Article 1 of the Hague Regulations.[49] However, this

[44] But see, eg, L Nurick and RW Barrett, 'Legality of Guerrilla Forces Under the Laws of War' (1946) 40 AJIL 563, 567 (arguing that the requirement that the individuals in question must serve a de jure or de facto state was 'a fundamental premise *implicit* in the Hague Regulations') (emphasis added); A Rosas, *The Legal Status of Prisoners of War* (Suomalainen Tiedeakatemia 1976) 296 (arguing that 'it must be *assumed*' that the parties did not want to depart from the requirement that the independent forces fight '*on behalf of* a belligerent State') (first emphasis added); GS Corn, 'Thinking the Unthinkable: Has the Time Come to Offer Combatant Immunity to Non-State Actors?' (2011) 22 Stanford Law & Policy Review 253, 258 (arguing that the fact that the treaty applied only to states implied a silent requirement that the individual be acting under the authority of a state).

[45] Conférence intergouvernementale, *Actes de la conférence de Bruxelles de 1874* (Librairie des publications législatives 1874) 29–30.

[46] See Section 7.3.3.

[47] WJ Ford, 'Resistance Movements and International Law (II)' (1967) 7 IRRC 579, 581–84.

[48] See Rosas (n 44) 298 fn 372 (opponents) and fn 373 (proponents); see also WJ Ford, 'Resistance Movements and International Law (IV)' (1968) 8 IRRC 7, 7–12.

[49] See, eg, *Bauer et al* (Judgment) (18 October 1945) (1949) 8 Law Reports of Trials of War Criminals 15 (French Permanent Military Tribunal in Dijon) 16–19; *List et al* (Judgment) (19 February 1948) (1949) 8 Law Reports of Trials of War Criminals 34 (US MT), 56–57 and 76–77; *von Leeb et al* (Judgment) (28 October 1948) (1949) 12 Law Reports of Trials of War Criminals 1 (US MT) 85–86.

was often not the case, especially due to the partisans' insufficient or inconsistent use of uniforms.[50]

In 1949, the adoption of the Third Geneva Convention removed some of these doubts. Subparagraphs 1, 2, 3, and 6 of article 4A of the Convention complemented and partially modified the Hague conditions:

> Prisoners of war, in the sense of the present Convention, are persons belonging to one of the following categories, who have fallen into the power of the enemy:
>
> (1) Members of the armed forces of a Party to the conflict, as well as members of militias or volunteer corps forming part of such armed forces.
> (2) Members of other militias and members of other volunteer corps, including those of organized resistance movements, belonging to a Party to the conflict and operating in or outside their own territory, even if this territory is occupied, provided that such militias or volunteer corps, including such organized resistance movements, fulfil the following conditions:
>   (a) that of being commanded by a person responsible for his subordinates;
>   (b) that of having a fixed distinctive sign recognizable at a distance;
>   (c) that of carrying arms openly;
>   (d) that of conducting their operations in accordance with the laws and customs of war.
> (3) Members of regular armed forces who profess allegiance to a government or an authority not recognized by the Detaining Power.
> [...]
> (6) Inhabitants of a non-occupied territory, who on the approach of the enemy spontaneously take up arms to resist the invading forces, without having had time to form themselves into regular armed units, provided they carry arms openly and respect the laws and customs of war.[51]

Unlike the previous texts, the Convention did not speak of conditions for combatant status; instead, it defined which persons should be considered POWs upon capture.[52] Nevertheless, the effect of the provision went beyond the attribution of POW status and it should also be understood as outlining which persons qualify as combatants.[53] Moreover, the text of Article 4A of GC III was also transposed to GC

[50] See further WJ Ford, 'Resistance Movements and International Law (III)' (1967) 7 IRRC 627, 627–39.

[51] Art 4A GC III.

[52] cf Art 4A, chapeau, GC III. The provision, in contrast to previous texts, does not use the term 'capture' but rather, and more accurately, 'fall[ing] into the power of the enemy'. This more cumbersome but also more precise wording was chosen in order to prevent conflict parties from denying POW status to persons detained following a mass capitulation, ie, those who were not, strictly speaking 'captured' by the detaining power. JS Pictet (ed), *Geneva Convention III relative to the Treatment of Prisoners of War: Commentary* (ICRC 1960) 50 (hereafter Pictet, *GC III Commentary*).

[53] See, eg, Y Sandoz, C Swinarski, and B Zimmermann (eds), *Commentary on the Additional Protocols of 8 June 1977 to the Geneva Conventions of 12 August 1949* (ICRC 1987) 515 [1677] (hereafter Sandoz et al, *APs Commentary*) (acknowledging that combatant status was not explicitly affirmed by Art 4A GC III, but considering it implicitly included in the recognition of POW status); E Crawford, *Identifying the Enemy: Civilian Participation in Armed Conflict* (OUP 2015) 17 ('Article 4A of the Third Geneva

I[54] and GC II[55] in order to specify the categories of protected persons under those Conventions.[56]

Returning to the regulation of combatancy, what were the most important changes introduced by the Third Convention? To begin with, an express reference to 'organized resistance movements' was added to the text of subparagraph 2 of Article 4A GC III in order to clarify the legal status of partisans.[57] Moreover, the newly adopted text now confirmed that it did not matter whether the partisans were operating in or outside their state's territory or whether that territory was occupied.[58] The requirement of 'belonging to a Party to the conflict' confirmed the heretofore tacit understanding that so-called 'independent forces'[59] could not operate without any link whatsoever to a belligerent state.[60] The ICRC Commentary, however, noted that this affiliation did not need to be official or even express; it was said to be sufficient 'if the operations are such as to indicate clearly for which side the resistance organization is fighting'.[61] The inclusion of the requirement of 'belonging' in Article 4A(2) GC III thus confirmed that non-state armed groups, 'based on their links to states, can enjoy the benefits of the law of IAC' including combatant status.[62] The prevailing liberal interpretation of the requirement of 'belonging' should also be underlined at this point, as it acquires crucial importance in the analysis of the entitlement to benefit from combatant status by non-state actors in conflicts internationalized by outside intervention.[63] At any rate, in order to benefit from the rights and privileges accorded to combatants, partisans still had to fulfil the four

Convention outline[s] who is entitled to POW status and, by extension, combatant status'); S Watts, 'Who Is a Prisoner of War?' in Clapham et al (n 1) 890 [2] (noting that Art 4A GC III 'has been perceived as a merger of sorts between conditions for POW status and conditions expected of combatants generally'); N Zamir, *Classification of Conflicts in International Humanitarian Law: The Legal Impact of Foreign Intervention in Civil Wars* (Edward Elgar 2017) 136 (considering that the original purpose of Art 4A GC III was to determine who was entitled to POW status and consequently to serve as a definition of a combatant).

[54] Art 13 GC I. [55] Art 13 GC II.

[56] See further JS Pictet (ed), *Geneva Convention I for the Amelioration of the Condition of the Wounded and Sick in Armed Forces in the Field: Commentary* (ICRC 1952) 144–45; JS Pictet (ed), *Geneva Convention II for the Amelioration of the Condition of Wounded, Sick and Shipwrecked Members of Armed Forces at Sea: Commentary* (ICRC 1960) 95; L Cameron, 'Article 13: Protected Persons', in ICRC (ed), *Commentary on the First Geneva Convention* (CUP 2016) 521 [1455] (hereafter Cameron, 'Article 13 GC I'); L Cameron, 'Article 13: Protected Persons', in ICRC (ed), *Commentary on the Second Geneva Convention* (CUP 2017) 535 [1497].

[57] See also Pictet, *GC III Commentary* (n 52) 52–61 (notably, the whole section devoted to subparagraph 2 is entitled 'Partisans' and on page 58, the Commentary confirms that 'this wording … constitutes a clear reference to the events of the Second World War and to the resistance movements which were active during that conflict').

[58] See further Pictet, *GC III Commentary* (n 52) 50 and 58–59; similarly Cameron, 'Article 13 GC I' (n 56) 520 [1453]. The new treaty text thus resolved the debates on this point referred to in note 48 in this chapter.

[59] Rosas (n 44) 300, drawing on EJS Castrén, *The Present Law of War and Neutrality* (Suomalainev Tiedeakemia 1954) 146.

[60] Watts (n 53) 897 [26]. [61] Pictet, *GC III Commentary* (n 52) 57.

[62] Zamir (n 53) 136. [63] See Section 7.2.2.1.2.

traditional conditions, which was already then known to be highly problematic for irregular groups relying on guerrilla methods of warfare.[64]

Also importantly for the present purposes, the new Convention included in subparagraph 3 a new category of 'regular armed forces who profess allegiance to a government or authority not recognized' by the opposing conflict party. In some of the subsequent writings, it was argued that this provision could be used to bring fighters in *internal* conflicts within the scope of the Convention.[65] It is submitted that such reading would take the thrust of the provision too far. The subparagraph in question was drafted to cover resistance troops akin to the Free French Forces (*Forces Françaises Libres*) who had been fighting the occupying German forces but who had not engaged in direct hostilities against the collaborating French government based in Vichy.[66] In more general terms, the provision was meant to cover cases of governments in exile, which continued to resist an occupying power from abroad.[67] Importantly, such conflicts were still understood as *international*—in fact, without an IAC in existence, the application of the GCs as a whole would not be triggered,[68] and so this subparagraph would not apply either.[69] Yet, the provision may be highlighted as another possible gateway through which members of entities that were arguably of a non-state nature could benefit from combatant status.

5.3.2 Additional Protocol I: equating regular and irregular forces

The decolonization period marked the appearance of national liberation movements as prominent and influential non-state actors on the international scene.[70] Those engaged in secession conflicts found it was nearly impossible to reconcile their characteristic method of guerrilla warfare based on stealth and ambush with the obligation to meet the four Hague conditions.[71] The combination of these factors—the influence of the liberation movements and the changing nature of warfare—led to a further development of the law regulating lawful combatancy.[72] At the 1974–77 Diplomatic Conference, notably attended by the representatives of eleven national

[64] See, eg, Castrén (n 59) 149 (admitting that 'most partisan movements similar to those appearing during the Second World War' would still fall short of protection on this basis); HS Levie, *Prisoners of War in International Armed Conflicts* (Naval War College Press 1979) 42 (arguing that 'this attempted enlargement of the provisions of prior conventions accomplished little or nothing').

[65] See, eg, RA Falk, 'Janus Tormented: The International Law of Internal War' in JN Rosenau (ed), *International Aspects of Civil Strife* (Princeton University Press 1964) 205 fn 26; T Farer, 'The Humanitarian Laws of War in Civil Strife: Towards a Definition of "International Armed Conflict"' (1971) 7 RBDI 21, 30.

[66] Pictet, *GC III Commentary* (n 52) 61–62; Rosas (n 44) 252–53.

[67] Pictet, *GC III Commentary* (n 52) 63; Rosas (n 44) 254.

[68] cf Common Art 2 GCs; see further Section 1.2.2.1.

[69] Similarly Rosas (n 44) 252; see also ibid fn 145 and references cited therein.

[70] See generally HA Wilson, *International Law and the Use of Force by National Liberation Movements* (Clarendon Press 1988).

[71] See, eg, Draper (n 5) 183 (observing that guerrilla warfare was a feature of the period) and 214 (arguing that guerrilla fighters were dissuaded from meeting the four conditions, because the conditions were stringent and because their fulfilment would likely lead to death, defeat, or capture).

[72] See Sandoz et al, *APs Commentary* (n 53) 383–84 [1370]–[73].

liberation movements,[73] two important changes were agreed insofar as the regulation of combatancy was concerned.

Firstly, the normative structure of the regulation was inversed. Article 43 AP I abandoned the differentiation between regular and irregular combatants as well as between regular armies and resistance movements.[74] All members of armed forces other than medical and religious personnel were declared to be combatants.[75] Accordingly, fighters no longer had to meet further conditions in order to qualify for combatancy. Article 44(3) AP I provided, inversely, that a combatant could *lose* his status if (1) he did not distinguish himself from the civilian population during the attack and its preparation, or (2) in situations where, owing to the nature of the hostilities, he cannot so distinguish himself, and he did not carry his arms openly during the attack and its preparation.[76]

Secondly, the Protocol expanded its scope to situations of wars of national liberation by including them in Article 1(4) AP I. While the importance of that provision for the internationalization of such conflicts has been discussed earlier in this work,[77] it should be emphasized here that this extension of applicability made provisions on combatant status clearly applicable to a certain class of non-state actors, ie, national liberation movements.[78] Although under the interpretation advanced here combatant status could in principle have been granted to some non-state actors already on the basis of Article 4A(3) GC III, they would nevertheless have had to meet the criterion of being 'regular' armed forces.[79] The adoption of the Protocol, by contrast, extended the privileges of combatancy also to irregular forces, albeit still only in conflicts that fell within the scope of this instrument.[80]

Needless to say, the relaxation of the requirements for obtaining the privileges of combatant status through the adoption of AP I was not universally welcomed at the time. In particular, the United States had strongly objected to the relevant provisions and made it clear subsequently that it had decided not to ratify the Protocol, 'in large part, because of them'.[81] Similarly, Israel voted against Article 44(3) AP I on grounds that it 'was contrary to the spirit and to a fundamental principle of humanitarian

[73] See Final Act of the Diplomatic Conference on the Reaffirmation and Development of International Humanitarian Law Applicable in Armed Conflicts (10 June 1977) [3] (listing liberation movements that took part in the conference).

[74] Wilson (n 70) 173; see also Sandoz et al, *APs Commentary* (n 53) 511–13 [1672]; M Bothe, KJ Partsch, and WA Solf, *New Rules for Victims of Armed Conflicts: Commentary on the Two 1977 Protocols Additional to the Geneva Conventions of 1949* (Martinus Nijhoff 1982) 236–38; J-M Henckaerts and L Doswald-Beck (eds), *Customary International Humanitarian Law* (CUP 2005) vol I, 16 (hereafter *ICRC CIHL Study*).

[75] Art 43(2) AP I.

[76] Art 44(3) AP I (argument *a contrario* 'he shall *retain* his status as a combatant ... ') (emphasis added).

[77] See Section 2.4.

[78] cf Sandoz et al, *APs Commentary* (n 53) 507 ('it is perfectly clear that the Protocol has extended its field of application to entities which are not States').

[79] See text to note 51 in this chapter for the text of the provision.

[80] cf Wilson (n 70) 174 (emphasizing that the import of Art 43 was that it 'extend[ed] the privileges of combatancy to irregular forces even when the authority commanding them is not recognized').

[81] US DoD, *Law of War Manual* (December 2016) 119 [4.6.1.2]; see also Letter of Transmittal from President Ronald Reagan (29 January 1987), reproduced in (1987) 81 AJIL 910.

law'.[82] Additionally, even some of the ratifying states chose to make a formal statement on ratification to the effect that the exception in Article 44(3) AP I could only apply in occupied territory or in Article 1(4) conflicts.[83] The continuing opposition to the new rules by non-ratifying states indicates that these provisions have not crystallized into customary law.[84] Nevertheless, in relation to the state parties to the Protocol, they must be recognized as amounting to an unequivocal extension of combatant status to members of at least some non-state armed groups.

5.4 Evaluation

This brief historical overview demonstrates that the development of conditions of combatant status has been strongly influenced by a state-sovereignty paradigm. States have so far been careful to maintain the exclusivity of application of the concept of combatancy to IACs. Indeed, as academics, case law, and the ICRC admit in a rare unison voice, combatancy is one of the concepts that has not benefited from the ongoing trend of confluence between the two types of conflict.[85] Nevertheless, as we have seen, at nearly all times in modern history, states were willing to extend this status to at least a limited set of non-state actors. Could this approach apply to non-state actors in internationalized armed conflicts more generally? In order to answer that question, Chapter 6 looks at the theoretical underpinnings of the present-day regulation of combatancy.

[82] Switzerland, *Official Records of the Diplomatic Conference on the Reaffirmation and Development of International Humanitarian Law Applicable in Armed Conflicts, Geneva (1974–1977)* (Federal Political Department 1978) vol VI, CDDH/SR.40, 121 [17] (Israel).

[83] See, eg, A Roberts and R Guelff (eds), *Documents on the Laws of War* (3rd edn, OUP 2000) 501 [7] (Belgium), 502 [F] (Canada), 504 [3] (Germany), 507 [C] (Italy), 510 [g] (United Kingdom). See further J Gadreau, 'The Reservations to the Protocols Additional to the Geneva Conventions for the Protection of War Victims' (2003) 85 IRRC 143, 152–53.

[84] cf US, Memorandum submitted in *United States v Shakur*, 690 F Supp 1291 (SDNY 1988), reproduced in M Nash Leich (ed), *Cumulative Digest of United States Practice in International Law 1981–1988* (Department of State 1995) vol III, 3441 ('Article 44 ... was not acceptable as a new norm of international law. It clearly does not reflect customary law'); ICRC, Report on the Practice of Israel (1997), Answers to additional questions on Chapter 1.1, cited in *ICRC CIHL Study* (n 74) ('Israel does not consider that Article 44(3) AP I reflects customary international law').

[85] See Crawford (n 1) 47; E Mikos-Skuza, 'International Law's Changing Terms: "War" becomes "Armed Conflict"' in ME O'Connell (ed), *What Is War?: An Investigation in the Wake of 9/11* (Martinus Nijhoff 2012) 28; D Fleck, 'The Law of Non-International Armed Conflicts' in Fleck (n 1) 604; Hill-Cawthorne (n 1) 26–27; *Prosecutor v Tadić* (Decision on Jurisdiction) IT-94-1-AR72 (2 October 1995) [126]–[27]; *ICRC CIHL Study* (n 74) vol 1, 384.

6

Normative Underpinnings

6.1 Introduction

Chapter 5 traced the historical development of the regulation of combatancy with a special focus on the eligibility of members of non-state armed groups for combatant status. It showed that throughout the modern age, at least some such persons could qualify as combatants under the law valid at the time.

This chapter builds on that conclusion to analyse whether extending combatant status to members of parties to internationalized armed conflicts is compatible with the law in force today. Conversely, the enquiry does not extend to questions of essentially non-legal nature such as the potential political and military advantages that a belligerent party may gain by granting this status to its adversaries.[1]

The chapter starts by considering the demands that the principles of distinction and equal application of international humanitarian law (IHL) place on the regulation of combatancy (Section 6.2). The outcome of this analysis is then confronted with objections that are commonly raised against the extension of combatant status to non-state actors (Section 6.3).

6.2 Regulation of Combatancy and Normative Principles of IHL

The gradual adoption of the Rousseauvian paradigm, namely that the object of armed confrontation is to prevail over the enemy through the defeat of its armed forces while excluding the non-fighting population,[2] allowed for the development of two countervailing first-order principles of IHL: the principle of military necessity and the principle of humanity.[3] These two 'diametrically opposed principles'

[1] On which see further A Rosas, *The Legal Status of Prisoners of War* (Suomalainen Tiedeakatemia 1976) 134–40.

[2] J-J Rousseau, *The Social Contract* (1762, GDH Cole tr, Cosimo 2008) 20; see further Section 5.2.2.

[3] See, eg, Y Sandoz, C Swinarski, and B Zimmermann (eds), *Commentary on the Additional Protocols of 8 June 1977 to the Geneva Conventions of 12 August 1949* (ICRC 1987) 392–93 [1389] (hereafter Sandoz et al, *APs Commentary*); MN Schmitt, 'Military Necessity and Humanity in International Humanitarian Law: Preserving the Delicate Balance' (2010) 50 VJIL 795, 798; ME O'Connell, 'Historical Development and Legal Basis' in D Fleck (ed), *The Handbook of International Humanitarian Law* (3rd edn, OUP 2013) 37; Y Dinstein, *The Conduct of Hostilities under the Law of International*

exist in 'a subtle equilibrium' with one another.[4] In other words, constraining the permissible use of armed force to what is necessary to bring about the defeat of the opponent (the principle of military necessity) translates into protecting the life, health, and property of the potential victims of wars in all other circumstances (the principle of humanity).[5]

The regulation of combatancy in IHL serves to instrumentalize the interplay of these two opposing principles by answering whom the belligerents may lawfully target as part of their effort to prevail over the enemy.[6] For this purpose, IHL has developed a second-order principle: the principle of distinction.[7] Moreover, in standard IACs, both conflict parties are subject to the same set of legal rights and obligations, which is expressed in another second-order principle, the principle of equal application.[8] The following text explores the impact of these two principles on the regulation of combatancy in internationalized armed conflicts.

6.2.1 Distinction

The answer to the question of who may lawfully be targeted in armed conflict finds its most powerful and clear expression in Art 48 AP I, entitled 'Basic Rule' and generally considered as reflective of customary law:[9]

> In order to ensure respect for and protection of the civilian population and civilian objects, the Parties to the conflict shall at all times *distinguish between the civilian population and combatants* and between civilian objects and military objectives and accordingly shall direct their operations only against military objectives.[10]

This requirement translates into two important consequences in relation to the regulation of warfare, strengthening the two first-order principles mentioned earlier.

Armed Conflict (3rd edn, CUP 2016) 9–10; see also *Ryuichi Shimoda et al v The State* (Judgment) (7 December 1963) 32 ILR 626 (District Court of Tokyo) 633–34.

[4] Dinstein (n 3) 9.

[5] JS Pictet, *Development and Principles of International Humanitarian Law* (Martinus Nijhoff 1985) 61–62.

[6] E Crawford, *Identifying the Enemy: Civilian Participation in Armed Conflict* (OUP 2015) 13–16.

[7] See generally N Melzer, 'The Principle of Distinction Between Civilians and Combatants' in A Clapham and P Gaeta (eds), *The Oxford Handbook of International Law in Armed Conflict* (OUP 2014) 296–331.

[8] See generally A Roberts, 'The Equal Application of the Laws of War: A Principle under Pressure' (2008) 90 IRRC 931.

[9] *Legality of the Threat or Use of Nuclear Weapons Case* (Advisory Opinion) [1996] ICJ Rep 226, 257 [78]–[79]; *Western Front: Eritrea's Claims 1, 3, 5, 9-13, 14, 21, 25 & 26* (Partial Award of 19 December 2005) (EECC) (2005) 26 RIAA 291, 326–27 [93]–[95]; J-M Henckaerts and L Doswald-Beck (eds), *Customary International Humanitarian Law* (CUP 2005) rules 1 and 7 (hereafter *ICRC CIHL Study*). The provision was adopted by consensus at the 1974–77 Diplomatic Conference in Geneva: see Switzerland, *Official Records of the Diplomatic Conference on the Reaffirmation and Development of International Humanitarian Law Applicable in Armed Conflicts, Geneva (1974–1977)* (Federal Political Department 1978) vol XIV, CDDH/III/SR.10, 79 [15] (hereafter *Official Records*); ibid, vol VI, CDDH/SR.41, 161 [107].

[10] Art 48 AP I (emphasis added).

This is true in all situations to which the rule on distinction applies, irrespective of the character of the conflict parties.[11]

Firstly, where followed, the rule improves the protection of civilians. In this sense, it should be read together with Article 51(3) AP I, which provides that civilians lose their protection from attack 'for such time as they take a direct part in hostilities'.[12] Together, these two provisions assure the conflict parties that attacks against them will come only through a certain identifiable class of persons and thus remove the need or the desire to target those who pose no danger—chiefly, the civilians.[13] This highlights the importance of maintaining the distinction at all times as otherwise, in Yoram Dinstein's words, '[i]f combatants were free to melt away amid the civilian population, every civilian would suffer the results of being suspected as a masked combatant'.[14]

Secondly, the Rousseauvian paradigm requires that combatants, understood as tools in the hands of the war-waging sovereign who wields them, are not to be punished for mere participation in hostilities.[15] It is ordinarily not by choice that they become involved in their state's war effort—many states rely on compulsory draft[16] and armed groups likewise resort to forced recruitment[17]—and even those who voluntarily decide to lend their life and limb to the military effort of their authority normally do not have a say in the original resolution to go to war.[18]

6.2.1.1 Combatants as rational subjects responding to incentives

Nevertheless, it would be wrong to consider, as some do, the combatants solely as instruments[19] or automatons,[20] or as persons who have traded their right to life for a

[11] cf also Melzer (n 7) 309 (summarizing that for the purposes of the principle of distinction, the pertinent rules of IHL distinguish essentially the same categories of persons in IACs and NIACs, respectively).

[12] On the customary status of Art 51(3) AP I, compare *ICRC CIHL Study* (n 9) rule 6 (virtually identical formulation) with US DoD, *Law of War Manual* (December 2016) 227 [5.8.1.2] (stating that the US does not consider Art 51(3) AP I as reflecting custom, but that it supports the customary principle on which that provision is based).

[13] See also OA Hathaway and SJ Shapiro, *The Internationalists: How a Radical Plan to Outlaw War Remade the World* (Simon & Schuster 2017) 77.

[14] Y Dinstein, 'The Distinction Between Unlawful Combatants and War Criminals' in Y Dinstein and M Tabory (eds), *International Law at a Time of Perplexity* (Martinus Nijhoff 1989) 103.

[15] Rousseau (n 2) 20.

[16] See CIA, 'The World Factbook: Military Service Age and Obligation' (2017) <www.cia.gov/library/publications/the-world-factbook/fields/2024.html>.

[17] This has been the practice of many armed groups, including, for example, Uganda's Lord's Resistance Army or Sierra Leone's Revolutionary United Front who were also known for forcibly conscripting children. See, eg, T Lyons, 'Governance: A Security Perspective' in J Spear and PD Williams (eds), *Security and Development in Global Politics: A Critical Comparison* (Georgetown University Press 2012) 123.

[18] This problem has been described as the question of the 'innocent soldier'. See, eg, RF Turner, 'Intentional Targeting of Regime Elites: The Legal and Policy Debate' (2002) 36 New England Law Review 785, 787 (claiming the authorship of the concept); see also M Walzer, *Just and Unjust Wars: A Moral Argument with Historical Illustrations* (4th edn, Basic Books 2006) 39; Roberts (n 8) 933 and 957–61.

[19] C McKeogh, *Innocent Civilians: The Morality of Killing in War* (Palgrave Macmillan 2002) 160–65.

[20] C Ceulemans, 'The Moral Equality of Combatants' (2007) 37 Parameters 99, 104.

supposed right to kill.[21] It has been correctly observed that such an approach would impermissibly objectify participants in warfare and devalue their lives.[22] Quite the contrary, combatant status serves an important function in relation to combatants themselves and their decisions with respect to their compliance with the law.

The general guarantee that combatants' participation in hostilities shall not as such be considered criminal after the conflict, translates into a strong incentive for these persons to adhere to the rules of IHL during their military deployment.[23] As long as a combatant follows the limitations imposed by IHL, the US Supreme Court Justice Hugo Black observed in *Johnson v Eisentrager*, the fact of his involvement in 'legitimate "acts of warfare," however murderous, do[es] not justify criminal conviction', because 'it is no "crime" to be a soldier'.[24] Therefore, the availability of combatant status contributes towards the general goal of securing compliance with IHL.[25]

6.2.1.2 Nature and extent of combatant privilege

The nature of the authority conferred in this respect by IHL upon combatants has been the subject of significant debate. Since the Grotian times, this notion has often been expressed in terms of a grant of a right or a privilege: a 'right of war',[26] 'licence to kill',[27] 'combatant privilege',[28] 'the right to participate directly in hostilities',[29] and so on.[30] Other writers have argued that the law of war only prohibits prosecutions but does not itself govern the legality of the underlying conduct; it is an

[21] W Abresch, 'A Human Rights Law of Internal Armed Conflict: The European Court of Human Rights in Chechnya' (2005) 16 EJIL 741, 757.

[22] K Watkin, 'Opportunity Lost: Organized Armed Groups and the ICRC "Direct Participation in Hostilities" Interpretive Guidance' (2010) 42 International Law and Politics 641, 647.

[23] WA Solf, 'The Status of Combatants in Non-International Armed Conflicts under Domestic Law and Transnational Practice' (1983) 33 AUILR 53, 64–65; J Callen, 'Unlawful Combatants and the Geneva Conventions' (2004) 44 VJIL 1025, 1026; ET Jensen, 'The Laws of War: Past, Present, and Future: Combatant Status: It is Time for Intermediate Levels of Recognition for Partial Compliance' (2005) 46 VJIL 209, 234; GS Corn, 'Thinking the Unthinkable: Has the Time Come to Offer Combatant Immunity to Non-State Actors?' (2011) 22 Stanford Law & Policy Review 253, 274.

[24] *Johnson v Eisentrager* (1950) 339 US 763, 793 (US Supreme Court) (diss op Black, J).

[25] On combatancy as an incentive to comply with IHL, see further Section 6.3.2.3.

[26] H Grotius, *The Law of War and Peace in Three Books* (FW Kelsey tr, 1625), book III, ch IV, s V, §1.

[27] See, eg, WA Solf, 'Commentator on the subject of Non-International Armed Conflicts' (1982) 31 AULR 927, 928; C Tomuschat, 'Human Rights and International Humanitarian Law' (2010) 21 EJIL 15, 16; Dinstein (n 3) 43; see also *Report on Terrorism and Human Rights*, OEA/Ser.L/-V/II.116 Doc 5 rev 1 corr (22 October 2002) (IACmHR) [68].

[28] See, eg, Solf (n 27) 928; M Evangelista, *Law, Ethics, and the War on Terror* (Polity 2008) 72; GD Solis, *The Law of Armed Conflict: International Humanitarian Law in War* (2nd edn, CUP 2016) 46; but see, eg, K Anderson, 'What to Do with Bin Laden and Al Qaeda Terrorists?: A Qualified Defense of Military Commissions and United States Policy on Detainees at Guantanamo Bay Naval Base' (2002) 25 Harvard Journal of Law and Public Policy 593 (using the term 'combatant's privilege' as the privilege to avoid prosecutions, thus in line with the more limited, immunity-based understanding discussed in the text to note 31 in this chapter).

[29] Art 43(2) AP I.

[30] On the broader question of the meaning of the notion of 'rights' under IHL and its historical development, see L Hill-Cawthorne, 'Rights under International Humanitarian Law' (2017) 28 EJIL 1187.

'immunity', not a right in itself.[31] Although this distinction may at first appear to be of an academic nature only,[32] it is submitted that it is imperative to understand the status as only a bar to prosecution, for profound moral and practical reasons.

To begin with, although Article 43 AP I speaks of a 'right' to participate in hostilities,[33] too much emphasis should not be placed on this wording. The history of the negotiations during the 1974–77 Diplomatic Conference shows that the formulation was chosen (to the expressly admitted relief among the delegates) in order to reach an agreement on the definition of a combatant.[34] By contrast, the official records from the conference do not suggest that the drafters intended to grant an *additional* right to the combatants.[35]

Therefore, IHL does not create a 'licence to kill'; its only import is to prevent prosecution for conduct with respect to which this body of law remains normatively neutral. Consequently, the better view is that combatant status should be construed as a pure instrumentality,[36] which allows for the alleviation of suffering in war, but does so without imposing an approbation of the law on violent acts widely perceived as morally problematic.[37] It is also more palatable for states as it does not displace their domestic laws that contain a prohibition of intentional killing of persons; instead, this interpretation only prevents the prosecution of such acts committed during armed conflicts.

In sum, the foregoing analysis of the principle of distinction supports a broad interpretation of the range of actors who should be deemed to have access to combatant status. This is because fighters are correctly seen as rational subjects who treat combatancy as a strong incentive in favour of compliance with IHL. Moreover, it has been shown that despite its name, 'combatant privilege' does not entail any additional rights for qualifying persons, nor does it invalidate the relevant prohibitions found in domestic criminal law. On that basis, it is submitted that the overall 'pull' of the said principle is in favour of granting combatant status to members of non-state armed groups in internationalized armed conflicts.

[31] See, eg, S Watts, 'Present and Future Conceptions of the Status of Government Forces in Non-International Armed Conflict' (2012) 88 International Law Studies 145, 152 (the rule 'merely prohibits prosecutions'); Roberts (n 8) 935 (arguing that IHL is not the source of the 'right' to participate in hostilities); R Baxter, 'So-Called Unprivileged Belligerency: Spies, Guerrillas, and Saboteurs' (1951) 28 BYBIL 323, 323–24 (arguing that international law contains limits on permissible behaviour in war but does not grant rights to that effect).

[32] Notably, some works in the area use the terms interchangeably. See, eg, R Kolb and R Hyde, *An Introduction to the International Law of Armed Conflicts* (Hart Publishing 2008) 203 (combatants enjoy 'immunity: they cannot be prosecuted under criminal law simply for having taken part in the hostilities') and 153 (IHL contains 'the licence to kill an enemy in combat').

[33] Art 43(2) AP I ('Members of the armed forces of a Party to a conflict . . . are combatants, that is to say, they have the *right* to participate directly in hostilities.') (emphasis added).

[34] See *Official Records* (n 9) vol XV, CDDH/236/Rev.1, 401 [85].

[35] cf ibid 401–04.

[36] cf Watts (n 31) 163.

[37] See further Roberts (n 8) 957–61 (discussing the moral problem of the 'innocent soldier' and its legal reverberations in light of modern warfare).

6.2.2 Equal application

Does the regulation of combatancy apply equally to all conflict parties? In principle, IHL is a symmetric body of law.[38] It prescribes the same duties and obligations to all belligerent parties irrespective of the legitimacy of their recourse to force.[39] This is certainly true in IACs where the equal application of IHL is considered as one of the key principles by the doctrine,[40] confirmed by case law[41] and the relevant treaty law.[42] However, this equality in law should not be mistaken for equality in fact. There is no doubt that, in reality, individual belligerents may be in vastly different positions as to the availability of human, material, and information resources. Consider the 1982 Falklands War as a relatively recent example of a typical interstate armed conflict.[43] Even though the UK's air and naval forces were unquestionably significantly superior to those available to Argentina, there was no call for a differentiated application of IHL to the conflict parties.[44]

Correspondingly, armed conflicts characterized by the participation of a non-state armed group will inevitably display an even stronger asymmetry of means and resources. That this asymmetry is not always one-sided and that it does not favour the state party in all respects has been highlighted very lucidly in a recent study:

> The state enters the war with a force advantage but with an information disadvantage. It has the strength to hit what it sees, but can see little of what it wishes to hit. The guerrilla fighters, on the contrary, have an information advantage but a force disadvantage. They can see what they wish to hit, but they have limited capabilities to hit what they see.[45]

Some see this inequality in fact as requiring unequal treatment in law, as well.[46] Indeed, states have found it notoriously difficult to accept that they should be subjected to the same regulation as their non-state counterparts.[47] In particular,

[38] D Murray, *Practitioners' Guide to Human Rights Law in Armed Conflict* (OUP 2016) 14.

[39] C Greenwood, 'The Relationship between Ius ad Bellum and Ius in Bello' (1983) 9 Review of International Studies 221, 225.

[40] See, eg, H Lauterpacht, 'The Limits of the Operation of the Law of War' (1953) 30 BYBIL 206, 212; Greenwood (n 39) 225–26; Roberts (n 8) 931–62; D Kritsiotis, 'War and Armed Conflict: The Parameters of Enquiry' in R Liivoja and T McCormack (eds), *Routledge Handbook of the Law of Armed Conflict* (Routledge 2016) 9–13.

[41] *The Hostages Trial, List et al* (Judgment) (19 February 1948) (1949) 8 Law Reports of Trials of War Criminals 34 (US MT) 59–60.

[42] AP I, preamble (IHL 'must be fully applied in all circumstances to all [protected] persons . . . without any adverse distinction based on the nature or origin of the armed conflict or on the causes espoused by or attributed to the Parties to the conflict').

[43] See generally S-S Junod, *Protection of the Victims of Armed Conflict Falkland-Malvinas Islands (1982): International Humanitarian Law and Humanitarian Action* (2nd edn, ICRC 1984).

[44] Although the UK denied that the operations in Falkland Islands had amounted to a 'state of war', it accepted that IHL applied to the situation. See Letter from Lord President of the Council, Mr John Biffen, to Mr George Foulkes, MP (20 May 1982), reproduced in (1982) 53 BYBIL 519–20.

[45] K Mulaj, 'The Kosovo Liberation Army and the Intricacies of Legitimacy' in K Mulaj (ed), *Violent Non-State Actors in World Politics* (Columbia University Press 2010) 103, paraphrasing GH McCormick, 'Terrorist Decision Making' (2003) 6 Annual Review of Political Science 473, 484.

[46] See, eg, R Provost, 'The Move to Substantive Equality in International Humanitarian Law: A Rejoinder to Marco Sassòli and Yuval Shany' (2011) 93 IRRC 437, 438–39.

[47] cf J Somer, 'Jungle Justice: Passing Sentence on the Equality of Belligerents in Non-international Armed Conflict' (2007) 89 IRRC 655, 656.

a number of delegations to the 1974–77 Diplomatic Conference in Geneva noted their concerns in this regard.[48] Perhaps the clearest expression of this sentiment came in the statement of the Zairian delegate who argued that law should not put on equal footing 'a sovereign State and a group of insurgent nationals, a legal Government and a group of outlaws, a subject of international law and a subject of domestic law'.[49] The delegate further added that, in his view, armed groups not only 'had not the same rights as the national Government', but, '[i]ndeed, they did not possess *any rights at all*, but simply had an obligation to deal humanely with all those who did not take part in hostilities'.[50]

This reluctance on the part of states has led some commentators to argue that the notion of equality does not apply to non-international armed conflicts (NIACs).[51] However, such a conclusion would be too hasty. In fact, the law of NIAC prescribes equivalent obligations to all conflict parties irrespective of their nature. Common Article 3 achieves this by requiring 'each Party to the conflict' to abide by its prescriptions equally.[52] Similarly, although Additional Protocol II was phrased in passive voice to respond to a concern that a mention of 'parties to the conflict … might be interpreted as a recognition of the insurgent party',[53] there is no doubt that on a principle level, its norms apply to all conflict parties in an equal fashion.[54]

Therefore, the better view is that even in NIACs, IHL prescribes equal rights and obligations for the parties.[55] In this regard, Jonathan Somer has helpfully distinguished the narrower equality of rights and obligations from a general equality of status, describing only the former as 'equality' and reserving the term 'parity' for the latter.[56] This restrictive understanding of equality in NIACs is also in line with the approach of the 1987 ICRC Commentary on the Additional Protocols.[57] Moreover, it appears to be a workable compromise, which simultaneously preserves the incentive function of the law while assuaging states' worries about raising the legal status of armed groups.[58] Still, it should be noted that even on this interpretation, according

[48] See, eg, *Official Records* (n 9) vol VIII, CDDH/I/SR.22, 212 [54] (Indonesia); ibid 231 [14] (Mexico); ibid 335 [64] (Iraq).

[49] ibid vol VII, CDDH/SR.56, 219 [124].

[50] ibid 219 [126] (emphasis added).

[51] See, eg, L Doswald-Beck, 'The Right to Life in Armed Conflict: Does International Humanitarian Law Provide All the Answers' (2006) 88 IRRC 881, 903; Watts (n 31) 151.

[52] Common Art 3(1) GCs. See also Common Art 3(4) GCs (clarifying that 'the legal status' of the conflict parties is not affected by IHL) and compare with the text to notes 55–59 in this chapter.

[53] Sandoz et al, *APs Commentary* (n 3) 1339 [4423].

[54] ibid 1345 [4437] (stating expressly that 'Protocol II and common Article 3 are based on the principle of the equality of the parties to the conflict').

[55] Accord Sandoz et al, *APs Commentary* (n 3) 1345 [4442]; Somer (n 47) 663; M Sassòli, AA Bouvier, and A Quintin, *How Does Law Protect in War?* (3rd edn, ICRC 2011), vol I, 121; S Sivakumaran, *The Law of Non-International Armed Conflict* (OUP 2012) 243; see also *Third Report on the Human Rights Situation in Columbia* OEA/Ser.L/V/II.102, Doc 9 rev 1 (26 February 1999) (IACmHR) ch 4 [13].

[56] Somer (n 47) 663.

[57] Sandoz et al, *APs Commentary* (n 3) 1351 [4458] ('in a non-international armed conflict the legal status of the parties involved in the struggle is fundamentally unequal').

[58] cf also J Pejić, 'Terrorist Acts and Groups: A Role for International Law?' (2004) 75 BYBIL 71, 82 (warning that advocates of the removal of the principle of equality of the parties under IHL 'should think twice, as they risk creating a monster that will come back to haunt them.').

to which the principle of equal treatment applies in NIACs, it most certainly does not, by way of IHL, extend to domestic law.[59]

The principle of equal application has thus retained its crucial importance in both main types of armed conflict under the framework of IHL. Internationalized armed conflicts, as NIACs that have developed into IACs, thus must also comport to the restrictions of this principle. By contrast, a straightforward denial of combatant status to one of the parties to an internationalized armed conflict would amount to an unequivocal breach of this principle. Importantly, like the principle of distinction analysed earlier in this section, the principle of equal application thus appears to support the extension of combatant status to members of non-state actors in internationalized conflicts. Accordingly, the next section examines reasons, which might be seen as pointing in the opposite direction.

6.3 Objections to the Extension of Combatant Status to Non-state Actors

The regulation of combatant status achieves the goals bestowed upon it by the principles of distinction and equal application through three cardinal consequences. Firstly, those who have combatant status become legitimate targets for the opposing forces. Secondly, the law provides a shield from prosecution to those combatants who participate in hostilities and by doing that perpetrate acts that would otherwise be criminal under domestic law. Thirdly, when a person with the status of a combatant is captured, they must be granted the status of a prisoner of war (POW) with the resultant protection guaranteed by IHL.[60]

The general understanding is that none of those consequences normally apply to fighters belonging to non-state armed groups. Internationalized armed conflicts, however, inevitably feature at least one non-state actor at the outset of the conflict. This section therefore considers arguments levelled against the extension of combatant status to non-state actors. Its main contention is that, however strong these arguments may be in traditional civil wars, their effect in internationalized armed conflicts is much weaker and does not generally prevent the extension of combatant status to fighters in these conflicts.

6.3.1 Sovereignty

On the face of it, at the two main diplomatic conferences aimed at the development of IHL after the Second World War, proposals that would have improved the

[59] Sassòli et al (n 55), vol I, 121 ('IHL treats parties to a non-international armed conflict equally, but cannot oblige domestic laws to do so.').

[60] See, eg, M Bothe, KJ Partsch, and WA Solf, *New Rules for Victims of Armed Conflicts: Commentary on the Two 1977 Protocols Additional to the Geneva Conventions of 1949* (Martinus Nijhoff 1982) 239–40 (hereafter Bothe et al, *New Rules*); R Goodman, 'The Detention of Civilians in Armed Conflict' (2009) 103 AJIL 48, 51; D Kretzmer, 'Civilian Immunity in War: Legal Aspects' in I Primoratz (ed), *Civilian Immunity in War* (Clarendon Press 2007) 89; US DoD, *Law of War Manual* (December 2016) 105 [4.4].

standing of fighters belonging to non-state armed groups were rejected on the basis of arguments invoking state sovereignty. In 1949, Norway proposed that even in NIACs as defined by the future Common Article 3 of the Conventions, no person should be punished 'merely for having taken part in the war on the one side or on the other'.[61] The proposal was vocally rejected by the British delegate as amounting to an 'abnegation of sovereignty'[62] and it was later quietly abandoned by the Norwegian delegation.[63]

At the time of drafting of the Additional Protocols, the idea of according combatant status across the board had already been abandoned. Accordingly, the original ICRC draft of AP II only contained an exhortation for the courts deciding upon a sentence for persons prosecuted for participation in hostilities in NIACs to 'take into consideration, to the greatest possible extent, the fact that the accused respected' IHL.[64] Many states re-emphasized their commitment to a conservative conception of sovereignty at the conference.[65] Correspondingly, when even the meekly worded provision[66] was removed from the final agreed text along with about a half of the draft Protocol,[67] the deletion was lauded as a triumph of the sovereignty-protective approach.[68]

6.3.1.1 Sovereignty objection and non-state actors

What lies behind these pro-sovereignty proclamations? The delegates actually did not refuse to extend combatant status or POW protection to *all* non-state armed groups. In fact, as shown in Chapter 5 of this work, in each historical period since the 1874 Brussels Declaration, members of some non-state armed groups could claim combatant status under the law valid at the time.[69] This was the case even after 1949 and 1977, respectively. Specifically, quasi-independent partisan forces who fulfilled the four conditions in Article 4A(2) GC III qualified as combatants, provided they

[61] Switzerland, *Final Record of the Diplomatic Conference of Geneva of 1949* (Federal Political Department 1949) vol II A, 322 (Norway) (hereafter *Final Record*).

[62] ibid, vol II A, 322 (United Kingdom).

[63] With little in the way of support for the proposal, the Norwegian delegation moved for it to be deferred during the 21st meeting of the Second Committee. However, Norway never submitted a formal amendment and thus the conference participants did not return to this issue afterwards. See *Final Record* (n 61), vol II A, 465 (reporting on the deferral).

[64] Art 10(5) of the draft AP II, reproduced in *Official Records* (n 9) vol I, part III, 36.

[65] See, eg, *Official Records* (n 9) vol VIII, CDDH/I/SR.22, 205 [17] (Argentina); ibid 211 [53] (Indonesia); ibid, CDDH/I/SR.23, 221 [33] (Romania).

[66] cf F Kalshoven, 'The Diplomatic Conference on Reaffirmation and Development of International Humanitarian Law Applicable in Armed Conflicts, Geneva, 1974–1977' in F Kalshoven (ed), *Reflections on the Law of War* (Martinus Nijhoff 2007) 187–88 (noting that the provision 'would in no way have affected the power of the State to punish such persons for the fact of their participation ... nor could it have been construed as even the beginning of an introduction of prisoner-of-war status into the [law of NIAC].').

[67] See Sandoz et al, *APs Commentary* (n 3) 1335 [4412]–[17].

[68] *Official Records* (n 9) vol VII, CDDH/SR.49, 61 [11] (Pakistan); see also ibid 62 [14] (Sudan); ibid 65 [33] (Saudi Arabia); ibid, CDDH/SR.56, 203 [51] (India); but see ibid, CDDH/SR.56, 206 [65] (Norway).

[69] See Section 5.2 and Section 5.3.

could be considered as fighting for a state party to the conflict, even if the government of that conflict party was ineffective or in exile.[70] Moreover, in conflicts falling under the purview of AP I, membership in irregular armed forces no longer constituted an obstacle to eligibility for combatant status.[71]

Statements invoking state sovereignty must therefore be seen against the particular context in which they were made. The drafters in the 1940s and 1970s were focused on the specific scenario of a 'traditional' civil war, which featured a contest for power in a particular state between its government and group of insurgents.[72] At the heart of the matter here was the internal aspect of sovereignty, in other words, the understanding that because the political power belongs to the sovereign state, the subjects of the state have no right to rebel against it.[73] However, the factual pattern of internationalized armed conflicts is markedly different. Therefore, the drafters' comments regarding state sovereignty should not be taken at their face value as equally applicable to conflicts that are the subject of the present work.

By contrast, there is little doubt that the drafters intended to preserve the states' sovereignty in dealing with 'traditional' insurrections. Admittedly, during the work on the Additional Protocols, certain states attempted to put forward an alternative humanitarian understanding of sovereignty that would be applicable to all armed conflicts. This interpretation was based on the argument that since sovereignty exists for the benefit of the whole people, IHL should apply in full and equally even in internal armed conflicts.[74] Needless to say, this view never gained much traction at the conference itself, nor in the international community in general. Instead, the general position had remained that 'to grant such protected status to rebels and insurgents [would be] fundamentally at odds with the modern system of the international law of sovereign States'.[75] Therefore, it is necessary to examine the impact of the sovereignty objection on the specific circumstances arising under the individual modalities of internationalization.

6.3.1.2 Impact on individual modalities of internationalization

On closer scrutiny, the sovereignty objection does not pose a major challenge to at least some types of internationalized armed conflicts. Wars of national liberation are the most straightforward case. States that accept this category of armed conflict—ie, first and foremost states parties to Additional Protocol I—do not object from the position of sovereignty against the members of national liberation movements

[70] See Section 5.3.1. [71] See Section 5.3.2.

[72] cf Kalshoven (n 66) 186–89 (summarizing the concerns over sovereignty expressed during the *travaux* on AP II to demonstrate that the drafters again focused on traditional civil wars occurring in the territory of one state).

[73] On the notion of 'internal sovereignty', see, eg, S Besson, 'Sovereignty' in R Wolfrum (ed), *Max Planck Encyclopedia of Public International Law* (OUP 2008) <www.mpepil.com> (updated April 2011) [56].

[74] See, eg, *Official Records* (n 9) vol VII, CDDH SR.56, 206 [65] (Norway); see also ibid, vol VIII, CDDH/I/SR.23, 218 [19] (New Zealand).

[75] E Crawford, *The Treatment of Combatants and Insurgents Under the Law of Armed Conflict* (OUP 2010) 154.

receiving privileged treatment as combatants. Rather, the extension of combatant status to such persons was one of the desired outcomes of the adoption of AP I[76]—and, equally, one of the main reasons for the harsh criticism and eventually rejection of the Protocol by a number of states, including the US and Israel.[77]

It is a matter of historical irony that this outcome has yet to fully materialize in an actual armed conflict that would meet the requirements of Article 1(4) AP I.[78] The scenario that has arguably come the closest in this regard is the situation in Western Sahara, particularly after Switzerland as the depositary of AP I accepted in 2015 that the Polisario Front was a national liberation movement in the sense of the Protocol.[79] Accordingly, members of the Polisario Front should be entitled to combatant status; however, the government of Morocco as the other supposed belligerent party has strongly objected to the qualification of the situation as a war of national liberation.[80] In any event, Morocco's position was not that fighters in wars of national liberation should not have access to combatant status *in general* due to sovereignty considerations; it was only that the particular situation of Western Sahara did not qualify as a war of national liberation (or, indeed, as an armed conflict at all).[81] Therefore, it appears that the sovereignty objection does not carry much force in the specific (and admittedly very rare) circumstances of Article 1(4) AP I conflicts.

Similarly, conflicts in which the government recognizes the belligerency of its adversary pose few problems from the perspective of the sovereignty objection. While the clash for sovereignty lies clearly at the heart of any such struggle, recognition of belligerency is a discretionary[82] unilateral act by the government in power that entails its tacit agreement to treat the rebels on par with a party to an IAC.[83] Accordingly, in the last unequivocal instances of recognition of belligerency by the territorial government, that is, in the American Civil War (1861–65) and in the Boer War (1899–1902),[84] the rebel fighters were extended combatant status and POW treatment.[85] The same analysis would hold, *a fortiori*, for the hypothetical conflicts that would

[76] Kalshoven (n 66) 195–96.

[77] See Letter of Transmittal from President Ronald Reagan (29 January 1987), reproduced in (1987) 81 AJIL 910; GH Aldrich, 'Prospects for United States Ratification of Additional Protocol I to the 1949 Geneva Conventions' (1991) 85 AJIL 1, 7–10; *Official Records* (n 9) vol VI, CDDH/SR.36, 41 [60] (Israel).

[78] cf T Meron, 'The Time Has Come for the United States to Ratify Geneva Protocol I' (1994) 88 AJIL 678, 683.

[79] Switzerland, 'Notification to the Governments of the States parties to the Geneva Conventions of 12 August 1949 for the Protection of War Victims' (26 June 2015) <www.eda.admin.ch/content/dam/eda/fr/documents/aussenpolitik/voelkerrecht/geneve/150626-GENEVE_en.pdf>, at 1.

[80] Communication by the Kingdom of Morocco (30 June 2015), annexed to Switzerland, 'Notification to the Governments of the States parties to the Geneva Conventions of 12 August 1949 for the Protection of War Victims' (9 July 2015) <www.eda.admin.ch/content/dam/eda/fr/documents/aussenpolitik/voelkerrecht/geneve/150709-GENEVE-avec-ann_e.pdf>.

[81] cf ibid 2.

[82] See Section 2.5.1.3.

[83] See, eg, YM Lootsteen, 'The Concept of Belligerency in International Law' (2000) 166 MLR 109, 109–10.

[84] See H McCoubrey and N White, *International Organizations and Civil Wars* (Dartmouth 1995) 7; Lootsteen (n 83) 110; E La Haye, *War Crimes in Internal Armed Conflicts* (CUP 2008) 14 fn 87.

[85] Q Wright, 'The American Civil War, 1861–65' in RA Falk (ed), *The International Law of Civil War* (Johns Hopkins Press 1971) 61–62; HA Wilson, *International Law and the Use of Force by National*

see state dissolution acknowledged and recognized by the parent state—something that never happens in practice.[86]

By contrast, situations in which the incumbent government disputes the legitimacy and any legal status of its opponent may indeed pose problems from the perspective of the sovereignty objection. Hence, non-state fighters in wars of secession that do not meet the conditions in Article 1(4) AP I and rebels assisted by outside intervening powers, to name the two main situations of this kind, would be the prime targets of the argument against their combatant status from the position of sovereignty.

State practice affirms this hypothesis. It has already been observed that states rarely make public the legal qualification of the conflicts they are involved in.[87] For some, it may in fact be a matter of policy *not* to do so.[88] Nevertheless, there has not yet been a conflict of the type described in the previous paragraph, in which a state would unequivocally recognize, as a matter of law and not just for reasons of policy, the combatant status of its opponents.[89] It is true that in a few cases, states agreed to accord their non-state adversaries some of the protections of the law of IAC, including POW treatment. With respect to the wars of secession outside of the decolonization context, a prominent example in this respect was the Nigerian practice during the conflict in Biafra.[90] As for foreign interventions, the US agreed to treat captured non-state fighters as POWs in Vietnam[91] and the French did so in Algeria.[92] However, all of these states expressly stated that they were acting out of policy considerations and not on the basis of a legal duty.[93]

On a doctrinal level, the objection may be overcome even in these conflicts by highlighting the competing sovereignty claims of the conflict party opposing the territorial state. In foreign interventions, these are espoused by the intervening state; in state dissolution scenarios by the newly emergent state. The fact remains, however, that the territorial states in these conflicts have been reluctant to accord combatant status to their non-state opponents regardless of these considerations. To understand their concern, the argument from sovereignty thus needs to be unpacked. In

Liberation Movements (Clarendon Press 1988) 38; Lootsteen (n 83) 115; N Higgins, *The Approach of International Law to Wars of National Liberation* (The Martin Institute 2004) 13.

[86] See Section 2.3.1.3. [87] See Section 1.1.2.

[88] See, eg, Letter from the Swiss Department of Defence to author (22 August 2011), on file with author (stating that Switzerland does not 'officially qualify conflicts under IHL', although an 'internal qualification' is undertaken); Letter from the Russian Embassy in the UK to author (7 October 2011), on file with author (stating that 'there hardly is a person who could have the authority to convey . . . an "official" position of the country on that issue'); Letter from the High Commission for the Republic of Cyprus to author (undated), on file with author (stating that Cyprus does not disclose its legal assessment of the legal effects of conflict internationalization).

[89] cf GH Aldrich, 'Customary International Humanitarian Law: An Interpretation on behalf of the International Committee of the Red Cross' (2005) 76 BYBIL 503, 507 (arguing that states 'will always oppose anything that appears to give rebels belligerent status').

[90] Solf (n 27) 929–30.

[91] MACV Directive Number 381-11 (5 March 1966), reproduced in GS Prugh, *Law at War, Vietnam, 1964–1973* (Department of the Army 1975) 127–31.

[92] Rosas (n 1) 149.

[93] See Solf (n 27) 929–930; MACV Directive Number 381-11 (5 March 1966), reproduced in Prugh (n 91) 127–31; Rosas (n 1) 149.

these cases, the governments in power perceive the insurrectionists' violent struggle as treasonous and thus, in an avowed aim to protect the state's sovereignty, they oppose any attempts to restrain their right to prosecute the rebel fighters.[94] The next subsection thus turns to this second objection from the perspective of internationalized armed conflicts.

6.3.2 Prosecution

Internationalized armed conflicts as understood in this work occur in the territory of a particular state with the participation of this state's forces. The activities of the armed group challenging that state will thus qualify as crimes under the domestic law of the state in question.[95] Combatant status as an instrument of international law does not change this qualification; instead, it provides a 'cloak of immunity' from prosecution at the domestic level.[96] This is a longstanding principle of the law of war, recognized already by Hugo Grotius, who wrote that a soldier 'who happens to be caught . . . cannot for that reason be punished as a murderer or a thief'.[97] And this brings us precisely to the core of the second objection: to grant combatant status to members of non-state armed groups would be to immunize them from prosecution for their participation in hostilities.[98] It has been claimed that 'no state will ever agree to rescind its right to prosecute non-state fighters who have fired at its military forces'.[99] This section accordingly looks at the force of this objection through analysing the relevant state practice and the theoretical justifications underpinning the objection.

6.3.2.1 Prosecution as a tool against non-state actors

The case in favour of the prosecution objection appears to be quite solid. A government facing an armed opponent has the incentive to utilize all means at its disposal to bring about its enemy's destruction. The domestic criminal justice mechanism as an instrument of internal sovereignty is one of such tools: prosecuting and sentencing rebel fighters to imprisonment or even execution is an effective way of preventing them from continuing the armed struggle as well as of discouraging others from

[94] C Greenwood, 'International Humanitarian Law (Laws of War)' in F Kalshoven (ed), *The Centennial of the 1st International Peace Conference: Reports & Conclusions* (Kluwer Law International 2000) 234; N Lubell, *Extraterritorial Use of Force against Non-State Actors* (OUP 2010) 137–38; Sivakumaran (n 55) 70–71.

[95] cf Lubell (n 94) 19; D Fleck, 'The Law of Non-International Armed Conflicts' in Fleck (n 3) 590; L Olson, 'Those Who Are Not POWs' in A Clapham, P Gaeta, and M Sassòli (eds), *The 1949 Geneva Conventions: A Commentary* (OUP 2015) 915–17 [13]–[16].

[96] Y Dinstein, 'The System of Status Groups in International Humanitarian Law' in W Heintschel von Heinegg and V Epping (eds), *International Humanitarian Law Facing New Challenges* (Springer 2007) 154; see also Solf (n 23) 57–58; D Jinks, 'The Declining Significance of POW Status' (2004) 45 Harvard International Law Journal 367, 376 fn 38; Crawford (n 75) 78; Melzer (n 7) 305–06.

[97] Grotius (n 26) book III, ch IV, s III, 2.

[98] cf, eg, Sandoz et al, *APs Commentary* (n 3) 1332 [4397]; A Clapham, 'Concept of International Armed Conflict' in Clapham, Gaeta, and Sassòli (n 95) 11 [22].

[99] AJ Carswell, 'Classifying the Conflict: A Soldier's Dilemma' (2009) 91 IRRC 143, 160.

joining.[100] As such, prosecution appears to have the important potential of weakening the enemy.

Indeed, some armed groups have been 'decapitated' this way following the capture of their leader, such as the Kurdish armed group PKK in Turkey after the capture of Abdullah Öcalan or the *Sendero Luminoso* (Shining Path) in Peru after the capture of Abimael Guzmán.[101] Sometimes states will attempt to do so even before any fighting might break out, as demonstrated by the issuance of an arrest warrant for the leader of the Catalonian independence movement Carles Puigdemont by a Spanish prosecutor in late 2017.[102]

On the basis of the foregoing, one would thus expect to see the prosecution of non-state fighters in every armed conflict featuring a confrontation between a state and a non-state actor operating in the same territory. However, the relevant practice is surprisingly patchy.

6.3.2.2 Modern practice: prevalence of amnesties and absence of prosecution

Although one might expect states to always rely on prosecution of their non-state opponents, an examination of practice actually reveals an important trend to the contrary. Several studies have shown that in many armed confrontations, states have in fact voluntarily refrained from prosecuting enemy fighters either on the basis of amnesty agreements between the belligerents or through domestic amnesty statutes.[103] This pattern can be observed in the most recent armed conflicts, too. For example, in May 2009, a law enacted by the Democratic Republic of the Congo provided for amnesty for about twenty illegal armed groups active in the North and South Kivu provinces.[104] A similar statute, albeit on its face limited to those individuals whose actions were aimed at 'promoting or protecting the revolution', was adopted soon after the conclusion of the 2011 conflict in Libya.[105] And in July

[100] See also S Watts, 'Who Is a Prisoner of War?' in Clapham et al (n 95) 909 [80].

[101] AH Sinno, 'Armed Groups' Organizational Structure and their Strategic Options' (2011) 93 IRRC 311, 318.

[102] See S Jones and D Boffey, 'European Arrest Warrant Issued for ex-Catalan Leader Carles Puigdemont', *The Guardian* (3 November 2017) <www.theguardian.com/world/2017/nov/03/european-arrest-warrant-issued-for-ex-catalan-leader-carles-puigdemont>. As this book went into press, Puigdemont had just been released on bail following a brief arrest in Germany. Interestingly, the domestic court had rejected 'rebellion' as grounds for extradition. See P Oltermann, 'Puigdemont Calls for Dialogue with Spain as He Leaves Jail on Bail', *The Guardian* (6 April 2018) <https://www.theguardian.com/world/2018/apr/06/carles-puigdemont-germany-prison-bail-spain-catalonia> accessed 30 April 2018.

[103] See Crawford (n 75) 104–09 (documenting a rich practice of amnesties granted in the decades prior to the publication); AG Reiter, 'Transitional Justice and Civil War: Exploring New Pathways, Challenging Old Guideposts' (2012) 1 Transitional Justice Review 137, 166 (concluding, on the basis of a dataset of civil war cases between 1970 and 2005, that states use amnesties, not prosecutions, to resolve ongoing civil wars); see also ICRC, 'Practice Relating to Rule 159. Amnesty' (2017) <https://ihl-databases.icrc.org/customary-ihl/eng/docs/v2_rul_rule159>.

[104] Reuters, 'Congo: Amnesty Passed for Illegal Armed Groups' *New York Times* (7 May 2009) <www.nytimes.com/2009/05/08/world/africa/08briefs-Congo.html?_r=0>.

[105] Libya, Law 38 (2012), On Some Procedures for the Transitional Period. See HRW, 'Libya: Amend New Special Procedures Law' (11 May 2012) <www.hrw.org/news/2012/05/11/libya-amend-new-special-procedures-law>.

2017, the president of Colombia signed a decree designed to complete the peace process in the country by granting amnesty to thousands of former members of the rebel group FARC.[106]

Admittedly, these amnesties are typically adopted only following the termination of the conflict and do not thus affect the conflict while it is underway.[107] Only exceptionally, amnesties are extended during an ongoing armed conflict, and this is usually done with the aim to induce the surrender of the non-state fighters and bring the conflict to a speedy end.[108] In any event, all amnesties of the recent history seem to have been adopted as voluntary acts not motivated by any sense of legal obligation.[109] In fact, the only legal provision that serves as a quasi-legal basis for post-conflict amnesties is Article 6(5) AP II, whose normative force is particularly weak: it only requires the authorities in power to 'endeavour' to grant the 'broadest possible' amnesty at the conflict's end.[110]

Nevertheless, the recurring reluctance of the post-conflict authorities in power to resort to blank prosecution of all persons participating in hostilities is worth examining. Emily Crawford has argued on the basis of a detailed analysis of this practice that the trend in question had 'gone some way to creating an *ex post facto* combatant status' for non-state fighters in NIACs.[111] While there is some force in her contention, it is submitted that that it slightly overstates the point. Notwithstanding the laudable aims of Article 6(5) AP II, neither this provision nor the trend it had commenced have conferred legitimate combatant status on members of dissident forces.[112] True, the prevalence of amnesties suggests that even the granting of '[a]n *ex ante* immunity would not ... necessarily constitute a fundamental change in practice'.[113] However, states have thus far remained staunchly unwilling to do so. Therefore, the existing amnesties should be seen as amounting to, at most, an *ex post facto* immunity from prosecution. However, such immunity is only one of the consequences of combatant status.[114] Therefore, it cannot be inferred that a novel type of combatant status with independent legal valence has emerged in the law of NIAC.

And yet, the trend of waiving criminal prosecutions after armed conflicts does provide a convincing counterargument to the prosecution objection analysed here. The fact that in actual practice, states often do not make use of their criminal justice system to deal with the persons who had opposed them in armed struggle, is a tacit

[106] BBC, 'Colombia: President Santos Grants Farc Members Amnesty' (11 July 2017) <www.bbc.com/news/world-latin-america-40564577>.

[107] However, it ought to be mentioned that depending on the particular definition of 'conflict termination', amnesties issued during the conflict may appear less exceptional: cf Reiter (n 103) 165 (finding that '[o]f the 36 conflicts [analysed in the study] that terminated in a peace agreement, half (18) granted amnesties to rebels before the conflict ended').

[108] See, eg, Algeria, Civil Harmony Law 1999 and Presidential Decree No 2000-03; Uganda, Amnesty Act 2000, s 3.

[109] Accord Crawford (n 75) 104.

[110] Art 6(5) AP II; see also *ICRC CIHL Study* (n 9) rule 159.

[111] Crawford (n 75) 79.

[112] H McCoubrey and N White, *International Organizations and Civil Wars* (Dartmouth 1995) 76.

[113] L Hill-Cawthorne, *Detention in Non-International Armed Conflict* (OUP 2016) 27.

[114] See text to note 60 in this chapter.

yet critical pronouncement on the efficacy of such measures. It is submitted that the authorities in power realize that to use the judicial branch to punish mere participation would often result in further backlash among the general population and that it might undermine national reconciliation.[115] From this perspective, the usefulness of prosecution thus appears limited at best and certainly not guaranteed in each conflict.

6.3.2.3 Fairness and efficiency of prosecution

In addition to the questionable utility of prosecution in many specific instances analysed previously, the problematic aspects of resorting to prosecution include important issues of general fairness and efficiency. Firstly, prosecution and punishment for mere participation may be criticized as fundamentally unfair. In IACs, the unfairness of prosecuting combatants is a central moral justification of this legal status. Provided that the combatants respect IHL and thus contribute towards the civilizing of war,[116] it is generally accepted it would be 'both inappropriate and unjust' to punish them for performing a duty imposed on them by their state.[117]

The situation of fighters in internationalized armed conflicts is comparable. They belong to (originally) non-state armed groups that are subject to a hierarchical structure and strict enforcement mechanisms approximating those of full-fledged states. The process of internationalization transforms the non-state actor in question, resulting in either its emergence as a state or making it legally equivalent to a state for the purposes of IHL or at least closely tied to a third state.[118] Its members are thus subjected to a duty to take part in the fighting by the state or the state-like entity they belong to without necessarily having a chance to opt out.[119] As long as they respect IHL, their prosecution would thus appear to be equally unfair.

Secondly, prosecution and punishment for mere participation may be seen as inefficient in attaining the humanitarian goal of IHL. It has been said that this body of law aims to 'civilize' or 'humanize' war.[120] In order to achieve that aim successfully,

[115] cf J Herman, O Martin-Ortega, and C Lekha Sriram, 'Beyond Justice versus Peace: Transitional Justice and Peacebuilding Strategies' in K Aggestam and A Björkdahl (eds), *Rethinking Peacebuilding: The Quest for Just Peace in the Middle East and the Western Balkans* (Routledge 2012) 49–50.

[116] cf H Meyrowitz, 'The Function of the Laws of War in Peacetime' (1986) 26 IRRC 77, 86 (highlighting the function of IHL as a means of civilizing war).

[117] cf Corn (n 23) 266. See also note 16 in this chapter and the accompanying text (concerning the obligation to serve in a state army).

[118] See Sections 2.2–2.5.

[119] Many non-state armed groups subject their members to the equivalent of a compulsory draft. See note 17 in this chapter for examples of practice.

[120] Meyrowitz (n 116) 86; J Meurant, 'Inter Arma Caritas: Evolution and Nature of International Humanitarian Law' (1987) 24 Journal of Peace Research 237, 238–39; W Banks, 'Toward an Adaptive International Humanitarian Law: New Norms for New Battlefields' in William Banks (ed), *New Battlefields/Old Laws: Critical Debates on Asymmetric Warfare* (Columbia University Press 2011) 5; see also Pictet (n 5) 1. Views sceptical of the humanizing function of IHL are quite rare today: for a mild example, see C af Jochnick and R Normand, 'The Legitimation of Violence: A Critical History of the Laws of War' (1994) 35 Harvard International Law Journal 49, 50 (arguing that, 'despite noble rhetoric to the contrary, the laws of war have been formulated deliberately to privilege military necessity at the cost of humanitarian values').

IHL should provide incentives for the actors to abide by its norms: an idea sometimes described as the 'benefits-burdens principle'.[121] Accordingly, lawful combatants in IACs know that if they obey the rules of IHL, they do not place themselves at risk of prosecution at the end of the conflict and that they may correspondingly avail themselves of the protections of IHL.[122] This serves as a powerful incentive for the combatants to distinguish themselves from non-combatants, thus protecting civilians, with the effect of contributing considerably to the humanitarian aim of the law.[123] By contrast, the denial of immunity from prosecution to non-state fighters translates into a disincentive to comply with the norms of IHL.[124]

There has been some debate whether this effect operates at the individual or at the group (organizational) level. The presumption in most of the writing on the subject is that individual fighters would be induced to comply with the law out of concern for the way in which they themselves would be treated in case of capture.[125] However, the American scholar Robert Sloane argued convincingly that it may be overly optimistic to expect individuals to conduct a rational calculation of this sort if they have not been educated in IHL and subjected to an effective military hierarchy.[126] In other words, the incentive effect operates primarily, or even exclusively, at the group level.

Sloane observed correctly that these conditions require the existence of an organizational structure superimposed over individual fighters.[127] He appeared to go too far, however, in equating compliance with the existence of 'professional state armies'.[128] Internationalized conflicts as well as large-scale civil wars prove that non-state armed groups can develop structures capable of providing instruction in IHL and enforcing compliance. For example, in the 2011 Libyan conflict the rebels unified by the National Transitional Council (NTC) adopted, with the help of Western experts,[129] a frontline manual on the fundamental rules of IHL[130] and arranged for

[121] US DoD, *Law of War Manual* (December 2016) 91 [3.6.3.2]. [122] ibid 118 [4.6.1].

[123] Solf (n 23) 64–65; Jensen (n 23) 233–34; Callen (n 23) 1026; Corn (n 23) 274.

[124] ML Mack and J Pejić, *Increasing Respect for International Humanitarian Law in Non-international Armed Conflicts* (ICRC 2008) 28; M Sassòli, 'Taking Armed Groups Seriously: Ways to Improve Compliance with International Humanitarian Law' (2010) 1 International Humanitarian Legal Studies 5, 48; Crawford (n 75) 157–58; Hill-Cawthorne (n 113) 26.

[125] See, eg, Solf (n 23) 64–65; Callen (n 23) 1063; D Jinks, 'The Temporal Scope of Application of International Humanitarian Law in Contemporary Conflicts (Background Paper)' [2003] International Humanitarian Law Research Initiative 1, 4; Jensen (n 23) 233–34.

[126] RD Sloane, 'Prologue to a Voluntarist War Convention' (2007) 106 Michigan Law Review 443, 459.

[127] ibid 459.

[128] ibid 459–60. He did admit for 'few exceptions' to his observation but did not specify what those would be.

[129] See I Scobbie, 'Operationalising the Law of Armed Conflict for Dissident Forces in Libya' (31 August 2011) <www.ejiltalk.org/operationalising-the-law-of-armed-conflict-for-dissident-forces-in-libya/>.

[130] NTC, 'Frontline Manual on the Fundamental Rules of Armed Conflict' (19 May 2011) <www.ejiltalk.org/wp-content/uploads/2011/08/Final-Libyan-LOAC-Guidelines-17-May-2011.ppt>; see also NTC, 'The Treatment of Detainees and Prisoners' (25 March 2011) <https://web.archive.org/web/20110416005255/http://www.ntclibya.org/english/prisoners> (confirming the issuance of 'codes of conduct' on the treatment of detainees early on after the commencement of the conflict).

its dissemination and enforcement among the troops.[131] Many other examples have been catalogued by the ICRC in an appendix to a 2011 issue of the *International Review of the Red Cross* dedicated to the topic of non-state armed groups.[132]

Ultimately, the question of the level at which this incentive mechanism functions primarily can only be resolved by an empirical study. For the present purposes, however, it is sufficient to observe that a plausible argument may be constructed in favour of a causal link between the prosecution of fighters for mere participation and (the lack of) their observance of IHL.[133] Therefore, it needs to be acknowledged that the denial of immunity to non-state fighters is in tension with the fundamental civilizing and humanizing aspirations of IHL.

6.3.3 Inability

Perhaps the most common objection against the extension of the law of IACs to non-state armed groups is the contention that they would be unable to fulfil the conditions of IHL.[134] It is claimed that the lack of material, administrative, and human resources inherent in the condition of being a non-state actor makes these entities incapable of meeting their obligations under IHL.[135] As summarized by Emily Crawford:

> By holding non-State groups to the level of obligation required under the Conventions, non-State groups are being asked to behave in a manner, which almost by definition, they cannot; to wit, as a properly constituted State.[136]

It is said that to demand compliance where it is not within the capacity of the subject concerned would be unwise as 'it reduces the law to hypocrisy and invites disregard of the entire legal regime'.[137]

However, this objection may bear more force in relation to other norms of the law of IACs than in relation to rules on combatancy.[138] It is submitted that the extension of combatant status to non-state fighters does not in and of itself pose problems of

[131] cf Statement of Alistair Burt, Parliamentary Under Secretary of State (Afghanistan/South Asia, counter terrorism/proliferation, North America, Middle East and North Africa), Foreign and Commonwealth Office, HC Deb, 12 September 2011, c1000W.

[132] See ICRC, 'A Collection of Codes of Conduct Issued by Armed Groups' (2011) 93 IRRC 483.

[133] Corn has argued persuasively that even if this link was not proven empirically, states ought to consider granting combatant immunity to non-state actors in NIACs to enhance the credibility of state action against such belligerents. See further Corn (n 23) 288–89 (section 'What if it didn't work?').

[134] See, eg, Crawford (n 75) 74–76 (discussing this specifically as a reason for denial of combatant status to non-state actors); see also *Official Records* (n 9) vol VIII, CDDH/I/SR.4, 28–29 [25] (United Kingdom); ibid, vol VI, CDDH/SR.36, 42 [62]–[63] (Israel).

[135] See, eg, A Clapham, 'Concept of International Armed Conflict' in Clapham et al (n 95) 25 [71]; see also *Official Records* (n 9) vol V, CDDH/SR.12, 124 [39] (Denmark); ibid, vol VIII, CDDH/I/SR.32, 337 [70]–[71] (Canada); ibid [76] (Mexico); but see ibid, vol VIII, CDDH/I/SR.33, 344 [7]–[8] (Belgium).

[136] Crawford (n 75) 75.

[137] JE Bond, 'Amended Article 1 of the Draft Protocol I to the 1949 Geneva Conventions: The Coming of Age of the Guerrilla' (1975) 32 Washington & Lee Law Review 65, 71.

[138] See Section 9.4 (concerning the law of belligerent occupation); see further Sivakumaran (n 55) 72–73 (discussing the capability question in general terms).

ability to apply IHL by the groups in which these persons are organized. To some extent, this is confirmed by the relevant positive law: as detailed in Chapter 5,[139] one of the four traditional criteria currently embodied in Article 4A(2) GC III is the requirement that the group in question conduct 'their operations in accordance with the laws and customs of war'.[140] Accordingly, by adopting a requirement that certain non-state actors comply with the law, states must be taken to have acknowledged that those actors were able to do so.[141] With that in mind, the remainder of this section considers the objection of inability more broadly. It argues (1) that the objection is based on an unwarranted generalization of non-state armed groups, and (2) that it is further undermined by the actual lack of resource-intensiveness of the norms in question.

6.3.3.1 Non-state actors and the assumed lack of resources

To begin with, the objection is based on the assumption of a lack of resources implicit in the non-state status of the armed groups in question. Such an assessment can only be made, however, on a case-by-case basis, and not by way of generalizing to all non-state actors.[142] After all, one of the arguments against the internationalization of Article 1(4) AP I conflicts was that due to 'the usual lack of resources and governmental infrastructure in the third-world countries' where such conflicts were 'most likely to occur', neither the government nor the insurgents would be able to comply with the full scope of the Geneva Conventions.[143] However, some non-state armed groups may in fact have more considerable resources at their disposal than their state counterparts.

This point is well exemplified by the so-called Croatian Republic of Herzeg-Bosnia (*Hrvatska Republika Herceg-Bosna*, HR H-B). This territorial unit, notably never recognized as an independent state[144] and hence[145] a non-state entity,[146]

[139] See Section 5.2.3 and Section 5.3.1.

[140] Art 4A(2)(d) GC III; see also Art 9(4) of the Brussels Declaration Concerning the Laws and Customs of War (27 August 1874), reproduced in D Schindler and J Toman (eds), *The Laws of Armed Conflicts* (3rd edn, Martinus Nijhoff 1988) 28; Art 1(4) of the (Hague) Regulations Respecting the Laws and Customs of War on Land, Annex to Hague Convention (IV) respecting the Laws and Customs of War on Land (signed 18 October 1907, entered into force 26 January 1910) 205 CTS 277.

[141] See also Sandoz et al, *APs Commentary* (n 3) 61 ('Partisans are . . . required to respect the Geneva Conventions to the fullest extent possible').

[142] cf Sivakumaran (n 55) 72–73 (arguing that 'armed groups have varying degrees of capability [and] are not monolithic entities').

[143] Bond (n 137) 71.

[144] See, eg, *Prosecutor v Hadžihasanović and Kubura* (Trial Judgment) IT-01-47-T (15 March 2006) 629 ('On 18 November 1991, the Croatian Community of Herceg-Bosna ([*Hrvatska zajednica Herceg-Bosna*,] "HZ H-B") proclaimed its independence. The community would never gain international recognition'); see also UNSC Res 787 (16 November 1992) [3] (affirming that no entity unilaterally declared in violation of the territorial integrity of Bosnia and Herzegovina would be accepted).

[145] See also Section 2.3.1, fn 216 (regarding the declaratory and constitutive theories of recognition).

[146] *Prosecutor v Naletilić and Martinović* (Trial Judgment) IT-98-34-T (31 March 2003) 265 [4]. But see *Prosecutor v Blaškić* (Transcript) IT-95-14 (30 June 1997) 316, 326, 336, (1 July 1997) 415–16, (2 July 1997) 437 (testimony of the Prosecution witness Zoran Pajić, an expert on international law and Yugoslavian constitutional law, to the effect that HR H-B was an independent state). For a persuasive summary of arguments against HR H-B's statehood, see, eg, *Prosecutor v Blaškić* (Decision on the

existed within the current borders of Bosnia and Herzegovina between 1991 and 1994.[147] Through its military arm, the Croatian Defence Council (*Hrvatsko vijeće obrane*, HVO), it engaged in an armed conflict against the government of Bosnia and Herzegovina.[148] Despite being a non-state actor, it commanded the administrative apparatus in thirty *opštinas* (municipalities) in Western Herzegovina and central Bosnia.[149] Therefore, it would be improper to speak of its inability to adhere to the rules of IHL due to a supposed lack of resources; in fact, its administrative and organizational structure closely mirrored that of states.[150] The ICTY was similarly undeterred from putting several of the key HR H-B and HVO representatives on trial and holding some of them responsible for violations of IHL applicable in IACs.[151] In fact, the HVO and the Bosnian army accepted in a 1993 ceasefire agreement that the law of IACs applied to the conflict in Bosnia and Herzegovina.[152]

By contrast, certain failing or failed states may be in a position more akin to those weaker non-state actors unable to meet all of their IHL obligations that are the object of this objection. By suffering a total or partial collapse of institutions, law, and order, the ability of these states to ensure the implementation and enforcement of law in general and IHL in particular is heavily impaired, in extreme cases to the point that has been described as *subjektive Unmöglichkeit* (or 'subjective impossibility').[153] As the fighting atomizes and group structures in the territory of a failed

Objection of the Republic of Croatia to the Issuance of Subpoena Duces Tecum) IT-95-14-T (18 July 1997) 27–29.

[147] Decision on the establishment of the HZ H-B (18 November 1991) (confirming the establishment of this entity and listing the municipalities which formed it in Art 2); Founding Decision on the Establishment and Declaration of the Croatian Republic of Herzeg-Bosnia (28 August 1993), Art 1 (declaring the establishment of the HR H-B as the successor entity of the HZ H-B); Washington Framework Agreement between the Government of the Republic of Bosnia and Herzegovina and the Government of the Republic of Croatia and Bosnian Croat party (signed 1 March 1994, entered into force 30 March 1994) (1994) 33 ILM 743 (putting an end, de facto and de jure, to this entity).

[148] *Naletilić and Martinović* Trial Judgment (n 146) [16]; *Prosecutor v Prlić et al* (Trial Judgment) IT-04-74-T (29 May 2013) vol 1 [436].

[149] R Kumar, *Divide and Fall? Bosnia in the Annals of Partition* (Verso 1997) 47–48; *Prlić* Trial Judgment (n 148) vol 1 [425].

[150] A Bebler, 'South-East European Federalism and Contemporary Bosnia and Herzegovina' (2007) 24 Acta Slavica Iaponica 1, 13. See further *Prlić* Trial Judgment (n 148) vol 1, 173–344 (examining in detail the political, administrative, military, and judicial structure of the HZ H-B and HR H-B).

[151] See, especially, *Prosecutor v Blaškić* (Appeal Judgment) IT-95-14-A (29 July 2004) (former colonel of the HVO); *Prosecutor v Kupreškić et al* (Appeal Judgment) IT-95-16-A (23 October 2001) (five members of the HVO and a Croatian military police commander); *Prosecutor v Kordić and Čerkez* (Appeal Judgment) IT-95-14/2-A (17 December 2004) (vice-president of the HR H-B and military commander of the HVO); case *Prosecutor v Ljubičić*, IT-00-41 (commander of the HVO military police units) (case referred to Bosnia and Herzegovina); *Prosecutor v Prlić et al* (Appeal Judgment) IT-04-74-A (29 November 2017) (top political and military officials of the HR H-B and HVO). The ICTY considered that the conflict between the HVO and the State army of Bosnia and Herzegovina was an IAC. See *Kordić and Čerkez* Appeal Judgment (*op cit*) [342]–[74]; *Prlić* Appeal Judgment (*op cit*) vol 1 [229]–[97].

[152] Agreement on the Application of IHL between the Parties to the Conflict in Bosnia and Herzegovina (22 May 1992), UN Doc S/25824, Annex (12 May 1993) 3 (confirming that the GCs and AP I were 'fully applicable' in the conflict). See also Section 2.5.2 (arguing that such bilateral agreements bring about the relative internationalization of the conflict between the conflict parties).

[153] M Herdegen, 'Der Wegfall effektiver Staatsgewalt im Völkerrecht: "The Failed State"' in D Thürer, M Herdegen, and G Hohloch (eds), *Der Wegfall effektiver Staatsgewalt: 'The Failed State' (The Breakdown of Effective Government)* (CF Müller 1996) 77.

state break down, 'every combatant is his own commander' and application of IHL becomes near-impossible.[154] Accordingly, in Somalia, with the outbreak of the civil war in the early 1990s, the state structure of power and authority all but disappeared, the professional state army ceased to exist,[155] and the compliance with IHL by state forces became illusory. In comparison with the admittedly *non-state* entity HR H-B, the Somali 'state'[156] controlled fewer, if any, resources and suffered indeed from the 'subjective impossibility' to uphold its international obligations.[157]

6.3.3.2 Resource-intensiveness of the rules on combatancy

In contrast to many other norms of the law of IACs, the rules governing combatant status are actually not strictly speaking resource-intensive. Of the three main consequences of combatant status (targeting, prosecution, detention),[158] the first two do not require the direct allocation of any material or personnel resources whatsoever. Their effect is regulatory only: the status permits a certain course of action for the opposing force, namely, to target the bearers of the status; and it simultaneously prohibits a different course of action, namely, to prosecute these persons for participation.

As for the third consequence, it may appear that the detention regime implicit in the grant of a POW status does indeed require considerable resources. Detained POWs are entitled to a range of resource-intensive rights during their captivity, including the provision of sufficient food,[159] clothing,[160] and medical attention,[161] as well as to procedural guarantees presupposing the existence of judicial infrastructure.[162] Thus, it may well be that the 'incapacity of an armed group to fulfil such state-like obligations' would make 'members of the government armed forces captured by these rebels ... unlikely to enjoy the full rights and privileges of POWs'.[163] However, in order to understand the flaw in this assumption, we need to revisit the target of the objection under scrutiny.

It is recalled that the objection targets the extension of combatant status to members of non-state armed groups. Assuming that this extension was granted, the persons (newly) entitled to the 'resource-intensive' rights would be those belonging to non-state actors and the entity (newly) vested with the corresponding obligations would be their opponent, that is, the state, which the non-state actor was fighting against. However, other than perhaps in the extreme cases of 'subjective impossibility'

[154] D Thürer, 'The "Failed State" and International Law' (1999) 81 IRRC 731, 745.

[155] Federal Research Division, *Somalia: A Country Study* (Kessinger Publishing 2004) 35.

[156] The continuity of the Republic of Somalia as a state de jure has been questioned by some commentators. See, eg, R Van Eijk, 'The United Nations and the Reconstruction of Collapsed States in Africa' (1997) 9 AJICL 573, 573; NL Wallace-Bruce, 'Of Collapsed, Dysfunctional and Disoriented States: Challenges to International Law' (2000) 47 NILR 53, 67; D Lalos, 'Between Statehood and Somalia: Reflections of Somaliland Statehood' (2011) 10 Washington University Global Studies Law Review 789, 789; contra J Crawford, *The Creation of States in International Law* (2nd edn, OUP 2006) 223 and 701 fn 3.

[157] Herdegen (n 153) 77.

[158] See text to note 60 in this chapter.

[159] Art 26 GC III.

[160] Art 27 GC III.

[161] Arts 29–31 GC III.

[162] Arts 99–108 GC III.

[163] Clapham (n 135) 25 [71].

discussed earlier,[164] no doubt is cast on the ability of states to comply with their IHL obligations even in time of resource shortage; it could even be argued that their duty to do so is a corollary of the general obligation to respect IHL in all circumstances.[165] At the same time, as we have seen, no new duties would be imposed on the non-state party in question. Even with respect to the third consequence of combatant status, the currently analysed objection thus proves to be unconvincing.

In sum, this section did not advocate a general dismissal of the objection of inability to comply with IHL with respect to all obligations under this body of law. As far as regulation of combatancy is concerned, however, its purpose was to demonstrate that non-state actors are not unavoidably unable to apply and follow the relevant rules. It can thus be said that, in the context of the present chapter, the objection of inability is not insurmountable.

6.4 Evaluation

This chapter has examined the normative underpinnings of the regulation of combatancy in the context of internationalized armed conflicts. It has shown that the two key normative principles of IHL militate in favour of granting combatant status to fighters belonging to parties to such conflicts. Firstly, the analysis of the principle of distinction has shown that extending combatancy to such fighters will incentivize their compliance with IHL without necessarily undermining the domestic law of the state in and against which they operate. Secondly, the principle of equal treatment has been shown as mandating the equality of rights and obligations of all parties to internationalized armed conflicts. This should include the equal availability of combatant status to members of such parties, unless a sufficiently strong countervailing reason could be identified.

Accordingly, the chapter turned to the analysis of the principal reasons of this kind that might be raised as objections against the extension of combatant status to non-state actors. It might be tempting to simply transpose the state/non-state bifurcation onto the issue of availability/denial of combatant status. However, as seen in the historical examination in Chapter 5, the matters are actually not that straightforward, and non-state actors have in fact had, for a long time, at least some access to this status. This chapter has built on that analysis to consider three main objections from the perspective of internationalized armed conflicts.

Firstly, it is true that states have frequently made pro-sovereignty proclamations to oppose possible extension of combatant status to non-state actors. However, this sovereignty objection has been shown to apply the strongest to non-state actors in 'traditional' civil wars, and much less so, if at all, to the specific circumstances of internationalized armed conflicts. Even in those internationalized conflicts, in

[164] See text to notes 153–157 in this chapter.

[165] See Common Art 1 GCs; *ICRC CIHL Study* (n 9) rule 139; cf also Bothe et al, *New Rules* (n 60) 43 ('It is not admissible to argue that a party to the conflict does not have at its disposal the material means or organization to comply with the Protocol.').

which that objection might be sustained, such as situations of state dissolution and/or foreign intervention, the true motivation behind the pro-sovereignty claims has been shown to be the states' desire to maintain their ability to prosecute their armed adversaries.

Accordingly, the chapter turned to this second objection—or the prosecution objection. It has then shown that states in fact resort to the prosecution of their armed adversaries much less frequently than what one might expect, as evidenced by a growing trend of granting amnesties at the close of or even during some armed conflicts. Moreover, the chapter argued that prosecuting fighters that have complied with IHL is fundamentally unfair and undermines the civilizing function of this body of law. Overall, the objection might carry some weight in specific situations, but it certainly does not suffice to justify the wholesale denial of combatant status to all fighters in all internationalized armed conflicts.

Finally, the chapter discussed the third common objection, namely, that non-state actors lack the ability to comply with IHL and therefore should be deemed ineligible for combatant status. In response, it was argued that such a claim is overbroad at its basis, because the universe of non-state armed groups is extremely diverse, with some of them commanding more resources than some of their state counterparts. Moreover, even those non-state actors that may be severely under-resourced should nonetheless be able to comply with the law on combatancy, as those norms that would apply to them have been shown not to be particularly resource-intensive.

7

Practical Application

7.1 Introduction

Chapter 6 demonstrated that the availability of combatant status to fighters in internationalized armed conflicts is, in principle, in accordance with the normative underpinnings of international humanitarian law (IHL). However, that certainly does not mean that every individual fighter participating in every internationalized armed conflict automatically qualifies as a combatant. Conversely, these persons still have to fulfil the criteria for this status,[1] a result that has been somewhat pessimistically described as 'virtually impossible'.[2]

Accordingly, this chapter analyses to what extent the conditions for combatancy may be fulfilled in practice by fighters in internationalized armed conflicts. In this regard, two sets of markedly different criteria arise from Geneva Convention III (GC III) and Additional Protocol I (AP I). On account of its universal ratification, the GC III requirements apply to all situations qualifying as IACs. These requirements are considered in detail in Section 7.2.

By contrast, a considerable group of countries have not ratified AP I, including the United States, Israel, India, and Pakistan.[3] Therefore, the requirements of combatancy under AP I have to be examined separately (Section 7.3). With one exception, the analysis in this chapter applies to all modalities of internationalization. That exception relates to wars of national liberation, a legal category only introduced by AP I and thus relevant only to discussion in the latter section.

[1] T Hoffmann, 'Squaring the Circle? International Humanitarian Law and Transnational Armed Conflicts' in MJ Matheson and D Momtaz (eds), *Rules and Institutions of International Humanitarian Law Put to the Test of Recent Armed Conflicts* (Brill 2010) 2010, 234; D Akande, 'Classification of Armed Conflicts: Relevant Legal Concepts' in E Wilmshurst (ed), *International Law and the Classification of Conflicts* (OUP 2012) 78; N Zamir, *Classification of Conflicts in International Humanitarian Law: The Legal Impact of Foreign Intervention in Civil Wars* (Edward Elgar 2017) 126.

[2] W Banks, 'Toward an Adaptive International Humanitarian Law: New Norms for New Battlefields' in W Banks (ed), *New Battlefields/Old Laws: Critical Debates on Asymmetric Warfare* (Columbia University Press 2011) 6.

[3] See ICRC, 'States Party to the Following International Humanitarian Law and Other Related Treaties' (14 December 2017) <https://ihl-databases.icrc.org/applic/ihl/ihl.nsf/vwTreaties1949.xsp>. By the time of writing, 174 states had ratified AP I.

7.2 Combatancy Criteria under Geneva Convention III

The legal framework of the Geneva Conventions (GCs) is based on a distinction between members of regular and irregular armed forces.[4] With respect to the former, Article 4A(1) GC III ascribes POW status to 'members of the armed forces of a Party to the conflict'. Except for membership in these formations, the Convention text does not prescribe any further conditions for eligibility to POW status. With respect to the latter category of irregular armed forces (such as guerrillas, partisans or resistance movements), Article 4A(2) GC III expressly makes members of these groups subject to specific conditions, which must be met in order for these persons to qualify for POW status. Accordingly, the rest of this section considers whether fighters in internationalized armed conflicts may fall into either of those categories and, if so, under what circumstances they may meet the requisite conditions for combatancy.

7.2.1 Regular armed forces

It is conceivable for some fighters in internationalized armed conflicts to fall into the category of regular armed forces in the sense of Article 4A(1) GC III. This is the case particularly in situations in which new states are being formed through the disintegration of the parent state.[5] In such cases, members of the armed forces of the newly emerged state would qualify for combatancy under the said provision.

For example, with Guinea-Bissau's achievement of statehood and independence of Portugal and the corresponding internationalization of the conflict between the two belligerents in 1973,[6] the army of Guinea-Bissau was a regular government army falling under Article 4A(1) GC III.[7] It was also under this understanding that Portugal allowed the ICRC to visit the Bissauan detainees as prisoners of war.[8]

The key question with respect to this category of armed forces is whether they must also meet the conditions expressly set out only with respect to irregular armed forces in Article 4A(2) GC III,[9] or whether mere membership in regular armed

[4] Of the four GCs, this chapter focuses on GC III, which deals with the protection of POWs. However, as explained in Chapter 5, the conditions established by GC III have been transposed virtually unchanged also to GC I (concerning the protection of the wounded and the sick in the field) and GC II (concerning the protection of the wounded, the sick, and the shipwrecked at sea) in order to specify the categories of protected persons under those Conventions. The distinction between regular and irregular forces can thus fairly be described as a general feature of the legal framework established by the GCs. See further Section 5.3.1, particularly text to fns 51–56.

[5] See Section 2.3.1. [6] See Section 2.3.1.1 for more a detailed analysis.

[7] Any doubts about the application of the Convention to the conflict were dispelled by Guinea-Bissau's accession to the GCs on 28 February 1974. C Pilloud, 'Reservations to the Geneva Conventions of 1949 (II)' (1976) 16 IRRC 163, 164.

[8] HA Wilson, 'Humanitarian Protection in Wars of National Liberation' (1987) 8 Arms Control 36, 41.

[9] For a detailed analysis of these conditions, see Section 7.2.2.1 and Section 7.2.2.2.

forces suffices to establish combatant status as it would appear from the strict text of Article 4A(1) GC III. Although there is some case-law support for the former extensive interpretation, it is submitted that a closer scrutiny of the judicial decisions in question reveals that they are in fact of limited assistance. By contrast, an examination of the drafters' intentions indicates that the restrictive mere membership approach is more compelling of the two possible interpretations.

7.2.1.1 Ex parte Quirin *and* Mohamed Ali*: apparent case-law support for the extensive interpretation*

Several scholars have suggested that the extensive interpretation is supported by judicial decisions that have considered the eligibility of members of state armed forces for POW status.[10] The two cases adduced in this regard are the 1942 judgment of the US Supreme Court in *ex parte Quirin*[11] and the 1969 decision of the Privy Council in *Mohamed Ali*.[12] In these cases, members of regular armed forces who had swapped their uniforms for civilian clothes to undertake a military operation were denied POW status precisely because they had not met one of the traditional conditions.[13] Yoram Dinstein argued on this basis that GC III should be read as only containing a presumption that regular forces meet the Hague conditions; whereas if this presumption is rebutted, the persons concerned should lose POW status.[14]

It is submitted that this analysis is unconvincing for both jurisdictional and substantive reasons. Firstly, these judgments—as decisions of domestic tribunals—carry only persuasive weight in international law and cannot be considered conclusive on the issue.[15] Furthermore, *Quirin* was decided several years before GC III was adopted, which further undermines its value in interpreting this instrument.[16] Also significantly, both cases focused on the question whether members of regular armed forces must meet the condition of wearing a fixed distinctive sign such as a uniform and did not specifically analyse the applicability of the remaining three conditions.[17] In any event, the available case law on point is not unanimous: for instance, in 1949, the British Military Court at Hamburg expressly held that 'regular soldiers' did not have to meet the four requirements in order to qualify as combatants.[18]

[10] See I Brownlie, 'Decisions of British Courts During 1968 Involving Questions of Public or Private International Law' (1969) 43 BYBIL 217, 238–39; GIAD Draper, 'The Status of Combatants and the Question of Guerrilla Warfare' (1971) 45 BYBIL 173, 182 fn 1; WT Mallison and SV Mallison, 'The Juridical Status of Irregular Combatants under the International Humanitarian Law of Armed Conflict' (1977) 9 Case Western Reserve Journal of International Law 39, 74; Y Dinstein, *The Conduct of Hostilities under the Law of International Armed Conflict* (3rd edn, CUP 2016) 51.

[11] *Ex parte Quirin* (1942) 317 US 1 (US Supreme Court) (hereafter *Quirin*).

[12] *Mohamed Ali et al v Public Prosecutor* [1969] 1 AC 430 (Privy Council) (hereafter *Mohamed Ali*).

[13] *Mohamed Ali* (n 12) 452; *Quirin* (n 11) 30–31.

[14] Dinstein (n 10) 51.

[15] cf A Rogers, 'Combatant Status' in E Wilmshurst and S Breau (eds), *Perspectives on the ICRC Study on Customary International Humanitarian Law* (CUP 2007) 114.

[16] cf JG Stewart, 'Rethinking Guantánamo: Unlawful Confinement as Applied in International Criminal Law' (2006) 4 JICJ 12, 20 fn 39 and the accompanying text; JJ Paust, 'War and Enemy Status after 9/11: Attacks on the Laws of War' (2003) 28 YJIL 325, 331.

[17] cf *Quirin* (n 11) 12; *Mohamed Ali* (n 12) 452.

[18] *In re von Lewinski (called von Manstein)* (1949) 16 ILR 509 (British Military Court at Hamburg) 515–16.

Secondly, substantive scrutiny demonstrates that reading the four conditions into the first paragraph of Article 4A would be incorrect. It should be reiterated at the outset that according to the ordinary meaning of the text of the provision,[19] no conditions except for membership attach to regular armed forces.[20] Therefore, it would appear that the burden of proof rests with the proponents of interpretations alternative to the strict text of the provision.[21] The Privy Council's judgment in *Mohamed Ali* is rather disappointing in this respect. It based the argument for the necessity to meet all four conditions on two main sources, the writings of James Molony Spaight and Jean Pictet.[22]

The quotation from Spaight's treatise *War Rights on Land* appears to be the more relevant of the two as it expressly required compliance with all four conditions for the recognition of combatant status.[23] However, it had predated the Convention by nearly forty years and it had thus only related to a differently worded provision on combatancy in the 1899 and 1907 Hague Regulations.[24] Even with regard to this different treaty text, a perusal of the quote from Spaight in its context reveals that his position remained ambiguous as to whether the four conditions should apply to also regular armies or only to irregular forces.[25]

As for Pictet, the judgment cited a virtually equivalent passage from his Commentary to the GCs.[26] However, this text also related only to the Hague Regulations (as it appeared in a section dealing with the history of the commented provisions), and not to the 1949 Conventions.[27] Another quote in the judgment taken from Pictet's commentary related to the third subparagraph of Article 4A governing forces belonging to governments not recognized by the adversary,[28] which Pictet *described* as having the characteristics of regular armed forces regulated by the first

[19] Vienna Convention on the Law of Treaties (concluded 23 May 1969, entered into force 27 January 1980) 1155 UNTS 331, Art 31(1) (hereafter VCLT).

[20] Art 4A(1) GC III.

[21] cf, eg, *Legal Status of Eastern Greenland (Denmark v Norway)* (Judgment) [1933] PCIJ Rep Series A/B No 53, 49; *Western Sahara* (Advisory Opinion) [1975] ICJ Rep 12, 52–53 [116].

[22] *Mohamed Ali* (n 12) 448–50.

[23] JM Spaight, *War Rights on Land* (Macmillan 1911) 56 ('The four conditions must be united to secure recognition of belligerent status'), cited in *Mohamed Ali* (n 12) 450.

[24] Regulations Respecting the Laws and Customs of War on Land, Annex to Hague Convention (II) with Respect to the Laws and Customs of War on Land (signed 29 July 1899, entered into force 4 September 1900) 32 Stat 1803, TS 403, Art 1 (hereafter Hague Regulations (1899)); Regulations Respecting the Laws and Customs of War on Land, Annex to Hague Convention (IV) respecting the Laws and Customs of War on Land (signed 18 October 1907, entered into force 26 January 1910) 205 CTS 277, Art 1 (hereafter Hague Regulations (1907)).

[25] Spaight (n 23) 56–57 (the relevant passage discussed irregular forces and *levées en masse*; it did not expressly attach the four conditions to regular forces).

[26] JS Pictet (ed), *Geneva Convention III relative to the Treatment of Prisoners of War: Commentary* (ICRC 1960) 48 (hereafter Pictet, *GC III Commentary*) ('The qualification of belligerent is subject to these four conditions being fulfilled.'), cited in *Mohamed Ali* (n 12) 450.

[27] cf Pictet, *GC III Commentary* (n 26) 47–48. The judgment remained silent as to the context in which this quote had appeared in the Commentary. cf *Mohamed Ali* (n 12) 450.

[28] Art 4A(3) GC III ('Members of regular armed forces who profess allegiance to a government or an authority not recognized by the Detaining Power.').

subparagraph.[29] The verb 'described' in the previous sentence is worthy of italics: by no means did Pictet insist on the conditionality of these characteristics in the text.[30] Similarly, the 2016 US DoD Law of War Manual stated that the four requirements 'were intended to *reflect* attributes of States' armed forces'.[31] Hence, even if the text of Article 4A(2) GC III indeed describes or reflects the typical attributes of armed forces, that still does not suffice to transform such attributes into legal requirements that all armed forces would have to meet.[32]

7.2.1.2 Drafters' intentions: express rejection of the extensive interpretation

To the extent that the meaning of the analysed provision could still be considered ambiguous or obscure, the issue should be resolved by considering the intentions of the drafters as evidenced in the *travaux préparatoires* of the Third Geneva Convention.[33] Pictet's commentary on the crucial first subparagraph of Article 4A is silent as to the reasons behind the exclusion of the four conditions from the final text.[34] Speculations have appeared in some writings that this was due to the drafters' consideration of the conditions as part of customary law and hence unnecessary to include in the treaty text.[35]

It is therefore necessary to examine the authentic record from the diplomatic conference in Geneva, where the text of this provision was the subject of a very lengthy and heated discussion.[36] On 21 June 1949, General Devijver of Belgium, the rapporteur of the Special Committee, proposed a 'working text', which unmistakably drew on Article 1 of the Hague Regulations[37] and which would have accorded POW status to '[m]embers of armed forces who are in the service of an adverse belligerent, *as well*

[29] Pictet, *GC III Commentary* (n 26) 63 ('These "regular armed forces" have all the material characteristics and all the attributes of armed forces in the sense of sub-paragraph (1): they wear uniform, they have an organised hierarchy and they know and respect the laws and customs of war.').

[30] See ibid 63. Pictet opined that the drafters had seen 'no need to specify' the requirements contained in the four conditions for such forces, apparently presuming that they would meet those criteria under ordinary circumstances. That is still, it is submitted, a position different from stating that the criteria should be read into the first and the third subparagraphs of Art 4A GC III.

[31] US DoD, *Law of War Manual* (December 2016) 120 [4.6.1.3] (emphasis added).

[32] But see ibid 119–20 [4.6.1.3] (despite acknowledging that members of state armed forces 'receive combatant status . . . by virtue of their membership', the following text then implies that the failure to meet one of the four conditions would result in the loss of combatant status).

[33] Art 32(a) VCLT.

[34] cf Pictet, *GC III Commentary* (n 26) 50–51.

[35] See, eg, Mallison and Mallison (n 10) 48; M Bothe, KJ Partsch, and WA Solf, *New Rules for Victims of Armed Conflicts: Commentary on the Two 1977 Protocols Additional to the Geneva Conventions of 1949* (Martinus Nijhoff 1982) 234–35 (hereafter Bothe et al, *New Rules*); JC Yoo, 'The Status of Soldiers and Terrorists under the Geneva Conventions' (2004) 3 Chinese JIL 135, 144.

[36] See, in particular, Switzerland, *Final Record of the Diplomatic Conference of Geneva of 1949* (Federal Political Department 1949) vol II A, 237–38, 244, 386–89, 413–37, 465–70 (hereafter *Final Record*); ibid, vol II B, 267–69, 340–42. Towards the end of the discussion, the rapporteur of Committee II quite appropriately labelled the later Art 4A as 'the main object' of the whole Convention. ibid, vol II B, 267; see also Pictet, *GC III Commentary* (n 26) 49 ('Article 4 is . . . the key to the Convention').

[37] See Section 5.3.1 for the historical background of this provision.

as members of militia or volunteer corps belonging to such belligerent, and fulfilling [the four conditions]'.[38]

At the session of Committee II devoted to the discussion of this text, General Slavin of the Soviet Union protested against this wording, arguing that as it stood then, 'it would appear that members of the Armed forces *would have to fulfil the four traditional requirements* ... in order to obtain prisoner of war status, *which was contrary to the Hague Regulations*'.[39] The rapporteur defended the draft as compliant with the Hague Regulations and argued that on his reading, the text 'carefully specified that only members of militia or volunteer corps should fulfil all four conditions'.[40] The discussion nonetheless brought to light two possible interpretations of the conjunction 'as well as'. Did it separate the category of (regular) armed forces from militias and volunteer corps for the purposes of meeting the four conditions, as argued by the rapporteur, or did members of both of these categories have to meet the requirements, as General Slavin had feared?

At this junction and to 'overcome the drafting difficulty',[41] in other words, to remove the ambiguity highlighted by the Soviet delegate, the provision was split up into two subparagraphs, forming the basis for the text finally adopted at the conference.[42] The final report of Committee II to the plenary assembly of the conference later confirmed that the aim of the division of subparagraph (1) was 'to show clearly' that the conditions were to apply to irregular forces only.[43] This examination of the preparatory work of the Convention therefore suggests that the strictly textual reading of Article 4A is the preferable one.[44]

Finally, this reading should also prevail over the admittedly ambiguous text of the Hague Regulations—this ambiguity being apparent in the uncertainty among the drafters in Geneva as well as in the potentially contrary interpretations by Spaight and Pictet discussed earlier—because GC III is the *lex posterior*[45] and on the basis of the principle that the Convention supplements and expands the protection granted by the Regulations, and not vice versa.[46]

7.2.1.3 *Consequences of the mere membership approach*

Where does this leave forces such as the Bissauan army in 1974 or the regular armed forces of the republics seceding from Yugoslavia in the 1990s? On the basis of the foregoing analysis, it is submitted that members of such armies do not have to meet all four conditions in order to be considered as combatants. However, a word of caution is in order.

[38] *Final Record* (n 36) vol II A, 465 (Belgium) (emphasis added).

[39] ibid 466 (Soviet Union) (emphases added).

[40] ibid 466 (Belgium).

[41] ibid 466.

[42] ibid 466–67.

[43] *Final Record* (n 36) vol II A, 561.

[44] See also W Hays Parks, 'Special Forces' Wear of Non-Standard Uniforms' (2003) 4 Chicago Journal of International Law 493, 509; A Rosas, *The Legal Status of Prisoners of War* (Suomalainen Tiedeakatemia 1976) 328; S Watts, 'Who Is a Prisoner of War?' in A Clapham, P Gaeta, and M Sassòli (eds), *The 1949 Geneva Conventions: A Commentary* (OUP 2015) 894 [14].

[45] cf Art 30(3) VCLT.

[46] Pictet, *GC III Commentary* (n 26) 5 and 51.

The analysis presented thus far does not in the least absolve these forces from observing other norms of IHL.[47] They still have to respect the fundamental principle of distinction which requires their members to distinguish themselves from civilians.[48] They also have to ensure their members' compliance with IHL in general.[49] If captured out of uniform, as the defendants in *Mohamed Ali* and *Quirin* were, these soldiers could still be tried for violating IHL, in particular its rules prohibiting perfidy.[50] It bears reiterating that the question of prosecution for war crimes or other violations of IHL is separate from the determination of combatant/POW status.[51]

Therefore, the key difference advocated here is that these persons should be deemed eligible for combatant and hence POW status solely on the basis of their membership in regular armed forces. This would be the case even if the other party to the conflict did not recognize the government under which such armed forces operated.[52] This result is mandated by Article 4A(3) GC III, which expressly grants POW status to 'members of regular armed forces who profess allegiance to a government or an authority not recognized by the Detaining Power'.[53] In sum, the mere membership approach endorsed here with respect to regular forces survives even in the face of the possible absence of recognition by the adverse conflict party.

7.2.2 Irregular armed forces

Those fighters in internationalized armed conflicts who do not qualify for combatant status as members of regular armed forces have to meet conditions attaching to irregular forces under the second subparagraph of Article 4A GC III. Although the literature often speaks of 'four traditional requirements',[54] the four conditions listed in *alinéas* (a) to (d) of Article 4A(2) GC III should be read together with a fifth one, which appears in the *chapeau* of that provision, namely, 'belonging to a Party

[47] cf also Watts (n 44) 895 [21].

[48] J-M Henckaerts and L Doswald-Beck (eds), *Customary International Humanitarian Law* (CUP 2005) rules 1 and 106 (hereafter *ICRC CIHL Study*); GD Solis, *The Law of Armed Conflict: International Humanitarian Law in War* (2nd edn, CUP 2016) 269.

[49] Hague Convention (IV) respecting the Laws and Customs of War on Land (signed 18 October 1907, entered into force 26 January 1910) 205 CTS 277, Art 1; Common Art 1 GCs; *ICRC CIHL Study* (n 48) rule 139.

[50] Art 23(b) Hague Regulations (1907) (n 24); *ICRC CIHL Study* (n 48) rule 65, especially at vol I, 224 ('simulation of civilian status [is perfidy] because civilians not taking a direct part in hostilities must be respected and may not be the object of attack'). Note that for an act to qualify as prohibited perfidy, it must be the proximate cause of death or injury; conversely, it would not qualify as such if it resulted only in the destruction of property. See further Bothe et al, *New Rules* (n 35) 203–04; K Ipsen, 'Combatants and Non-Combatants' in D Fleck (ed), *The Handbook of International Humanitarian Law* (3rd edn, OUP 2013) 106–07.

[51] Art 85 GC III.

[52] cf Pictet, *GC III Commentary* (n 26) 63.

[53] Art 4A(3) GC III; on the provenance of this provision, see Section 5.3.1.

[54] See, eg, Mallison and Mallison (n 10) 74; JS Pictet, *Development and Principles of International Humanitarian Law* (Martinus Nijhoff 1985) 39; I Detter, *The Law of War* (2nd edn, CUP 2000) 139; Yoo (n 35) 140; G Cadwalader, 'The Rules Governing the Conduct of Hostilities in Additional Protocol I to the Geneva Conventions of 1949: A Review of Relevant United States References' (2011) 14 YIHL 133, 140.

to the conflict'.[55] This qualification reflects the historical fact of exclusion of armed bands of marauders or pirates acting for private purposes from combatant and POW status.[56] As such, the condition was included intentionally by the drafters in 1949.[57] Therefore, it should be seen as part and parcel of the other requirements pertaining to irregular forces under the Convention.[58] The following text first considers the said requirement of belonging and then proceeds to discuss the four traditional requirements. It finally considers the argument that there is a further—either implied or customary—sixth condition of foreign nationality that would apply to irregular forces.

7.2.2.1 The criterion of belonging to a party to the conflict

The requirement of belonging is qualitatively different from the other four conditions. While the fulfilment of the traditional four conditions depends primarily on the internal structure and organization of the armed group itself, the criterion of belonging concerns the group's external relations with a party to the armed conflict in question.[59] Whether and how this requirement may be fulfilled by non-state armed forces in internationalized armed conflicts depends on the specific modality of internationalization. In this sense, it is useful to focus specifically on conflicts internationalized *inter partes*[60] and those internationalized by outside intervention.[61] By contrast, the criterion is less (or not at all) applicable to other modalities of internationalization. This is because armed forces fighting in conflicts internationalized by state dissolution[62] will ordinarily fall under the category of regular armed forces discussed earlier,[63] and the notion of wars of national liberation[64] is unknown to the legal framework of the GCs.[65]

7.2.2.1.1 Internationalization *inter partes*

Internationalization *inter partes* arises from a voluntary act of a State through which it makes the entirety of the law of IAC applicable to the relations between itself and a non-state armed group. If the acting state is in fact itself a belligerent in what was originally a NIAC, its consent to internationalize the conflict therefore extends to treating its non-state adversary as a 'Party to the conflict' in the full meaning of the term under the law of IAC. It goes without saying that the forces of the recognized party 'belong' to that party itself and thus the criterion of 'belonging' will always be met.

[55] Art 4A(2), chapeau, GC III. [56] Solis (n 48) 211; Mallison and Mallison (n 10) 50.
[57] *Final Record* (n 36) vol II A, 478–79.
[58] See further K Del Mar, 'The Requirement of "Belonging" under International Humanitarian Law' (2010) 21 EJIL 105, 109–13.
[59] cf Watts (n 44) 897 [27]. [60] See generally Section 2.5.
[61] See generally Section 2.2. [62] On which see generally Section 2.3.
[63] See Section 7.2.1. [64] On which see generally Section 2.4.
[65] The practical application of the criteria of combatancy under AP I to armed groups including national liberation movements is discussed in Section 7.3.

This interpretation is also supported by state practice during the American Civil War (1861–65) and the Boer War (1899–1902). During both of these conflicts, the recognition of belligerency by the territorial state was followed by a grant of POW status to the recognized forces.[66] Indeed, the extension of combatant and POW status was considered to be one of the main intended consequences of such recognition.[67]

Moreover, it has been shown that conflicts may also be internationalized *inter partes* by an act of a neutral third state, most commonly by a recognition of belligerency issued by that state.[68] While such recognition would not normally pose any challenges with regard to targeting and prosecution, as these aspects of combatancy do not reach third uninvolved states, it could complicate matters in relation to the detention of the fighters participating in the conflict.

GC III contains a number of provisions regulating the position of neutral countries vis-à-vis POWs detained in IACs.[69] Most of them are based on the implicit assumption that the conflict is considered as an IAC also in the mutual relationship of the belligerent parties and as such they would be inapplicable due to the relative nature of the internationalization process.[70] For instance, the selection and appointment of a Protecting Power under Article 8 GC III requires the cooperation and ultimately consent of both conflict parties.[71] This would, however, not be required in law as for the territorial state, the conflict would not be internationalized, which would render the said provision inoperable.

Conversely, other provisions do not hinge upon the territorial state's recognition of the international nature of the conflict and can be applied of their own standing. Accordingly, the law of neutrality provides that if troops belonging to one of the conflict parties appear in the territory of a neutral state, that state is obliged to intern them for the duration of the conflict.[72] GC III then prescribes that these troops be given treatment equivalent to POWs under the same Convention.[73] There is little practice on this basis, one of the last reported cases being the Swiss internment of about 15,000 foreign military personnel from both sides of the conflict during the Second World War.[74] Nevertheless, third-state recognition of belligerency has been a sporadic occurrence after 1945.[75] It would thus appear that the recognizing states were in violation of their neutrality obligations if they did not intern or, *a fortiori*,

[66] YM Lootsteen, 'The Concept of Belligerency in International Law' (2000) 166 MLR 109, 115; N Higgins, *The Approach of International Law to Wars of National Liberation* (The Martin Institute 2004) 13; HA Wilson, *International Law and the Use of Force by National Liberation Movements* (Clarendon Press 1988) 38.

[67] cf Lootsteen (n 66) 110; Rosas (n 44) 292 fn 350; SC Neff, *War and the Law of Nations* (CUP 2005) 257.

[68] See Section 2.5.1.

[69] See, eg, Arts 4(B)(2), 8, 10(2) and (4), 109–17, 122(1) and (2), and 123 GC III.

[70] On the relative nature of recognition of belligerency, see Section 2.5.1.2.

[71] Pictet, *GC III Commentary* (n 26) 100.

[72] Art 57 Hague Regulations (1899) (n 24); Hague Convention (V) respecting the Rights and Duties of Neutral Powers and Persons in Case of War on Land (signed 18 October 1907, entered into force 26 January 1910) 205 CTS 299, Art 11.

[73] Art 4B(2) GC III. [74] Solis (n 48) 216.

[75] See Section 2.5.1.1 (summarizing the post-1945 practice of third-state recognition of belligerency).

if they provided support to the fighters of the party recognized as belligerent as was reportedly the case with Venezuela and FARC after 2008.[76]

Therefore, it can be summarized that, due to the relative character of third-state recognition, only those provisions relating to combatancy that can be applied without the territorial state's consent or cooperation would be triggered by such recognition.

7.2.2.1.2 Outside intervention

As for conflicts internationalized by foreign intervention, it is submitted that the non-state actor there would always meet the criterion of 'belonging to a Party to the conflict'. It bears reminding that a NIAC is internationalized if an outside state uses force against the territorial state through a non-state armed group in its territory. Under the understanding advanced in this book, this condition is met if the outside state participates in organizing and coordinating the rebel group.[77] Therefore, there must by definition be a certain connection between the non-state armed group and the intervening state, one that has been described by the ICTY as 'overall control'.[78] However, does that connection suffice to consider the non-state actor as 'belonging' to the outside state in question for the purposes of Article 4A(2) GC III?

Pictet's Commentary to the Third Convention made it clear that the requirement of belonging should be interpreted very liberally.[79] It highlighted that the drafters had had in mind diverse cases of resistance movements active during the Second World War and that the provision was supposed to cover all of these cases.[80] The affiliation that would fulfil the analysed criterion could thus 'find expression merely by tacit agreement' insofar as it was clear for which side the irregular forces were fighting or it could, conversely, be 'confirmed by official recognition' by an outside state.[81] This liberal interpretation also finds strong support in the academic literature[82] and some official statements.[83]

Importantly, in comparison with the 'overall control' standard, the 'belonging' requirement sets a much lower threshold. While the former standard requires the

[76] C Kraul, 'Chavez Keeps Up Campaign to Get Rebels Off Terrorist List' *Los Angeles Times* (20 January 2008) (reporting on a 17 January 2008 recognition of belligerency for FARC and ELN by Venezuela); BBC, 'Colombian FARC Rebels' Links to Venezuela Detailed' (10 May 2011) <www.bbc.co.uk/news/world-latin-america-13343810> (summarizing a report by the International Institute for Strategic Studies according to which Venezuela provided sanctuary to FARC members and allowed them to operate on its territory).

[77] See Section 2.2.2.4.

[78] *Prosecutor v Tadić* (Appeal Judgment) IT-94-1-A (15 July 1999) [131]; for a critical analysis of the ruling, see Section 2.2.2.3.4.

[79] Pictet, *GC III Commentary* (n 26) 57–58. [80] ibid 57. [81] ibid.

[82] D Bindschedler-Robert, 'A Reconsideration of the Law of Armed Conflicts' in *Conferences on Contemporary Problems of International Law: The Law of Armed Conflicts* (Carnegie Endowment for International Peace 1971) 40; H Meyrowitz, 'Le statut des guérilleros dans le droit international' (1973) 107 Journal du droit international 875, 901–02; Rosas (n 44) 258; Del Mar (n 58) 111; A Clapham, 'Concept of International Armed Conflict' in Clapham et al (n 44) 18 [44]; Zamir (n 1) 139–40; but cf Watts (n 44) 897–98 [30] (accepting *de facto* relationships in principle, but only if they surpass 'mere logistical support').

[83] See, eg, US DoD, *Law of War Manual* (December 2016) 120–21 [4.6.2] ('The State's authority may be granted by its representatives orally').

outside power to have a share in the organization, coordination or planning of the operations of the armed group in question, the requirement of 'belonging' only demands an acceptance, whether express or tacit, that the armed group is fighting on behalf of the outside power.[84] Hence, in any conflict internationalized by a connection qualifying as 'overall control', this connection will always meet the requirement of belonging, as well.

7.2.2.2 Four traditional criteria of combatancy

The four traditional conditions can easily be assessed together. This is because the question whether a non-state actor in an internationalized armed conflict meets these requirements depends primarily on its internal structure and organization. Larger forces that are well organized and subjected to a strict military hierarchy following the army model may fit the criteria quite easily.

For example, the non-state armed group known as the Croatian Defence Council (*Hrvatsko vijeće obrane*, HVO) was created by separation from the Croatian State army in 1992.[85] They have thus maintained the original military hierarchy, while adopting own uniforms and insignia.[86] There seems to be no doubt that their members carried their arms openly.[87] Finally, although some of their members, including the commanding officers, have been prosecuted for violations of IHL,[88] this does not bear on the capacity of the armed group as such to conduct itself in accordance with IHL.[89] In fact, the HVO military command issued orders emphasizing the importance of the lawful conduct of its troops, confirming that the leadership was aware of the significance of this requirement while at the same time believing that the HVO fighters were capable of fulfilling it.[90] Leaving aside the factual question to what extent the HVO actually did respect IHL as a group, it can nevertheless be observed on the basis of the foregoing that armed groups similar to it[91] may be able to meet all four traditional conditions.[92]

[84] Del Mar (n 58) 112.

[85] Despite the separation, both the HVO and its enemy, the Bosnian Army, accepted that the conflict in Bosnia and Herzegovina was to be governed by the law of IACs. See Agreement on the Application of IHL between the Parties to the Conflict in Bosnia and Herzegovina (22 May 1992), UN Doc S/25824, Annex (12 May 1993) 3.

[86] *Prosecutor v Naletilić and Martinović* (Trial Judgment) IT-98-34-T (31 March 2003) [195]; *Prosecutor v Prlić et al* (Trial Judgment) IT-04-74-T (29 May 2013) vol 1 [775].

[87] cf *Prlić* Trial Judgment (n 86) vol 1 [769]–[844].

[88] See examples cited in Section 6.3.3.1 at fn 151.

[89] cf Watts (n 44) 902–03 [52] (arguing that rare or episodic violations of IHL by some members of an armed group do not disqualify the entire group from meeting this requirement).

[90] See, eg, *Prosecutor v Kordić and Čerkez* (Trial Judgment) IT-95-14/2-T (26 February 2001) [699] (referring to an order issued by Mario Čerkez on 18 March 1993); *Prlić* Trial Judgment (n 86) vol 1 [697] (referring to the 'Book of Service Rules for the Armed Forces of the HZ H-B' issued by Mate Boban on 3 July 1992); ibid [707] (referring to an order issued by Mate Boban on 15 September 1993).

[91] See also *Prosecutor v Blaškić* (Trial Judgment) IT-95-14-T (3 March 2000) [147] (ascribing POW status to the 'Bosnian Muslim combatants held by the HVO').

[92] See also F Kalshoven, 'The Position of Guerrilla Fighters under the Law of War' in F Kalshoven (ed), *Reflections on the Law of War: Collected Essays* (Martinus Nijhoff 2007) 494; *Official Records Switzerland, Official Records of the Diplomatic Conference on the Reaffirmation and Development of International Humanitarian Law Applicable in Armed Conflicts, Geneva (1974–1977)* (Federal Political

Of course, many such groups will choose not to, and sometimes even make that explicit: for example, Hezbollah claimed in 2006 that they would not comply with IHL due to perceived previous violations by Israel.[93] It has been correctly said that questions about the lawfulness of Hezbollah's military operations 'cast doubt' as to whether its members should be considered combatants.[94] Nevertheless, it can be concluded that those groups that do meet the conditions in the context of internationalized armed conflicts, to which the GCs apply, should benefit from combatant status.

7.2.2.3 Foreign nationality as an additional criterion?

It is sometimes suggested that an additional condition of foreign nationality is either implied by the structure of GC III[95] or that such a condition is part of customary international law.[96] If correct, this would mean that persons who have the same nationality as their enemy would not qualify for combatant status even if they met all the other conditions of combatancy.[97] In practice, this could be especially problematic in internationalized armed conflicts, in which members of all conflict parties often have the same nationality.

It is submitted, however, that there are strong reasons against the existence of such a condition in the present state of the law. Firstly, consider the argument that the condition can be 'inferentially deduced' from the framework established by the Conventions.[98] The principal authority for this argument is the *Koi* case decided by the Privy Council in 1967.[99] In it, Lord Hodson, speaking for the majority of the judges, relied on Articles 87 and 100 GC III, both of which deal with criminal sanctions that may be imposed by a detaining power on POWs in its hands.[100] These provisions contain an identical stipulation that the detaining power must take into account that the prosecuted POW 'is not bound to it by any duty of allegiance'.[101] Lord Hobson described these provisions as resting 'upon the assumption that a "prisoner of war" is not a "national of the detaining power"' and on that basis he inferred that a person who owes a duty of allegiance to a detaining power is not entitled to POW status.[102]

Department 1978) vol VIII, CDDH/I/SR.4, 32 [46] (Mozambique Liberation Front—FRELIMO) (hereafter *Official Records*).

[93] See, Statement of Hezbollah Secretary-General Hassan Nasrallah (16 July 2006), reproduced in HRW, 'Civilians under Assault: Hezbollah's Rocket Attacks on Israel in the 2006 War' (August 2007) <www.hrw.org/reports/2007/iopt0807/iopt0807web.pdf>, at 12.

[94] N Lubell, *Extraterritorial Use of Force Against Non-State Actors* (OUP 2010) 138–39; but see ibid 251–54 (concluding that the 2006 conflict between Israel and Lebanon was a NIAC, thus mooting the issue of combatancy).

[95] See, eg, Rosas (n 44) 384; Dinstein (n 10) 55; Zamir (n 1) 143–44.

[96] See, eg, H Lauterpacht (ed), *Oppenheim's International Law: Disputes, War and Neutrality* (7th edn, Longmans 1952) vol II, 268 [86]; Rosas (n 44) 383; Brownlie (n 10) 235; M Sassòli, AA Bouvier, and A Quintin, *How Does Law Protect in War?* (3rd edn, ICRC 2011) vol I, 177.

[97] cf Hoffmann (n 1) 234 fn 67.

[98] Dinstein (n 10) 55.

[99] *Public Prosecutor v Oie Hee Koi and connected appeals* [1968] AC 829 (Privy Council) (hereafter *Koi*).

[100] *Koi* (n 99) 856–57.

[101] Arts 87(2) and 100(3) GC III.

[102] *Koi* (n 99) 857 [C].

However, the references to nationality in Articles 87 and 100 GC III are descriptive, not normative in nature: they 'describe a feature (rather than a requirement) worthy of lenient treatment that is common among POWs'.[103] By contrast, Article 4A GC III is the relevant normative provision, which lists the applicable conditions of POW status. In that respect, its silence with regard to the nationality requirement is telling, and particularly so when contrasted with the corresponding provision of GC IV, which expressly excludes states' own nationals from the scope of that Convention.[104] The drafters' failure to address nationality as a condition of POW status under Article 4A(2) GC III thus confirms that no such condition should be read into the Convention framework.[105]

Secondly, the claim that the condition of foreign nationality has gained the force of custom falters in the face of contrary practice. Already in 1946, a US Court of Appeals held *in re Territo* that it found no support 'for the contention ... that citizenship in the country of either army in collision necessarily affects the status of one captured on the field of battle'.[106] In 1947, a commission composed of government experts from multiple countries stated in its comments on the ICRC draft convention on POWs that '*as a rule*, [POWs] are not nationals of the [detaining power], to which they owe no allegiance'.[107] By extension, this must be taken to mean that the experts considered that there was a possible exception to the rule; in other words, that at least exceptionally, the detaining state's own nationals could qualify as POWs.

There is no indication that a customary rule to the contrary has evolved in the meantime. In particular, today's 'military legal manuals do not widely include foreign nationality as a prerequisite to POW status'.[108] Moreover, as recently as 2004, the US Supreme Court reaffirmed the *Territo* case and held that '[t]here is no bar to this Nation's holding one of its own citizens as an enemy combatant'.[109] Overall, these instances show that the practice in favour of the supposed condition of foreign nationality can in no way be described as 'extensive and virtually uniform'.[110] It can thus be concluded that there is no implied condition of foreign nationality under GC III, nor is it required as a matter of customary law.

[103] KH Tse, 'The Relevancy of Nationality to the Right to Prisoner of War Status' (2009) 8 Chinese JIL 395, 401.

[104] cf Art 4(1) GC IV.

[105] cf Watts (n 44) 904 [58]; contra Zamir (n 1) 144; D Jinks, 'The Declining Significance of POW Status' (2004) 45 Harvard International Law Journal 367, 422 fn 302.

[106] *In re Territo*, 156 F.2d 142, 145 (9th Cir. 1946); see also *Quirin* (n 11) 37–38.

[107] ICRC, *Report on the Work of the Conference of Government Experts for the Study of the Conventions for the Protection of War Victims* (ICRC 1947) 203.

[108] Watts (n 44) 904 [58].

[109] *Hamdi v Rumsfeld* (2004) 542 US 507, 519 (US Supreme Court).

[110] cf *North Sea Continental Shelf cases (Federal Republic of Germany v Denmark; Federal Republic of Germany v Netherlands)* (Judgment) [1969] ICJ Rep 3, 43 [74] (considering the existence of extensive and virtually uniform state practice to be an indispensable requirement for the formation of a new rule of custom).

7.3 Combatancy Criteria under Additional Protocol I

7.3.1 Membership approach and the question of forfeiture of combatant status

By and large, the 1977 Additional Protocol I to the GCs has significantly loosened the conditions for combatancy. The Protocol was newly based on a membership approach, equalizing members of regular and irregular military structures.[111] Under Article 43(2) AP I, all members of the armed forces of a Party to the conflict except medical and religious personnel were defined as combatants. Although this process of assimilation of regular and irregular armed forces has certainly been influential in the period since the adoption of AP I, it is doubtful whether it has reached the level of customary law.[112] For the time being, it thus remains the case that there are 'two different standards of what constitutes lawful combatancy': one under GC III (discussed in the previous section) and another one binding on states parties to AP I.[113]

Under the terms of the Protocol, a combatant could only forfeit the legal status of a combatant and the related right to be a POW upon capture if the combatant failed to distinguish themselves from the civilian population.[114] Much ink has been spilled about this duty to distinguish oneself, especially in specific situations, in which the 'nature of the hostilities' renders it impossible to follow the general duty to do so during the preparation for or while engaged in an attack.[115] In these situations, Article 44(3) AP I only requires combatants to carry their arms openly during each military engagement and while they are visible to their adversaries during the military deployment prior to launching an attack.[116] Personal accounts of those participating in the Diplomatic Conference as well as later academic analyses have clarified that these specific situations were understood to be limited to fighting in occupied territories and wars of national liberation as defined in Article 1(4) of the Protocol.[117]

[111] Wilson (n 66) 173.

[112] cf Rogers (n 15) 110; but see *ICRC CIHL Study* (n 48) 16 (arguing that the Article 43 AP I definition 'is now generally applied' and that it 'is therefore no longer necessary to distinguish between regular and irregular armed forces').

[113] C Greenwood, 'The Law of War (International Humanitarian Law)' in MD Evans (ed), *International Law* (2nd edn, OUP 2006); see also Dinstein (n 10) 64.

[114] Art 44(2)–(4) AP I.

[115] See, eg, GH Aldrich, 'Prospects for United States Ratification of Additional Protocol I to the 1949 Geneva Conventions' (1991) 85 AJIL 1, 7–10; F Kalshoven, 'The Diplomatic Conference on Reaffirmation and Development of International Humanitarian Law Applicable in Armed Conflicts, Geneva, 1974–1977' in F Kalshoven (ed), *Reflections on the Law of War: Collected Essays* (Martinus Nijhoff 2007) 201–05; H-P Gasser, 'An Appeal for Ratification by the United States' (1987) 81 AJIL 912, 919–22; GB Roberts, 'New Rules of Waging War: The Case Against Ratification of Additional Protocol I' (1985) 26 VJIL 109, 133–34; ET Jensen, 'The Laws of War: Past, Present, and Future: Combatant Status: It is Time for Intermediate Levels of Recognition for Partial Compliance' (2005) 46 VJIL 209, 228–30.

[116] Art 44(3) AP I.

[117] RR Baxter, 'Humanitarian Law or Humanitarian Politics? The 1974 Diplomatic Conference on Humanitarian Law' (1975) 16 Harvard International Law Journal 1, 12; Gasser (n 115) 920; Aldrich (n 115) 10; Kalshoven (n 115) 202.

In any event, the focus of the present analysis is on the question whether combatant status may apply to non-state actors in internationalized armed conflicts falling within the framework of AP I. It is therefore not necessary to go into detail with respect the factual circumstances under which that status would be *lost*, as is the case with the failure to comply with the requirements of Article 44(3) AP I.[118] Rather, the aim is to examine whether there are situations in which the status would be *granted* in the first place.

7.3.2 Relaxation of the original criteria by Additional Protocol I

In general, the conditions in AP I are more relaxed than the traditional requirements that had been incorporated in GC III.[119] The duties to have a fixed distinctive sign[120] and to carry arms openly[121] have been replaced by a more general duty to distinguish oneself from civilians.[122] The obligation to conduct operations lawfully,[123] often seen as applicable also to individual members of an armed formation,[124] has been replaced by a more easily satisfiable group-level-only condition of being subject to an internal disciplinary system enforcing compliance with IHL.[125] It can thus be observed that, *a minori ad maius*, if a non-state group satisfies the GC III conditions, it would also meet the conditions of AP I.[126] For the same reason, if it is accepted that the criterion of foreign nationality is inapplicable under the scheme of GC III,[127] it would equally not apply to conflicts governed by AP I.[128]

The sole exception appears to be the original requirement of 'belonging' to a conflict party,[129] which was transformed into the requirement that the force in question be 'under a command responsible' to a party to the conflict.[130] Although not always recognized in the literature as such,[131] this is in fact a higher standard, requiring a stronger connection to a conflict party than what was mandated by GC III.[132] It is therefore useful to examine this criterion more closely.

[118] Art 44(3) AP I (argument *a contrario* 'he shall *retain* his status as a combatant ...') (emphasis added).

[119] cf R Kolb, *Advanced Introduction to International Humanitarian Law* (Edward Elgar 2014) 16; Watts (n 44) 900 [39]; L Olson, 'Those Who Are Not POWs' in Clapham et al (n 44) 917 [17].

[120] Art 4A(2)(b) GC III. [121] Art 4A(2)(c) GC III.

[122] Art 44(3), first sentence, AP I. [123] Art 4A(2)(d) GC III.

[124] See, eg, GIAD Draper, 'The Status of Combatants and the Question of Guerrilla Warfare' (1971) 45 BYBIL 173, 196; HS Levie, *Prisoners of War in International Armed Conflict* (Naval War College Press 1977) 44–45; Dinstein (n 10) 59–60.

[125] Art 43(1), second sentence, AP I.

[126] See also Art 44(6) AP I and the text to notes 141–45 in this chapter.

[127] On which see Section 7.2.2.3.

[128] But see, eg, Zamir (n 1) 143 fn 122 (arguing that 'the requirement of non-allegiance should be deemed as applicable alongside the other requirements of Articles 43 and 44 of API').

[129] Art 4A(2), chapeau, GC III. [130] Art 43(1), first sentence, AP I.

[131] See, eg, Dinstein (n 10) 61 (equating the link required under GC III and AP I); R Kolb and R Hyde, *An Introduction to the International Law of Armed Conflicts* (Hart Publishing 2008) 202 (considering that the requirement from GC III had remained intact in AP I).

[132] cf L Cameron and V Chetail, *Privatizing War: Private Military and Security Companies under Public International Law* (CUP 2013) 389 fn 14 (observing that 'belonging' is a much looser standard than where the conflict party exercises command and control over a non-state group).

7.3.3 The criterion of being under a responsible command

Although the requirement of being under a command responsible to a conflict party has raised the particularly low bar set by the requirement of 'belonging', it is submitted that this is actually not problematic in most conflicts within the scope of this study. In wars of national liberation, brought under the scope of Additional Protocol I by way of its Article 1(4), the non-state actor in question, in other words the authority representing a people exercising its right to self-determination, is itself considered a Party to the conflict and no further connection or attribution to a third party is necessary.[133]

Likewise, in situations of state dissolution and internationalization *inter partes*, the newly emerged state or the recognized belligerent, respectively, are to be considered as a 'Party to the conflict' in the meaning of the Protocol.[134] The question of the existence of a responsible command thus arises only in relation to the internal hierarchy and structure of such forces. Since these actors, through their acquisition of a degree of international legal personality, become a party to the conflict, they do not need to be connected to another subject of international law for the purposes of combatant status.

However, the same would not be the case in conflicts internationalized by outside intervention. In these situations, the role of the 'Party to the conflict' in the sense prescribed by the Protocol is held by the outside intervening power.[135] For the non-state actor to be under a 'command responsible' to this outside power is, however, a threshold higher than that required by the criterion of 'belonging' or even that of the 'overall control' test.[136] It implies that the non-state group must be subject to direct hierarchical military subordination by the outside power[137] and to a system of sanctions imposed by that power.[138] In such circumstances, the situation would notably also have to be treated as a single internationalized armed conflict due to the resulting loss of autonomy on part of the non-state actor.[139] This may be true for certain private military contractors operating alongside foreign forces,[140] but it will not be the norm with respect to those rebel groups that are functioning more independently.

In any event, members of such groups would not be left without any status due to the operation of the 'savings clause'[141] in Article 44(6) AP I. This provision stipulates that the entire article of which it forms part 'is without prejudice to the right of any

133 See Art 96(3)(a) AP I; see further Section 2.4.

134 cf ICRC, *Draft Additional Protocols to the Geneva Conventions of August 12, 1949: Commentary* (ICRC 1973) 50; Y Sandoz, C Swinarski and B Zimmermann (eds), *Commentary on the Additional Protocols of 8 June 1977 to the Geneva Conventions of 12 August 1949* (ICRC 1987) 508 [1662] (hereafter Sandoz et al, *APs Commentary*).

135 See further Section 2.2.2.4.

136 Compare with the text to notes 79–84 in this chapter.

137 See Sandoz et al, *APs Commentary* (n 134) 513 [1672]; *ICRC CIHL Study* (n 48) vol I, 15.

138 Ipsen (n 50) 86.

139 See Section 3.3.

140 For specific examples of practice, see, eg, N Boldt, 'Outsourcing War: Private Military Companies and International Humanitarian Law' (2005) 47 GYIL 502, 527; Cameron and Chetail (n 132) 409.

141 *Official Records* (n 92) vol XV, CDDH/236/Rev.1, 403 [92].

person to be a prisoner of war pursuant to Article 4 of the Third Convention'.[142] This text thus confirms that the Protocol's aim was to expand, not limit access to POW and combatant status.[143] Therefore, the effect of the provision is that no one who qualifies as a combatant under GC III may be denied status under AP I.[144] Accordingly, even if the interconnection between the internal non-state actor and the external intervening power fell below the level of the former being 'under a command responsible' to the latter, members of the non-state group could still qualify for combatant status provided that the criteria under GC III were met.[145]

7.4 Evaluation

The idea that members of non-state armed groups do not normally benefit from combatant status is part of the conventional wisdom among IHL scholars and practitioners. Yet, the legal position of non-state actors involved in internationalized armed conflicts is fundamentally different from that of their counterparts in traditional civil wars.

Chapter 5 and Chapter 6 explored this difference and demonstrated, on the basis of a historical analysis and through the consideration of the normative underpinnings of the regulation of combatancy, that fighters belonging to these formations are in principle eligible for combatant status.

The present chapter then examined the specific conditions for this status as prescribed by the two applicable legal frameworks established by GC III and AP I, respectively. On the basis of that examination, the chapter has demonstrated that it is not only theoretically plausible, but also practically feasible for fighters engaged in internationalized armed conflicts to actually qualify for combatant status.

This chapter thus rounds off Part II of this book dedicated to the regulation of combatancy in internationalized armed conflicts. Part III turns to the law of belligerent occupation, which is considered to be the other principal area of IHL whose applicability is contingent on the legal qualification of the conflict at hand.

142 Art 44(6) AP I.

143 cf Bothe et al, *New Rules* (n 35) 256.

144 Olson (n 119) 919 [24].

145 See Section 7.2.

PART III

BELLIGERENT OCCUPATION

8

Historical Development

8.1 Introduction

Although belligerent occupation is sometimes perceived as a notion associated with the large-scale wars of the past, the recent conflicts in ex-Yugoslavia, Iraq, the Democratic Republic of the Congo (DRC), Eritrea and Ethiopia, or Georgia prove that to think that it is becoming obsolete would be 'no more than utopian dreaming'.[1] At the same time, belligerent occupation is a concept firmly rooted in the law of international armed conflict (IAC), so much so that the orthodox writing uses it as a prime example of a notion that cannot be transplanted into non-international armed conflicts (NIACs).[2]

The reasoning behind the conventional position is certainly understandable. The triangular relationship at the heart of the law of belligerent occupation between the occupying power, the ousted power, and the occupied population cannot be easily transposed into the reality of a conflict occurring in the territory of a single state.[3] While 'classic' IACs reflect a duality of states, their territories and populations, it is more problematic to associate these attributes with conflict parties if at least one of them is a non-state actor. Yet this is precisely how an internationalized armed conflict begins: as an armed contestation between a state and a non-state armed group. Does that mean that the law of belligerent occupation must remain inapplicable to these conflicts?

[1] Y Dinstein, *The International Law of Belligerent Occupation* (CUP 2009) xiii.

[2] See, eg, R Baxter, 'Comments' in PD Trooboff (ed), *Law and Responsibility in Warfare: The Vietnam Experience* (University of North Carolina Press 1975) 65; M Sassòli, 'The Legal Qualification of the Conflicts in the Former Yugoslavia: Double Standards or New Horizons for International Humanitarian Law?' in S Yee and W Tieya (eds), *International Law in the Post-Cold War World: Essays in Memory of Li Haopei* (Routledge 2001) 312; R Kolb and R Hyde, *An Introduction to the International Law of Armed Conflicts* (Hart 2008) 69; E Crawford, *The Treatment of Combatants and Insurgents Under the Law of Armed Conflict* (OUP 2010) 47; Y Sandoz, 'Land Warfare', 117, and P Spoerri, 'The Law of Occupation', 185, both in A Clapham and P Gaeta (eds), *The Oxford Handbook of International Law in Armed Conflict* (OUP 2014); M Sassòli, 'The Concept and the Beginning of Occupation' in A Clapham, P Gaeta, and M Sassòli (eds), *The 1949 Geneva Conventions: A Commentary* (OUP 2015) 1415 [57]; E Crawford and A Pert, *International Humanitarian Law* (CUP 2015) 159.

[3] S Sivakumaran, *The Law of Non-International Armed Conflict* (OUP 2012) 529.

Chapter 8, Chapter 9, and Chapter 10 of this book advance a negative, yet nuanced, answer to this question. Together, they stand for the proposition that the law of occupation should be seen as *in principle* applicable to the situations of internationalized armed conflict, with the actual extent of applicability depending on the specific circumstances of a particular conflict. Specifically, this chapter examines the historical development of the law of belligerent occupation in order to identify trends relevant to the applicability of this body of law to internationalized armed conflicts. Chapter 9 and Chapter 10 then consider respectively the theoretical and practical ramifications of extending the law of belligerent occupation to such conflicts.

The overall argument presented in this part runs against the conventional wisdom that occupation as a notion of the law of IAC is not transferrable into single-territory conflicts. However, it does benefit from prior scholarship, in which positions partially supportive of the present argument have been put forward. In particular, certain writers have considered (some of) the law of occupation as applicable to NIACs.[4] Moreover, some have posited that it would apply to several of the conflicts designated as internationalized in this book.[5] The present part considers these academic positions and, where appropriate, develops the analysis they contain. The overall aim of this and the following two chapters can thus be described as constructing a comprehensive, practice-informed, and workable pro-applicability case covering all types of internationalized armed conflict.

This chapter begins to build that case by examining the history of the law of belligerent occupation from the perspective of the regulation of internationalized armed conflicts. It explores two main questions. Firstly, to what extent can the evolution of the law support the notion of application of the concept of belligerent occupation to non-state actors? Secondly, how has the underlying aim of the law of belligerent occupation evolved with the ongoing emancipation of the individual on the international plane? Overall, it uncovers the historical reasons that support an extensive view of the applicability of this body of law to modern internationalized armed conflicts.

[4] See, eg, A Roberts, 'What Is a Military Occupation?' (1984) 55 BYBIL 249, 296–97; L Zegveld, *The Accountability of Armed Opposition Groups in International Law* (CUP 2002) 71; Sivakumaran (n 3) 529–32; D Fleck, 'The Law of Non-International Armed Conflicts' in D Fleck (ed), *The Handbook of International Humanitarian Law* (3rd edn, OUP 2013) 605.

[5] See, eg, Roberts (n 4) 292–93 (stating that '[o]ne may hazard the opinion' that the law of occupation should apply to situations, in which a liberation movement occupies a state's territory); Dinstein (n 1) 34 (stating that the law of belligerent occupation would apply to wars of national liberation and conflicts in which the insurgents obtain recognition of belligerency from the government); T Ferraro, 'Determining the Beginning and End of an Occupation under International Humanitarian Law' (2012) 94 IRRC 133, 158–60 (arguing that the law of occupation applies to situations of 'occupation by proxy', ie, occupations carried out by forces under the control of an outside state).

8.2 Before 1949

8.2.1 Origins of the law of occupation

Despite its breadth, the law of occupation is a relatively novel addition to the regulation of armed conflicts. Under the traditional Westphalian paradigm of international law,[6] war between states was a legitimate manifestation of state sovereignty, and for some writers even 'a right inherent in sovereignty itself'.[7] According to Clausewitz, war could be waged for one of two principal aims. Firstly, the objective could be to completely overthrow the enemy, forcing it to accept any terms desired by the victorious power. Secondly, it could be 'merely' to subjugate parts of its territory with the goal of their eventual annexation.[8] In both of these kinds of war it was understood that enemy territory under control of the victorious side at the end of the war was fair game for conquest.[9] In some instances this could mean the total obliteration of a previously existing state, such as during the 1795 Third Partition of Poland, which saw the forcible split of the Polish-Lithuanian Commonwealth among Prussia, Austria, and Russia.[10] It bears reminding that in line with the Rousseau doctrine, war was in that period seen as a relationship between states, with little heed given to the needs or the protection of their inhabitants.[11] As King William of Prussia famously stated during the Prussian invasion of France in 1870: 'I conduct war with the French soldiers, not with the French citizens'.[12] The combination of this disregard for the plight of individuals with the conception of conquest as legitimate spoils of war meant that there was little need for the regulation of the conduct of the foreign armies in enemy territory before annexation could be effectuated.

The origins of the legal regulation, which would apply before the final decision on annexation but after the outside army acquired control over enemy territory, can be traced back to Vattel's writings. Although he accepted conquest as a valid precondition for the transfer of legal title, he considered it desirable to accord protection to the property of the private individuals.[13] He thus proposed that the conqueror would only lawfully seize the public possessions, while individuals would be allowed to keep their private property.[14] This solution laid the groundwork for the future law

[6] See also Section 1.2.1.2 and particularly fns 56–57 (referring to the debate concerning the role of the Peace of Westphalia in the transition towards modern international law).

[7] AS Hershey, *The Essentials of International Public Law* (Macmillan 1912) 349.

[8] C von Clausewitz, *On War* (1832, M Howard and P Paret ed and tr, Princeton University Press 1976) 7 (hereafter Clausewitz, *On War*).

[9] See, eg, E de Vattel, *The Law of Nations or the Principles of Natural Law* (J Chitty tr, 1758), book III, ch XIII, §§195, 197; R Phillimore, *Commentaries upon International Law* (T&JW Johnson 1854) vol I, 233 [*300]; ibid (1857) vol III, 468 [*682].

[10] N Davies, *God's Playground: A History of Poland* (2nd edn, OUP 2005) vol 1 ('The Origins to 1795') 386–411.

[11] J-J Rousseau, *The Social Contract* (1762, GDH Cole tr, Cosimo 2008) 19–20; see further Section 5.2.2.

[12] EL Feilchenfeld, *The International Economic Law of Belligerent Occupation* (Carnegie Endowment for International Peace 1942) 12 fn 2.

[13] de Vattel (n 9), book III, ch XIII, §200.

[14] ibid.

of occupation as it made it clear that even in armed conquest, the victorious army remained under the constraints of the law. Vattel's proposition was motivated equally by humanitarian considerations and by a desire to provide for legal certainty in extremely volatile times.[15] Yet it was still believed that the sovereignty of the defeated state was transferred to the victor and that the victor was not obliged to conserve the institutions or the laws of the territory under its control.[16]

A breakthrough in the conceptualization of occupation came a century later with the publication of the 1844 treatise written by the German lawyer August Wilhelm Heffter.[17] Heffter was the first author to describe occupation as an interim phase which brought about the temporary suspension of the exercise—but not the transfer—of the sovereignty of the occupied state.[18] On this understanding, the purpose of legal regulation during occupation was not just to govern the conduct of the foreign hostile army towards the inhabitants of the occupied territory. Unlike the previous writers, Heffter's conception of occupation was novel in that it took into consideration also the interests of the ousted sovereign. The victorious side was thus obliged—until the final resolution of the matter could be made either in the form of a peace treaty, a complete defeat (*debellatio*), or a withdrawal by the occupant—to conserve the laws, institutions, and property of the ousted sovereign.[19] Nevertheless, it is a testament to his period that even Heffter still considered that the occupying state held a legitimate expectation that it would acquire sovereignty after a successful military campaign.[20]

There is no doubt that this conception of the law of occupation was predicated on the premise that the warring parties would be states and states only. The notion of sovereignty, whose protection lay at the heart of the novel conception of occupation propounded by Heffter, was inextricably linked with the existence of states. This also reflected the reality of the nineteenth century. The concept of internationalized armed conflict was not to appear for another hundred years.[21] And yet, one conceivable type of conflict meeting the criteria of an internationalized conflict as proposed in this book would have been a civil war featuring the recognition of belligerency of the non-state party.[22] Remarkably, it was precisely in the context of such a conflict that the next major development of the law of occupation took place.

[15] See R Giladi, 'A Different Sense of Humanity: Occupation in Francis Lieber's Code' (2012) 94 IRRC 81, 85.

[16] See, eg, GF von Martens, *Précis du Droit des Gens Moderne de l'Europe* (JC Dieterich 1789) 348–49.

[17] AW Heffter, *Das Europäische Völkerrecht der Gegenwart* (1st edn, Schroeder 1844).

[18] See E Benvenisti, *The International Law of Occupation* (2nd edn, OUP 2012) 27–28.

[19] Heffter (n 17) 220–21; see also Benvenisti (n 18) 27–28 and Y Arai-Takahashi, 'Preoccupied with Occupation: Critical Examinations of the Historical Development of the Law of Occupation' (2012) 94 IRRC 51, 56–57.

[20] Heffter (n 17) 308; see also Benvenisti (n 18) 28.

[21] See Section 1.3.1.

[22] See Section 2.5.1.

8.2.2 Lieber Code: a non-state-permissive conception

Francis Lieber, the principal author of the 1863 Lieber Code, was a veteran of the Napoleonic Wars and a professor at the Columbia College in New York.[23] The Code that bears his name was not solicited by the US government; it was Lieber in his private capacity who proposed its preparation, which was accepted by President Lincoln.[24] The final text, approved by the president, was promulgated in General Orders No. 100 under the title 'Instructions for the Government of Armies of the United States in the Field'.[25] As a compilation of legal norms that the US government considered to apply in times of war, it constituted an important statement of *opinio juris* in this area, with a significant part devoted to the law of occupation.[26] It has even been described as 'the first successful attempt to codify a branch of international law'.[27]

Some of the terminology used in the Code as well as the fact of its adoption during a civil war may nevertheless raise doubts as to the applicability of its provisions on occupation as a matter of international law. First, with respect to the terminology, the Code stipulated in its first article that an occupation of a territorial unit results in the application of 'Martial Law' to that territory,[28] a term nowadays normally considered as a concept of domestic law.[29] However, Rotem Giladi correctly pointed out that 'Martial Law' was simply 'Lieber's code word for the occupant's military authority'.[30] This is consistent with the contextual and historical interpretation of this term. The following articles in the Code make it clear that 'Martial Law' entailed the conservation of civil and penal law in force in the occupied territories insofar as permitted by military necessity[31] and that it was seen as applicable in hostile countries.[32] Similarly, the contemporary American case law used 'Martial Law' as a broader concept encompassing all 'kinds of military jurisdiction', including, in particular, that 'exercised in time of foreign war without the boundaries of the United States, or in time of rebellion and civil war within states or districts occupied by rebels treated as belligerents'.[33] It is therefore submitted that Lieber's term 'Martial Law' should simply be understood as the period reference to the law of belligerent occupation;[34] this interpretation has recently been further confirmed by the 2016

[23] R Baxter, 'The First Modern Codification of the Law of War: Francis Lieber and General Orders No. 100' (1963) 3 IRRC 171, 172.

[24] ibid 182.

[25] Instructions for the Government of Armies of the United States in the Field, prepared by Francis Lieber, General Orders No 100 (24 April 1863) (hereafter Lieber Code).

[26] cf DA Graber, *The Development of the Law of Belligerent Occupation, 1863–1914: A Historical Survey* (Columbia University Press 1949) 15 (noting that roughly one third of the articles of the Lieber Code concerned occupation).

[27] JB Scott, *The Hague Peace Conferences of 1899 and 1907* (Johns Hopkins Press 1909) 525.

[28] Lieber Code (n 25), Art 1.

[29] See, eg, J Wallace and SE Wild, *Webster's New World Law Dictionary* (Houghton Mifflin Harcourt 2010) 176 ('martial law n. Civil law exerted over citizens by military, generally in times of war or emergency.'); see also *United States v Minori Yasui*, 48 F.Supp. 40, 49 (D. Ore. 1942).

[30] Giladi (n 15) 89.

[31] Lieber Code (n 25), Arts 3 and 6.

[32] Lieber Code (n 25), Arts 1, 3, and 6.

[33] *Ex parte Milligan* (1866) 71 US 2, 141–42 (US Supreme Court).

[34] FB Freidel, *Francis Lieber: Nineteenth-century Liberal* (Louisiana State University Press 1947) 550; Giladi (n 15) 89.

US Department of Defense Law of War Manual, which had expressly equated the two notions.[35]

Second, although it was admittedly adopted during the American Civil War, the Code should properly be understood as applicable to both main types of conflict. Paradoxically, Lieber's original aim was to regulate inter-state conflict; in his own words, he 'disrelished'[36] the addition of the last section which was the only one expressly covering internal conflict.[37] That the Code would be workable in an international conflict was confirmed a few years later when both France and Prussia applied it in their mutual war of 1870–71.[38] Nevertheless, the section was maintained in the promulgated text which, moreover, expressly foresaw that the law of occupation could also be applied to the territory controlled by the rebel forces.[39] The Lieber Code is thus a landmark legal instrument which, in spite of its principal inter-state orientation, allowed for the application of the law of belligerent occupation also to non-state actors.[40] The United States' practice during the Civil War reflected this interpretation and it thus provides a very instructive source for the potential application of the law of occupation to internationalized armed conflicts.[41]

The Lieber Code entailed a non-formalistic conception of occupation.[42] The application of occupation law was not contingent on proclamations or other formal requirements being met by the occupation army; its presence in the occupied territory was sufficient.[43] The Code confirmed that the local law continued to apply[44] but it did not provide yet for a duty to restore and maintain public order and safety.[45] The occupant's authority was limited not by the authority of the displaced government, but only by the war aims of the occupant as operationalized by the concept of military necessity.[46] This conception of occupation, detached from the fulfilment of formal conditions and from the status of the ousted power, could be applied to both main types of armed conflict with relative ease.

Nevertheless, the non-state-permissive conception of the law of occupation was destined to remain an aberration for a long time. Although occupation law and the Lieber Code were applied in a number of conflicts after the end of American Civil War, these were exclusively inter-state conflicts like the Franco-Prussian War (1870–71) or the Spanish-American War (1898).[47]

[35] US DoD, *Law of War Manual* (December 2016) 755 [11.1.1.1] ('The conduct of military occupation has also been characterized as an exercise of "military government" or "*martial law.*" ') (footnotes omitted, emphasis added). Notably, the Manual cited Article 1 of the Lieber Code to support this proposition: see ibid, 756 fn 6.

[36] Baxter (n 23) 184.

[37] Lieber Code (n 25), section x ('Insurrection—Civil War—Rebellion'). [38] Scott (n 27) 526.

[39] Lieber Code (n 25), Art 153.

[40] cf Giladi (n 15) 89; Y Arai-Takahashi, 'Law-Making and the Judicial Guarantees in Occupied Territories' in Clapham et al (n 2) 1450 [95].

[41] See Section 10.3.2.2 and Section 10.3.3.2.

[42] See also M Zwanenburg, 'The Law of Occupation Revisited: The Beginning of an Occupation' (2007) 10 YIHL 99, 101 (describing the Lieber Code as promulgating a 'factual character of the concept of occupation').

[43] Lieber Code (n 25), Art 1. [44] Lieber Code (n 25), Art 6. [45] Giladi (n 15) 105.

[46] ibid 106. [47] Arai-Takahashi (n 19) 76–77.

8.2.3 Post-Lieber Code codifications: return to the state-centric model

The non-binding though influential texts adopted in the late nineteenth century confirmed this trend. The first of them was the 1874 Brussels Declaration.[48] On the one hand, it filled the gap left open by the Lieber Code by codifying the duty of the occupant to restore and maintain public order and safety.[49] This way, the regulation of occupation came to reflect the modern conception of occupation as a *transition* of public power from the legitimate ousted power to the occupant, as opposed to the Lieber Code's understanding of occupation as an *original* source of the occupant's power.[50] On the other hand, unlike the Lieber Code, the Declaration was designed to regulate inter-state relations only.[51] Its drafting history leaves no doubt that the representatives of 15 European powers were preparing for possible wars among themselves and there is no indication that—as contrasted to the provisions on combatants[52]—the regulation of occupation was contemplated to apply either to occupation by non-state actors or to the occupation of territories held by such entities.[53]

The 1880 Oxford Manual on the Laws of War on Land,[54] the second of these texts, was even clearer in its terms. While the text of the Brussels Declaration had spoken merely of '[the] occupied territory',[55] 'the army of occupation',[56] and 'the hostile Power',[57] which would perhaps still have allowed for a strictly linguistic interpretation permitting the extension of the application of the relevant norms to non-state actors, the Oxford Manual revealed a much more unambiguously state-centric approach also from a purely textual perspective. Accordingly, the corresponding provisions in the Manual already referred respectively to the '[t]erritory [of] the *State* to which it belongs',[58] 'the invading *State*',[59] and 'the enemy *State*'.[60]

[48] Brussels Declaration Concerning the Laws and Customs of War (27 August 1874), reproduced in D Schindler and J Toman (eds), *The Laws of Armed Conflicts* (3rd edn, Martinus Nijhoff 1988) 27–34 (hereafter Brussels Declaration). See Section 5.2.3 for a more detailed discussion of the historical background of this document.

[49] Brussels Declaration (n 48) Arts 2–3:

> Article 2. The authority of the legitimate Power being suspended and having in fact passed into the hands of the occupants, the latter shall take all the measures in his power to restore and ensure, as far as possible, public order and safety.
>
> Article 3. With this object he shall maintain the laws which were in force in the country in time of peace, and shall not modify, suspend or replace them unless necessary.

[50] cf Giladi (n 15) 105.

[51] See Conférence intergouvernementale, *Actes de la conférence de Bruxelles de 1874* (Librairie des publications législatives 1874) 4 (hereafter *Actes de la conférence de Bruxelles*).

[52] See Section 5.2.3. [53] See generally *Actes de la conférence de Bruxelles* (n 51).

[54] The Laws of War on Land, Manual (adopted by the Institute of International Law at Oxford, 9 September 1880), reproduced in Schindler and Toman (n 48) 35–48 (hereafter Oxford Manual).

[55] Brussels Declaration (n 48) Arts 36, 37, and 41. [56] ibid, Arts 5 and 6.

[57] ibid, Art 37. [58] Oxford Manual (n 54) Art 41 (emphasis added).

[59] ibid, Art 41 (emphasis added).

[60] ibid, chapeau to section II.C.a (emphasis added), Art 52 (emphasis added), chapeau to section II.C.b (emphasis added).

The Hague Regulations changed little in this regard. Admittedly, several of their provisions spoke of 'belligerent parties', which would again seemingly permit an extensive interpretation similar to that suggested earlier with respect to the Brussels Declaration.[61] However, Article 2 of Hague Convention IV, to which the Regulations were appended, stated clearly that the Regulations were to apply only between 'Contracting powers' and only if all the belligerents were parties to the Convention.[62] The Convention, like other Hague Conventions, was only open for ratification to states,[63] and thus it cannot be doubted that references to 'belligerent parties' were supposed to relate to states only.

Therefore, for the present purposes, the Hague Regulations served primarily to confirm that the old, conquest-based view of occupation had been definitively abandoned.[64] As summarized by a US Court of Appeals, '[s]ince the adoption of these Regulations it is generally agreed that the occupant does not succeed to sovereignty over the occupied territory, but has only limited administrative authority'.[65] The Regulations implemented this understanding by combining two 'apparently incongruous'[66] provisions of the Brussels Declaration[67] in one, namely Article 43 of the Hague Regulations. The delegates of the First Peace Conference at The Hague had thus laid down the 'cornerstone'[68] or the 'gist'[69] of the modern law of occupation:

> The authority of the legitimate power having in fact passed into the hands of the occupant, the latter shall take all the measures in his power to restore, and ensure, as far as possible, public order and [civil life],[70] while respecting, unless absolutely prevented, the laws in force in the country.[71]

[61] See, eg, Regulations Respecting the Laws and Customs of War on Land, Annex to Hague Convention (IV) respecting the Laws and Customs of War on Land (signed 18 October 1907, entered into force 26 January 1910) 205 CTS 277, Arts 3 and 36 (hereafter Hague Regulations). But see, eg, ibid, Arts 37 and 39 (referring instead to 'belligerent States' and 'Contracting Parties', respectively). It can be concluded that the Regulations used these terms interchangeably as synonyms.

[62] Hague Convention (IV) respecting the Laws and Customs of War on Land (signed 18 October 1907, entered into force 26 January 1910) 205 CTS 277, Art 2.

[63] cf ibid, preamble (listing the High Contracting Parties) and Art 5 (detailing the ratification procedure).

[64] See text to notes 9–16 in this chapter.

[65] *Netherlands v Federal Reserve Bank of New York et al*, 201 F.2d 455, 461 (2d Cir. 1953); see also *South West Africa cases (Ethiopia v South Africa; Liberia v South Africa)* (Judgment) [1966] ICJ Rep 6, 418 (diss op Jessup) ('It is a commonplace that international law does not recognize military conquest as a source of title').

[66] Arai-Takahashi (n 19) 60.

[67] Brussels Declaration (n 48) Arts 2–3. See note 49 in this chapter and the accompanying text.

[68] E Benvenisti, *The International Law of Occupation* (1st edn, Princeton University Press 1993) 9.

[69] Benvenisti (n 18) 68.

[70] The phrase used in the authoritative French text was 'l'ordre et *la vie publics*' (emphasis added). This work uses the English translation, which is generally accepted in the literature, and as opposed to the first English translation, which had used the words 'public order and *safety*' (emphasis added). See, eg, EH Schwenk, 'Legislative Power of the Military Occupant under Article 43, Hague Regulations' (1945) 54 Yale Law Journal 393, 393 fn 1; MS McDougal and FP Feliciano, *Law and Minimum World Public Order: The Legal Regulation of International Coercion* (Yale University Press 1961) 746–47; M Sassòli, 'Legislation and Maintenance of Public Order and Civil Life by Occupying Powers' (2005) 16 EJIL 661, 663–64; Benvenisti (n 18) 68 fn 1.

[71] Art 43 Hague Regulations (n 61).

This provision specifies two main duties of the occupying power: first, a positive obligation to restore and ensure public order and civil life in the occupied territory as far as possible, and, second, a negative obligation to respect the laws in force except where absolutely prevented.[72] Both were written from the perspective of the interests of the occupying state and the occupied state, balancing the security interests of the former with the stability interests of the latter.

This is in line with the understanding of the Hague Regulations as an instrument concerned solely with inter-state warfare.[73] The aim of the protection provided for in times of belligerent occupation was therefore also state-centric, focusing mainly on the preservation of the European public order rather than on the humanization of warfare per se.[74] Unlike the instrument considered in the next section, the Hague Regulations were not directly concerned with the rights of individuals.[75]

8.3 After 1949

8.3.1 Geneva Convention IV: individualization of the law of occupation

The 1949 Fourth Geneva Convention brought about the latest substantial change in the regulation of belligerent occupation. In that regard, Eyal Benvenisti described two of the major achievements of the Convention as the shift of emphasis from the political interests of the ousted regime to the protection of the occupied population; and the adoption of what is essentially a 'bill of rights' for the population in the enemy's hands.[76] It is submitted that both changes are in reality just different aspects of a single yet profound paradigm shift in international law dating back to the end of the Second World War. This has been described as the individualization or humanization of international law; in other words, the gradual rise of the prominence attributed to the individual *qua* human being in international law, including as a bearer of legal rights and obligations.[77]

[72] cf Dinstein (n 1) 90–91. [73] See, eg, Scott (n 27) 539. [74] Giladi (n 15) 83.

[75] cf, eg, Switzerland, *Final Record of the Diplomatic Conference of Geneva of 1949* (Federal Political Department 1949) vol II A, 675 (hereafter *Final Record*) ('Mr. Pilloud ([ICRC]) pointed out that the Hague Convention was intended to regulate relations between States, whereas [GC IV] was concerned with the rights of individuals').

[76] Benvenisti (n 18) 72–73.

[77] See, eg, A-M Slaughter, 'Rogue Regimes and the Individualization of International Law' (2001–2002) 36 New England Law Review 815, 815–23; T Meron, *The Humanization of International Law* (Martinus Nijhoff 2006); AAC Trindade, 'The Humanization of Consular Law: The Impact of Advisory Opinion No. 16 (1999) of the Inter-American Court of Human Rights on International Case-law and Practice' (2007) 6 Chinese JIL 1, 1–3; S Murphy, 'Evolving Geneva Convention Paradigms in the "War on Terrorism": Applying the Core Rules to the Release of Persons Deemed "Unprivileged Combatants"' (2007) 75 George Washington Law Review 1105, 1140–48; M Benzing, 'Sovereignty and the Responsibility to Protect in International Criminal law' in D König et al (eds), *International Law Today: New Challenges and the Need for Reform?* (Springer 2008) 44; G Simpson, 'Punishing Human Rights Violators' in C Gearty and C Douzinas (eds), *The Cambridge Companion to Human Rights Law* (CUP 2012) 125; P Gaeta, 'Geneva Conventions and International Criminal Law' in Clapham et al (n 2) 740 [6]–[7]; but see L Arimatsu, 'Territory, Boundaries and the Law of Armed Conflict' (2009) 12 YIHL 157, 161 (suggesting that 'the "humanization of war through law" claim is, perhaps, overstated') (internal quotation marks kept).

It is thus symptomatic that the above-mentioned 'bill of rights' in GC IV[78] begins with Article 47, which guarantees conventional rights to the protected persons against any institutional, administrative, or territorial changes introduced by the occupying power.[79] Pictet's commentary described it as a provision of 'essentially humanitarian character' with the object 'to safeguard human beings and *not to protect the political institutions and government machinery* of the State as such'.[80] Although the applicability provisions of GC IV leave no doubt that an IAC must exist in order for the rules on occupation to operate,[81] this novel humanitarian individual-centric approach acquires fundamental importance in the consideration of the extent to which the rules in the Convention may be viewed as adaptable to the reality of internationalized conflict.[82]

The Convention also amplified and clarified[83] the scope of the negative obligation in Article 43 of the Hague Regulations, originally formulated as the duty to respect, 'unless absolutely prevented, the laws in force in the country'.[84] In contrast to the Hague Regulations, which contained nothing more on when exactly the occupier could consider itself as 'absolutely prevented' from respecting these laws, Article 64 GC IV authoritatively defined the situations in which the occupying power was permitted to depart from the laws in force in the occupied territory. The occupying power could newly repeal or suspend the existing laws if and only if they constituted a threat to its security or an obstacle to the application of the Convention.[85] Conversely, it could adopt new laws if these were essential to safeguard its security, to fulfil its conventional obligations, or to maintain the orderly government of the territory.[86]

The existence of a duty[87] to modify laws incompatible with the Convention and to adopt new ones in order to procure its proper application further underlines the individualized conception of the law of occupation propounded by the Convention as opposed to the state-centric conception protective of institutions and elites espoused by the Hague Regulations.[88] Its enactment should be seen as the drafters' reaction to the atrocious discriminatory laws adopted by the Nazi Germany and the legitimization of their subsequent repeal by the Allied occupying powers in 1945.[89] Such laws would run counter to Article 27(3) GC IV, which prescribes that all protected persons are to receive the same standard of treatment, without any discrimination based on prohibited criteria such as race, religion, or political opinion.[90]

78 Arts 47–78 GC IV. 79 Art 47 GC IV.

80 JS Pictet (ed) *Geneva Convention IV relative to the Protection of Civilian Persons in Time of War: Commentary* (ICRC 1958) 273–4 (hereafter Pictet, *GC IV Commentary*) (emphasis added).

81 See Section 1.2.2.1. 82 See Chapter 9 and Chapter 10.

83 cf JAC Gutteridge, 'The Geneva Conventions of 1949' (1949) 26 BYBIL 294, 324; RT Yingling and RW Ginnane, 'The Geneva Conventions of 1949' (1952) 46 AJIL 393, 422.

84 Art 43 Hague Regulations (n 61). 85 Art 64(1) GC IV. 86 Art 64(2) GC IV.

87 Dinstein (n 1) 113.

88 See also Benvenisti (n 18) 203 fn 19 ('the primary objective and overriding purpose of the Civilian Convention is the protection of civilians—not the preservation, intact and unchanged, of the institutions, bases of power, and laws of the ousted sovereign.').

89 *Final Record* (n 75) vol II A, 670 (United States); ibid 771 (India); ibid 833 (summarizing the view of the Third Committee that laws that 'constitute an obstacle to the application of the Convention' would include those that 'provid[e] for racial discrimination').

90 See also Pictet, *GC IV Commentary* (n 80) 207.

The occupying power would now, in fact, have a *duty* to repeal them under the new individual-centric framework introduced by the Geneva Convention.[91]

8.3.2 Additional Protocol I: occupation and national liberation movements

The 1977 Additional Protocol I is most relevant for the present purposes due to its extension of the scope of the law of belligerent occupation to wars of national liberation. Its Article 1 (4) subjects armed conflicts in the exercise of the right of self-determination to the application of the Protocol and all four Geneva Conventions. This mechanism has been dealt with elsewhere in this book.[92] Suffice it to say here that the adoption of this provision allowed again, for the first time since the Lieber Code, for the express application of the law of occupation to non-state actors, specifically to the so-called national liberation movements.

The Protocol did not otherwise greatly amend the scope of occupation law applicable under GC IV, adding only 'a few details' to the overall legal regime.[93] Nonetheless, from the perspective of the present argument, an important addition was Article 75 AP I. This provision, entitled 'Fundamental Guarantees', is a veritable mini-convention of human rights applicable in armed conflicts[94] and generally accepted as reflective of customary law.[95] Its inclusion affirms the trend of individualization of IHL in general and, additionally, the applicability of this provision to situations of belligerent occupation[96] further confirms the interpretive approach proposed in this part of the book.

8.3.3 Post-Additional Protocols period: implementation issues

With the adoption of the Additional Protocols, the treaty-driven process of development of the law of belligerent occupation came to a halt. This area of law had emerged as a well-developed and consolidated body of rights and duties applicable during a situation of armed occupation. The key issue has become one of the application of the law.

[91] cf Dinstein (n 1) 113–14 (inferring this duty from the obligation to respect and ensure respect for the Convention stipulated in Common Art 1 read together with the proscription to invoke the provisions of internal law as justification for the failure to perform a treaty found in Art 27 VCLT).

[92] See Section 2.4.

[93] M Bothe, 'Occupation, Belligerent' in R Bernhardt (ed), *Encyclopedia of Public International Law* (Elsevier 1997) vol III, 764; see further Dinstein (n 1) 7 (listing the few examples in which Geneva provisions relevant to belligerent occupation were amended or abrogated by the Protocol).

[94] cf Y Sandoz, C Swinarski, and B Zimmermann (eds), *Commentary on the Additional Protocols of 8 June 1977 to the Geneva Conventions of 12 August 1949* (ICRC 1987) 865 [3007] (describing Art 75 AP I as 'a sort of "summary of the law"' and comparing it to Common Art 3, 'which was called "mini Convention"') (all internal quotation marks kept).

[95] See, eg, *Civilian Claims: Eritrea's Claims 15, 16, 23 & 27–32* (Partial Award of 17 December 2004) (2004) 26 RIAA 195 (EECC) 212 [30]; JM Henckaerts and L Doswald-Beck (eds), *Customary International Humanitarian Law* (CUP 2005) rules 87–105; H-P Gasser and K Dörmann, 'Protection of the Civilian Population' in Fleck (n 4), 232.

[96] See Art 72 AP I.

In the modern period, the law of occupation has very seldom been relied on and applied by the states involved in belligerent occupations.[97] Such reliance does, of course, entail in itself the acceptance of the label of an occupying power, which may result in a number of consequences viewed as undesirable by the state in question. Firstly, these states may have been reluctant to bring upon themselves the 'litany of onerous positive duties' entailed in modern occupation law.[98] Secondly, some of this reluctance may also be attributed to the perception that occupation is internationally 'unlawful'.[99] Given that many UN General Assembly resolutions, starting with Resolution 3314 on the Definition of Aggression,[100] have condemned foreign occupation as a moral equivalent or even a legal subspecies of aggression, states may fear that acknowledging the status of an occupant may bring upon them international opprobrium.[101] Thirdly, this reluctance was also an aspect of the Cold War reality. Despite the frequent interventions and proxy wars of the period, neither of the two main superpowers was willing to publicly describe these situations as amounting to belligerent occupation. Such a step could have invited a *tu quoque* response: in poignant shorthand, Nazil Bhuta wrote that 'if the Soviet Army in Budapest and Prague was an "army of occupation", so too was US military presence in Saigon and Seoul'.[102]

The law of occupation was expressly acknowledged as applicable directly by the occupying powers only twice in the post-1977 era: by Israel with respect to the Occupied Palestinian Territories (although only by its judicial branch and only with respect to the Hague Regulations,[103] but not Geneva Convention IV[104]) and by the US and the UK with respect to Iraq after 2003.[105] There is thus a dearth of direct statements made by the states from which specific *opinio juris* regarding the law of occupation could be discerned. This shortage further complicates the analysis

[97] Benvenisti (n 18) 202; N Bhuta, 'The Antinomies of Transformative Occupation ' (2005) 16 EJIL 721, 734–35; Zwanenburg (n 42) 130.

[98] Arai-Takahashi (n 19) 69.

[99] ICRC, 'Expert Meeting: Occupation and Other Forms of Administration of Foreign Territory - Report' (2012) <www.icrc.org/eng/assets/files/publications/icrc-002-4094.pdf>, at 4; see also *Armed Activities on the Territory of the Congo (Democratic Republic of the Congo v Uganda)* (Judgment) [2005] ICJ Rep 116 (sep op Kooijmans) [62]–[63].

[100] UNGA Res 3314 (XXIX) (Definition of Aggression) (14 December 1974), Art 3(a) (qualifying as aggression, inter alia, 'any military occupation, however temporary' that results from an invasion or attack on the territory of another state).

[101] See, eg, UNGA Res S-9/2 (Declaration on Namibia) (3 May 1978) [12]; UNGA Res ES-9/1 (The Situation in the Occupied Arab Territories) (5 February 1982) [2]; UNGA Res 37/123 (The Situation in the Middle East) (16 December 1982) [2]; UNGA Res 43/26 (Question of Namibia) (17 November 1988) [4].

[102] Bhuta (n 97) 734.

[103] *Affo v Commander Israel Defence Force* (1988) 83 ILR 121 (Israel, Supreme Court) 165–66 (holding that customary international law of belligerent occupation did apply to Gaza on account of Israel's effective control over that area).

[104] cf *Legal Consequences of the Construction of a Wall in the Occupied Palestinian Territory* (Advisory Opinion) [2004] ICJ Rep 136 [93] (noting that Israel's position is to deny the de jure applicability of GC IV).

[105] Letter from the Permanent Representatives of the United Kingdom of Great Britain and Northern Ireland and the United States of America to the United Nations Addressed to the President of the Security Council, UN Doc S/2003/538 (8 May 2003).

undertaken later in this book especially with respect to the application of the law of occupation to internationalized conflicts.[106]

8.4 Evaluation

The historical examination of the development of the law of occupation reveals two important observations. The first one is the strong grounding of this area of law in a state-centric paradigm. The vast majority of regulation adopted to govern the reality of occupied territories is based on a presumption of the existence of two established and comparable independent states interlocked in a war against each other. Nevertheless, several isolated developments going against this general trend can be identified. These include the 1863 Lieber Code and the 1977 Additional Protocol I, both of which foresaw the application of the rules on occupation also to territories controlled by non-state actors. Accordingly, these instruments provide for important exceptions that serve as vehicles for the extension of the applicability of the law of belligerent occupation to some types of internationalized conflicts.

The second observation relates to a trend, parallel with the general development of public international law, of individualization of the law of belligerent occupation. What was at first essentially a legal void dominated by the right of conquest gradually evolved into a complex sub-area of the law of armed conflict, concerned chiefly with states' interests, such as the preservation of their elites, institutions, and structures in time of war. The said trend of individualization then brought individuals' interests to the fore, putting persons before institutions and individuals before states. The existence of this trend also serves as a powerful argument in favour of the applicability of occupation law to novel situations brought about by internationalized conflicts.

[106] See Chapter 10.

9

Normative Underpinnings

9.1 Introduction

Chapter 8 discussed the historical development of the regulation of belligerent occupation with a special focus on the position of individuals and non-state actors. It identified historical trends that support an extensive application of the law of occupation in internationalized armed conflicts.

This chapter builds on that conclusion to analyse whether the extensive approach is compatible with the modern law of belligerent occupation. In this regard, it is necessary to examine the central normative assumptions underlying this area of the law. There is an 'inextricable tie' between belligerent occupation and standard inter-state wars.[1] However, in contrast to such situations, internationalized armed conflicts necessarily feature a non-state actor as one of the conflict parties.

Accordingly, this chapter considers three logically connected assumptions that seemingly militate against the applicability of the law of occupation to non-state actors. These could be summarized as claims that non-state actors lack the capacity to have rights and duties arising from the law of occupation (Section 9.2); that they may not become subjects of the law of occupation due to their sovereignty deficit (Section 9.3); and that in any event, they would be unable to comply with the rules of this body of law (Section 9.4).

9.2 Personality

Unlike the rules on combatancy, which ultimately relate to each putative combatant individually, the law of belligerent occupation is predicated on the existence of group-level entities with specific rights and obligations, both in the role of the removed and the occupying authorities. As the removed authority, this entity must have been in control of a distinct territory until the commencement of the occupation. As the occupier, it must have come to control such territory through the act of military occupation. In both of these potential positions, it must then have

[1] Y Dinstein, *The International Law of Belligerent Occupation* (CUP 2009) 31.

the capacity to have rights and obligations arising from the law of occupation. Of course, with respect to states as primary subjects of international law endowed *ex definitione* with territories and the means to control them, all of this is assumed without the need for further discussion.[2] However, such capacity—in other words, legal personality—is not automatically accepted with regard to non-state actors.

9.2.1 Traditional international law: states as the exclusive bearers of legal personality

The traditional view conferred legal personality on states only. In the classical formulation by Lassa Oppenheim, '[s]overeign States exclusively are International Persons—i.e. subjects of International Law'.[3] This conception of international legal personality was supported by other pre-Second World War writers,[4] including Heinrich Triepel[5] and Dionisio Anzilotti.[6] Although this position finds much less doctrinal support in modern scholarship, traces of its acceptance exist well into the second half of the twentieth century,[7] including in reference to armed groups.[8] On this view, non-state actors, including those acting in internationalized conflicts, would not be eligible to accrue rights and responsibilities directly from international law as they do not benefit from legal personality in that legal system.

9.2.2 Modern international law: pragmatic conception of legal personality

The traditional view can be countered both on the level of general international law and specifically with respect to international humanitarian law (IHL). From the perspective of general international law, the states-only conception of personality was based on the idea of an international community composed solely of states.[9] If that had ever been an accurate description of the reality, it is certainly not the case

[2] On the criteria for statehood, see further Montevideo Convention on the Rights and Duties of States (signed 26 December 1933, entered into force 26 December 1934) 165 LNTS 19, Art 1; J Crawford, *The Creation of States in International Law* (2nd edn, OUP 2006) 37–95.

[3] L Oppenheim, *International Law: A Treatise* (Longmans, Green & Co. 1905 & 1906) vol I, 99 (hereafter Oppenheim, 1st edn); L Oppenheim, *International Law: A Treatise* (2nd edn, Longmans, Green & Co. 1912) vol I, 107 (identical formulation).

[4] See further R Portmann, *Legal Personality in International Law* (CUP 2010) 42–64.

[5] See H Triepel, *Droit International et Droit Interne* (A de Lapradelle ed, A Pédone 1920) 20.

[6] See D Anzilotti, *Opere di Dionisio Anzilotti: Corso di diritto internazionale* (Cedam 1955) 112.

[7] See, eg, Case 26/62 *Van Gend en Loos v Nederlandse Administratie der Belastingen* [1963] ECR 1; for further discussion see, in particular, O Spiermann, 'The Other Side of the Story: An Unpopular Essay on the Making of the European Community Legal Order' (1999) 10 EJIL 763, 766; Portmann (n 4) 77–79.

[8] See, eg, Switzerland, *Official Records of the Diplomatic Conference on the Reaffirmation and Development of International Humanitarian Law Applicable in Armed Conflicts, Geneva (1974–1977)* (Federal Political Department 1978) (hereafter *Official Records*) vol VII, CDDH/SR.50/Annex, 104 (Zaire) (reproduced in full in text to note 21 in this chapter).

[9] Portmann (n 4) 43–44.

today. Even Oppenheim and the later editors of his work had to acknowledge the 'sui generis' role of the newly established League of Nations, admitting it possessed a degree of personality because it was endowed with specific rights and duties.[10] Several decades later, the International Court of Justice (ICJ) introduced a pragmatic needs-based conception of legal personality in the landmark advisory opinion on *Reparation for Injuries*.[11] Specifically, the Court held that the nature of an entity as a participant in a legal system is determined by the needs of the community.[12] As the requirements of international life evolved to embrace organized and institutionalized collective action, with the United Nations at its apex, the attribution of international legal personality to international organizations became indispensable.[13]

A similar argument may be advanced with respect to non-state armed groups. These actors are now a regular presence on the international plane as they play a prominent role in numerous armed conflicts.[14] The growing regulation of conduct during such conflicts and the legal protection of interests and rights implicated by these conflicts attest to the fact that the needs of the international community have evolved and now require for the non-state armed groups to be capable of holding rights and duties. Due to this development, the attribution of international legal personality to non-state actors has likewise become indispensable.[15]

9.2.3 International humanitarian law: non-state actors as bearers of limited legal personality

In addition to general international law considered in the previous section, IHL provides additional grounds for the rejection of the traditional view. It is generally accepted that IHL applies to and binds armed groups.[16] This is certainly true of

[10] L Oppenheim, *The League of Nations and its Problems: Three Lectures* (Longmans, Green & Co 1919) 22; L Oppenheim, *International Law: A Treatise* (RF Roxburgh ed, 3rd edn, Longmans, Green & Co 1920 & 1921) vol I, 125; L Oppenheim, *International Law: A Treatise* (A McNair ed, 4th edn, Longmans, Green & Co 1926 & 1928) vol I, 133 (hereafter Oppenheim, 4th edn).

[11] *Reparation for Injuries Suffered in the Service of the United Nations* (Advisory Opinion) [1949] ICJ Rep 174.

[12] ibid 178. [13] ibid.

[14] See, eg, M Allansson, E Melander, and L Themnér, 'Organized Violence, 1989–2016' (2017) 54 Journal of Peace Research 574.

[15] Accord S Sivakumaran, 'Binding Armed Opposition Groups' (2006) 55 ICLQ 369, 373–74; see also A Clapham, *Human Rights Obligations of Non-State Actors* (OUP 2006) 278; D Murray, 'How International Humanitarian Law Treaties Bind Non-State Armed Groups' (2014) 19 JCSL 1, 3.

[16] See, eg, L Zegveld, *The Accountability of Armed Opposition Groups in International Law* (CUP 2002) 9–12; L Moir, *The Law of Internal Armed Conflict* (CUP 2004) 52–58 and 96–99; J Pejić, 'Procedural Principles and Safeguards for Internment/Administrative Detention in Armed Conflict and Other Situations of Violence' (2005) 87 IRRC 375, 376; N Lubell, *Extraterritorial Use of Force Against Non-State Actors* (OUP 2010) 18; M Sassòli, 'Taking Armed Groups Seriously: Ways to Improve Compliance with International Humanitarian Law' (2010) 1 JIHLS 5, 10–14; D Tuck, 'Detention by Armed Groups: Overcoming Challenges to Humanitarian Action' (2011) 93 IRRC 759, 767; D Fleck, 'The Law of Non-International Armed Conflicts' in D Fleck (ed), *The Handbook of International Humanitarian Law* (3rd edn, OUP 2013) 598; S Sivakumaran, *The Law of Non-International Armed Conflict* (OUP 2012) 236–37; Murray (n 15) 1; L Hill-Cawthorne, *Detention in Non-International Armed Conflict* (OUP 2016) 100–01.

customary IHL in general.[17] In addition, core IHL treaties also ascribe rights and duties directly to non-state actors. For instance, Common Article 3 lists provisions which bind directly 'each Party to the [non-international] conflict', at least one of whom must logically be a non-state actor. The fact that these actors are bound by the rules of IHL confirms that they have the capacity to have rights and duties under this body of law: the latter is the prerequisite of the former.[18]

It is of interest that this pro-personality understanding was challenged at the 1974–77 Diplomatic Conference. Several developing states protested against the inclusion of the expression 'parties to the conflict' as the subject of the rights and duties imposed by AP II. Apart from the fears that this wording might affect the sovereignty of states parties or that its adoption would lead to the formal death of the instrument as it would never be applied,[19] it was also argued that this phrase would unacceptably place the entities involved in the conflict on an equal footing.[20] The delegate from Zaire was the most explicit in linking the issue with that of legal personality:

> As far as my delegation is concerned, *only a sovereign State can claim to have international legal personality* and, as such, it enjoys all the prerogatives of sovereignty, including that of entering into international agreements and conventions, that is to say, of becoming a party to them. Accordingly, dissident armed forces are primarily a group of rebels with no international legal personality. Their only legal status is that granted them under the domestic laws of their national State. *To claim otherwise is to place a sovereign State on the same footing as a rebel movement, and that would imply de facto recognition of the movement.*[21]

Although the initiative to delete all references to 'parties to the conflict' succeeded in Geneva as the drafters replaced them with somewhat inelegant formulations in passive voice,[22] it is submitted that this deletion did not in fact affect the legal status of non-state armed groups in international law.[23] Although the drafters could not agree

[17] Zegveld (n 16) 19; F Hampson, 'The Impact of the War on Terror on the Accountability of Armed Groups' in HM Hensel (ed), *The Law of Armed Conflict: Constraints on the Contemporary Use of Military Force* (Ashgate 2007) 158 fn 67; Sivakumaran (n 16) 239.

[18] But see *Prosecutor v Kallon and Kamara* (Decision on Challenge to Jurisdiction: Lomé Accord Amnesty) SCSL-2004-15-AR72(E) (13 March 2004) [45]–[47] (distinguishing the existence of international legal personality of armed groups from their capacity to be bound by Common Article 3, apparently denying the former but accepting the latter). For a convincing critique of this aspect of the decision, see A Cassese, 'The Special Court and International Law: The Decision Concerning the Lomé Agreement Amnesty' (2004) 2 JICJ 1130, 1132–35.

[19] See, eg, *Official Records* (n 8) vol VII, CDDH/SR.49, 61 [11] (Pakistan) (summarizing the reasons behind the proposed deletion of about a half of the draft Protocol); see also Section 6.3.1 (discussing this deletion in more detail).

[20] See, eg, *Official Records* (n 8) vol VIII, CDDH/I/SR.40, 426 [29] (Iraq); ibid, vol VII, CDDH/SR.49, 65 [33] (Saudi Arabia); ibid, CDDH/SR.56, 219–20 [124]–[29] (Zaire).

[21] ibid, vol VII, CDDH/SR.50, 104 (emphases added, paragraphs collapsed).

[22] Compare, eg, Art 29(1) of the draft AP II, reproduced in *Official Records* (n 8) vol I, part III, 41 ('Should the parties to the conflict undertake such displacements, they shall take all possible measures ...') with Art 17(1) AP II ('Should such displacements have to be carried out, all possible measures shall be taken ...').

[23] See also A Cassese, 'The Status of Rebels under the 1977 Geneva Protocol on Non-International Armed Conflicts' (1981) 30 ICLQ 416, 421–28 (hereafter Cassese, 'Status of Rebels'); Moir (n 16) 96; Sivakumaran (n 16) 236.

on a common denominator for the entities involved in a non-international armed conflict (NIAC), it is clear that the Protocol—like Common Article 3 which it 'develops and supplements'[24]—contains binding obligations and not mere exhortations.[25] Someone therefore must be the subject of these obligations.[26] Accordingly, the only entities that can plausibly be required to carry them out are those that are engaged in an armed struggle against one another.[27] Moreover, as discussed in Chapter 6, rules of IHL apply equally to all conflict parties irrespective of the type of the conflict in question.[28] We have, therefore, returned back to square one: non-state actors, like states, are bound by obligations contained in Additional Protocol II.[29] By implication, on the basis of the analysis outlined earlier, they must have a limited legal personality.

If it is accepted that non-state actors have a certain legal personality even in NIACs, which are marked by the states' deep-seated fear of any erosion of their sovereign status and the concomitant rights, then this should all the more so be the case in internationalized conflicts where any such concern is naturally much allayed. This is exemplified by the ease with which the doctrine,[30] case law,[31] and even some states[32] have ascribed legal personality to national liberation movements.[33] Similarly,

[24] Art 1(1) AP II.

[25] Cassese, 'Status of Rebels' (n 23) 424; but see, eg, *Official Records* (n 8) vol VII, CDDH/SR.52, 136 [81] (Holy See) (claiming that by deleting the term 'parties to the conflict' from the draft Protocol, the delegates had restricted it to a non-mandatory 'statement of good intentions').

[26] See H Kelsen, *On the Pure Theory of Law* (University of California Press 1978) 114–17 (arguing that a precondition for any legal obligation is the existence of one or more individuals bound by the obligation, ie, the 'subject(s) of the obligation').

[27] cf *Official Records* (n 8) vol VII, CDDH/SR.49, 76 (Belgium) (stating that since 'the entire philosophy' of Common Art 3 has been included in AP II, the obligations contained in the latter bind equally both parties to the conflict).

[28] See Section 6.2.2.

[29] This interpretation is generally accepted in the scholarship. See, eg, Y Sandoz, C Swinarski, and B Zimmermann (eds), *Commentary on the Additional Protocols of 8 June 1977 to the Geneva Conventions of 12 August 1949* (ICRC 1987) 1345 [4442] (hereafter Sandoz et al, *APs Commentary*); Zegveld (n 16) 10–11; Moir (n 16) 96–99; Sivakumaran (n 16) 236–37; Hill-Cawthorne (n 16) 100–01.

[30] See, eg, HA Wilson, *International Law and the Use of Force by National Liberation Movements* (Clarendon Press 1988) 130–36; P Malanczuk, *Akehurst's Modern Introduction to International Law* (7th edn, Routledge 2002) 104–05; J Crawford (ed), *Brownlie's Principles of Public International Law* (8th edn, OUP 2012) 123–24; K Mastorodimos, 'National Liberation Movements: Still a Valid Concept (with Special Reference to International Humanitarian Law)?' (2015) 17 Oregon Review of International Law 71, 88.

[31] See, eg, *Yasser Arafat and Kalaf Salah* (Judgment no 1981, 28 June 1985) (Italy, Court of Cassation) 884, reproduced in A Cassese, *International Law* (2nd edn, OUP 2005) 141.

[32] See, eg, *Official Records* (n 8) vol VIII, CDDH/I/SR.4, 28 [23] (Syria); ibid, CDDH/I/SR.6, 45 [12] (Senegal); Report of the Working Group on a Draft Declaration on the Right and Responsibility of Individuals, Groups and Organs of Society to Promote and Protect Universally Recognized Human Rights and Fundamental Freedoms, UN Doc E/CN.4/1986/40 (13 March 1986) 5 [28] (German Democratic Republic).

[33] This liberal understanding has also translated to the states' willingness to permit some national liberation movements to participate as observers alongside the states' representatives in international conferences and even permanent international institutions including the UN. See, eg, Final Act of the Diplomatic Conference on the Reaffirmation and Development of International Humanitarian Law Applicable in Armed Conflicts (10 June 1977) [3] (listing the liberation movements that had taken part in the Conference).

an armed group recognized as a belligerent is understood to acquire a limited international legal personality vis-à-vis the recognizing state.[34]

It can thus be concluded that non-state actors in internationalized armed conflicts are eligible for rights and duties under international law. As such, they may, from a conceptual perspective, take on the role of both the occupier and the occupied. However, a non-state actor, even one endowed with legal personality under international law, by definition lacks sovereignty, which is an attribute reserved exclusively to states.[35] It is therefore essential to consider the implications of the relationship between sovereignty and the law of occupation for internationalized armed conflicts.

9.3 Sovereignty

Occupation and sovereignty are often seen as closely related concepts. In the context of classic inter-state conflicts, the modern law of occupation has even been described as having been shaped by the development of the concept of sovereignty. For example, Eyal Benvenisti wrote that '[t]he obligation to respect the sovereign rights of the ousted government ... reflects the final stages of the crystallization of the concept of sovereignty as a nation's claim for exclusive control over its territory and nationals.'[36] But does that mean that the law of occupation may only regulate relationship between two sovereign bodies?

9.3.1 Disentangling the law of occupation and sovereignty

An affirmative answer would rule out the application of the law on occupation to internationalized conflicts except those in which a new sovereign state has emerged through the process of state dissolution.[37] This is because sovereignty is a defining attribute of states.[38] According to the traditional understanding of sovereignty, the state is sovereign because it is a state and, therefore, an entity that is not a state cannot be sovereign.[39] As a result, non-state actors—even in internationalized conflicts—cannot be considered sovereign.[40] The extent of interdependence

34 See Oppenheim, 1st edn (n 3) vol I, 99–100; H Lauterpacht, 'The Subjects of the Law of Nations' (1947) 63 LQR 438, 444–45; see further Section 2.5.1.

35 cf, eg, H Hannum, *Autonomy, Sovereignty, and Self-Determination: The Accommodation of Conflicting Rights* (University of Pennsylvania Press 2011) 15 ('One principle upon which there seems to be universal agreement is that sovereignty is an attribute of statehood, and that only states can be sovereign.').

36 E Benvenisti, *The International Law of Occupation* (2nd edn, OUP 2012) 21.

37 On which see Section 2.3.1.

38 See, eg, CW Morris, *An Essay on the Modern State* (CUP 2002) 172; Crawford (n 2) 32; Hannum (n 35) 15.

39 cf J Crawford, 'Sovereignty as a Legal Value' in J Crawford, M Koskenniemi, and S Ranganathan (eds), *The Cambridge Companion to International Law* (CUP 2012) 117 ('[T]he state is sovereign because it is a state; not one of a kind but one of a species, the species of states.').

40 cf *Al-Bihani v Obama* (2010) F.3d 866, 873 (US, DC Circuit Court). In this case, a US federal court refused to apply the rules of co-belligerency to a non-state armed group. Like the presently considered arguments related to occupation law, the court considered those rules as rooted in the concept

between the requirement of sovereignty and the applicability of occupation law therefore needs to be examined.

The argument that both sides of the conflict must be sovereign states in order for the law of occupation to apply has been the subject of debate in relation to the Israeli–Palestinian conflict. In that context, David Ball argued that unlike general IHL, which applies to such conflicts also on the basis of customary international law, 'the specific laws of war regarding belligerent occupancy [sic] may not'.[41] His argument was based on three considerations. First, the law of occupation as set out by the Hague Regulations speaks exclusively in terms of 'States'.[42] Second, without a displaced sovereign, the law could only apply directly to individual persons, which Ball considered problematic.[43] Finally, the civilian population not belonging to any sovereign—ie, the Palestinians—would not qualify as 'affected citizens'.[44]

It is submitted that, on a closer scrutiny, none of these contentions prove convincing. Firstly, as discussed in Chapter 8, the reference to states is a testament to the period in which the Regulations were adopted.[45] The content of the norms set out by the Regulations is now almost universally considered to constitute customary international law.[46] As soon as the law of international armed conflict (IAC) applies, therefore, the norms contained in the Regulations apply, as well. Accordingly, the ICJ rightly considered the Regulations applicable by force of custom[47] to the Palestinian territories without conducting a specific enquiry into the status of those territories[48] while being fully cognizant of—although not expressly acknowledging—the fact that the Palestinian side was represented by a non-state actor.[49]

The second concern is equally misplaced. Ball did not show in what sense the direct application of the law to individual persons should be problematic. In fact, in

of state sovereignty, and thus inapplicable to non-sovereign non-state actors: 'Any attempt to apply the rules of co-belligerency to such a force would be folly, akin to this court ascribing powers of national sovereignty to a local chapter of the Freemasons.'

41 D Ball, 'Toss the Travaux? Application of the Fourth Geneva Convention to the Middle East Conflict—A Modern (Re)assessment' (2004) 79 New York University Law Review 990, 1001.

42 ibid. 43 ibid. 44 ibid 1002. 45 See Section 8.2.3.

46 See, eg, *Judgment of the International Military Tribunal for the Trial of German Major War Criminals* (30 September 1946) (IMT) 254; *Krupp et al* (Judgment) (30 June 1948) (1949) 10 Law Reports of Trials of War Criminals 69 (US MT) 133; *Judgment of the International Military Tribunal for the Far East* (12 November 1948) (IMTFE), reproduced in J Pritchard and SM Zaide (eds), *The Tokyo War Crimes Trial* (Garland 1981) vol 22, 491; JS Pictet (ed) *Geneva Convention IV Relative to the Protection of Civilian Persons in Time of War: Commentary* (ICRC 1958) 614; *R v Finta (No 1)* (1989) 82 ILR 424 (Canada, High Court of Justice) 439; *Affo v Commander Israel Defence Force* (1988) 83 ILR 121 (Israel, Supreme Court) 163; *Polyukhovich v Commonwealth of Australia* (1991) 91 ILR 1 (Australia, High Court) 123; *Legal Consequences of the Construction of a Wall in the Occupied Palestinian Territory* (Advisory Opinion) [2004] ICJ Rep 136 [89]; *Prosecutor v Prlić et al* (Appeal Judgment) IT-04-74-A (29 November 2017) vol 1 [317]; contra Benvenisti (n 36) 131 (arguing that because of the disregard of the law of occupation during the Second World War, the Regulations had *lost* their customary status by the end of the war).

47 Israel was not a party to the Hague Convention (IV) respecting the Laws and Customs of War on Land (signed 18 October 1907, entered into force 26 January 1910) 205 CTS 277, to which the Regulations were annexed. See *Wall* Advisory Opinion (n 46) [89].

48 *Wall* Advisory Opinion (n 46) [89]; see also ibid [101].

49 ibid [91]; *Legal Consequences of the Construction of a Wall in the Occupied Palestinian Territory* (Order) [2003] ICJ Rep 428 [2]; see also text to notes 59–66 in this chapter.

the Israeli conditions, the government's observance of the law of occupation (or the lack thereof) has been a constant source of litigation before the domestic courts.[50] These cases, which relate precisely to the application of occupation law to individuals, have been brought primarily by Palestinian petitioners who considered that their individual rights arising from occupation law had been violated.[51] What is more, it is not accurate to say that there would, by definition, be no equivalent entity to the displaced sovereign. The non-state actor to whom the civilians owe their allegiance may perform equivalent or quasi-equivalent functions to those of the former territorial sovereign.

Finally, the argument that the Palestinian civilians' lack of full citizenship precluded their qualification as 'affected citizens' concerned the extent of personal scope of application of the law of occupation. Accordingly, this issue is dealt with in more detail in a later section, where the criterion of allegiance is put forward as an appropriate alternative in the determination of protected person status.[52] Suffice it to say at this point that the consideration of the claims brought by the inhabitants of the occupied territories by the Israeli courts amounts to a tacit acknowledgement by the occupying power that these individuals do fall within the law's remit *ratione personae*. In other words, the absence of association with a sovereign entity does not exclude the applicability of the law of occupation to the affected persons.

9.3.2 Sovereignty-agnostic nature of the law of occupation

The foregoing analysis suggests that the modern law of occupation should properly be seen as sovereignty-agnostic. Its role is chiefly conservationist and humanitarian: it serves to conserve the status quo ante[53] and to protect the humanitarian needs of the population.[54] It does not, however, affect the sovereignty of the territory brought under the occupant's control.[55] To an extent, this was already recognized by Oppenheim, who wrote that there was 'not an atom of sovereignty in the authority of the Occupying Power.'[56] Today, this interpretation is confirmed by Article 4 AP I, which sets out the 'undisputed principle of international law'[57] that the occupation of a territory does not affect its legal status.[58]

[50] See generally D Kretzmer, 'The Law of Belligerent Occupation in the Supreme Court of Israel' (2012) 94 IRRC 207.

[51] See ibid 215–36.

[52] See Section 10.4.3.

[53] A Roberts, 'Transformative Military Occupation: Applying the Laws of War and Human Rights' (2006) 100 AJIL 580, 580.

[54] O Ben-Naftali, 'PathoLAWgical Occupation: Normalizing the Exceptional Case of the Occupied Palestinian Territory and Other Legal Pathologies' in Orna Ben-Naftali (ed), *International Humanitarian Law and International Human Rights Law: Pas de Deux* (OUP 2011) 161.

[55] Oppenheim, 4th edn (n 10) vol I, 445; MS McDougal and FP Feliciano, *Law and Minimum World Public Order: The Legal Regulation of International Coercion* (Yale University Press 1961) 752; Dinstein (n 1) 49.

[56] L Oppenheim, 'The Legal Relations between an Occupying Power and the Inhabitants' (1917) 33 LQR 363, 364.

[57] Sandoz et al, *APs Commentary* (n 29) 72.

[58] Art 4 AP I.

The ICJ likewise did not consider it necessary to enquire into the exact status of the Palestinian territories in its *Wall* advisory opinion and the non-existence of two separate sovereign entities did not prevent it from holding that the law of belligerent occupation did in fact apply to those territories.[59] This approach, separating the issue of applicability of the law of belligerent occupation to a certain territory from the question of the title to that territory, is standard in the international jurisprudence concerning situations of occupation.[60] As noted in the new ICRC Commentary on GC I, '[a]ny other interpretation would lead to a result that is unreasonable as the applicability of the law of occupation would depend on the invading State's subjective considerations.'[61]

In this regard, Yoram Dinstein agreed that the fact that one of the conflict parties may be a non-state entity is 'immaterial', but he suggested that the problem is 'handle[d]' by the regulation of unilateral undertakings in Common Article 2(3).[62] To the extent that his suggestion might be interpreted as a proposition that such an undertaking would be *necessary* for the application of the law of occupation to situations involving non-state actors, the present author would respectfully disagree. (A unilateral declaration may, however, be one of the routes bringing about the relative internationalization of an armed conflict.[63]) It is true that the Court noted that the Palestinians had issued such a declaration.[64] However, the existence of the declaration was not decisive for the ICJ.[65] Instead, the determinative factor was the existence of a trigger of application of the law of IAC.[66] This trigger exists, by definition, in each of the subtypes of internationalized conflict.

The same rationale should be followed here, irrespective of the existence (or not) of two sovereign bodies on the opposite sides of the conflict. This understanding is in line with the trend of individualization of humanitarian law described previously,[67] as well as with a more recent tendency, identified by Adam Roberts, 'to think of war as a set of minimum rules to be observed in the widest possible range of situations and not to worry excessively about the precise legal definition of military occupation'.[68]

In conclusion, the potential lack of sovereignty characterizing one of the conflict parties should not, contrary to the traditional view, be seen as preventing the application of the law of belligerent occupation. It thus remains to be seen whether this conclusion needs to be modified in any way due to the perceived or real lack of

[59] *Wall* Advisory Opinion (n 46) [95].

[60] See, eg, *Central Front—Ethiopia's Claim 2* (Partial Award of 28 April 2004) (2004) 26 RIAA 155 (EECC) 169–70 [28]–[29].

[61] T Ferraro and L Cameron, 'Article 2: Application of the Convention' in ICRC (ed), *Commentary on the First Geneva Convention* (CUP 2016) 115 [325].

[62] Dinstein (n 1) 24.

[63] See Section 2.5.2.

[64] *Wall* Advisory Opinion (n 46) [91]; Dinstein (n 1) 25.

[65] cf *Wall* Advisory Opinion (n 46) [91]–[92] (commencing the paragraph mentioning the declaration with the qualifier 'Furthermore' and proceeding to the following paragraph, in which the Court cited Common Article 2, without any further analysis of the declaration or its legal relevance).

[66] ibid [95] (holding that if the conditions of applicability in Common Article 2 are fulfilled, the Geneva Conventions apply in full).

[67] See Chapter 8.

[68] A Roberts, 'What Is a Military Occupation?' (1984) 55 BYBIL 249, 258.

capacity on part of non-state actors to abide by the norms of the law of occupation, which is the subject of the following section.

9.4 Inability

A typical recurring objection to the extension of the application of IHL to non-state actors is the claim that even if conceptually such an extension was possible, in any event armed groups would be unwilling and/or unable to comply with the more demanding norms of the law of IAC.[69] There is some force in this objection. After all, the maxim *impossibilium nulla obligatio est* (there is no obligation to do the impossible) has been recognized since the Roman times[70] by many modern legal systems.[71] Equally, there is no fundamental reason why this maxim would not operate in international law, as well.[72]

9.4.1 Inability and unwillingness distinguished

At the outset, it is essential to distinguish the objection of inability—which is the true focus here—from the frequently mentioned twin consideration of unwillingness.[73] It is true that, just as any other subject of law, armed groups may be reluctant to accept the applicability of particular (or all) norms of IHL.[74] Sometimes, they

[69] See also Section 6.3.3 (concerning the regulation of combatant status).

[70] A Watson (ed) *The Digest of Justinian* (rev edn, University of Pennsylvania Press 2009) vol 4, 482 (book 50, 17, 185).

[71] J Gordley, 'Impossibility and Changed and Unforeseen Circumstances' (2004) 52 American Journal of Comparative Law 513, 513.

[72] See, eg, *Case Concerning Pulp Mills on the River Uruguay (Argentina v Uruguay)* (Merits) [2010] ICJ Rep 14, 254 [65] (sep op Torres Bernárdez) (referring to the principle as applicable to the resolution of the case without further analysis); *Prosecutor v Blaškić* (Decision on the Objection of the Republic of Croatia to the Issuance of Subpoena Duces Tecum) IT-95-14-T (18 July 1997) [95] (referring to the related principle *ultra posse nemo tenetur*—defined as 'one should not be compelled to engage in a behaviour that is nearly impossible'—as applicable to the resolution of the case without further analysis); see also JE Bond, 'Amended Article 1 of the Draft Protocol I to the 1949 Geneva Conventions: The Coming of Age of the Guerrilla' (1975) 32 Washington & Lee Law Review 65, 71 (noting that demanding the impossible 'reduces the law to hypocrisy and invites disregard of the entire legal regime').

[73] There certainly are areas of international law where the use of these two considerations together clearly is or at least may plausibly be justified. These include the determination of admissibility of cases before the ICC; state responsibility to protect victims of large-scale human rights violations; or rules governing self-defence against non-state actors acting from a third state's territory. The argument presented in this section is not intended as a judgment on any of those uses of the dual criteria of unwillingness and inability. See further, eg, Rome Statute of the International Criminal Court (adopted 17 July 1998, entered into force 1 July 2002) 2187 UNTS 3, Art 17 (hereafter Rome Statute); ICISS, *The Responsibility to Protect: Report of the International Commission on Intervention and State Sovereignty* (International Development Research Centre 2001), at xi; AS Deeks, '"Unwilling or Unable": Toward a Normative Framework for Extraterritorial Self-Defense' (2012) 52 VJIL 483.

[74] Similarly, it is a matter of empirical fact that for various reasons, states are reluctant to be labelled as occupying powers and thus frequently contest the applicability of the law of occupation to situations of effective foreign control over territory. See further ICRC, 'Expert Meeting: Occupation and Other Forms of Administration of Foreign Territory - Report' (2012) <www.icrc.org/eng/assets/files/publications/icrc-002-4094.pdf>, at 4 (hereafter ICRC, 'Expert Meeting: Occupation').

may even go so far as to proclaim in advance their intention to ignore these rules, as Hezbollah did in 2006,[75] or issue guidelines openly condoning conduct in clear violation of IHL, as ISIS has been doing at least since 2013.[76] Happily, other armed groups have been warmer to the idea of compliance with IHL.[77] For example, a representative of the FRELIMO, speaking at Geneva in March 1974, on the eve of the Mozambican War of Independence, stated that compliance by armed groups is not contingent on 'the technical apparatus or the material means' but rather on 'the will to apply the principles of humanitarian law'.[78]

It should certainly be admitted that the potential lack of voluntary submission to the law is relevant from the policy perspective and, if empirically confirmed, should inform any decisions concerning the future development of the legal norms in question (ie, from the perspective of *lex ferenda*). However, it is an unacceptable argument for the purposes of *lex lata*. To uncover the flaw at the heart of this claim, one only needs to be reminded that not much more than a century ago, the celebrated Russian jurist Fyodor Fyodorovich Martens himself dismissed the application of the law of war to non-European *states* along very similar lines. In his book *La Paix et la Guerre*, he wrote that 'it would be impossible to expect Turks or Chinese to observe the laws and customs of war as elaborated by the common efforts of the Christian and civilised nations'.[79] This language not only jars the sensitivities of the modern reader (commendably, international law has long put to rest any distinction between 'civilized' and 'uncivilized' states[80]), but it also highlights how the exclusion of a category of subjects from the remit of the law may fatally undermine the prospect of the effectiveness of the legal regime as a whole. By way of example, Martens's dismissive attitude appears to have been shared by the 'civilized' states of his era engaged in the Boxer Expedition in 1900–01 in China (a broad ad hoc alliance of eight nations consisting of Austria-Hungary, France, Germany, Great Britain, Italy, Japan,

[75] See Statement of Hezbollah Secretary-General Hassan Nasrallah (16 July 2006), reproduced in HRW, 'Civilians under Assault: Hezbollah's Rocket Attacks on Israel in the 2006 War' (August 2007) <www.hrw.org/reports/2007/iopt0807/iopt0807web.pdf>, at 12.

[76] See M Revkin, *The Legal Foundations of the Islamic State* (Brookings 2016) 23 (noting that ISIS 'has published guidelines, either as official fatwas or independent legal opinions authored by Islamic State-affiliated clerics, specifying the conditions under which enemy combatants may be targeted, tortured, mutilated, or killed, as well as rules governing the ransom of non-Muslim hostages') (footnotes omitted).

[77] For further examples and analysis see O Bangerter, 'Reasons Why Armed Groups Choose to Respect International Humanitarian Law or Not' (2011) 93 IRRC 353.

[78] *Official Records* (n 8) vol VIII, CDDH/I/SR.5, 36 [18] (Mozambique Liberation Front—FRELIMO); see also ibid 44 [34] (PLO); ibid 45 [41] (Guinea-Bissau).

[79] FF Martens, *La paix et la guerre: la Conférence de Bruxelles 1874; Droit et devoirs des belligérants (leur application pendant la guerre d'Orient 1874–1878); La Conférence de La Haye 1899* (N de Sancé tr, A Rousseau 1901) 46–47, quote translated into English and reproduced in Y Arai-Takahashi, 'Preoccupied with Occupation: Critical Examinations of the Historical Development of the Law of Occupation' (2012) 94 IRRC 51, 77 fn 161.

[80] See, eg, *Maritime Delimitation in the Area between Greenland and Jan Mayen (Denmark v Norway)* (Merits) [1993] ICJ Rep 38, 236 fn 9 (sep op Weeramantry); H Lauterpacht, *Recognition in International Law* (CUP 1947) 31 fn 1. For a more detailed discussion of the civilized/uncivilized distinction, see L Obregón Tarazona, 'The Civilized and the Uncivilized' in B Fassbender and A Peters (eds), *The Oxford Handbook of the History of International Law* (OUP 2012) 917–39.

Russia, and the US).[81] As a consequence, IHL was not deemed applicable to the conflict, resulting in repeated cases of looting, pillage, and denial of quarter by the expeditionary troops.[82] In sum, individual unwillingness to apply IHL is not an excuse for unlawful conduct of any given actor and it should likewise be rejected as a potential systemic justification for the disapplication of IHL to a class of actors.

9.4.2 Inability and effectiveness of the law

Having set aside the question of unwillingness, the remainder of the analysis accordingly focuses on inability in a narrow sense. This objection is based on the argument that it should not be expected of non-state armed groups to act in a manner akin to that expected of states as the primary addressees of the IHL norms on occupation.[83] In an expert meeting on Occupation and Other Forms of Administration of Foreign Territory organized by the ICRC in 2003, two experts further substantiated this argument with reference to the goal of effectiveness of IHL.[84] It is worth restating their contention in full:

> [The] experts pointed out that another important reason for classifying as a non-international armed conflict a confrontation opposing the occupying forces to organized armed groups not belonging to the occupied State was the groups' capacity to comply with the relevant IHL rules. They argued that the law governing non-international armed conflict, particularly because of its limited number of provisions, was better suited to dealing with such situations as it was specifically designed for dealing with armed violence involving non-State actors. In fact, *the limited resources of these groups, combined with the absence of the apparatus necessary to implement the law of international armed conflict, would limit their ability to comply with the full set of norms applicable in international armed conflict*. Since IHL efficiency was notably based on its effectiveness and the ability of the parties to respect its provisions, choosing the law governing non-international armed conflict as the legal framework applicable to the fighting between the occupying power and organized armed groups was deemed fitting and practical.[85]

Although the experts' argument was made in the context of a discussion of the legal classification of hostilities on occupied territory,[86] its thrust obviously applies to the present scrutiny as well. Would it therefore be correct to say that the effectiveness of IHL demands the inapplicability of the IAC law of occupation to conflicts featuring a non-state party? It is submitted that such a position should be rejected as overbroad. While there certainly are *some* armed groups that may be unable to comply with *some* norms of the law of belligerent occupation, it is not the case that

[81] See further JK Fairbank and K-C Liu (eds), *The Cambridge History of China. Volume 11: Late Ch'ing, 1800–1911, Part 2* (CUP 1980) 115–30.

[82] F Grob, *The Relativity of War and Peace* (Yale University Press 1949) 72–73.

[83] See, eg, E Crawford, *The Treatment of Combatants and Insurgents Under the Law of Armed Conflict* (OUP 2010) 75; T Gal, 'Unexplored Outcomes of *Tadić*' (2014) 12 JICJ 59, 73; see also *Official Records* (n 8) vol VIII, CDDH/I/SR.4, 28–29 [25] (United Kingdom); ibid, vol VI, CDDH/SR.36, 42 [62]–[63] (Israel).

[84] ICRC, 'Expert Meeting: Occupation' (n 74) 128.

[85] ibid (emphasis added).

[86] See ibid 124–28.

the potential inability to apply the norms in question somehow renders the whole body of law inapplicable. Accordingly, the following text aims to demonstrate that (1) not all non-state actors in internationalized conflicts are equal in their capacity to comply with the law of occupation; (2) not all norms of occupation law are equally onerous; and (3) the law of belligerent occupation itself contains safeguards capable of bolstering the occupying power's capacity to comply with it.

9.4.2.1 Actor-dependent compliance

Firstly, it is inaccurate to characterize all non-state actors in internationalized armed conflicts as fundamentally lacking in resources. As it was argued in Chapter 6 at length, and demonstrated on the respective examples of the Croatian Republic of Herzeg-Bosnia and Somalia, some armed groups may have significantly more resources at their disposal than full-fledged states do.[87] Moreover, this objection does not relate to all types of internationalized armed conflicts equally. In particular, in the cases of state dissolution, the emerging state—due to its fulfilment of the criteria of statehood—can be expected to wield sufficient resources to ensure the full applicability of the IAC law of occupation. Accordingly, the ICTY determined on a number of occasions that the successor states of the Socialist Federal Republic of Yugoslavia (SFRY) had acted as both occupying and occupied states during the Yugoslavian War of 1991–95.[88] The capacity of these newly emergent states to abide by IHL was not questioned by the ICTY. Actors in the remaining types of internationalized conflicts might, of course, be significantly less able to observe the law of occupation, especially at the outset of the conflict.

9.4.2.2 Rule-dependent compliance

Secondly, the duties under the law of belligerent occupation are not all equally onerous and some may lend themselves more easily than others to full compliance by non-state actors.[89] For example, Tom Gal has argued that it would be 'unreasonable' to force armed groups to comply with the more demanding norms exemplified by 'provisions discussing legislation and requirements for the treatment of internees'.[90] By contrast, many protections and prohibitions contained in the law of belligerent occupation also have their equivalents in the law of NIAC.[91] For

[87] See Section 6.3.3.1.

[88] See, eg, *Prosecutor v Rajić* (Rule 61 Decision) IT-95-12-R61 (13 September 1996) [38]–[43] (holding that Croatia was in belligerent occupation of a part of the Bosnian territory in 1993); *Prosecutor v Blaškić* (Trial Judgment) IT-95-14-T (3 March 2000) [149]–[50] (holding that Croatia was in belligerent occupation of a part of the Bosnian territory in 1993); *Prosecutor v Gotovina* (Trial Judgment) IT-06-90-T (15 April 2011) vol 1 [1218] and vol 2 [2014], [2309] (acknowledging that the Federal Republic of Yugoslavia was in belligerent occupation of parts of Croatia in 1995).

[89] cf Roberts (n 68) 293. [90] Gal (n 83) 73.

[91] cf Sivakumaran (n 16) 530 ('Certain general protections and prohibitions contained in the law of belligerent occupation—for example, *the protections afforded to the wounded and the sick; the protection of civilian hospitals; the principle of humane treatment; the prohibition of collective penalties, pillage, and reprisals; the taking of hostages; the prohibitions of deportation and forcible transfer; and the right to due process*

instance, the prohibition of forcible displacement of civilians under the law of occupation[92] is paralleled by both treaty[93] and customary[94] rules applicable in NIACs.[95] As seen on this example, obligations contained in these norms are chiefly negative in nature; in other words, they demand the addressee simply to refrain from conduct amounting to international crimes or from otherwise infringing individual rights.[96]

It can therefore be assumed that compliance with such norms is within the power of even the least organized armed groups in internationalized armed conflicts. Accordingly, in the *Martić* case, the ICTY considered norms of the law of belligerent occupation permitting the forcible seizure of property by the occupying power as applicable in its consideration of the elements of the crime of plunder.[97] The Tribunal did not inquire into the nature of the armed conflict during which the acts in question had been committed,[98] nor did it place any importance on the fact that the defendant represented a non-recognized political entity 'Republic of Serbian Krajina', in other words, a non-state actor.[99] A similar approach was followed in the *Mrkšić* case.[100] It is submitted that this approach is in line with the relative ease of application of the prohibitory norms entailing negative obligations such as to abstain from unlawful acts against protected persons and their property.

Furthermore, in many cases, it will be possible for the armed group in question to comply even with the relatively more onerous requirements of the law of belligerent occupation. As a prime example of norms the application of which to non-state actors has been described as 'unreasonable', consider those rules of the law of belligerent occupation that discuss legislation.[101] It is submitted that a blanket

and judicial guarantees—are already applicable to non-international armed conflicts, whether through comparable treaty provisions or through customary international law.') (emphasis added).

92 Art 49 GC IV.

93 Art 17 AP II; Art 8(2)(e)(viii) of the Rome Statute (n 73).

94 J-M Henckaerts and L Doswald-Beck (eds), *Customary International Humanitarian Law* (CUP 2005) rule 129B (hereafter *ICRC CIHL Study*).

95 See further G Dawson and S Faber, *Forcible Displacement Throughout the Ages: Towards an International Convention for the Prevention and Punishment of the Crime of Forcible Displacement* (Brill 2012) 54.

96 On the distinction between positive and negative obligations, see generally D Shelton and A Gould, 'Positive and Negative Obligations' in D Shelton (ed), *The Oxford Handbook of International Human Rights Law* (OUP 2013) 562–83.

97 *Prosecutor v Martić* (Trial Judgment) IT-95-11-T (12 June 2007) (ICTY) [102]–[03]. The defendant was found guilty on the count of plunder of public or private property, as a violation of the laws or customs of war. See ibid [518].

98 cf ibid [347] ('The Trial Chamber finds that a state of *armed conflict* existed in the relevant territories of Croatia and [Bosnia and Herzegovina] during the time relevant to the crimes charged in the Indictment.') (emphasis added); but see *Prosecutor v Sesay et al* (Trial Judgment) SCSL-04-15-T (2 March 2009) [982] (holding expressly that '[t]he rights and duties of occupying powers, as codified in the 1907 Hague Convention and the Fourth Geneva Convention, apply only in international armed conflicts').

99 See *Martić* Trial Judgment (n 97) [2].

100 *Prosecutor v Mrkšić et al* (Trial Judgment) IT-95-13/1-T (27 September 2007) [422] and [457] (refusing to make a finding on the nature of the conflict); ibid [458] fn 1711 (referring to Art 70 GC IV, which contains a general prohibition of the arrest of protected persons for acts or opinions expressed *before the occupation*, to establish the content of the offence of imprisonment as a crime against humanity for the purposes of that case).

101 cf Gal (n 83) 73 (arguing that 'forcing' non-state actors to comply with, inter alia, 'provisions discussing legislation' in GC IV would be 'unreasonable'). Although Gal did not provide a specific list,

rejection of their applicability proves to be too sweeping upon closer analysis. In fact, legislation has been issued by non-state actors in internationalized armed conflicts in the past and sometimes it has even been accepted *ex post facto* by the eventually victorious enemy.

For instance, in the archetypal conflict internationalized by the recognition of belligerency, the American Civil War (1861–65), the Confederate states continued to issue legislative acts during the period of the ongoing hostilities.[102] In a string of post-war cases, the US Supreme Court acknowledged the general validity of the Confederate legislation.[103] Therefore, it may be observed that although a conflict party whose belligerent rights were recognized by the territorial state may formally be a non-state actor, it will likely be capable of issuing and enforcing legislation. It will have these capabilities due to its high degree of organization and territorial control, both of which are implicit in the criteria for belligerency.[104]

Similarly, some armed groups acting in conflicts internationalized by outside intervention have been known to enact and enforce their own 'laws'. For example, the Croatian Republic of Herzeg-Bosnia (*Hrvatska Republika Herceg-Bosna*, HR H-B)[105] issued its own legislation during the armed conflict in Bosnia and Herzegovina,[106] although the validity of these enactments was later put into doubt due to the non-recognition of this entity by the post-war Bosnian constitution.[107] Similarly, the so-called National Transitional Council (NTC) had started promulgating its own 'laws' months before it consolidated power over the whole territory of Libya in October 2011.[108] Since—unlike the HR H-B—the NTC emerged victorious at the end of the conflict,[109] all of these enactments remained in force

it can be assumed she was referring to Articles 51(3), 64(1), 67, 68(2), 70(2), and 73 GC IV, as well as Article 43 of the Hague Regulations, all of which speak of 'law', 'the law', or 'the laws' valid in the occupied territory.

[102] See, eg, WW Lester, *A Digest of the Military and Naval Laws of the Confederate States* (Evans and Cogswell 1864).

[103] See, in particular, *Texas v White* (1868) 74 US 700, 733 (US Supreme Court); *Horn v Lockhart* (1873) 84 US 570, 573 (US Supreme Court); *United States v Insurance Companies* (1874) 89 US 99, 103 (US Supreme Court); see also *Taylor v Thomas* (1874) 89 US 479, 491 (US Supreme Court); *Williams v Bruffy* (1877) 96 US 176, 192 (US Supreme Court); *Keith v Clark* (1878) 97 US 454, 476 (US Supreme Court); *Baldy v Hunter* (1898) 171 US 388, 401 (US Supreme Court).

[104] See Section 2.5.1.1 for a discussion of the traditional criteria for belligerency.

[105] See Section 6.3.3.1 for a discussion of the historical background and the legal nature of this entity.

[106] HR H-B, Founding Decision On the Establishment and Declaration of the Croatian Republic of Herzeg-Bosnia, 28 August 1993, Art 6 ('Legislative authority is invested in the House of Representatives of the Republic.').

[107] cf UNHCR, 'Amnesty Laws in Bosnia and Herzegovina' (19 March 1998) <www.refworld.org/docid/3ae6b33214.html>, section III.2; see also Constitution of Bosnia and Herzegovina (Annex 4 of The General Framework Agreement for Peace in Bosnia and Herzegovina) (14 December 1995), Art I(3).

[108] See Temehu, 'Declarations, Laws & Resolutions Issued By The NTC' (2017) <www.temehu.com/ntc.htm> (tab 'NTC Laws'); see also Chatham House, 'Libya: Establishing the Rule of Law' (May 2012) <www.chathamhouse.org/publications/papers/view/184599>, at 11–14 (discussing the history and legitimacy of the laws passed by the NTC during the transitional phase).

[109] See further K Mačák and N Zamir, 'The Applicability of International Humanitarian Law to the Conflict in Libya' (2012) 14 ICLR 403, 429–35 (arguing that the armed conflict in Libya terminated in late October 2011 and discussing the obligations of IHL that remained applicable after that date).

following the election of the General National Congress in July 2012,[110] subject only to their potential future invalidation by Libya's Supreme Court.[111] These two armed groups are not at all an exception to the rule; in fact, as observed by Sandesh Sivakumaran, armed groups that exercise control over territory or which constitute de facto states are particularly prone to enacting legislation.[112] The worries about their capacity to do so expressed in part of the scholarship are thus in many instances misplaced.

The remaining unresolved point here, therefore, is the nature of these enactments. It could be argued that because these materials are issued by non-state entities, they do not in fact qualify as 'legislation' for the purposes of the law of belligerent occupation.[113] Nevertheless, the fact that non-state armed groups may have the capacity to enact their own legislation has been acknowledged by states at least since the time of the negotiation of the two Additional Protocols.[114] While this evolving understanding admittedly does not amount to subsequent practice regarding the interpretation of the law of belligerent occupation in general in the sense of Article 31(3)(b) of the VCLT, it may nevertheless be relevant for the purposes of the present analysis. After all, states must be presumed to have agreed the provisions of the law of belligerent occupation with a desire to enable their effectiveness.[115] In fact, the obligation to ensure respect for the Geneva Conventions in all circumstances features prominently in the very first common article to the Conventions[116] and is considered to be part of customary international law.[117]

Therefore, if it is accepted that these provisions of the law of occupation apply, at least to some degree, to conflicts that are characterized by the participation of non-state actors, then, since these provisions are based on an understanding that a conflict party enacts legislation, their application should not be rejected only on the basis of a formalist argument that non-state laws are not laws at all. Similarly, in the context of due process requirements imposed on non-state armed groups by the law of NIAC, Jonathan Somer has argued that '[t]o the extent that the fair trial provisions of IHL require the right to legislate in order to establish courts and enact penal provisions covering conduct related to the conflict, such capacity should exist

[110] Chatham House (n 108) 12.

[111] See, eg, BBC, 'Libya Revokes Muammar Gaddafi Praise Law' (14 June 2012) <www.bbc.co.uk/news/world-africa-18446110> (reporting that the Supreme Court overturned Law 37, enacted by the NTC in May 2011, for its unconstitutionality).

[112] Sivakumaran (n 16) 140.

[113] cf Zegveld (n 16) 187; Sivakumaran (n 16) 140.

[114] Sandoz et al, *APs Commentary* (n 29) 1399 [4605]. A number of domestic judgments issued even earlier had confirmed the general willingness to give effect to the laws issued by unrecognized entities. See, eg, *Hausner v Banque Internationale de Commerce de Petrograd* (1924) BGE 50 II 507, 511–13 (BGer) (giving effect to the laws of as-of-then unrecognized Soviet regime); *Salimoff v Standard Oil Co* (1933) 262 NY 220, 227–28 (US, CA NY) (ditto); *Banco de Bilbao v Sancha* [1938] 2 KB 176 (CA) 195–96 (giving effect to the laws enacted by the nationalist insurgents in the Spanish Civil War).

[115] cf Cassese, 'Status of Rebels' (n 23) (1981) 434 (describing it as a 'basic legal principle' that 'international treaties are always to be interpreted in such a way as to render their provisions effective').

[116] Common Art 1 GCs; see also Art 1(1) AP I.

[117] *Military and Paramilitary Activities in and against Nicaragua (Nicaragua v US)* (Merits) [1986] ICJ Rep 14 [220]; *ICRC CIHL Study* (n 94) rule 139.

independent of the state party.'[118] The present author respectfully agrees with this approach. To deny that non-state armed groups have the capacity to enact legislation, even if they actually *do* pass laws, only by refusing that what they actually adopt is legislation at all, would be to endorse the 'logic' of the Belgian surrealist René Magritte's painting of a pipe captioned '*Ceci n'est pas une pipe*'.[119]

9.4.2.3 Capacity-strengthening safeguards in the law of occupation

Thirdly, while the experts cited in the ICRC report may be correct that the non-state actor would normally lack the necessary resources at the outset of the conflict,[120] it should be recognized that an armed conflict is not a constant situation that does not undergo any development. Quite the contrary: the relative strength of the parties, their control over territory and population, as well as their general capacity for action are all subject to persistent variation. 'War is dynamic; things change, and change quickly.'[121] It is thus possible that in and of itself, the non-state party may not readily possess, for example, the 'food and medical supplies, ... clothing, bedding, means of shelter, [and] other supplies essential to the survival of the civilian population' it is required to provide under the terms of Article 69 AP I. Nevertheless, one solution to the problem of the alleged lack of resources, lying at the heart of the inability objection, may be found within the law of belligerent occupation itself.

Accordingly, it is submitted that the law of belligerent occupation contains safeguards aimed precisely at bolstering the capacity of the occupying authority to abide by the rules contained in this area of law. These are implicit particularly in rules on taxation and use of enemy property. Taxation in occupied territories is governed by Articles 48 and 49 of the Hague Regulations. Together, these provisions permit the occupier to maintain and impose taxes and other compulsory payments in the occupied territory.[122] They also contain an inseparable obligation to use such collected monies only 'for the needs of the [occupying] army' and 'the administration of the territory'.[123] However, as the Israeli High Court of Justice noted in *Abu Aita*, this restriction on the permissible purpose of the collected payments still 'leaves a very wide opening' and thus allows for much flexibility on part of the occupying authority.[124]

[118] J Somer, 'Jungle Justice: Passing Sentence on the Equality of Belligerents in Non-international Armed Conflict' (2007) 89 IRRC 655, 658; see also F Hampson, 'Fundamental Guarantees' in E Wilmshurst and SC Breau (eds), *Perspectives on the ICRC Study on Customary International Humanitarian Law* (CUP 2007) 287 fn 20; Sivakumaran (n 16) 75–76.

[119] 'This is not a pipe.' See R Magritte, *La Trahison des Images* [The Treachery of Images] (1929).

[120] See text to note 85 in this chapter.

[121] J Storr, 'Neither Art Nor Science: Towards a Discipline of Warfare' (2001) 146 RUSI Journal 39, 40; see also J Storr, *The Human Face of War* (Continuum 2009) 57 (discussing the dynamic and evolutionary nature of war).

[122] See, eg, C Phillipson (ed), *Wheaton's Elements of International Law* (5th edn, 1916) 534–35.

[123] Regulations Respecting the Laws and Customs of War on Land, Annex to Hague Convention (IV) respecting the Laws and Customs of War on Land (signed 18 October 1907, entered into force 26 January 1910) 205 CTS 277, Art 49 (hereafter Hague Regulations).

[124] *Abu Aita et al v Commander of the Judea and Samaria Region et al*, HCJ 69 & 493/81, (1983) 37(2) PD 197, 273.

Additionally, requisitions in kind and services may be demanded from the population.[125] The US Military Tribunal at Nuremberg confirmed in *Krupp* that this includes 'urgently needed equipment and supplies for the proper functioning of the occupation authorities'.[126] Articles 53 and 55 of the Hague Regulations further permit the seizure of all movable public property and the use of immovable public property in the occupied territory, respectively.[127] Article 55 specifies that as regards the immovables, the occupying power must use them as 'administrator and usufructuary' only.[128] As interpreted by the Institute of International Law, the combined effect of all of these provisions is that the occupant may 'dispose of the resources of the occupied territory to the extent necessary for the current administration of the territory and to meet the essential needs of the population'.[129]

These permissive clauses should accordingly be seen as enabling provisions, channelling the necessary resources towards a party constrained by their absence. James Stewart noted that as a matter of *policy*, rebel groups should be allowed to seize certain types of property during the war as 'there is little basis for expecting [them] to comply with the laws of war without offering certain *privileges*'.[130] This may be true in NIACs, but the argument presented here for the purposes of internationalized armed conflicts goes even further. Since internationalization triggers the applicability of the law of IAC,[131] the provisions permitting taxation and seizure and use of property should be seen as serving a reinforcing function vis-à-vis the remainder of the law of belligerent occupation by strengthening the capacity of non-state actors to implement this body of law.[132] Similar enabling provisions exist in relation to particular detailed obligations of the occupier, confirming this broad approach.[133] Their application should thus not be constrained to the realms of policy or seen as a privilege offered to the non-state actor, but it should rather be interpreted as an essential facet and a *requirement* of the law as such.

In sum, although arguments for IHL's limited applicability to armed groups are sometimes based on a concern for the effectiveness of the law due to these groups' supposed inability to apply it, in reality a more effective result may actually be achieved by accepting an extended application of the law. It has been shown that

[125] Art 52 Hague Regulations (n 123).

[126] *Krupp* (n 46) 137.

[127] See further Benvenisti (n 36) 81–82.

[128] Art 55 Hague Regulations (n 123).

[129] Institute of International Law, 'Bruges Declaration on the Use of Force' (2003) 70-II AIDI 285, 287.

[130] JG Stewart, *Corporate War Crimes: Prosecuting the Pillage of Natural Resources* (Open Society Foundations 2011) 21–22 (emphasis added).

[131] See Section 1.3.2.

[132] See also German Ministry of Defence, *ZDv 15/2, Humanitäres Völkerrecht in bewaffneten Konflikten: Handbuch [Humanitarian Law in Armed Conflicts: Manual]* (2013) 89 [553]; Peru, *Manual de Derecho Internacional Humanitario para las Fuerzas Armadas [Manual of International Humanitarian Law for Armed Forces]*, Resolución Ministerial No 1394-2004-DE/CCFFAA/CDIH-FFAA (1 December 2004) [91.c(2)]; UK Ministry of Defence, *The Manual of the Law of Armed Conflict* (OUP 2004) 304 [11.88(c)]; US DoD, *Law of War Manual* (December 2016) 827 [11.22.1.3] and 828–29 [11.22.2].

[133] See, eg, Art 63(5) AP I (permitting the requisitioning or diversion of resources belonging to civil defence organizations in occupied territories as long as such measures are necessary for the needs of the civilian population).

many non-state armed groups in internationalized armed conflicts are in fact capable of applying many of the relevant obligations. Additionally, the law of occupation itself endows these actors with further means to facilitate law-compatible conduct. As in Chapter 6, it should be emphasized here as well that the present argument is not meant as a general dismissal of the inability objection with respect to all obligations under IHL.[134] Nevertheless, insofar as the law of belligerent occupation in internationalized conflicts is concerned, it is submitted that the actual effect of the objection of inability is significantly limited.

9.5 Evaluation

This chapter has examined the normative underpinnings of the law of belligerent occupation in the context of internationalized armed conflicts. Admittedly, the binary nature of the law of armed conflict may be an uneasy match with the reality of modern conflicts marked by the participation of non-state entities.[135] However, this chapter has shown that the obstacles to the application of the law of occupation to internationalized armed conflicts are not insurmountable.

Accordingly, the present chapter has argued that non-state actors have at least a limited legal personality, which includes the capacity to have rights and duties under occupation law. It has then defended a sovereignty-agnostic conception of the law of belligerent occupation, demonstrating that the absence of sovereignty on part of non-state actors does not rule out the applicability of this body of law to such entities. Finally, the chapter has shown that the supposed inability of non-state actors to abide by the law of occupation may actually in many cases be exaggerated, or at any rate it may be addressed by the in-built legal safeguards that strengthen an occupier's ability to comply with its duties.

Overall, the chapter stands for the proposition that the law of belligerent occupation may in principle apply to internationalized armed conflicts. Chapter 10 turns to the practical ramifications of this view by examining the precise scope of application of this body of law in such conflicts.

[134] See Section 6.3.3.

[135] cf Y Shany, 'Binary Law Meets Complex Reality: The Occupation of Gaza Debate' (2008) 41 Isr L Rev 69, 77–78.

10
Practical Application

10.1 Introduction

This chapter puts forward a tripartite positive case for the application of the law of belligerent occupation to internationalized armed conflicts. It considers three traditional aspects of applicability, namely the temporal, geographical, and personal scope of application of the law.

By contrast, the chapter does not devote a separate section to the material scope of application. This is because the material applicability of the law of belligerent occupation has been confirmed in principle by the analysis presented in the previous chapter. Nevertheless, references to specific rules of the law of occupation are used throughout the text to illustrate the analysis.

As a general guiding principle, it can be said that to 'leave the local population bereft of legal protection ... would run counter to the object and purpose of the law of occupation'.[1] However, it is still necessary to identify the point in time from which the law of belligerent occupation applies in internationalized armed conflicts (Section 10.2); the precise territory or territories in which it applies (Section 10.3); and the persons who are protected by this body of law in such conflicts (Section 10.4).

10.2 Temporal Scope

One of the essential characteristics of internationalized armed conflicts is that, by definition, they originate through the transformation of a previously existing non-international armed conflict (NIAC). In other words, an internationalized armed conflict never commences without an antecedent NIAC.[2] At the same time, due to the attributes of the mechanism of internationalization, at the point of this transformation, both (or all) conflict parties will likely be in the possession of some part

[1] T Ferraro and L Cameron, 'Article 2: Application of the Convention' in ICRC (ed), *Commentary on the First Geneva Convention* (CUP 2016) 112 [313] (hereafter Ferraro and Cameron, 'Article 2').

[2] See Section 1.3.2.

of the territory of the 'parent' state.[3] The extent to which these territorial segments may qualify as enemy territory under the law of belligerent occupation is considered elsewhere in this chapter.[4] However, presuming that they do so qualify, should it be accepted that the trigger of applicability of the law of belligerent occupation is coterminous with the moment of internationalization? The present section argues in favour of a negative and, therefore, more nuanced answer to this question. The answer proposed here is that the law of occupation applies from the point in time when the parties have sufficiently consolidated their control over a given territory, while recognizing that this moment may (and typically will) arrive later than when the conflict in question is internationalized.

10.2.1 The Pictet theory: uncertainty in the law of IAC

In order to determine the point at which the law of belligerent occupation starts to apply in internationalized armed conflicts, it is necessary to revisit the rules on the temporal scope of this body of law in 'standard' or 'simple' IACs. In his seminal work on the international law of occupation, Eyal Benvenisti devoted to this issue a one-paragraph section entitled 'When occupation begins'.[5] He then answered the eponymous question with a pithy statement: 'Once control is established, occupation begins'.[6] While commendable for its brevity, this conclusion conceals the vigorous debate as to the exact point at which the control in question is sufficient to trigger the application of the law of belligerent occupation.[7]

[3] See, eg, Section 2.3.1, text to fns 212–16 (discussing the requirement of territorial control with respect to conflicts internationalized by state dissolution); Section 2.5.1.1, text to fn 353 (noting the requirement of territorial control in the context of conflicts internationalized by recognition of belligerency).

[4] See Section 10.3.

[5] E Benvenisti, *The International Law of Occupation* (2nd edn, OUP 2012) 55.

[6] ibid.

[7] See, in particular, H Lauterpacht (ed), *Oppenheim's International Law* (7th edn, Longmans 1952) 434; JS Pictet (ed), *Geneva Convention IV relative to the Protection of Civilian Persons in Time of War: Commentary* (ICRC 1958) 60 (hereafter Pictet, *GC IV Commentary*); A Roberts, 'What Is a Military Occupation?' (1984) 55 BYBIL 249, 256; LC Green, *The Contemporary Law of Armed Conflict* (3rd edn, Manchester University Press 2008) 285; M Zwanenburg, 'The Law of Occupation Revisited: The Beginning of an Occupation' (2007) 10 YIHL 99 (hereafter Zwanenburg, 'The Law of Occupation Revisited'); Y Dinstein, *The International Law of Belligerent Occupation* (CUP 2009) 38–42; D Akande, 'Classification of Armed Conflicts: Relevant Legal Concepts' in E Wilmshurst (ed), *International Law and the Classification of Conflicts* (OUP 2012) 45–46; M Zwanenburg, 'Challenging the Pictet Theory' (2012) 94 IRRC 30 (hereafter Zwanenburg, 'Challenging the Pictet Theory'); M Bothe, 'Effective Control During Invasion: A Practical View on the Application Threshold of the Law of Occupation' (2012) 94 IRRC 37; M Sassòli, 'A Plea in Defence of Pictet and the Inhabitants of Territories Under Invasion: The Case for the Applicability of the Fourth Geneva Convention During the Invasion Phase' (2012) 94 IRRC 42 (hereafter Sassòli, 'A Plea in Defence of Pictet'); T Ferraro, 'Determining the Beginning and End of an Occupation under International Humanitarian Law' (2012) 94 IRRC 133, 139–58; H-P Gasser and K Dörmann, 'Protection of the Civilian Population' in D Fleck (ed), *The Handbook of International Humanitarian Law* (3rd edn, OUP 2013) 273–74; P Spoerri, 'The Law of Occupation' in A Clapham and P Gaeta (eds), *The Oxford Handbook of International Law in Armed Conflict* (OUP 2014) 187–92; M Sassòli, 'The Concept and the Beginning of Occupation' in A Clapham, P Gaeta, and M Sassòli (eds), *The 1949 Geneva Conventions: A Commentary* (OUP 2015) 1389–419 (hereafter Sassòli, 'The Concept and the Beginning of Occupation').

With respect to standard IACs, this debate reflects the uncertain conceptual distinction between invasion and occupation. Specifically, at what point since the entry of a hostile army into a state's territory ('invasion phase') does the army exercise such control that it is bound by the law of occupation ('occupation phase')? On the one hand, some believe that there is in fact no distinction between the two phases for applying the rules in question; instead, what is decisive is whether the invading forces exercise control over protected persons.[8] This position is often referred to as the 'Pictet theory', as it was Jean Pictet who had first expressed it:

> There is no intermediate period between what might be termed the invasion phase and the inauguration of a stable regime of occupation. Even a patrol which penetrates into enemy territory without any intention of staying there must respect the Conventions in its dealings with the civilians it meets.[9]

On the other hand, there are those who maintain that until such time as the invading army stabilizes its control over the territory in question, the law of occupation would not apply at all.[10] It has been suggested that during the 'invasion phase' it would be materially impossible to apply certain norms of occupation law which involve a degree of civil-military cooperation,[11] with examples including the obligation to facilitate the proper working of all institutions devoted to the care and education of children[12] or to ensure and maintain medical and hospital establishments and services.[13]

10.2.2 When occupation begins in internationalized conflicts

Attempting to resolve the debate on the 'Pictet theory' would be beyond the scope of the present work. As internationalized armed conflicts by definition evolve from NIACs, they are in any event normally not characterized by an 'invasion phase'.[14] Nevertheless, the debate relating to standard IACs is particularly relevant for the present purposes as it highlights the considerations that determine the exact point at which the law of belligerent occupation becomes applicable.

Accordingly, what both sides agree on is that a degree of consolidation of power is necessary for the entirety of the law of belligerent occupation to become operative (whether this is described as a formal condition of applicability[15] or a simple consequence of the conflict party's capability to abide by certain more onerous norms[16]).

[8] See, eg, Pictet, *GC IV Commentary* (n 7) 60; Roberts (n 7) 256; R Kolb and S Vité, *Le droit de l'occupation militaire: perspectives historiques et enjeux juridiques actuels* (Bruylant 2009) 148–49; Akande (n 7) 46; Sassòli, 'A Plea in Defence of Pictet' (n 7); Sassòli, 'The Concept and the Beginning of Occupation' (n 7) 1409–13 [42]–[51].

[9] Pictet, *GC IV Commentary* (n 7) 60.

[10] See, eg, Lauterpacht (n 7) 434; Zwanenburg, 'The Law of Occupation Revisited' (n 7) 107–08; Dinstein (n 7) 41; Zwanenburg, 'Challenging the Pictet Theory' (n 7) 30; Bothe (n 7) 37–39.

[11] Zwanenburg, 'Challenging the Pictet Theory' (n 7) 34–36.

[12] Art 50 GC IV.

[13] Art 56 GC IV.

[14] cf also *Prosecutor v Prlić et al* (Appeal Judgment) IT-04-74-A (29 November 2017) vol 1 [339] (holding that 'invasion is not a prerequisite for the determination of a state of occupation').

[15] Zwanenburg, 'Challenging the Pictet Theory' (n 7) 35.

[16] Sassòli, 'A Plea in Defence of Pictet' (n 7) 46.

Mere presence in the hostile territory is patently insufficient for these purposes. As demonstrated on the examples mentioned earlier, the armed forces would simply not be in the position to apply those norms of occupation law that entail specific positive obligations such as the duty to maintain child care and health care institutions.[17] This applies equally to internationalized armed conflicts, even though they are not characterized by an 'invasion phase' as such.

Consequently, it is essential that the control over the territory in question persists for a material period of time. As expressed by the ICTY in *Naletilić and Martinović*, 'battle areas may not be considered as occupied territory'.[18] However, once control is established and maintained by the occupying power, the territory is considered occupied even in the face of continuing resistance and sporadic fighting.[19] Although there is 'no hard and fast rule as to … a minimal duration of belligerent occupation',[20] international jurisprudence has accepted periods of control lasting from 24 hours,[21] to 'a few days'[22] to 'almost six weeks'[23] as sufficient in this respect. At the moment of internationalization, this condition will likely not be met yet, and it certainly will not be met automatically merely due to the transformation of the conflict nature.

In sum, the threshold of internationalization is *not* in and of itself coterminous with the moment at which the law of belligerent occupation begins to apply in internationalized armed conflicts. Similarly to standard IACs, the conflict party in question must consolidate its control over the territory of its enemy, putting an end to the fighting there and substituting its own authority for that of the displaced enemy.[24] Once these requirements are fulfilled, the law of belligerent occupation commences to apply in an internationalized armed conflict.

10.3 Geographical Scope

Simply put, the fundamental problem with the geographical scope of application of the norms of belligerent occupation in internationalized conflicts is the absence

[17] Arts 50 and 56 GC IV; but see Sassòli, 'The Concept and the Beginning of Occupation' (n 7) 1411 [46] (arguing that such obligations should be interpreted flexibly before control is established, which translates primarily into a negative duty of non-interference with the relevant institutions); Ferraro and Cameron, 'Article 2' (n 1) 114 [322] (arguing that the law of occupation is subject to 'a gradual application' and that positive obligations of the occupying power 'take effect over time').

[18] *Prosecutor v Naletilić and Martinović* (Trial Judgment) IT-98-34-T (31 March 2003) [217].

[19] *The Hostages Trial, List et al* (Judgment) (19 February 1948) (1949) 8 Law Reports of Trials of War Criminals 34 (US MT) 56; *Prlić* Appeal Judgment (n 14) vol 1 [319]; Ferraro and Cameron, 'Article 2' (n 1) 108–09 [302]; but see Sassòli, 'The Concept and the Beginning of Occupation' (n 7) 1396–97 [17] (arguing that acts of resistance that result in the occupying power losing control over a part of a territory terminate the occupation in that part of the territory).

[20] Dinstein (n 7) 39.

[21] *Naletilić and Martinović* Trial Judgment (n 18) [587].

[22] *Central Front—Eritrea's Claims 2, 4, 6, 7, 8, and 22* (Partial Award of 28 April 2004) (2004) 26 RIAA 115 (EECC) 136 [57].

[23] *Issa and Others v Turkey* (App no 31821/96) (2004) 41 EHRR 27 (ECtHR) [45] *juncto* [73]–[74].

[24] cf Roberts (n 7) 274–75; *Naletilić and Martinović* Trial Judgment (n 18) [217]; Dinstein (n 7) 39; US DoD, *Law of War Manual* (December 2016) 764 [11.2.2.1].

of a clear delineation between what could be described as the 'home field' and the 'away field'.[25] In a standard IAC, the whole territory of a state is eligible to become occupied.[26] For the original sovereign, this is the 'home field', which benefits from the protection of the law of belligerent occupation. For the occupying power, this is the 'away field', which it must treat in accordance with the obligations provided for in the same body of law. In internationalized conflicts, such designation is more problematic.

With respect to internal armed conflicts, the territory-designation problem was well summarized by Richard Baxter:

> Territory cannot be belligerently occupied by the lawful government or the rebels. There is no starting point which divides territory into friendly and enemy areas, so that, when the latter type of area is occupied, it will be belligerently occupied. It surely cannot be maintained that the insurgents should be required to treat all territory over which they exercise control as being belligerently occupied or that the lawful government should be forced to treat territory liberated from the control of rebels as belligerently occupied. It is of the essence of belligerent occupation that it should be exercised over foreign, enemy territory. Such requirements as that of Article 43 of the Hague Regulations that the occupant must respect, 'unless absolutely prevented, the laws in force in the country' are simply unworkable in domestic conflict.[27]

Although it may be tempting to simply extend this reasoning to internationalized armed conflicts due to the fact that they begin as internal conflicts themselves, it is submitted that such an approach would be insufficiently nuanced. Instead, it should be recognized that the territory-designation problem does not affect all internationalized armed conflicts equally.

In particular, conflicts internationalized by state dissolution should not pose any problems in this respect;[28] the emerging states will likely have reasonably well-defined borders to determine which territory belongs to the respective conflict parties.[29] For example, the successor states of the former Socialist Federal Republic of Yugoslavia (SFRY) had maintained their existing borders from the pre-war federal period.[30] Consequently, when situations of belligerent occupation came about in

[25] I am grateful to Dapo Akande for this metaphor.

[26] cf Common Art 2(2) GCs ('The Convention shall ... apply to all cases of *partial or total* occupation of the territory of a High Contracting Party') (emphasis added).

[27] R Baxter, 'Ius in Bello Interno: The Present and Future Law' in JN Moore (ed), *Law & Civil War in the Modern World* (Johns Hopkins University Press 1974) 531.

[28] Conversely, prior to the moment of internationalization, the situation remains a NIAC. Some commentators have argued that even in such cases, if a secessionist authority gained control over parts of metropolitan territory which it did not claim, it should apply the law of belligerent occupation there. However, such suggestions are better seen as proposals of policy or arguments *de lege ferenda* rather than interpretations of the law in force. cf M Bothe, 'Occupation, Belligerent' in R Bernhardt (ed), *Encyclopedia of Public International Law* (Elsevier 1997) vol III, 765 and Benvenisti (n 5) 61 (both in favour of such interpretation); but see Sassòli, 'The Concept and the Beginning of Occupation' (n 7) 1415 [57] (arguing the interpretation is without legal basis).

[29] See generally Section 2.3.1.

[30] cf Badinter Arbitration Committee, Opinion No 3 (14 January 1991), reproduced in A Pellet, 'The Opinions of the Badinter Arbitration Committee: A Second Breath for the Self-Determination of Peoples' (1992) 3 EJIL 178, Appendix, 184–85 (taking the view that after the breakup of Yugoslavia, the former internal borders would become international borders protected by international law).

the internationalized conflicts occurring between pairs of ex-Yugoslavian states, the determination of the occupied territory did not prove any more problematic than in standard IACs.[31]

However, the other three main types of internationalized armed conflicts do occur in the territory of a single state even after the moment of internationalization. Hence, in order to determine whether or not parts of that state's territory may be considered occupied under the law of belligerent occupation, three consecutive questions need to be answered. First, does international law foresee that a state would occupy its own territory? Second, may such occupation relate to a territory previously held by a non-state group? Third, may a non-state armed group occupy a state's territory? It is submitted that with respect to the specific circumstances of internationalized conflicts, all three questions should be answered in the affirmative.

10.3.1 Occupation of a state's own territory

As to the first point, it has been suggested that it is 'axiomatic that a state can never occupy its own territory as a belligerent'.[32] With respect to NIACs, such a view certainly remains the prevailing orthodoxy[33]—although even in this context, it may be gradually becoming 'less axiomatic'.[34] Be that as it may, that view does not square with the available international practice and jurisprudence concerning internationalized armed conflicts and standard IACs.

There are admittedly some instances of practice supporting the interpretation that a state may not occupy its own territory. Of the publicly available military manuals, those issued at various times by the UK and the US have examined the issue at some length. To begin with, the 2004 UK military manual took the view that upon 'liberation' of a state's own territory and before the restoration of normal government, the situation would be a matter for the domestic law of the state concerned.[35] Two cases were cited in a footnote following this proposition.[36] The first one was the *Battat v R* case decided by the Privy Council in 1951.[37] However, it is unclear why this judgment was cited at this point, given that its text did not discuss IHL or the

[31] See, eg, *Prosecutor v Rajić* (Rule 61 Decision) IT-95-12-R61 (13 September 1996) [38]–[43] (holding that Croatia was in belligerent occupation of a part of the Bosnian territory in 1993); *Prosecutor v Blaškić* (Trial Judgment) IT-95-14-T (3 March 2000) [149]–[50] (holding that Croatia was in belligerent occupation of a part of the Bosnian territory in 1993); *Prosecutor v Gotovina* (Trial Judgment) IT-06-90-T (15 April 2011) vol 1 [1218] and vol 2 [2014], [2309] (acknowledging that the Federal Republic of Yugoslavia was in belligerent occupation of parts of Croatia in 1995).

[32] M Milanovic, 'Lessons for Human Rights and Humanitarian Law in the War on Terror: Comparing *Hamdan* and the Israeli *Targeted Killings* Case' (2007) 89 IRRC 373, 383 fn 47.

[33] See, eg, M Sassòli, 'The Legal Qualification of the Conflicts in the Former Yugoslavia: Double Standards or New Horizons for International Humanitarian Law?' in S Yee and Wang Tieya (eds), *International Law in the Post-Cold War World: Essays in Memory of Li Haopei* (Routledge 2001) 312; R Kolb and R Hyde, *An Introduction to the International Law of Armed Conflicts* (Hart 2008) 69; Benvenisti (n 5) 61; Spoerri (n 7) 185; E Crawford and A Pert, *International Humanitarian Law* (CUP 2015) 159.

[34] cf S Sivakumaran, *The Law of Non-International Armed Conflict* (OUP 2012) 531.

[35] UK Ministry of Defence, *The Manual of the Law of Armed Conflict* (OUP 2004) [11.1.2] (hereafter *UK Military Manual*).

[36] ibid fn 8. [37] *Battat v R* [1951] AC 519 (Privy Council).

notion of belligerent occupation at all, and thus it is of little use for the present purposes.[38] The second cited case was *Tan Tuan et al v Lucena Food Control Board et al*, a 1949 *en banc* decision of the Philippines Supreme Court.[39] This case concerned a brief period at the end of the Second World War when a part of the territory of the Philippines (which had, since the 1898 Treaty of Paris, been a US colony[40]) was reconquered by the US from the Japanese.[41] In fact, *Tan Tuan* directly contradicts the position expressed in the manual, as evidenced by the following passage:

> The Province of Tayabas had been declared liberated ... on June 14, 1945.... *The fact that this was not foreign territory did not deprive the United States Army of the status of belligerent occupant.* ... A nation can not [sic] conquer its own territory, but it may subdue and occupy such portions of it as are made the theater of an insurrection against its authority ..., or, for that matter, of foreign invasion.[42]

The ratio from *Tan Tuan* was confirmed in a later case before the same court.[43] Moreover, other post-Second World War cases also held that IHL applied to the territory reconquered from a common enemy.[44] The position taken by the UK military manual thus appears to be contradicted by the available case law, including at least one decision cited in the manual itself.

By contrast, the US Field Manual on the Law of Land Warfare accepted the applicability of the law of belligerent occupation to 'territory liberated from the enemy' and also expressly to '[d]omestic territory recovered from rebels treated as belligerents'.[45] This seems to have been the US position at least since the time of the American Civil War.[46] The Lieber Code expressly provided for the theoretical possibility that belligerent occupation could be established in the state's own territory.[47] Equally, in practice during the Civil War, the territory of the seceding states was recognized by the Union army as enemy territory and once control over it was established, it was automatically subject to the law of occupation.[48] This much was

[38] cf ibid. [39] *UK Military Manual* (n 35) [11.1.2] fn 8.

[40] See N Tarling (ed), *The Cambridge History of Southeast Asia, Volume 2: The Nineteenth and Twentieth Centuries* (CUP 1993) 260–61.

[41] See ibid 329–36 and 349.

[42] *Tan Tuan et al v Lucena Food Control Board, Federico Marquez, Godofredo Reyes, Alfredo Bonus, Teotimo Atienza and the Court of Appeals*, GR No L-1451 (6 October 1949) (Supreme Court of the Republic of the Philippines).

[43] *Saura Import and Export Co, Inc v Bibiano L Meer*, GR No L-2927 (26 February 1951) (Supreme Court of the Republic of the Philippines).

[44] See, eg, *Public Prosecutor v X (Eastern Java)* (1948) 15 Annual Digest 535, 535 (Case No 176) (Temporary Court Martial at Surabaya).

[45] US, Field Manual No 27-10, The Law of Land Warfare (18 July 1956, as amended on 15 July 1976) 10.

[46] But see US DoD, *Law of War Manual* (December 2016) 760 [11.1.3.2] ('The law of belligerent occupation does not apply to the liberation of friendly territory.'). Although the relevant footnote in the Law of War Manual refers to the earlier Field Manual, it does not reconcile the apparently different views taken by the two documents: ibid fn 30. However, even the newer text allows for the application of the law of belligerent occupation 'by analogy' provided a civil affairs agreement has not been reached with the friendly government: ibid.

[47] Instructions for the Government of Armies of the United States in the Field, prepared by Francis Lieber, General Orders No 100 (24 April 1863) Art 5 (hereafter Lieber Code).

[48] Q Wright, 'The American Civil War, 1861–65' in RA Falk (ed), *The International Law of Civil War* (Johns Hopkins Press 1971) 62.

acknowledged by express presidential statements during the war[49] as well as by the post-bellum jurisprudence of the US Supreme Court.[50] Importantly, with regard to recognized belligerency, the recently issued US DoD Law of War Manual re-endorsed the same view again.[51]

It is also of some significance that this issue was briefly addressed by the ICTY in *Hadžihasanović et al*, although the tribunal did not ultimately take a view on it. It arose as a preliminary matter in relation to a count in the indictment charging one of the accused with unlawful labour in violation of the law of belligerent occupation.[52] The acts in question were alleged to have occurred in the territory of Bosnia and Herzegovina while the accused was a general of the Bosnian Army.[53] The tribunal was thus directly faced with the question whether the law of occupation could apply to a state's occupation of its own territory.[54] Instead of rejecting it outright as axiomatically wrong, it considered it as an open question of substantive law, which was to be determined at trial.[55] However, in the subsequently amended indictment in that case, the prosecution removed the count in question and thus the issue was not ultimately adjudicated upon.[56]

Nonetheless, it is submitted that the totality of the cases and opinion cited significantly undermines the position that a state may under no circumstances become an occupying power in relation to its own territory. On the contrary, it is submitted that it is more consistent with the analysed line of judicial and extrajudicial views, as well as with the humanizing and individualizing trend dominating this area of law[57] to allow for such a possibility. It is on this assumption that the analysis proceeds to the second question.

10.3.2 Occupation of territory belonging to a non-state actor

10.3.2.1 Wars of national liberation

Provided that a state may in law become the occupying power of its own territory, the next question is whether it can acquire this position vis-à-vis a non-state actor. With respect to so-called wars of national liberation, the answer can be inferred

[49] See, eg, Executive Order of President Abraham Lincoln (20 October 1862), reproduced in *Burke v Miltenberger* (1873) 86 US 519, 519 (US Supreme Court).

[50] See, eg, *New Orleans v The Steamship Company* (1874) 87 US 387, 387 (US Supreme Court); see also *The Venice* (1863) 69 US 258, 276–77 (US Supreme Court).

[51] US DoD, *Law of War Manual* (December 2016) 761 [11.1.3.3]. However, the Manual also stated that 'the law of belligerent occupation would not apply to the use of military forces to control a State's own territory, such as in cases of domestic emergency, insurrection, or non-international armed conflict'. ibid 767 [11.2.2]. It is submitted that the examples given (ie, domestic emergency, insurrection, and NIAC) suggest that the drafters of the Manual had different factual patterns in mind than those present in internationalized armed conflicts.

[52] *Prosecutor v Hadžihasanović et al* (Indictment) IT-01-47 (5 July 2001) [22]–[24] (charging Enver Hadžihasanović with unlawful labour) and [46]–[48] (alleging that conduct charged as grave breaches of the GCs occurred, inter alia, during the 'partial occupation' of Bosnia and Herzegovina).

[53] *Prosecutor v Hadžihasanović et al* (Decision on Form of Indictment) IT-01-47-PT (7 December 2001) [32].

[54] ibid [32]–[34].

[55] ibid [35].

[56] cf *Prosecutor v Hadžihasanović et al* (Amended Indictment) IT-01-47-PT (11 January 2002).

[57] See Chapter 8.

directly from Article 1(4) AP I. Given that the provision extends the applicability of the entire body of IHL to this type of conflict, this must also include the law of belligerent occupation.[58] This is also apparent from the express inclusion of multiple rules relating to belligerent occupation in the Protocol itself:[59] it must be assumed that an international treaty applies in its entirety to all situations falling within its material scope[60] unless an express provision modifying this general principle can be identified.[61]

Some commentators have objected that neither of the parties in an Article 1(4) AP I conflict would be willing to accept that the territory under their control should be regarded as belligerently occupied.[62] However, it is impossible to anticipate in advance the attitude of the conflict parties towards their legal obligations in specific cases. Moreover, the parties' potential unwillingness to apply the law is at any rate irrelevant with regard to the actual applicability of the norms in question, and especially so with rules of IHL, the application of which is independent of the subjective views of conflict parties.[63] Therefore, it is submitted that the better view is that the territory belonging to the people engaged in the conflict is eligible to be belligerently occupied by the enemy state.

The precise designation of that territory would depend on which of the three permissible purposes under Article 1(4) AP I the conflict would be waged for.[64] It would pose little difficulty in a conflict fought against 'colonial domination', as in that case, the entirety of the colony would qualify as the territory belonging to the people in question.[65] Similarly, in a conflict fought against 'alien occupation', the territory in which the alien occupier deprives a distinct people of their right to self-determination would so qualify.[66] Apparently, in 2015, Switzerland as the depositary of AP I considered the situation in Western Sahara to qualify as an Article 1(4) AP I conflict because '[l]e Front POLISARIO lutte contre le Maroc en tant

[58] cf also E Milano, *Unlawful Territorial Situations in International Law: Reconciling Effectiveness, Legality and Legitimacy* (Martinus Nijhoff 2006) 156; Dinstein (n 7) 34; Sassòli, 'The Concept and the Beginning of Occupation' (n 7) 1415 [55].

[59] See, eg, Arts 3(b), 4, 14, 15(3), 18(3), 33(2), 34(1)–(2), 45(3), 46(3), 63, 64(3), 66(3), 67(2), 69, 85(4)(a), and 99(1) AP I.

[60] cf Y Sandoz, C Swinarski, and B Zimmermann (eds), *Commentary on the Additional Protocols of 8 June 1977 to the Geneva Conventions of 12 August 1949* (ICRC 1987) 34 [35] (hereafter Sandoz et al, *APs Commentary*) (confirming that paragraphs 3 and 4 of Art 1 AP I 'define the material scope of application of the Protocol').

[61] See, eg, Arts 6(1) and 83(1) AP I (extending the applicability of those provisions also to peacetime); Art 70(1) AP I (restricting the applicability of that provision to territories 'other than occupied territory').

[62] R Baxter, 'Humanitarian Law or Humanitarian Politics? The 1974 Diplomatic Conference on Humanitarian Law' (1975) 16 Harvard International Law Journal 1, 15–16; Sassòli, 'The Concept and the Beginning of Occupation' (n 7) 1415 [55].

[63] JK Kleffner, 'Scope of Application of International Humanitarian Law' in D Fleck (ed), *The Handbook of International Humanitarian Law* (3rd edn, OUP 2013) 45; see also Ferraro and Cameron, 'Article 2' (n 1) 115 [325] (arguing that it would be unreasonable to base the applicability of the law of occupation on the invading state's subjective considerations).

[64] On which see further Section 2.4.2.

[65] Sassòli, 'The Concept and the Beginning of Occupation' (n 7) 1415 [55].

[66] cf Kolb and Vité (n 8) 86–87; Sassòli, 'The Concept and the Beginning of Occupation' (n 7) 1415 [55].

que puissance occupante étrangère'.[67] On that view, the territory of Western Sahara should be considered as belligerently occupied by Morocco, which is consistent with the interpretation favoured here.[68]

In contrast to the first two privileged purposes under Article 1(4) AP I, the determination of the relevant territory would be more problematic in conflicts waged against 'racist regimes'. It has been suggested that 'a racist regime would likely be considered as occupying *the entire territory of the state* it governs',[69] but it is questionable whether it would be consistent with the object and purpose of the law of occupation to extend it to the entirety of the territory affected by an armed conflict. This would mean dispensing completely with the distinction between the 'home field' and the 'away field', which is central to the law of occupation.[70] At best, it can be said that the law is unclear in this regard; as shown elsewhere in this work, it is unlikely that the category of conflicts fought against 'racist regimes' is capable of application in practice,[71] and thus this issue is probably of limited practical significance.

10.3.2.2 Recognition of belligerency

Although conflicts internationalized by way of recognition of belligerency are largely a thing of the past, practice supporting the applicability of the law of belligerent occupation to occupied territory was more forthcoming in these situations. The delineation of the relevant territory in these conflicts is facilitated by the fact that one of the customary requirements of belligerent recognition is that the 'insurgents ... are in possession of a *certain part* of the territory of the legitimate Government'.[72] Should this territory come under the control of the state party to the conflict *after* the recognition of belligerency has been granted, the applicability of the law of IAC dictates that this land be subjected to the law of belligerent occupation.

The paradigmatic example is, again, the American Civil War (1861–65). The territory of the Southern secessionist states was easy to determine due to the federal structure of the country at war. And in practice, both the executive and the judicial institutions of the North acknowledged the applicability of occupation law to those parts of the Confederate territory (such as the city of New Orleans) that had come under the control of the Union army.[73]

[67] Switzerland, 'Déclaration unilatérale du Front POLISARIO d'application des Conventions de Genève et de leur premier Protocole additionnel dans son conflit avec le Maroc' (25 June 2015, completed and updated 30 June 2015) 2 (internal memorandum, on file with author).

[68] See also ibid ('Le Maroc occupe le Sahara occidental, respectivement le territoire à l'époque colonisé par l'Espagne. Dans le cas d'une occupation militaire, il ne saurait être exigé en outre que subsiste actuellement une résistance armée. L'existence d'un accord de cessez-le-feu ne change dès lors rien à la qualification du conflit.').

[69] Sassòli, 'The Concept and the Beginning of Occupation' (n 7) 1415 [55].

[70] See text to note 25 in this chapter.

[71] See Section 2.4.2.

[72] L Oppenheim, *International Law: A Treatise* (Longmans, Green & Co. 1905 & 1906) vol II, 86 (emphasis added).

[73] See text to notes 48–50 in this chapter.

Another example is the Boer War of 1899–1902, the locus of the last-known express recognition of belligerency by the territorial state.[74] In that conflict, protections of the law of belligerent occupation were similarly considered applicable to the occupied Boer territory, as evidenced both by the period criticism of the violations of this body of law committed by the British forces,[75] as well as by the accounts of their compliant behaviour.[76]

10.3.2.3 Outside intervention

Finally, there are only very isolated instances of practice supporting the applicability of the law of belligerent occupation to the territory of a non-state armed group in a conflict internationalized by an outside intervention. This scarcity of practice is likely attributable to a variety of reasons. States' reluctance to bestow upon their non-state opponents any legal status[77] certainly ranks high among these reasons, and the problem is further compounded by the usual uncertainty concerning the legal qualification of these conflicts.[78]

Nonetheless, limited examples of practice do exist. One may be found in connection with the non-state armed group Croatian Defence Council (*Hrvatsko vijeće obrane*, HVO) active in Central Bosnia in the early 1990s and subsequently found to have acted under the overall control of Croatia.[79] Its representative Dario Kordić (and a later defendant before the ICTY[80]) issued a written statement during the conflict according to which 'the HVO was the only military force allowed [in a particular part of the Bosnian territory] and *any other force would be treated as an occupying force*'.[81] Another separate example arose in the same broad context in relation to the Bosnian city of Mostar, which had formed a part of the territory of the Croatian Community of Herzeg-Bosnia (*Hrvatska zajednica Herceg-Bosna*, HZ H-B), an ethnically Croatian enclave defended by the HVO. When Mostar temporarily fell under the control of the Serb-Montenegrin forces in 1992, the city authorities issued a decision stating that 'the Mostar municipality is *under partial*

[74] See, eg, HP Gasser, 'International Humanitarian Law' in H Haug (ed), *Humanity for All: The International Red Cross and Red Crescent Movement* (P Haupt 1993) 559; E La Haye, *War Crimes in Internal Armed Conflicts* (CUP 2008) 14 fn 87.

[75] See, eg, JM Spaight, *War Rights on Land* (Macmillan 1911) 332, 340–41, 343, 350–53.

[76] See, eg, ibid 396 and 407.

[77] See, eg, Switzerland, *Official Records of the Diplomatic Conference on the Reaffirmation and Development of International Humanitarian Law Applicable in Armed Conflicts, Geneva (1974–1977)* (Federal Political Department 1978) (hereafter *Official Records*) vol VII, CDDH/SR.50/Annex, 104 (Zaire); S Watts, 'Present and Future Conceptions of the Status of Government Forces in NonInternational Armed Conflict' (2012) 88 International Law Studies 145, 163 (stating that 'historical experience of NIACs, and [the States'] clearest self-interest' weigh against any grant of legal status to the rebels).

[78] See further Section 1.1.2.

[79] *Blaškić* Trial Judgment (n 31) [122]; *Prosecutor v Prlić et al* (Trial Judgment) IT-04-74-T (29 May 2013) vol 3 [568].

[80] See *Prosecutor v Kordić and Čerkez*, IT-95-14/2-T.

[81] *Prosecutor v Kordić and Čerkez* (Trial Judgment) IT-95-14/2-T (26 February 2001) [508] (emphasis added).

occupation by units of the so-called Yugoslav People's Army'.[82] More recently, in the context of the conflict in eastern Ukraine, the Russian representative on the Security Council accused the Ukrainian governmental forces of possessing the 'intention to *occupy*' and of having actually 'beg[u]n to *occupy*' towns and territories in Donbas.[83]

However, too much should not be inferred from these proclamations. They were made by military and political representatives who may or may not have wanted to endow their statements with any legal significance. What is more, they are too infrequent and unaccompanied by any complementary statements by the other party to the conflict in question. Therefore, it cannot be said that these proclamations have occasioned any discernible change in the law. However, they demonstrate well the *possibility* of identifying a territory of an armed group which subsequently comes under control of a state. It is thus submitted that even conflicts internationalized by an outside intervention may, under certain circumstances, come under the scope of the law of belligerent occupation.

10.3.3 Occupation of state territory by a non-state actor

10.3.3.1 Wars of national liberation

The final of the three questions asks whether a non-state armed group may come to occupy a state's territory. Many of the considerations discussed in regard to the second question apply here as well. This is true particularly with respect to conflicts potentially internationalized by operation of Article 1(4) AP I where the analysis is chiefly theoretical due to the dearth of available practice.[84] The relevant *travaux préparatoires* also did not consider the possibility of a liberation movement acting as an occupying power, 'perhaps because liberation movements are widely viewed as underdogs, not overlords'.[85] In this connection, Eyal Benvenisti suggested that the national liberation movement, acting in the exercise of the right of self-determination, would be entitled to consider itself 'the rightful sovereign, not subject to any limitations on its powers stemming from the law of occupation'.[86] However, it is submitted that, the question of 'rightfulness' (or the absence thereof) is irrelevant for the applicability of the modern law of belligerent occupation due to its sovereignty-agnostic nature.[87]

This interpretation is further supported by the recent case-law of the ICTY. In the context of the *Prlić* case, one of the defendants argued that the principle of self-determination negated the possibility that the Croatia-controlled HVO could be subject to the law of occupation in Bosnia and Herzegovina because Croats had been living there 'for centuries'.[88] Dismissing the argument, the Appeals Chamber

[82] *Naletilić and Martinović* Trial Judgment (n 18) [17], citing a decision of the Mostar Municipal Assembly, Municipal Crisis staff Number 427/92 (29 April 1992) (emphasis added).

[83] UN Doc S/PV.7683 (28 April 2016) 21 (Russian Federation) (emphases added).

[84] See further Section 2.4.

[85] Roberts (n 7) 293.

[86] E Benvenisti, *The International Law of Occupation* (1st rev edn, Princeton University Press 2004) 185. cf also Benvenisti (n 5) 167–202 (abandoning this line of argument).

[87] See Section 9.3.2.

[88] *Prlić* Appeal Judgment (n 14) vol 1 [310].

held in late 2017 that 'the test for occupation is actual authority over the territory and population and not the motivation behind such an occupation'.[89] To be sure, it was not argued that the conflict in Bosnia and Herzegovina was a war of national liberation in the sense of Article 1(4) AP I. However, the *Prlić* ruling confirmed that even acting in pursuance of the right to self-determination would not release the entity in question from the applicability of the law of belligerent occupation to enemy territories under its actual authority.

Therefore, the better view is that the law of occupation would apply in any territory under the effective control of a liberation movement other than such territory for which the people in question has the right to self-determination.[90] This may include the metropolitan territory of the state characterized as a colonial dominator or an alien occupier[91] or even the territory of a neighbouring third state.[92] As explained earlier, the designation of the territories belonging to the parent state and the liberation movement respectively would be much more problematic in conflicts waged against 'racist regimes'.[93] However, overall it may be concluded that national liberation movements can, in principle, become occupying powers vis-à-vis the state territory.

10.3.3.2 Recognition of belligerency

As for conflicts internationalized by belligerent recognition, practice is scarcer than that discussed with respect to occupation by the territorial state. This is hardly surprising. Rebels are, after all, typically in a weaker starting position than the incumbent government. In addition, in both of the most recent conflicts, in which recognition had been granted by the territorial state, the rebels were ultimately defeated. It is therefore more likely that they would not establish sufficient control over enemy territory in order to trigger the law of occupation. This seems to have been the case both in the Boer War as well as in the American Civil War, especially after belligerent recognition had been granted.[94]

Interestingly, during the American Civil War, the secessionist states did come in temporary control of portions of the northern states of Missouri, Kentucky, and Maryland, but as Quincy Wright observed, '[t]hese controls were, however, short lived and were treated as "invasion" rather than "occupation."'[95] Nevertheless, it is implied in this statement that if the South's control over parts of the Union territory had been more permanent, it would have been treated as occupied territory. This is in line with the Lieber Code's conception of belligerent occupation.[96]

[89] ibid [341].

[90] Sassòli, 'The Concept and the Beginning of Occupation' (n 7) 1415 [55].

[91] cf ibid.

[92] Roberts (n 7) 292–93.

[93] See text to notes 69–71 in this chapter.

[94] Prior to the recognition of belligerency in the Boer War, the Boer militias staged an invasion into the British-held Natal and Cape Colony areas. However, even in this early phase of the war, the Boers were not able to maintain their hold over the British territory long enough to substitute the British control over these areas. See further D Judd and K Surridge, *The Boer War: A History* (IB Tauris 2013) 105–58 (discussing the early stages of the war).

[95] Wright (n 48) 63 (internal quotation marks kept).

[96] Lieber Code (n 47), Art 153; see also Section 8.2.2.

As mentioned earlier, due to the customary requirements of recognition of belligerency,[97] the identification of the territory of the non-state party will be relatively easy.[98] By necessary implication, the remaining territory should be considered as the territory of the state party to the conflict. In these conflicts, therefore, logic as well as practice supports an affirmative answer to the analysed question.

10.3.3.3 Outside intervention

The final category is represented by conflicts internationalized by outside intervention. There is a wealth of judicial opinion and findings of international organs, which have considered non-state armed groups as having established sufficient control to occupy state territory. The key question is whether it is the non-state group that should be considered the occupying power in such a situation of 'indirect effective control',[99] or rather the third state that supports the said armed group.

Several relevant examples of practice may be given. The Independent International Fact-Finding Mission on the Conflict in Georgia (IIFFMCG) considered parts of the Georgian territory to have been occupied by the Abkhaz forces, triggering the applicability of the law of belligerent occupation.[100] Both the UN General Assembly and Security Council have considered the Azerbaijani territory under the control of Armenian-supported separatists in the Nagorno Karabakh region as occupied.[101] Similarly, with respect to the conflict in eastern Ukraine, Ukrainian representatives on the Security Council have repeatedly complained that parts of Ukrainian territory were under occupation by 'Russian proxies'.[102]

Further examples abound in the jurisprudence of the ICTY. Specifically, the Tribunal held that parts of the territory of Bosnia and Herzegovina controlled at various times by Bosnian Serbian and Bosnian Croatian non-state armed groups qualified as occupied territories.[103] In addition, in *Prlić*, a trial chamber of the Tribunal expressly confirmed that as a matter of law, in circumstances characterized

[97] See Section 2.5.1.1 for a discussion of the traditional criteria for belligerency.

[98] See text to note 72 in this chapter.

[99] Ferraro and Cameron, 'Article 2' (n 1) 116 [331].

[100] IIFFMCG, *Independent International Fact-Finding Mission on the Conflict in Georgia: Report* (September 2009) vol 2, 213, 290, and 311.

[101] UNGA Res 62/243 (The Situation in the Occupied Territories of Azerbaijan) (14 March 2008) [2] and [3]; ibid, preambular [5]; UNSC Res 884 (12 November 1993) preambular [5].

[102] See, eg, UN Doc S/PV.7365 (21 January 2015) 17–18 (Ukraine); UN Doc S/PV.7576 (11 December 2015) 26 (Ukraine); UN Doc S/PV.7876 (2 February 2017) 7 (Ukraine).

[103] *Prosecutor v Karadžić and Mladić* (Review of the Indictment Pursuant to Rule 61 of the Rules of Procedure and Evidence) IT-95-5-R61 & IT-95-18-R61 (11 July 1996) [1.31] (finding that the VRS had occupied parts of Bosnian territory); *Blaškić* Trial Judgment (n 31) [149]–[50] (finding that the HVO had occupied parts of Bosnian territory); *Prosecutor v Hadžihasanović and Kubura* (Trial Judgment) IT-01-47-T (15 March 2006) [400] and [643] (finding that the VRS had occupied parts of Bosnian territory); ibid [955] (finding that the HVO had occupied a part of the Bosnian territory); *Prlić* Trial Judgment (n 79) vol 3 [589] (finding that the HVO had occupied several parts of the Bosnian territory); see also *Prosecutor's Office of Bosnia and Herzegovina v Radomir Vuković and Zoran Tomić*, X-KR-06/180-2, Verdict (22 April 2010) (Court of Bosnia and Herzegovina) 7 (finding that the Srebrenica Safe Area in Bosnia and Herzegovina had been subject to 'total occupation by the VRS').

in this book as a conflict internationalized by outside intervention,[104] the territory under the control of a non-state armed group is to be considered as being occupied:

> [I]f the Prosecution proves that the party to the armed conflict under the overall control of a foreign State fulfils the criteria for control of a territory . . . , a state of occupation of that part of the territory is proven.[105]

The remaining question concerns the identification of the occupying power in these complex conflict situations. It is submitted that as long as the non-state party in question maintains a degree of operational autonomy, it should be considered the occupying power for the purposes of the law of belligerent occupation. This is a necessary consequence of the conceptualization of the relationship between the law of state responsibility and the rules on conflict qualification put forward in this book.[106]

This issue bears closer examination. In situations in which the non-state party maintains its operational autonomy in full, the conflict between itself and the territorial state remains non-international in nature in spite of the involvement of the third state.[107] Therefore, the law of belligerent occupation would not apply to the territory under its control at all.[108] At the other end of the spectrum, if the entirety of the non-state party's operational autonomy had been sacrificed in favour of the intervening (and thus controlling) state, it is this state that should be considered to be the occupying power.[109] The non-state actor acts as the agent of the intervening state in the sense of Article 29 GC IV[110] and Article 8 ILC ASR.[111]

In the middle between these two extreme types of situations lie conflicts which are internationalized on account of the sufficient control of the outside party, but which do not yet trigger the responsibility of the intervening state for the conduct of the armed group in question.[112] In other words, these are the situations, in which the non-state actor controls a part of the home state's territory, but is not itself subject to 'effective control' of the outside state.[113] In this middle-type of situation, which seemed to have been the case in some of the ex-Yugoslavian conflicts, for some time during the 2011 Libyan conflict, and possibly in the Abkhaz-controlled territory of Georgia, the semi-autonomous non-state actor should be seen as the occupying power.

[104] See Section 2.2.2.4.

[105] *Prlić* Trial Judgment (n 79) vol 1 [96].

[106] See Section 2.2.2.4.

[107] See Section 3.3.

[108] See note 28 in this chapter; see also, eg, Kolb and Hyde (n 33) 69; Benvenisti (n 5) 61; Sassòli, 'The Concept and the Beginning of Occupation' (n 7) 1415–16 [57].

[109] See Section 3.3.

[110] Art 29 GC IV ('The Party to the conflict in whose hands protected persons may be, is responsible for the treatment accorded to them by its agents, irrespective of any individual responsibility which may be incurred.'). See also T Gal, 'Unexplored Outcomes of *Tadić*' (2014) 12 JICJ 59, 65 (arguing, on the analysis of the ICRC commentary to Art 29 GC IV, that the notion of 'agent' in that provision applies to non-state actors).

[111] ILC, Draft Articles on Responsibility of States for Internationally Wrongful Acts, with commentaries Yearbook of the ILC (2001) vol II, part two, 47, Art 8.

[112] See Section 3.3.

[113] See further Section 2.2.2.3.

To the extent that this admittedly complex matter is discussed in the literature at all, commentators tend to conflate the middle and one of the extreme positions. For instance, Tristan Ferraro argued that '*a state* would be an occupying power for the purposes of IHL when it exercises *overall control* over de facto local authorities or other local organized groups that are themselves in effective control of a territory or part thereof'.[114] However, this approach unacceptably strains the law of state responsibility. It would make the outside state responsible under IHL for acts for which it does not have to answer on the international plane because they were performed by an independent third party.[115]

It is proposed that the better approach is to separate the question of conflict qualification (determined by a test akin to the 'overall control' test propounded by the ICTY[116]) from the question of the identification of the occupying power (determined by a case-by-case consideration of the facts on the ground and the degree of operational autonomy of the individual actors).[117] Admittedly, the ICTY has nominally maintained its problematic[118] state responsibility-oriented approach to conflict qualification developed in its earlier case-law.[119] Nevertheless, its later jurisprudence actually lends support to the approach proposed here with respect to the law of occupation. In particular, the *Naletilić and Martinović* case drew a clear distinction between the tests concerning conflict qualification and the determination of the existence of occupation, respectively.[120] Moreover, a trial chamber of the Tribunal accepted in *Prlić* that the HVO (and *not* Croatia, which had exercised overall control over the former[121]) should be treated as the occupying power with respect to the relevant territories.[122] Although that interpretation was later rejected on appeal,[123] the case demonstrates that it is conceptually possible to delimit the territory subject to belligerent occupation by a non-state party as well as to consider this actor to be the actual occupying power.

[114] Ferraro (n 7) 158 (emphases added); similarly see, eg, Gal (n 110) 77; Ferraro and Cameron, 'Article 2' (n 1) 116–17 [329]–[32].

[115] See further Section 2.2.2.4. See also Gal (n 110) 77–78 (criticizing this gap in responsibility from a normative perspective); but see Ferraro and Cameron, 'Article 2' (n 1) 99 [271] (arguing in favour of the test of 'overall control' as the correct standard for *both* conflict qualification and the law of state responsibility on the grounds that the law 'must avoid a situation where some acts are governed by the law of international armed conflict but cannot be attributed to a State').

[116] *Prosecutor v Tadić* (Appeal Judgment) IT-94-1-A (15 July 1999) [131].

[117] See text to notes 107–13 in this chapter.

[118] See Section 2.2.2.3.4.

[119] See, eg, *Prlić* Trial Judgment (n 79) vol 1 [85]–[86] and vol 3 [518].

[120] *Naletilić and Martinović* Trial Judgment (n 18) [214] ('The Chamber is of the view that there is an essential distinction between the determination of a state of occupation and that of the existence of an international armed conflict. The application of the overall control test is applicable to the latter. A further degree of control is required to establish occupation.').

[121] *Prlić* Trial Judgment (n 79) vol 3 [545].

[122] ibid [589]; see also ibid [575] fn 1175 ('The Chamber recalls that the occupation by the HVO can be established, inasmuch as Croatia/the HV wielded overall control over the HVO.').

[123] *Prlić* Appeal Judgment (n 14) vol 1 [325].

10.4 Personal Scope

The final question concerning the scope of application relates to the designation of protected persons under the law of occupation. In the law of IAC, these are defined by Article 4(1) GC IV as individuals who find themselves 'in the hands of [an] Occupying Power *of which they are not nationals*'.[124] At the beginning of an internationalized armed conflict, however, all inhabitants except for foreign residents share the same nationality, ie, that of the territorial state. Does this mean that the concept of protected persons does not extend to internationalized armed conflicts? This section argues that the designation of protected persons may be founded in internationalized conflicts on the concept of allegiance in lieu of the traditional approach based on nationality.

10.4.1 Traditional view: nationality as the sole criterion

Similarly to territory, population is one of the defining characteristics of a state in international law.[125] 'The sum of its nationals, and thus the concept of nationality as such, determines the "personal dimension" of a State in its international relations and gives rise to specific rights and duties of States'.[126] Under ordinary circumstances, international law does not further atomize the concept of nationality.[127] Therefore, there is only and exactly one population associated with one state, namely, all those who share the same nationality.[128] However, a situation of armed conflict can hardly be described as ordinary and internationalized armed conflicts pose further challenges of their own.

Nonetheless, the traditional view was that all provisions of IHL that protect persons of another nationality were 'fundamentally unworkable in internal conflict'.[129] Richard Baxter gave two reasons in support of this view:

> It is not possible to say that rebels should be treated *as if* they were enemy nationals. In the first place, this is not what the Convention says. In the second place, how can this status be determined, when the allegiance of civilians is sought by both belligerents and cannot readily

[124] Art 4(1) GC IV (emphasis added).

[125] Montevideo Convention on the Rights and Duties of States (signed 26 December 1933, entered into force 26 December 1934) 165 LNTS 19, Art 1.

[126] O Dörr, 'Nationality' in R Wolfrum (ed), *Max Planck Encyclopedia of Public International Law* (OUP 2008) <www.mpepil.com> (updated November 2006) [1].

[127] cf European Convention on Nationality (signed 6 November 1997, entered into force 1 March 2000) 2135 UNTS 213, Art 2(1) ('"nationality" means the legal bond between a person and a State and does not indicate the person's ethnic origin').

[128] J Crawford, *The Creation of States in International Law* (2nd edn, OUP 2006) 52–55; see also *Nottebohm (Liechtenstein v Guatemala)* (Second Phase) [1955] ICJ Rep 4 [57].

[129] Baxter (n 27) 530; see also ICRC, *Conference of Government Experts on the Reaffirmation and Development of International Humanitarian Law Applicable in Armed Conflicts, 24 May–12 June 1971* (ICRC 1971) (hereafter ICRC, *Conference of Government Experts*) vol V, 69 (observing that the concept of nationality is 'not consistent' with the nature of a NIAC).

be ascertained in individual cases? *Nationality is a fixed legal status; loyalty or allegiance is quite another thing.*[130]

Baxter thus juxtaposed nationality and allegiance as two alternative criteria of association of civilians with a conflict party and then dismissed the latter without further analysis. Importantly, the jurisprudence of the ICTY has since departed from the traditional view based on nationality, endorsing instead precisely allegiance as the 'decisive criterion for determining the status of a protected person'.[131]

10.4.2 The ICTY approach: replacing nationality with allegiance

The ICTY developed this 'original approach'[132] to the interpretation of Article 4 GC IV already in the *Tadić* case.[133] The defence had argued in that case that in the context of the armed conflict occurring solely in the territory of Bosnia and Herzegovina, the victims could not be regarded as protected persons under IHL because they had been of the same nationality as the alleged perpetrators.[134] Although the victims as well as the alleged perpetrators including the defendant in the case were indeed all of Bosnian nationality, they did differ in their ethnicity: the former were Bosnian Muslims or Bosnian Croats while the latter were Bosnian Serbs.[135]

The Appeals Chamber of the ICTY rejected the nationality-based approach as excessively formalistic.[136] On the basis of a textual, historical, and teleological analysis of the relevant provisions in GC IV, it considered the allegiance-based approach as the decisive legal test.[137] With respect to the case before it, the Appeals Chamber concluded that the victims and the perpetrators did not owe allegiance to the same conflict party, and thus it deemed Article 4 GC IV as applicable to the situation.[138] This approach thus places the substance of relations between individual actors before the formal legal characterization of their mutual bonds.[139] It was confirmed by a host of later decisions of the ICTY and it has become an indelible part of the Tribunal's stable jurisprudence.[140] It has also been accepted

[130] Baxter (n 27) 530–31 (first emphasis original, second emphasis added).

[131] *Prlić* Trial Judgment (n 79) vol 1 [100], citing *Tadić* Appeal Judgment (n 116) [166].

[132] W Schabas, *The UN International Criminal Tribunals: The Former Yugoslavia, Rwanda and Sierra Leone* (CUP 2006) 247.

[133] *Tadić* Appeal Judgment (n 116) [166].

[134] *Prosecutor v Tadić* (Defence Motion on the Jurisdiction of the Tribunal) IT-94-1-T (23 June 1995) 2; *Prosecutor v Tadić* (Defence Brief to Support the Motion on the Jurisdiction of the Tribunal) IT-94-1-T (23 June 1995) [9.4]; *Prosecutor v Tadić* (The Respondent's Brief of Argument on the Brief of Argument of the Prosecution) IT-94-1-A (19 January 1999) [2.9] and [2.18].

[135] *Prosecutor v Tadić* (Trial Judgment) IT-94-1-T (7 May 1997) [180] (concerning the accused's ethnicity) and [726], [730], [734], [742], [752] (concerning the ethnicity of some of the victims).

[136] *Tadić* Appeal Judgment (n 116) [165]–[66]; see also ibid [96] ('[IHL] is not grounded on formalistic postulates.').

[137] ibid [164]–[69]. [138] ibid [169]. [139] ibid [168].

[140] See, eg, *Blaškić* Trial Judgment (n 31) [125]–[26]; *Prosecutor v Aleksovski* (Appeal Judgment) IT-95-14/1-A (24 March 2000) [151]; *Prosecutor v Delalić et al* (*Čelebići* Appeal Judgment) IT-96-21-A (20 February 2001) [81]–[83]; *Prosecutor v Blaškić* (Appeal Judgment) IT-95-14-A (29 July 2004) [167]–[82]; *Prosecutor v Kordić and Čerkez* (Appeal Judgment) IT-95-14/2-A (17 December 2004) [329]–[30]; *Prlić* Appeal Judgment (n 14) vol 1 [354]–[55].

by the ICC,[141] the ECCC,[142] and—albeit indirectly—the Belgrade War Crimes Chamber.[143]

10.4.3 The traditional view and the ICTY approach juxtaposed: in defence of allegiance

10.4.3.1 Locating the criterion of allegiance in Geneva Convention IV

Given the marked discrepancy between the traditional view and the recent case-law produced and inspired by the ICTY, it is necessary to appraise the objections given against such a development. Firstly, it is true that the alternative view is prima facie incompatible with the text of the Convention,[144] which limits the protection to those individuals who are 'not nationals' of the occupying power.[145] However, the *Tadić* appeal judgment correctly noted that there are other provisions in the same Convention, which detract from the importance of the formal legal bond of nationality.[146] Specifically, Article 44 GC IV forbids the states in their capacity as detaining powers to treat refugees as enemy aliens solely on the basis of their *de jure* nationality of an enemy state when these refugees do not, de facto, enjoy the protection of any state.[147] In addition, Article 70(2) GC IV prohibits the occupying power to arrest, prosecute, convict, or deport its own nationals who have sought refuge in the territory of the occupied state.[148] The inclusion of these provisions indicates that the drafters did not consider the fact of shared nationality as a conclusive factor which would remove such persons from the protection of the law in all situations.

Although many commentators have commended the ICTY for its extensive interpretation of the concept of protected persons,[149] its approach has not been free from criticism.[150] For example, Tamás Hoffmann argued, on the basis of the

[141] *Prosecutor v Thomas Lubanga Dyilo* (Decision on the Confirmation of Charges, Pre-Trial Chamber I) ICC-01/04-01/06 (29 January 2007) [277]–[80]; *Prosecutor v Germain Katanga and Mathieu Ngudjolo Chui* (Decision on the Confirmation of Charges, Pre-Trial Chamber I) ICC-01/04-01/07 (30 September 2008) [290]–[91]; see also ICC, Elements of Crimes (2000) UN Doc PCNICC/2000/1/Add.2, fn 33.

[142] *Case of Kaing Guek Eav alias 'Duch'* (Trial Judgment) 001/18-07-2007/ECCC/TC (26 July 2010) [419] and [425]–[26]; cf also *Case of Nuon Chea et al* (Closing Order) 002/19-09-2007-ECCC-OCIJ (15 September 2010) [1482] (doubting whether the 'allegiance test' applies to IACs in general but acknowledging its applicability to 'internecine armed conflicts occurring pursuant to the dissolution of a pre-existing state and in the context of the formulation of new states').

[143] *Anton Lekaj* (Judgment) KV 4/05 (18 September 2006) (WCC) 26 and 39.

[144] cf Baxter (n 27) 531.

[145] Art 4(1) GC IV.

[146] *Tadić* Appeal Judgment (n 116) [165].

[147] Art 44 GC IV.

[148] Art 70(2) GC IV.

[149] See, eg, WJ Fenrick, 'The Application of the Geneva Conventions by the International Criminal Tribunal for the former Yugoslavia' (1999) 81 IRRC 317, 327; T Meron, 'The Humanization of Humanitarian Law' (2000) 94 AJIL 239, 260; K Kittichaisaree, *International Criminal Law* (OUP 2001) 140–41; N Wagner, 'The Development of the Grave Breaches Regime and of Individual Criminal Responsibility by the International Criminal Tribunal for the former Yugoslavia' (2003) 85 IRRC 351, 375–76; D Fleck, 'Shortcomings of the Grave Breaches Regime' (2009) 7 JICJ 833, 843.

[150] See, eg, M Sassòli and LM Olson, 'The Judgment of the ICTY Appeals Chamber on the Merits in the Tadić Case' (2000) 82 IRRC 733, 743–44; T Hoffmann, 'The Perils of Judicial Construction of Identity—A Critical Analysis of the International Criminal Tribunal for the Former Yugoslavia's Jurisprudence on Protected Persons' in F Jenkins, M Nolan, and K Rubinstein (eds), *Allegiance and*

principle *inclusio unius est exclusio alterius*, that Article 70(2) GC IV should be seen as an exception that confirms the general rule based on nationality.[151] However, this provision is not the only IHL norm adopting a more nuanced approach to the criterion of nationality. Apart from Article 44 GC IV cited earlier, two further rules merit express mention in this connection.

Firstly, already the Hague Regulations proclaimed that '[i]t is forbidden to compel the inhabitants of occupied territory to swear allegiance to the hostile Power'.[152] Secondly, Article 68(3) GC IV provides that before the imposition of the death penalty against a protected person, the court must take into account that 'since the accused is not a national of the occupying power, he is not bound to it by any duty of allegiance'.[153]

These provisions further demonstrate that the law of belligerent occupation places weight not only on the formal bonds inherent in nationality, but also on the actual allegiance owed by the protected persons. The former provision protects the inhabitants from interference with their allegiance by the occupying power and the latter provision highlights the importance of the fact that the inhabitants are not bound by a duty of allegiance to the occupying power.[154] Additionally, several further provisions of GC IV refer to allegiance instead of nationality as a method of associating protected persons with a conflict party.[155]

It is therefore submitted that the better view is that the regulation of protected persons in the law of belligerent occupation, and particularly in GC IV, is based on a delicate balance between, on the one hand, the interests of states manifested in the adoption of the nationality criterion as the general rule[156] and, on the other hand, the humanitarian aims of this body of law[157] reflected in those provisions that complement this criterion with the consideration of allegiance in specific cases.[158] Internationalized armed conflicts should equally be seen as specific cases because they are characterized by an international element bringing them within the scope of the law of IAC. The concern for the effectiveness of the law thus militates in favour of a complementary allegiance-based approach to the identification of protected persons in such conflicts.

Identity in a Globalised World (CUP 2014) 497–521; E Salmón, 'Who is a Protected Civilian?' in Clapham, Gaeta, and Sassòli (n 7) 1145 [33]–[34].

151 Hoffmann (n 150) 511; see also Sandoz et al, *APs Commentary* (n 60) 46.

152 Regulations Respecting the Laws and Customs of War on Land, Annex to Hague Convention (IV) respecting the Laws and Customs of War on Land (signed 18 October 1907, entered into force 26 January 1910) 205 CTS 277, Art 45.

153 Art 68(3) GC IV; see also KH Tse, 'The Relevancy of Nationality to the Right to Prisoner of War Status' (2009) 8 Chinese JIL 395, 401 (arguing, in the context of the right to POW status, that '[t]he fact that most POWs do not owe a duty of allegiance to their detaining power does not necessarily imply that those who owe such a duty should be taken out of the category of POWs').

154 Dinstein (n 7) 52–53.

155 Arts 98(2), 105, 107(1), and 135(2) GC IV.

156 See Pictet, *GC IV Commentary* (n 7) 46 (stating that the Convention is 'faithful' to the principle of international law proscribing the interference in a state's relations with its own nationals).

157 See ibid 21 (stating that 'the Conventions have been drawn up first and foremost to protect individuals, and not to serve State interests').

158 Contra Hoffmann (n 150) 512.

Hoffmann further took issue[159] with the argument made in *Tadić* that the modern reality of interethnic armed conflicts necessitated the use of criteria other than nationality for the determination of allegiance.[160] He argued that interethnic conflicts had in fact broken out on a number of occasions in the twentieth century, and thus it would be 'difficult to imagine the drafting states were unaware of them in 1949'.[161] However, even if the phenomenon of interethnic violence is less novel than the *Tadić* Appeals Chamber may have made it out to be, the legal implications of this observation should not be overstated.

Specifically, Hoffmann claimed that 'the problem was clearly considered by states during the treaty negotiations', but that 'they refused to give any concessions in extending the scope of Geneva Convention IV to their own civilian population'.[162] However, the drafters' debates he referred to had actually related only to the possibility of extending the application of IHL to *non-international* armed conflicts.[163] For example, a statement by the Canadian representative cited in Hoffmann's piece expressly rejected that the GC IV concept of protected persons would apply 'in a large-scale *civil* war'.[164] By contrast, the ICTY's allegiance-based approach is predicated on the existence of an international (or internationalized, as understood in this book) armed conflict. Therefore, the fact that the drafters were not ready to accept the extension of the protected person status to their own citizens in NIACs is not directly relevant to the issue upon consideration.

10.4.3.2 Overcoming the practical obstacles to the determination of allegiance

Even if it is accepted that the allegiance test is compatible with the text of GC IV and its drafting history, it might be queried to what extent this test may in fact be relied upon in practice. This was the crux of Baxter's concern when he argued that allegiance could not readily be ascertained in individual cases.[165] Similarly, several commentators have contended that it would be difficult to apply the allegiance test 'in the heat of the conflict'[166] and that, in any event, representations made by the concerned persons about their true allegiance would be 'virtually impossible to verify'.[167] In reality, these practical obstacles are not insurmountable for at least three main reasons.

Firstly, more than four decades after the publication of Baxter's article in 1974, we have the benefit of the constant international jurisprudence spearheaded by the ICTY. The Tribunal held in *Naletilić and Martinović* that it would 'review, on a case by case basis, the effective allegiance of the victims'.[168] It has been considerably active in this sense and, as noted earlier, its approach has since been endorsed by other international and domestic courts.[169] The ICTY's line of cases since the 1999 *Tadić*

[159] Hoffmann (n 150) 514–16. [160] *Tadić* Appeal Judgment (n 116) [166].
[161] Hoffmann (n 150) 514. [162] ibid 516. [163] cf ibid 514–16.
[164] Switzerland, *Final Record of the Diplomatic Conference of Geneva of 1949* (Federal Political Department 1949) vol II-B, 13 (Canada) (emphasis added); cf Hoffmann (n 150) 515.
[165] Baxter (n 27) 531. [166] Sassòli and Olson (n 150) 744; Fleck (n 149) 843.
[167] Salmón (n 150) 1145 [33].
[168] *Naletilić and Martinović* Trial Judgment (n 18) [207].
[169] See notes 141–43 in this chapter.

Appeal Judgment[170] has therefore by now become a 'persuasive precedent' for the determination of the protected person status in similar cases in the future.[171] It can thus no longer be said that there are no criteria or indicators for the determination of allegiance during armed conflicts.

Secondly, with respect to the more modern objections about the practical difficulty of applying and verifying these criteria while fighting a battle, it suffices to say that this is hardly the only difficult determination that IHL prescribes the commanders to make in the midst of an armed conflict.[172] Whether or not a particular legal test is easier or more difficult to apply is irrelevant as a question of *lex lata.*[173] If the allegiance test renders uncertain results under volatile circumstances even after a 'careful assessment',[174] the commander should err on the side of caution and treat the individual in question as a protected person;[175] in short, *in dubio pro humanitate.*[176]

Thirdly, the determination of allegiance will normally be ascertainable by the conduct of the conflict party in question towards a putative protected person. If they are treated as a potential threat to the relevant conflict party, such treatment would amount to a good indication that the person is perceived as owing their allegiance to the enemy. This can be well illustrated on the example of the Bosnian Muslim members of the HVO during the armed conflict in Bosnia and Herzegovina. Initially, these persons joined the HVO of their own will, having even reportedly sworn allegiance to this non-state armed group.[177] However, after an attack on an HVO military base, in which some of them had participated, the HVO authorities started perceiving this whole group as a threat.[178] The leadership of the HVO then ordered the Muslim members to be disarmed and detained *en masse.*[179] On the basis of this factual pattern, a trial chamber of the ICTY held in *Prlić* that these persons 'were perceived by the HVO as loyal to the [Bosnian state army]' and thus qualified as protected persons within the meaning of Article 4 GC IV.[180]

It is true that this approach—based on 'the detaining authority's view of the victims' allegiance'[181]—may mean that in practice almost all victims of internationalized

[170] *Tadić* Appeal Judgment (n 116).
[171] Wagner (n 149) 367–68.
[172] See, eg, A Carswell, 'Classifying the Conflict: A Soldier's Dilemma' (2009) 91 IRRC 143 (discussing the challenges of legal classification of armed conflicts for the military commanders).
[173] cf N Zamir, *Classification of Conflicts in International Humanitarian Law: The Legal Impact of Foreign Intervention in Civil Wars* (Edward Elgar 2017) 102.
[174] cf J-M Henckaerts and L Doswald-Beck (eds), *Customary International Humanitarian Law* (CUP 2005) 24 (hereafter *ICRC CIHL Study*).
[175] See Art 50(1) AP I ('In case of doubt whether a person is a civilian, that person shall be considered to be a civilian.'). Note that the customary nature of the presumption of civilian status codified in this rule is not universally accepted. Compare, eg, *ICRC CIHL Study* (n 174) 23–24 and MN Schmitt (ed), *Tallinn Manual 2.0 on the International Law Applicable to Cyber Operations* (CUP 2017) 424–25.
[176] cf XIXth International Red Cross Conference, *Draft Rules for the Limitation of the Dangers incurred by the Civilian Population in Time of War* (ICRC 1956) 82 (citing the principle *in dubio pro humanitate* as applying in the event of doubt as to the extent of anticipated civilian loss caused by an attack); but see Hoffmann (n 150) 517 (arguing that the ICTY's approach was wrongly based on the principle *in dubio pro humanitate*, given that as a criminal court, it should have instead acted *in dubio pro reo*).
[177] *Prlić* Trial Judgment (n 79) vol 3 [609].
[178] ibid.
[179] ibid.
[180] ibid [610]–[11].
[181] *Prlić* Appeal Judgment (n 14) vol 1 [355].

armed conflicts would benefit from the protected persons status. As Sassòli and Olson observed, 'a State will only rarely abuse those who maintain their allegiance to it'.[182] Conversely, once a conflict party perceives a person as effectively loyal to the enemy, the probability of adverse consequences for that person will increase exponentially. Nevertheless, the approach is well in tune with the ongoing trend of humanization of IHL discussed in Chapter 8, as well as with a growing body of international jurisprudence.[183] As such, it is submitted that the expanded scope of protection is an advantage, not a disadvantage, of this line of argument.

Elizabeth Salmón has raised the question whether the criterion of allegiance would also be available in 'conflicts that are devoid of an ethnic component'.[184] Although the focus here has been on ethnicity given the detailed treatment this factor has received in the international case-law thus far, it is submitted that allegiance may also be determined by reference to other comparable factors. In particular, if the conflict in question is not interethnic in nature, but it instead arises from ideological confrontation, allegiance may be determined by political or ideological factors.[185] For example, in the *Duch* case, the ECCC considered certain Cambodian nationals as protected persons due to the perception on the side of the government that they had been 'Vietnamese sympathizers' and the court did not further elaborate on their actual ethnicity.[186]

On the basis of the foregoing analysis, it is thus submitted that the designation of protected persons in internationalized armed conflicts on the basis of the allegiance test is not only conceptually viable and generally compatible with the text of GC IV, but that it is also practically possible. Therefore, the personal scope of the law of belligerent occupation in such conflicts should be understood to include persons who hold the same nationality as the occupier, but who owe their effective allegiance to the displaced enemy.

10.5 Evaluation

Together with combatant status, belligerent occupation is one of the two main concepts that have resisted the trend of confluence between IACs and NIACs. This part of the book has considered whether and to what extent the law of belligerent occupation may apply to conflicts internationalized in one of the ways put forward in this study.

The main challenge identified in this part arises out of the fact that, similarly to traditional NIACs, internationalized armed conflicts begin in the territory of

[182] Sassòli and Olson (n 150) 744.

[183] See, in particular, *Čelebići* Appeal Judgment (n 140) [98]; *Prlić* Appeal Judgment (n 14) vol 1 [355]; *Duch* Trial Judgment (n 142) [426].

[184] cf Salmón (n 150) 1145 [34].

[185] Tse (n 153) 419 (referring in this connection to 'commitment to communism' as such an ideological factor potentially applicable in the context of the conflict in Malaysia, in which the Malaysian leftist insurgents were supported from the outside by Indonesia).

[186] *Duch* Trial Judgment (n 142) [426].

a single state, whereas according to the orthodox understanding of the law of belligerent occupation, this body of law is based on a duality of warring states, their territories and populations. In response, Chapter 8 and Chapter 9 argued, on the basis of a historical analysis and through the consideration of the normative underpinnings of the law of occupation, that this body of law is in principle applicable to internationalized armed conflicts.

This chapter then examined the precise scope of application of the law of occupation to internationalized armed conflicts. It argued that the temporal trigger for the application of this body of law is at the moment when one of the conflict parties consolidates its control over the enemy territory and substitutes its own authority for that of the displaced enemy. It then assessed the geographical scope of the law and drew specific guidelines for the determination of the territory subject to the law of occupation in various types of internationalized armed conflicts. Finally, the chapter endorsed the allegiance based approach to the designation of protected persons under the law of belligerent occupation and applied it to the reality of internationalized armed conflict.

This chapter thus completes Part III of this book. On the whole, the conclusion of this part is that it is indeed possible to apply the law of belligerent occupation to modern internationalized armed conflicts, while the precise scope of its application should be determined in line with the criteria outlined in this chapter. Chapter 11 concludes this book by summarizing its overall argument and considering the potential for further development of the relevant law.

PART IV
CONCLUSION

11

Conclusion

This book has argued that the concept of internationalized armed conflict has a continuing relevance in international law. It serves to denote those situations of armed violence that have undergone a fundamental conversion of their legal qualification, having transformed from a non-international armed conflict (NIAC) to an international armed conflict (IAC).

In principle, this transformation makes the entirety of the law of IAC applicable to internationalized conflicts. However, in practice, the application of rules predicated on the existence of inter-state warfare to internationalized conflicts is not always straightforward. This is particularly so with the regulation of combatant status and belligerent occupation, both analysed in detail in the preceding chapters.

The purpose of this conclusion is not to provide a detailed digest of each of the chapters in this book. Rather, it aims to briefly summarize the argument of the book and to make some more general observations about the process and effects of internationalization in international law.

11.1 A Challenge to the Classic Understanding

This book started with a simple observation. The law of armed conflict that is in force today is an uneasy match for conflicts that break out in the territory of a single state and gradually acquire international dimensions. Given how many modern conflicts fit this factual pattern, the status quo is perhaps startling, and certainly often problematic. The main cause for this mismatch is well-known and understandable when seen from the historical perspective. It is that the law forces every situation of armed violence into one of two straitjackets sewn after the Second World War and adapted very little since then: for international humanitarian law (IHL) to apply, the situation must qualify as either a NIAC or an IAC.

The choice is of much more than just semantic consequence. Even though the famous *Tadić* decision on jurisdiction[1] set in motion a process of confluence between these two legal categories, a number of major differences have remained. In that regard, various writers have placed emphasis on different areas of IHL, but two matters are most generally accepted as those that have withstood this trend of

[1] *Prosecutor v Tadić* (Decision on Jurisdiction) IT-94-1-AR72 (2 October 1995).

confluence, namely, the regulation of combatancy and the law of belligerent occupation. When a conflict changes its nature from a NIAC to an IAC (in other words, becomes 'internationalized'), the consequences in these areas are, in principle, most profoundly felt.

That such a transformation of the legal nature of a conflict is conceivable is not a novel observation. Over 250 years ago, Emmerich de Vattel argued that if an internal conflict acquires a certain set of characteristics—focusing on the strength of the rebels and the intensity of the fighting—it must be treated in the same way as an international conflict.[2] As international reality and international law developed, so did these conditions. However, Vattel's principle remains: the accumulation of certain prerequisites alters the nature of an internal conflict and renders the norms governing IACs applicable to the conflict in question. This, at the core, is the meaning of conflict internationalization.[3]

However, the law of IAC, of which the regulation of combatant status and belligerent occupation forms a central part, was drafted with 'standard' (or 'classic') inter-state armed conflicts in mind. A classic IAC—such as, for instance, the 1980–88 war between Iraq and Iran—is characterized by the participation of two sovereign states, each with an effective government and a clearly defined territory and population. Classic IACs are symmetric in nature and engage 'state armies of roughly equal military strength and of comparable organizational structures'.[4] By contrast, internationalized armed conflicts start in the territory of one state only, involve at least one non-state actor as a conflict party, and their character is invariably asymmetric.

11.2 Process of Internationalization

In order to respond to the challenge that internationalized armed conflicts pose to IHL, it is first necessary to understand the process of internationalization and its various modalities. This was the focus of Part I of the book. Specifically, Chapter 2 argued that four distinct modalities of internationalization have emerged thus far in international law. The first two of them bring about situations that may be subsumed under the terms of Common Article 2. Since these are the closest to the notion of standard IACs discussed earlier, they may be described as instances of 'standard internationalization'. The remaining two modalities are seen as cases of 'complementary internationalization', because they are to be treated as international although they ostensibly do not meet the conditions in Common Article 2, and as such, they complement the two standard modalities.

The first modality of internationalization occurs when a third state or an international organization intervenes in a NIAC ('external standard internationalization').[5]

[2] E de Vattel, *The Law of Nations or the Principles of Natural Law* (J Chitty tr, 1758), book III, ch XVIII, 292–95.

[3] See Section 1.3.

[4] W Banks, 'Toward an Adaptive International Humanitarian Law: New Norms for New Battlefields' in W Banks (ed), *New Battlefields/Old Laws: Critical Debates on Asymmetric Warfare* (Columbia University Press 2011) 5.

[5] See Section 2.2.

In order to bring about the internationalizing effect, the intervention must be conducted without the consent of the territorial state. It may be direct or indirect, but if it is the latter, the involvement of the outside actor must amount to a use of force through a non-state armed group engaged in the conflict. A good example is the 2011 Libyan conflict: assuming the veracity of the reports concerning the establishment of a joint operations centre for the coordination of NATO and rebels' military operations, the conflict should be seen as internationalized by NATO's indirect intervention.[6]

Second, a NIAC is internationalized if the parent state disintegrates within the duration of the conflict. Under traditional international law, stability and permanence of control—conditions by definition incompatible with the existence of an armed conflict—were required for the emergence of a new state. However, the post-1945 era was marked by situations in which new states were formed during an armed conflict, both within and outside of the context of decolonization, including the cases of Guinea-Bissau in the 1970s and ex-Yugoslavia in the 1990s. These examples highlight the situations in which internal development brings about a Common Article 2 situation and hence can be described as instances of 'internal standard internationalization'.[7]

Third, a NIAC waged in furtherance of the self-determination of a people ('war of national liberation') may become international *ex lege* on the basis of Article 1(4) of Additional Protocol I (AP I). In theory, this provision was designed to internationalize qualifying conflicts inside the territories of states parties to the Protocol without the need for any further international element. In reality, the provision was heavily criticized for its political and subjective nature and it has seen very limited application in practice. Still, Article 1(4) AP I does provide for an additional modality of internationalization of armed conflicts. Because it takes effect irrespective of the reaction of the territorial state and vis-à-vis all subjects of international law, this modality can be denoted as 'absolute complementary internationalization'.[8]

Fourth, an internal conflict may be internationalized on a relative basis. This means that the effects of internationalization are limited to the non-state actor engaged in the conflict and a third party acting towards such non-state actor in a way designed to activate the law of IAC as between these two subjects. It was argued that this result may be brought about by way of the customary doctrine of recognition of belligerency; through a unilateral decision of the territorial state; and by the conclusion of a special agreement under Common Article 3. The archetypal examples of instances of this 'relative complementary internationalization' have included the 1861–65 American Civil War (recognition of belligerency) and some subconflicts in the Yugoslavian Civil War in the 1990s (special agreements).[9]

Together, these four modalities represent a comprehensive map of conflict internationalization in contemporary international law. The relationship between the 'standard' and 'complementary' forms of internationalization exemplifies the

[6] See further K Mačák and N Zamir, 'The Applicability of International Humanitarian Law to the Conflict in Libya' (2012) 14 ICLR 403, 418–23.

[7] See Section 2.3. [8] See Section 2.4. [9] See Section 2.5.

horizontal nature of international law. Even though Common Article 2 contains a (standard) definition of IACs, states in their law-creating capacity may generate norms, conventional and customary, which complement that definition. Therefore, in the two latter-mentioned cases, conflicts are internationalized even if they do not involve two states as belligerent parties.

It is certainly possible that further complementary modalities will emerge in the future. However, their creation would have to follow the rules on the formation of international law. In other words, a new multilateral treaty might define a new class of conflicts as international, just as Article 1(4) AP I did in 1977. Likewise, with sufficient state practice and *opinio juris* to the effect that some conflicts, such as those in which the belligerency of the non-state party is recognized, should additionally be treated as international, a corresponding norm of customary law may emerge. However, without such development, the nature of the conflict must be considered on the basis of the primary mechanism of standard internationalization and by reference to Common Article 2.

Situations featuring more than two conflict parties pose additional complications. In the first place, such situations are a necessary attribute of conflicts internationalized by outside intervention. However, it is conceivable that other forms of internationalization develop into these complex conflict situations, as well. A workable model is thus necessary in order to determine whether to consider such situations as a single internationalized armed conflict or a number of independent IACs and NIACs. Accordingly, Chapter 3 put forward a model based on the retention of autonomy of the allied conflict parties: once the autonomy is foregone and replaced with a single use of force, the law of IAC applies 'globally' to the situation at hand. Until then, the situation should be seen as 'mixed', in other words, as a set of mutually independent conflict pairs.

A final consideration concerns the question whether the process of internationalization may be reversed at all. This is the issue of de-internationalization or, in other words, the question whether it is possible for a situation of armed violence to transform from an IAC into a NIAC. Chapter 4 demonstrated that this is not simply a matter of the conflict 'losing' its international character. Instead, for a conflict to be de-internationalized, it must fulfil the independent criteria for the existence of a NIAC, while maintaining the identity of the conflict parties and the continuity of the hostilities in question. It was argued that with respect to several modalities of internationalization, the hypothetical corresponding modality of de-internationalization is not actually available in law. However, given that de-internationalization by and large involves a general reduction in the protection afforded to victims of armed conflicts, the unavailability of this process in some circumstances is better seen as a strength than as a flaw of the existing law.

11.3 Effects of Internationalization

Once the process of internationalization is understood, it is then possible to turn to the effects this process generates. The study has focused on two areas of IHL that are governed by markedly different normative frameworks in NIACs and IACs respectively. These are the matters of combatant status and belligerent occupation. The study has subjected each to a close scrutiny from the perspective of their historical development, normative underpinnings, and practical application, all with respect to the reality of internationalized armed conflicts.

11.3.1 Combatant status

In Part II, it was argued that fighters belonging to non-state armed groups participating in internationalized armed conflicts are, in principle, eligible for combatant status. This is not an uncontroversial position. Indeed, the conventional understanding is that members of armed groups do not normally benefit from combatant status. Moreover, states have generally been portrayed as very reluctant to extend the benefits of such status to persons fighting for non-state armed groups. This has variously been justified by the states' interest in safeguarding their sovereignty; their desire to subject such fighters to prosecution; and by the purported inability of non-state actors to abide by the supposedly onerous norms of IHL.

However, historical scrutiny offers a more nuanced account. Accordingly, Chapter 5 demonstrated that practically since the time the distinction between combatants and civilians solidified into law, the applicable rules have permitted members of at least some non-state armed groups to benefit from combatant status. At various times in the history of the regulation of armed conflicts, these have included militias and volunteer corps; armed forces professing allegiance to a non-recognized authority; and national liberation movements. Therefore, the historical development of this area of the law suggests that it would be erroneous to interpret the rules on eligibility for combatancy in an unduly restrictive manner.

Building on that interim conclusion, Chapter 6 provided further support to an extensive interpretation of the applicable law by examining its normative underpinnings. It was submitted that a wholesale denial of combatant status to fighters in internationalized armed conflicts is incongruous with the principles at the core of this area of law, namely the principles of distinction and equal application. Furthermore, the three main objections against the extension of combatant status to non-state actors have been shown as unconvincing in the specific context of internationalized conflicts. The strongest of these objections related to states' sovereignty or, more precisely, to the fear that their sovereignty would be impermissibly diluted by placing non-state fighters on par with state armed forces. However, it was argued that this first objection is misplaced in some types of internationalized conflicts and that in the remaining ones, it actually reflects the desire to protect one's sovereignty by retaining the right to prosecute these fighters, ie, it is better seen as a separate second objection of prosecution. Still, states often refrain from prosecution in practice, and for good reason. In particular, the threat of prosecution for mere participation in hostilities amounts to a formidable disincentive to comply with the law for the non-state actors in question. Therefore, concerns of efficiency were shown to operate strongly against the objection of prosecution. Finally, it was argued that the third possible objection—relating to the supposed inability of non-state armed groups to comply with IHL—was erroneous because the compliance with the rules relating to combatant status is not in fact particularly onerous for non-state actors under scrutiny.

Although the three key objections were shown not to exclude the extension of combatancy to non-state actors in internationalized conflicts in principle, it is another matter to determine whether a specific member of a non-state armed group should benefit from this extension in practice. Accordingly, Chapter 7 put forward a three-pronged approach dependent on the applicable legal framework and the nature of the armed forces of the non-state actor. Firstly, the criteria for combatancy are the most lenient for members of regular armed forces in conflicts governed only by Geneva Convention III (GC III), as these persons need not meet the 'four traditional conditions' in Article 4A(2) of that Convention. Secondly, members of irregular armed forces in such conflicts must meet these conditions, as well as the criterion of belonging to a party to a conflict. Nevertheless, it is conceivable that they would qualify for combatancy, as demonstrated on examples from internationalized conflicts ranging from the antiquated Boer War to the relatively recent Yugoslavian Civil War. Thirdly, fighters in conflicts to which AP I applies as well may paradoxically find the requirements under that legal framework more difficult to meet. Although the Protocol does not distinguish between regulars and irregulars anymore, its requirement of being 'under a command responsible' to a conflict party[10] may be harder to satisfy for some non-state armed groups than the GC III requirement of 'belonging'.[11] Nonetheless, such armed groups would be assisted by the savings clause in Article 44(6) AP I, which may pave the way to combatant status even for them.

11.3.2 Belligerent occupation

Part III of the book presented an argument in favour of the applicability of the law of belligerent occupation to internationalized armed conflicts. Again, it cannot be said that this view benefits from universal acceptance. After all, the law of belligerent occupation is premised on the 'classic' inter-state symmetric warfare characterized by a duality of territories, populations, and legal orders. In contrast, at the outset of an internationalized conflict, such a duality is noticeably absent, seemingly supporting the conventional view of restricted applicability.

However, as Chapter 8 argued, the restrictive view is at odds with the trends apparent in the historical development of the law of belligerent occupation. Firstly, in spite of the general grounding of this branch of law in a state-centric paradigm, several isolated developments have contemplated the possibility of non-state actors becoming belligerent occupants of a portion of the state territory. The Lieber Code foresaw this effect with respect to armed groups recognized as belligerents and AP I extended rights and duties of occupation law to qualifying national liberation

[10] Art 43(1) AP I. [11] Art 4A(2) GC III.

movements. Secondly, the law of belligerent occupation has undergone a fundamental transformation as part of a general trend of individualization and humanization of international law. As a result, it should no longer be seen as a simple brake on inter-state relations and a protector of states' interests, elites, and institutions. Instead, the law has gradually brought individuals' interests to the fore, putting persons before institutions and individuals before states.

These historical trends should be seen together with the normative underpinnings of the law of belligerent occupation, analysed in Chapter 9. Specifically, three logically connected assumptions about this area of the law seemingly militate against its applicability to non-state actors. The first one is of a conceptual nature, doubting the non-state actors' capacity to have rights and duties under the law of occupation at all. In response, it was argued that armed groups have at least limited legal personality under IHL and thus are eligible for rights and duties stemming from occupation law. The second assumption is based on the understanding that the law of occupation may only apply to the relationship of two sovereigns. However, the modern law of occupation should better be seen as sovereignty-agnostic: conservationist and humanitarian, but in principle blind to the sovereign status of the conflict parties. The third assumption concerns the supposed inability of non-state actors to comply with the law of occupation in reality. However, its import is limited only to some armed groups and, moreover, it is neutered to some extent by the safeguards inherent in the law of occupation, which bolster the occupant's capacity to comply with the law.

Finally, Chapter 10 put forward a tripartite positive case for the application of the law of belligerent occupation to internationalized armed conflicts. First, from a temporal perspective, the law applies once the parties have sufficiently consolidated their territorial control. Notably, this moment may and typically will arrive later than the point of internationalization itself. Second, the designation of territory subject to the law of belligerent occupation is heavily dependent on the type of internationalization in question, but specific guidelines have been identified confirming that making this determination is not an insurmountable obstacle. Third, the personal scope of application of this body of law benefits from the rich jurisprudence of the ICTY. On its basis, it was argued that the concept of nationality, a fixed legal status firmly associated with standard IACs, may in internationalized armed conflicts give way to the newer legal standard of allegiance.

11.3.3 Common features

Although the regulation of combatant status and belligerent occupation belong to separate areas of IHL, insofar as their applicability to internationalized armed conflicts is concerned, some common features can be identified.

Firstly, the historical analysis of the development of both of these areas has confirmed that the extension of the law of IAC to non-state actors is not an unprecedented novelty. On the contrary: at various points in modern history, members of some categories of non-state armed groups have had access to combatant status.[12]

[12] See Chapter 5.

Likewise, at least some international instruments have foreseen the application of the law of occupation to non-state actors.[13] Additionally, it can be said that the possibility and desirability of such a conceptual reinterpretation for the purposes of internationalized conflicts is underscored by the ongoing trend of humanization of international law.[14]

Secondly, objections that could conceivably be or have been raised against such an extension on a general level do not appear convincing upon closer scrutiny of the normative underpinnings of the relevant parts of IHL. Some objections, such as the various arguments invoking state sovereignty, are better seen as limited in their effect to traditional NIACs.[15] Others have been shown to apply to various types of internationalized conflicts to a varying extent (or not at all): for instance, conflicts internationalized by state disintegration pose few difficulties in this regard.[16] In addition, IHL's internal safeguards further weaken the practical import of some of these objections, particularly with respect to the availability of resources necessary to comply with the law.[17]

Thirdly, moving to the practical level, it has been shown that this conceptual approach is robust enough to withstand application to concrete circumstances arising in actual internationalized armed conflicts. To this effect, the study has put forward a specific applicability approach for each of the two areas under scrutiny informed by examples of state practice. The concept of internationalized armed conflicts is thus more than just a theoretical category; rather, it is capable of practical application vis-à-vis the relevant rules of IAC, including the regulation of combatant status[18] and belligerent occupation.[19]

11.4 Final Remarks

On the whole, this book can be said to have presented an argument in favour of extensive application of IHL to internationalized armed conflicts. However, in this regard, 'extensive' should certainly not be confused with 'exhaustive'. In addition to the moderately optimistic picture painted thus far, the study has also uncovered some gaps in the legal regulation. A number of examples stand out. With respect to combatancy, the modification of the GC III criterion of 'belonging' to one of 'responsible command' in AP I may limit the availability of combatant status in certain internationalized conflicts.[20] Furthermore, in conflicts internationalized by outside intervention, the *lex lata* concerning the belligerent occupation by the parent state of a territory held by a non-state actor is uncertain at best, and the virtual absence of practice gives little hope for much change in the future.[21] Finally, some, although definitely not all, non-state actors do indeed lack the ability to abide by some of the

[13] See Chapter 8. [14] See, in particular, Section 6.3.2.3 and Section 8.3.1.
[15] See Section 6.3.1 and Section 9.3.2. [16] See Section 6.3.1.2 and Section 9.4.2.1.
[17] See Section 6.3.3 and Section 9.4.2. [18] See Chapter 7. [19] See Chapter 10.
[20] See Section 7.3.3. [21] See Section 10.3.2.3.

relevant IHL norms, undercutting the general goal of compliance with the law in internationalized armed conflicts.[22]

It remains open for future research whether these gaps can be filled and, if so, how that can be achieved. One such vehicle is the presumption in favour of protection in case of doubt as to how exactly the law applies in specific circumstances.[23] This has been advocated on a number of occasions throughout the book. For instance, if it is uncertain whether a given IAC has transformed into a NIAC, it is advisable to err against de-internationalization.[24] Similarly, if the test of allegiance renders uncertain results during a belligerent occupation in an internationalized armed conflict, it should be presumed that the individual in question is a protected person.[25] However, it must be conceded that the effect of this presumption is limited to cases characterized by actual doubt and that its application may indeed be controversial in specific instances.

What, then, is to be done with the remaining lacunae in the law? The sceptic would say that we should simply acknowledge that they are an unfortunate corollary of the Westphalian paradigm still prevailing in international law. Even though this view may appear to be morally problematic—as it leads to glaring discrepancies in the protection of victims of acts that are similar or even identical—perhaps it is inevitable given the enduring distinction between IACs and NIACs in international law.[26] Maybe these gaps do not in fact amount to a diagnosis of any severe predicament and we should not succumb to normative hypochondria: 'Humanitarian law is basically fine'.[27]

Conversely, the optimist could respond that challenges brought about by internationalized armed conflicts should be addressed by the adoption of a new multilateral instrument, perchance a fourth Additional Protocol to the Geneva Conventions. Calls for such development have been made on a number of occasions.[28] Yet their humanitarian desirability appears to be indirectly proportionate to their prospects of success. Any revision of IHL in this area would have to get a broad coalition of states on board,[29] reconcile the views of some of them with those propounded by the

[22] See Section 6.3.3.1 and Section 9.4.2.1.

[23] cf A Rogers, 'Combatant Status' in E Wilmshurst and SC Breau (eds), *Perspectives on the ICRC Study on Customary International Humanitarian Law* (CUP 2007) 112 (arguing that '[s]ince the law of war is concerned with making room for humanity, there should always be a presumption in favour of protection').

[24] See Section 4.4. [25] See Section 10.4.3.2. [26] See Section 1.2.

[27] G Rona, 'Interesting Times for International Humanitarian Law: Challenges from the "War on Terror"' (2003) 27 Fletcher Forum of World Affairs 55, 69.

[28] See, eg, H-P Gasser, 'Internationalized Non-International Armed Conflicts: Case Studies of Afghanistan, Kampuchea, and Lebanon' (1983) 33 AULR 145, 157; MC Bassiouni, 'The New Wars and the Crisis of Compliance with the Law of Armed Conflict by Non-State Actors' (2007–2008) 98 Journal of Criminal Law and Criminology 711, 808; G Rose, 'Preventive Detention of Individuals Engaged in Transnational Hostilities: Do We Need a Fourth Protocol Additional to the 1949 Geneva Conventions?' in W Banks (ed), *New Battlefields/Old Laws: Critical Debates on Asymmetric Warfare* (Columbia University Press 2011) 63; S Watts, 'Present and Future Conceptions of the Status of Government Forces in Non-International Armed Conflict' (2012) 88 International Law Studies 145, 165; E Crawford, *Identifying the Enemy: Civilian Participation in Armed Conflict* (OUP 2015) 206.

[29] cf Rose (n 28) 63; see also G Marston, 'United Kingdom Materials on International Law 1998' (1998) 69 BYBIL 433, 605 (reproducing a statement of the UK delegate to a periodical meeting of states

ICRC,[30] and probably also bring non-state armed groups to the negotiating table.[31] In sum, in the foreseeable future, the adoption of such an instrument will most likely remain the subject of academic imagination.

The most realistic prescription, then, is to focus on enhancing compliance with the law as it stands. After all, states generally and parties to any armed conflict specifically are under a general duty to respect and ensure respect for IHL in all circumstances.[32] A key factor in ensuring compliance with IHL is its precise and accurate understanding by the relevant actors.[33] This book has offered a specific conceptualization of the modern phenomenon of internationalized armed conflicts and applied it to two controversial areas of IHL. Accordingly, it is hoped that it will contribute to the general understanding of this subject matter and thereby also to overall compliance with the law in this area.

parties to the GCs, in which he doubted that the adoption of a new instrument would be 'a worthwhile exercise').

[30] cf Y Dinstein, *The Conduct of Hostilities Under the Law of International Armed Conflict* (3rd edn, CUP 2016) 24–26 (noting that the passage of nearly forty years without a substantial revision of the body of IHL is the result of a 'Great Schism' that had split the international community in the post-1977 era, with the ICRC and the US frequently finding themselves on the opposing sides of the divide).

[31] cf M Sassòli, 'Engaging Non-State Actors: The New Frontier for International Humanitarian Law' in J-D Gasanabo (ed), *Exploring Criteria & Conditions for Engaging Armed Non-State Actors to Respect Humanitarian Law & Human Rights Law* (Geneva Call 2007) 9.

[32] Common Art 1 GCs; Art 1(1) AP I; J-M Henckaerts and L Doswald-Beck (eds), *Customary International Humanitarian Law* (CUP 2005) rule 139.

[33] See S Vöneky, 'Implementation and Enforcement of International Humanitarian Law' in D Fleck (ed), *The Handbook of International Humanitarian Law* (3rd edn, OUP 2013) 698–99.

Index

Note: please see tables of authorities for references to cases, treaties, and other documents.

The manufacturer's authorised representative in the EU for product safety is Oxford University Press España S.A. of el Parque Empresarial San Fernando de Henares, Avenida de Castilla, 2 28830 Madrid (www.oup.es/en or product.safety@oup.com). OUP España S.A. also acts as importer into Spain of products made by the manufacturer.

www.ingramcontent.com/pod-product-compliance
Lightning Source LLC
LaVergne TN
LVHW011915200926
848484LV00002B/636

9780198819868